EMBRACE CHANGE

Unlock the mysteries of the universe as you astrally travel the 88 initiatory paths of the Enochian Cube. A fresh approach to Enochian magic, *The Angels' Message to Humanity* heralds the dawn of a new era of magical exploration and experimentation similar to Dr. Dee's own mystical revelations. Unique, innovative, powerful—this book will forever change the way you look at Enochian magic and the world itself.

The Angels' Message to Humanity is a remarkable synthesis of two of the most powerful systems of self-transformation known—Enochian Magic and Tantric Sex Magic. Discover the unearthly beauty and symmetry hidden within Dr. Dee's letter squares and tablets as they are expanded into three-dimensional temples on the astral plane. Explore the deepest secrets of the Watchtowers and the Tablet of Union—and the newly revealed Tablet of Chaos. Experience the incomparable ecstasy of union with angelic and divine beings through a truly unique, Western form of Tantra.

Go beyond visualization and meditation—*The Angels' Message to Humanity* is your key to direct, personal experience of the astral realms of the Enochian universe. Transform your life through other planar contacts and experience an incredibly interactive series of initiations taking you from the depths of human experience to the unparalleled heights of divinity and enlightenment. Intense and rewarding, the rituals and exercises of the 88 paths through the Enochian Cube will challenge you, invigorate you, and illuminate you.

The sexual and magical techniques presented in this book are some of the most potent means of attaining union with divinity available to humanity. No other book offers as complete and thorough a system of self-transformation and magical development as *The Angels' Message to Humanity*. Are you ready to experience the radical truths that await you at the summit of this path to personal evolution?

ABOUT THE AUTHORS

Gerald J. Schueler, Ph.D., born in Darby, Pennsylvania, and his wife, Betty Sherlin Schueler, Ph.D., born in Washington DC, currently reside in Maryland. Jerry is a retired systems analyst, free-lance writer, editor, and artist. Betty is a computer consultant, free-lance writer, editor and artist. The Schuelers have co-authored many articles on anthropology, computers, dogs, philosophy, science, magick, and other subjects.

TO WRITE TO THE AUTHORS

If you wish to contact the authors or would like more information about this book, please write to the authors in care of Llewellyn Worldwide, and we will forward your request. The authors and the publisher appreciate hearing from you and learning of your enjoyment of this book and how it has helped you. Llewellyn Worldwide cannot guarantee that every letter written to the authors can be answered, but all will be forwarded. Please write to:

Gerald and Betty Schueler
c/o Llewellyn Worldwide
P.O. Box 64383, Dept. K 605–X,
St. Paul, MN 55164-0383, U.S.A.

Please enclose a self-addressed, stamped envelope for reply, or $1.00 to cover costs.
If outside the U.S.A., enclose international postal reply coupon.

FREE CATALOG FROM LLEWELLYN

For more than 90 years Llewellyn has brought its readers knowledge in the fields of metaphysics and human potential. Learn about the newest books in spiritual guidance, natural healing, astrology, occult philosophy and more. Enjoy book reviews, new age articles, a calendar of events, plus current advertised products and services. To get your free copy of *Llewellyn's New Worlds of Mind and Spirit*, send your name and address to:

Llewellyn's New Worlds of Mind and Spirit
P.O. Box 64383, Dept. K 605–X,
St. Paul, MN 55164-0383, U.S.A.

LLEWELLYN'S HIGH MAGICK SERIES

THE ANGELS' MESSAGE TO HUMANITY

ASCENSION TO DIVINE UNION

POWERFUL ENOCHIAN MAGICK

Gerald Schueler, Ph.D. and Betty Schueler, Ph.D.

Foreword by Donald Tyson

1996
Llewellyn Publications
St. Paul, MN 55164–0383, U.S.A.

Angels' Message to Humanity. Copyright © 1996 by Gerald Schueler, Ph.D., and Betty Schueler, Ph.D. All rights reserved. Printed in the United States of America. No part of this book may be reproduced in any manner whatsoever without written permission from Llewellyn Publications, except in the case of brief quotations embodied in critical articles and reviews.

FIRST EDITION
First Printing, 1996

Cover Design by Tom Grewe
Interior Art by Gerald Schueler, Ph.D.
Interior Design and Layout by Darwin Holmstrom

Library of Congress Cataloging-in-Publication Data
Schueler, Gerald J., 1942–
    The angels' message to humanity : ascencion to divine union,
  powerful enochian magick / Gerald and Betty Schueler. -- 1st ed.
        p.   cm. -- (Llewellyn's high magick series)
  Includes index.
  ISBN 1-56713-605-X (pbk.)
  1. Enochian magic. 2. Mandala. 3. Rites and ceremonies.
I. Schueler, Betty, 1944– . II. Title. III. Series.
BF1623.E55S33 1996
133.4'3--dc20   95-42656
                                                                     CIP

Llewellyn Publications
A Division of Llewellyn Worldwide, Ltd.
St. Paul, Minnesota 55164-0383, U.S.A.

About Llewellyn's High Magick Series

Practical Magick is performed with the aid of ordinary, everyday implements, is concerned with the things of the Earth and the harmony of Nature, and is considered to be the magick of the common people. High Magick, on the other hand, has long been considered the prerogative of the affluent and the learned. Some aspects of it certainly call for items expensive to procure and for knowledge of ancient languages and tongues, though that is not true of all High Magick. There was a time when, to practice High Magick, it was necessary to apprentice oneself to a Master Magician, or Mage, and to spend many years studying and, later, practicing. Throughout the Middle Ages there were many high dignitaries of the Church who engaged in the practice of High Magick. They were the ones with both the wealth and the learning.

High Magick is the transformation of the Self to the Higher Self. Some aspects of it also consist of rites designed to conjure spirits, or entities, capable of doing one's bidding. Motive is the driving force of these magicks and is critical for success.

In recent years there has been a change from the traditional thoughts regarding High Magick. The average intelligence today is vastly superior to that of four or five centuries ago. Minds attuned to computers are finding a fascination with the mechanics of High Magical conjurations (this is especially true of the mechanics of Enochian Magick).

The Llewellyn High Magick Series has taken the place of the Mage, the Master Magician who would teach the apprentice. *Magick* is simply making happen what one desires to happen—as Aleister Crowley put it: "The art, or science, of causing change to occur in conformity with will." The Llewellyn High Magick Series shows how to effect that change and details the steps necessary to cause it.

Magick is a tool. High Magick is a potent tool. Learn to use it. Learn to put it to work to improve your life. This series will help you do just that.

Also by Gerald Schueler, Ph.D., and Betty Schueler, Ph.D.

Enochian Magick
An Advanced Guide to Enochian Magick
Enochian Physics
Egyptian Magick
Enochian Tarot
Enochian Yoga
The Enochian Workbook

TABLE OF CONTENTS

List of Color Plates	viii
Foreword	ix
Introduction	xxvii
1. Invisible Worlds and the Five Elements	1
2. The Four Great Watchtowers and the Tablet of Union	3
3. The Mandala	9
4. The Pentagram Ritual and Magic Circle	13
5. Assuming a God-form	17
6. The Six Enochian Mandalas	19
7. The Mantras	27
8. Sex and Bliss	29
9. The Preparation	33
10. Pathworking the Watchtower of Earth	39

The Path of Innoculation—40; The Path of Wealth—42; The Path of Physical Sustenance—45; The Path of Physical Security—47; The Path of Physical Love—49; The Path of Fertility—51; The Path of True Vision—53; The Path of Births and Deaths—56; The Path of Physical Magic—58; The Path of Physical Healing—60; The Path of Magical Knowledge—62; The Path of Physical Creativity—64; The Path of Grounding—66; The Path of Physical Harmony—68; The Path of Physical Health—71; The Path of Physical Insight—73

11. Pathworking the Watchtower of Water	77

The Path of Dream Control—78; The Path of Sexual Attraction—81; The Path of Emotional Protection—84; The Path of Sexual Desire—87; The Path of the Mystery of Love—89; The Path of the Power of Love—92; The Path of Love—94; The Path of Peace—97; The Path of Universal Love—99; The Path of Psychic Power—102; The Path of Love Magic—104; The Path of Transmutation—107; The Path of Love Visions—109; The Path of Enchantment—112; The Path of Visions—114; The Path of Emotions—117

12. Pathworking the Watchtower of Air	121

The Path of Mental Stability—122; The Path of The Psychic Shield—125; The Path of Sexual Energy—127; The Path of Psychism—129; The Path of Prosperity—132; The Path of Fortune—134; The Path of Eloquence—136; The Path of Communication—138; The Path of Telepathy—141; The Path of Pyschic Protection—143; The Path of Contentment—145; The Path of Insulation—147; The Path of Intelligence—149; The Path of Psychic Knowledge—151; The Path of Mental Health—154; The Path of Longevity—156

The Angels' Message to Humanity

13. Pathworthing the Watchtower of Fire — 159

   The Path of Healing—160; The Path of Security—163; The Path of Regeneration—165; The Path of Spirituality—167; The Path of Foreknowledge—169; The Path of Spiritual Peace—171; The Path of Healing Others—173; The Path of Healing Power—175; The Path of Purification—177; The Path of Happiness—180; The Path of Joy—182; The Path of Bliss—184; The Path of Benevolence—186; The Path of Power—188; The Path of Riches—190; The Path of Prophecy—192

14. Pathworking the Tablet of Union — 197

   The Path of Retribution—197; The Path of Judgement—201; The Path of Fruitfulness—202; The Path of Past Lives—203; The Path of Altruism—204; The Path of Will—205; The Path of Dream Control—206; The Path of Self-expression—207; The Path of Sexual Currents—208; The Path of Sensitivity—209; The Path of Compassion—210; The Path of Magical Power—211; The Path of Warding—212; The Path of Understanding—213; The Path of Pattern—214; The Path of Intuition—215; The Path of Wisdom—216; The Path of Courage—217; The Path of Lust—218; The Path of Versatility—219; The Path of Appearances—220; The Path of Imagination—222; The Path of Enthusiasm—223; The Path of Desire—224;

15. The Tablet of Chaos — 227

Glossary of God-forms — 235

Index — 245

Color Plates

   I. The Watchtower of Earth Mandala; II. The Watchtower of Water Mandala; III. The Watchtower of Air Mandala; IV. The Watchtower of Fire Mandala; V. The Complete Enochian Mandala; VI. The Six Mandalas of the Directional Enochian Cube; VII. The Six Mandalas of the Serial Enochian Cube; VIII. Pathworking Foldout of the Serial Enochian Cube.

Foreword

John Dee and Edward Kelley

The Great Table was delivered to John Dee and Edward Kelley at Cracow, Poland, on the morning of June 25, 1584. It was a crowning moment for Dee. For years he had sought occult knowledge that might be put to use in the service of his native England and his sovereign Elizabeth I, in order to further her plans for colonial expansion and the domination of the high seas. The Great Table was a magical tool that could be used to rule the spirits of the various far-flung nations of the Earth, the very instrument Dee had searched after with such single-minded diligence. It was also much more than this, but despite his vast learning, Dee was never fully aware of the larger significance of the Table.

There is good reason to believe that Dee's father had been a gentleman sewer (a kind of wine steward and food taster) at the table of Henry VIII—Elizabeth's father—which explains Dee's extraordinary intimacy with the queen. He remained her friend and trusted advisor throughout her lifetime.

In addition to serving Elizabeth as court astrologer and consultant on all things to do with witchcraft and sorcery, he acted as her political liaison and espionage agent on continental Europe. His knowledge was unparalleled in matters of navigation, cartography (having studied under the great Mercator himself), and world geography. Drake, Hawkins, and other English adventurers consulted with him, seeking to benefit from his encyclopedic mind and the huge library of obscure, ancient books and manuscripts he had assembled, at great personal expense, at his house at Mortlake, near London. He was world-famous for his introduction to Euclid's geometry, and wrote learned papers on such matters as establishing English sovereignty over recently discovered lands in the New World, and his projected reform of the Gregorian calendar.

However, his many talents were by no means limited to the material plane. It was his greatest ambition to yoke into service the very angels of heaven, and enlist their support on the side of his beloved sovereign.

In 1581, after experiencing strange dreams and mysterious poltergeist phenomena at his house in Mortlake, Dee attempted to contact higher spiritual intelligences by scrying in a small globe of crystal. He recorded in his diary on May 25, 1581:

The Angels' Message to Humanity

"Today I had sight offered me in chrystallo, and I saw" (Laycock, *The Complete Enochian Dictionary* [London: Askin Publishers, 1978], p. 23).

Despite some limited success, Dee was quickly forced to acknowledge that he had no real talent for spirit communication, and began to employ professional psychics who would dictate to him the words and images presented by the spirits in his crystal, or in his black mirror of polished obsidian.

Edward Kelley was the second of these paid seers, and by far the most gifted. He arrived at Dee's door on March 10, 1582, calling himself Edward Talbot (which may, in fact, have been his birth name), seeking to pick Dee's brain concerning the secrets of alchemy. The son of a Worcester apothecary, he had received his formal education at Oxford (probably under the name of Talbot) and had taken up the practice of law in London and later Lancaster. In this latter practice he had been accused of forging false title deeds for a client and fled to Wales (probably under the name of Kelley) to avoid punishment. While walking through Wales he is reputed to have purchased a portion of the fabled alchemical powders of projection for a ridiculously low price from an innkeeper who had stolen them from the tomb of an ancient bishop. The white powder was capable of transforming base metals into silver, and the red powder (of which Kelley was able to buy only a small amount) turned base metals into gold. It was to better understand the use of these powders that he came to call upon John Dee.

Kelley himself had some familiarity with magic. In 1577 he had been accused of performing a necromantic ritual, with the help of a man named Paul Waring, in the graveyard attached to Law Church in the park of Wotton-in-the-Dale in Lancaster county. With the help of a serving-man, Kelley and Waring had dug up the corpse of a poor man recently buried and induced his spirit to speak prophetic matters regarding the political future of a local young nobleman, who paid them for the service. Ebenezer Sibly writes that they were looking for treasure hidden by the dead man, and that only the shade of the corpse was summoned out of the grave, but the first account seems more probable to me. In any case, when Dee suggested to Kelley that he try his hand at scrying in the crystal, Kelley needed little persuasion.

Almost immediately Kelley was able to establish communication with a potent group of spiritual beings who claimed to be angels of God, and who promised Dee the revelation of profound mysteries that would tend to the greater glory of England and his own personal advantage.

These spirits all seem to have been related to a single nameless goddess, who hovered in the background of all the scrying sessions conducted by Dee and Kelley. One of the spirits, Madimi, who acted as a spirit guide for Kelley, referred to this mysterious goddess only as "my Mother." Kelley was never able to actually see this exalted goddess in the crystal, but he heard her voice. When Dee asked the Mother her name, she replied in anger: "I AM; What will you more?" and flew away like a flame, while Madimi lay prostrate in awe and terror (Casaubon, *A True And Faithful Relation*, p. 27).

Who exactly is Madimi's mother (also kinswoman to some, if not all, of the other Enochian spirits)? This question is crucial to understanding Enochian magic. It seems to me that she is identical with the Soul of the World of the Greeks and Romans, Aima of the Kabbalists, Robert Graves' White Goddess, and Shakti of Hindu Tantric doctrines. She is Barbelo of the Gnostics, who appears in the Revelation of St. John

Foreword

the Divine as "a woman clothed with the sun, and the moon under her feet, and upon her head a crown of twelve stars" (Revelation 12:1). She is the "Queen of Heaven" mentioned by the prophet Jeremiah. In her darker, or shadowed, aspect she is also Lilith and Babylon the Great.

At the urging of the spirits, Dee and Kelley departed with their wives from Mortlake on September 21, 1583 to travel to the continent, where great occult revelations were promised. After their arrival in Poland, Madimi's Mother herself ordered Dee and Kelley to travel from their temporary residence in Lasko, where they had set up their ritual apparatus, to Cracow. Dee did not want to undertake this further extension of their journey, for which he had no money, but the spirits threatened him with horrible consequences if he disobeyed.

On February 18, 1584, Kelley saw a vision in the crystal of their house in Lasko beset by eight demons:

> These shadows go up and down the side of the house, thrusting their Torches into the sides of it. The house is very like this house. There are eight of them. They have claws like Eagles. When they sit, they are like Apes. They set a fire on it, and it burneth mightily; Now your wife runneth out, and seemeth to leap over the Galery Rayl, and to lay as dead. And now come you out of door, and the Children stand in the way toward the Church. And you come by the yern door; and kneel, and knock your head on the earth. They take up your wife; her head waggleth this way and that way. You look up to heaven still, and kneel upon one of your knees. The stone house quivereth and quaketh, and all the roof of the house falleth into the house, down upon the Chests. And one of these baggage things laugheth. The house burneth all off. Your wife is dead, all her face is battered. She is bare-legged, she hath a white Peticote on. Now the apparition is all gone (*A True And Faithful Relation*, p. 66).

Madimi told Dee through Kelley: "My mother would have you dwell at Cracovia. And I consent unto it. Let them that be wise understand" (Casaubon, p. 67). Dee asked anxiously if the terrible vision of his wife's death could be avoided if he moved his household, and Madimi answered that it was merely a warning of what would happen if he remained:

> DEE: But if I go to Cracovia, no such thing shall happen, I trust.
> MADIMI: No, Sir. Therefore, This is your warning.
> DEE: It is not, then, the will of God, that I shall set up the Table here, as you see, we have prepared.
> MADIMI: Be contented. This wilderness is not forty years. My Mother saith, It must not be here (*A True And Faithful Relation*, p. 68).

At long last, at Cracow, the spirits started to make good on their promises. On April 13, the spirit Nalvage began to dictate to Dee through Kelley the text of a series of ritual evocations, known as "Keys," in a previously unknown angelic language. Only five days before the transmission of the Great Table, Kelley received an astonishing vision of four castles, or "Watchtowers," that stood at the extremities of the world (this vision is described in chapter 4, Note 7, below).

Although neither Dee nor Kelley realized it at the time, both the Keys and the vision of the Watchtowers were related to the Great Table, along with many other cryptic fragments communicated by the angels. It was only after receiving the initial

The Angels' Message to Humanity

communications that Dee, with his immense genius for ciphers and mathematics, was able to assemble these numerous pieces into the fabric of the magical system that came to be known as Enochian.

Just prior to revealing the Great Table, the Angel Ave said through Kelley (who is able to see Ave in the crystal showstone):

> The Lord appeared unto Enoch, and was mercifull unto him, opened his eyes, that he might see and judge the earth, which was unknown unto his Parents, by reason of their fall: for the Lord said, Let us shew unto Enoch, the use of the earth: And lo, Enoch was wise, and full of the spirit of wisdom.
>
> And he sayed unto the Lord, Let there be remembrance of thy mercy, and let those that love thee taste of this after me: O let not thy mercy be forgotten. And the Lord was pleased (*A True And Faithful Relation*, p. 174).

This was the knowledge sought by Dee, the sacred wisdom promised to him by the spirits: the overt function of Enochian magic was to teach "the use of the earth."

The Great Table is the key to that knowledge. Every other aspect of Enochian magic relates back to the Table, because the Table is a magical schematic diagram of the universe—a more abstract and also a more complete expression of Kelley's mystical vision of the four Watchtowers. Since the mandalas in this book are based upon the Great Table, it will be useful to examine it in some detail here.

THE GREAT TABLE

Physically, the Great Table is a grid of small squares divided into four equal quadrants by a cross, called by Dee the Black Cross, which occupies the middle row and column. Each quadrant, called a Watchtower, is made up of twelve columns and thirteen rows. Each quadrant is further subdivided by a Great Cross through its center, which consists of the middle row of the quadrant and the two middle columns. The Great Cross divides each Watchtower into four sub-quadrants, each composed of five columns and six rows. Upon each sub-quadrant stands a small cross that occupies the second row and the middle column of that sub-quadrant. All the small squares of the quadrants are occupied by individual letters, which, taken in various orderings, make up the names of spirits.

It is the quadrants of the Great Table that formed the rainbow crosses that issued forth upon white clouds from the castles, or Watchtowers, in Kelley's vision. In the margin of his diary Dee wrote: "These Crosses seemed not to be on the ground, but in the air in a white Cloud. The great Crosse seemed to be of a Cloud, like the Rainbow" (Casaubon, p. 168). In the corners of each Great Cross lie four lesser crosses. Of these lesser crosses Kelley reported: "These Crosses had on them, each of them ten, like men, their faces distinctly appearing on the four parts of the Crosse, all over" (ibid.). The many other remarkable figures in Kelley's vision were the spirits whose names are extracted from the letters of the Watchtowers of the Great Table.

It is worth tracing through the process by which Kelley perceived the Great Table, since it provides an understanding of the structure and use of the Table (upon which the mandalas are based). At seven in the morning on June 25, 1584, while Dee and Kelley sat talking about Kelley's mysterious vision of the Watchtowers, the angel Ave ordered Dee to "bring up the shew-stone." Dee set the crystal upon a cushion

Foreword

decorated with crosses on a small table covered with a cloth and illuminated by candles. Ave appeared in the stone in the form of a standing figure dressed in a flowing white garment with a white circlet about his head.

Ave demanded: "Who is he that is rich?" Dee responded: "The Lord of all." Ave said: "He it is that openeth the four store-houses, not such as fly away with the winde, but such as are pure and without end" (Casaubon, p. 172). The spirit burst into flame and crumbled into a pile of ashes. From the ashes he rose up again, like the phoenix—as Kelley said: "brighter than he was before."

Ave parted the air to reveal a small square table and took from its top a black cloth. Then he removed a green cloth that lay under it, and a white cloth under the green, and a red cloth under the white, so that the bare tabletop was revealed. This, Kelley said, was made of earth "as Potter's Clay, very raw earth" (Casaubon, p. 173).

These four colored cloths represented the four quarters of the world. Ave unveiled them widdershins, beginning in the north (black) and proceeding to the west (green), the south (white), and finally the east (red). The four tablecloths correspond with the four cloths that issued from the Watchtowers in Kelley's vision. The "raw earth," or clay, is the *prima materia* of alchemy, the ground of all matter.

Kelley described the table in this way: "The Table hath four feet, of which two touch the ground, and two do not: The feet seem also to be of the earth. The Table is square." Upon the bare surface of the table appeared successively four symbols. First, in the upper left corner, "did a T appear on the Table: Out of the top of this T do four beams issue of clear colour bright." Second, in the upper right corner, "a Crosse like an Alphabet Crosse." Third, in the lower right corner, "appeareth another Crosse, somewhat on this fashion, and there appear'd these Letters and Numbers: b I 6 ." From 4 I b Fourth, in the lower left corner, "appeareth a little round smoke, as big as a pin's head." As Kelley observed these symbols, he also remarked that the earthen surface of the table "seemeth to be scribled and rased with new lines."

The raised lines that seemed to cover the table are the lines of the grid that divides the Great Table into letter squares. It is clear from this account that the surface of the earthen table was intended by Ave to represent the Great Table itself. Each of the four symbols stands for one of the Watchtowers. The first in the form of the T, with four beams of clear light issuing from its top, is the symbol of the Watchtower of the east (red), which is to be located upon the Great Table in the upper left quadrant, the quadrant of the east. The second symbol, the alphabet cross, stands for the Watchtower of the south (white), which is to be located upon the Great Table in the upper right quadrant, the quadrant of the south. The third symbol, the curious square of numbers and letters, stands for the Watchtower of the west (green), which is to be located upon the Great Table in the lower right quadrant, the quadrant of the west. The fourth symbol, the small, round smoke, stands for the Watchtower of the north (black), which is to be located upon the Great Table in the lower left quadrant, the quadrant of the north.

It is quite evident that the surface of the square table of clay revealed by Ave is intended to represent the Great Table of letters. In describing the four quarters of the world, the Enochian spirits always begin in the east and proceed sunwise around the circle of the Earth to the north (Casaubon, pp. 167 and 171); or, as in the gradual unveiling of the table by the successive removal of the cloths, they proceed backwards

The Angels' Message to Humanity

from the north widdershins around the circle of the Earth to its beginning, the east. The Great Table is designed to lie flat in the circle of the world, with its corners pointing to the four directions in space. Therefore the Watchtower of the east must be opposite the Watchtower of the west, and the Watchtower of the north must be opposite the Watchtower of the south.

This fact was not appreciated by the founders of the Golden Dawn, who through their Order papers popularized Enochian magic. In the Golden Dawn system, the four quadrants of the Great Table are associated with the corresponding Fixed signs of the zodiac:

Upper Left	Upper Right
Aquarius (Air—East)	Scorpio (Water—West)
Lower Left	Lower Right
Taurus (Earth—North)	Leo (Fire—South)

This assignment fits the Great Table nicely into the complex and subtle magical system evolved by the Golden Dawn, but it is not the assignment revealed to Dee and Kelley by the spirit Ave. However, its use is nearly universal in modern occultism, and it is the assignment of the quadrants of the Great Table to the four quarters that appears in the present work. It is a perfectly workable system; I merely wished to point out that it differs from the original assignment.

Notice that I am talking about the quadrants of the Great Table, upon which the Watchtowers—the actual squares of letters—reside. In the Golden Dawn system, the Watchtowers are linked primarily with the elements, and these elements supply them with their associated directions. In the original system of Dee and Kelley, the Watchtowers are linked primarily to the quadrants of the Great Table, which lie in the four quarters of the world, and which receive their elemental associations from the directions of space. This is an important distinction.

After Dee had recorded the symbols of the Watchtowers, the earthen table was covered with lines again. Kelley counted thirteen rows and twelve columns, so it appears to have been a grid of one of the Watchtowers; but whether he saw all four Watchtower grids at once upon the earthen table or whether they appeared to him successively is not clear from the account in the diary. It was probably the latter. Upon the grid a small point appeared in the center of each empty cell; convoluted lines then connected the cells in sets of seven. Each of these lines formed the sigil of a powerful spirit set to rule over a different region of the world.

Kelley reported to Dee: "Now come upon these squares like Characters." The spirit Ave explained: "They be the true Images of God his spiritual Creatures," and ordered Kelley to "Write what thou seest" (Casaubon, p. 175). When Kelley complained that he could not write them, he perceived a bright flash of fire before his face, and suddenly he found himself able to draw the sigils easily by tracing the line of each from point to point in the middle of the cells on the grid it occupied.

Only after the sigils of the geographical spirits had been completed did Ave reveal the letters of the Watchtowers upon which these sigils were based. Each sigil is formed by drawing a line upon the grid of the Watchtower from letter to letter in the name of the spirit it signifies. Since there are 156 (12x13) cells in each Watchtower, and each of the twenty-two spirit names has seven letters, there are two cells in each Watchtower not touched by the sigils (22x7=154). On three of the Watchtowers these pairs of cells fall together, and with a solitary unattached letter on the Watchtower of Water (Golden Dawn attribution) they constitute the name of the sixty-fifth geographical spirit, Paraoan (P[inverted]A; RA; OA; N [inverted]). The other unattached letter in the Watchtower of Water, L [inverted], stands at the head of the names of the geographical spirits of the Aether ZAX, whose three names are formed from the letters in the upper and right arms of the Black Cross. Curiously, one of the sigils on the Great Table has no corresponding name in the list of geographical spirits attached to the thirty Aethers.

There are thus ninety-one spirit sigils, eighty-seven formed from sets of seven-letter cells, three made by joining the solitary inverted L to twenty letters on the Black Cross (spirits twenty-eight, twenty-nine, and thirty), and one formed from the solitary inverted N added to the end of the three unattached pairs of letters P[inverted]A, RA, OA, to form the spirit name Paraoan, the sixty-fifth geographical spirit. This leaves one sigil on the Watchtower of Water without a name, but a name is easily extracted from the sigil (Laxdizi), and might be added to the list of geographical spirits.

These spirits are divided into groups of three and placed under the authority of the thirty Aethers, or Airs, which form the basis for the Key of the Thirty Aethers, an evocation in the Enochian language received by Dee before the delivery of the Great Table. The exception is the thirtieth Aether, TEX, which receives four geographical spirits. Were the unnamed sigil (Laxdizi) to be added to the list of ninety-one geographical spirits, there would be two Aethers with four spirits.

In this way the Great Table fulfilled Dee's primary ambition to achieve magical dominion over the far-flung regions of the Earth. By evoking a spirit of a particular region such as Assyria, Dee could use its name, its sigil, and the authority of its ruling Aether to control it, and thus influence the fortunes of the nations of that region. Each spirit is, in effect, the genius or tutelary daemon of its appointed region, responsible for its fortune or misfortune. Since a sovereign shares the fate of his or her nation, these spirits could be employed to benefit or hinder the plans of the various princes and potentates of the world, and in this way forward the ambitions of Elizabeth I.

THE REFORMED TABLE OF RAPHAEL

There are two recognized orderings of the four Watchtowers upon the quadrants of the Great Table. The first, which may be called the Table of Ave, is that originally set down by Dee and Kelley in Cracow. The second was received on April 20, 1587, while Dee and Kelley were in Trebona enjoying the hospitality of the emperor, Rudolph II, King of Hungary and Bohemia, who fervently desired that Kelley should manufacture alchemical gold for his depleted treasury. The second version of the Table was delivered by the angel Raphael, and for this reason is referred to as the "Reformed Table of Raphael."

It is significant that April 20, 1587 was a Monday, since all of the most important Enochian communications were received on Monday, the Sabbath of Madimi's Mother. Monday is the day of the Moon, which indicates that this figure was a lunar goddess.

There is very little difference between the lettering of the individual cells in the Watchtowers, but in the Reformed Table, the Watchtower originally in the upper right quadrant (south) has been moved to the lower left (north); the Watchtower originally in the lower right quadrant (west) has been moved to the upper right (south); and the Watchtower that was originally in the lower left quadrant (north) has been moved to the lower right (west). Only the Watchtower in the upper left quadrant (east) has remained in its original position.

This is a very radical change. Dee accepted it because he was, himself, very unsure of the correct placement of the Watchtowers on the Great Table. He wrote: "And in the first placing of them together, I remember that I had doubt how to joyn them; for they were given apart each by themselves" (Casaubon, *Actio Tertia*, p. 15). The Golden Dawn also adopted the placement of the Watchtowers on the Reformed Great Table of Raphael, but as I said earlier, they assigned the quadrants of the Table in accordance with the Fixed signs of the zodiac and the Kerubic figures that appear on the Tarot trump card The Universe: XXI. It is the Golden Dawn pattern of the Watchtowers that is adhered to in the present work.

I should note in passing that I believe both the original Table of Ave and the Reformed Table of Raphael to be in error. It seems clear to me that the Watchtowers were intended to be assigned to the quadrants of the Great Table in the order east, south, west, north, which prevails whenever the Watchtowers appear in Dee's diary. This being so, the first Watchtower received at Cracow (with the angelic names ORO, IBAH, AOZPI on the arm of the Great Cross) should be applied to the east and the upper left quadrant, as indeed is the case; the second Watchtower received (MOR, DIAL, HCTGA) should appear in the south on the upper right quadrant, which is also so on the original Table; the third Watchtower received (OIP, TEAA, PDOCE) should appear in the west on the lower right quadrant, as it does in the Reformed Table (but not in the original Table); and the fourth Watchtower received at Cracow (MPH, ARSL, GAIOL) should appear in the north on the lower left quadrant (but does not do so on either version of the Table).

This is my own personal interpretation, which disagrees both with Dee's own placement and with the placement of the Golden Dawn which the authors have followed in the present work. I offer it here only so that readers can consider the logic upon which it is based—not as the definitive authority on the Great Table. The assignment of the Watchtowers to the quarters and elements used by the Golden Dawn has been practiced with great success for a century, and should not be rashly discarded. However, I wish to point out that in Dee's diagram of the twelve Enochian banners (see Geoffrey James, *The Enochian Magick of Dr. John Dee* [St. Paul: Llewellyn, 1994], p. 119), the assignment of the Watchtowers to the quarters, which I have advocated here for the first time, has indeed been followed. At any rate, it is a matter for consideration.

In addition to the geographical daemons, all of the spirits described in Kelley's vision of the Watchtowers may be extracted from the letters on the quadrants of the Great Table by using methods set forth by the spirit Ave in Casaubon's *A True And Faithful Relation* (pp. 179-88). This is the source for Regardie's description of these spirits in *Golden Dawn* (pp. 630-38), and it forms the method used by almost all modern students of Enochian magic. It is these spirits that are encountered on the paths of the Enochian mandalas.

As I said above, the Great Table is more than a two-dimensional magic square of letters. It is a schematic diagram of the universe. Like all schemata, it requires study before sense can be made of its parts. The four Watchtowers are the castles of Kelley's

Foreword

vision, and symbolize the magical pillars that support the heavens and keep them separate from the Earth, thereby defining creation. Were these pillars to fail, the result would be the indiscriminate mingling of what is above and what is below: chaos.

The Watchtowers are kept rigorously separate from each other by the Black Cross that divides the center of the Great Table. This is a gulf that cannot be passed, but can in certain cases be transcended dimensionally, even as a wall that permits no progress can be climbed. On the Enochian cube described in this book, the barrier of the Black Cross is defined by the edges of the cube. To pass from one face of the cube to another, it is necessary to describe a right angle, in effect leaving the dimension of the first face and entering that of the second, which lies at right angles to the first. Of course this is only a metaphor, but it is useful in understanding the significance of the Black Cross which lies between the four Watchtowers.

Enochian Mandalas

Although it has always been recognized that the Great Table echoes the overall structure of Kelley's vision of the four Watchtowers and their spiritual inhabitants, hitherto it has been employed merely to extract the names of these spirits for the purpose of evoking them into the world and employing them for specific magical purposes. The Table itself has been regarded as little more than a storehouse of these names.

Gerald and Betty Schueler, the authors of this book, have achieved what in my estimation is a brilliant and wholly original insight. They have chosen to regard each Watchtower as a mandala. In Eastern occultism and religion a mandala is more than just a pretty diagram: it is the map of a magical place which a magician actually enters during ritual meditation. Having entered the mandala, the magician is able to interact with its inhabitants and travel across its various regions. Each mandala is an entire world on the astral level, with its own unique environment and inhabitants.

Even as the Great Table can either be considered as four separate Watchtowers, or as a single whole, so can the Enochian mandalas in this book be viewed individually, or taken together as one great mandala. The Enochian cube is one possible form of this great mandala. A two-dimensional illustration of the cube appears in this book, in which each Watchtower is connected by a fifth mandala formed from the Tablet of Union.

The Tablet of Union consists of four Enochian names revealed to Dee by the spirit Ave the day after the transmission of the four Watchtowers. It is called a "tablet" because Dee wrote the names in his diary one above the other. Since each name has five letters, they form another, smaller, letter square:

E	X	A	R	P
H	C	O	M	A
N	A	N	T	A
B	I	T	O	M

In fact, they were never intended to be used in this form; they were designed by the spirits to be written upon the Black Cross, which both divides and unites the four Watchtowers. The names EXARP and HCOMA are written upon the vertical arm of

The Angels' Message to Humanity

the Cross, while the names NANTA and BITOM are written on its horizontal arm. Each pair of names is written twice, in mirror inversion, on both sides of the central intersection of the Cross. As the spirit Ave puts it: "That shall make the crosse that bindeth the four Angles of the Table together. The same that stretcheth from the left to the right, must also stretch from the right to the left" (Casaubon, p. 179).

In transforming the Tablet of Union into a fifth Enochian mandala, the authors of the present work have presented it in the form of a square and placed it in the center of the other four mandalas of the Watchtowers. It thus maintains its function of both uniting and separating the Watchtowers.

Each Watchtower mandala has been broken down graphically into its essential components, and these placed at various levels indicate a progression of relative importance. It may be useful to examine these briefly to show how they relate to Dee's Great Table and Kelley's seminal vision of the four Watchtowers.

Each Watchtower is surrounded by a square wall. Within each wall's side is a double gate permitting entry into the Watchtower. Having passed through one of the four gates, the path-worker walks in upon the first level, which is the ground or foundation of the structure of the mandala. This is equivalent to the four colored cloths (in Kelley's vision) that were thrown out of the doors of the four castles for the spirits of the castles to walk upon. The colors represent the four directions and the four elements. In the present work, the Golden Dawn colors of the elements and quarters are used on this first (and lowest) level of the mandalas.

On the Great Table this level is occupied by the letters in the cells that lie under the arms of the lesser crosses of each Watchtower, called in the Golden Dawn the "Sephirothic Crosses." These letters, sixteen under each Sephirothic Cross, form the names of four spirits, which by permutation are increased to sixteen spirits for each sub-quadrant, or sixty-four spirits for the entire Watchtower.

The second level of each mandala is ascended by short flights of stairs. It consists of eight platforms, represented in the Great Table by the pairs of Kerubic Squares that are to be found above the arms of each Sephirothic Cross. The sixteen letters in these cells make up the names of sixteen angels (called "dispositors" by Ave) who attend after every cross and dispose the will of the king of the castle (or Watchtower) whence they issue. Kelley described these spirits of his vision as sixteen "white Creatures" (Casaubon, p. 168). They rule over the sixty-four spirits of the first level.

The third level of each Enochian mandala is reached by ascending short flights of stairs from the platforms of the second level. It consists of four elevated platforms, one for each sub-quadrant of the Watchtower, in the shape of unequal Christian crosses. This level is represented upon the Great Table by the four Sephirothic Crosses of each Watchtower. In Kelley's vision these are the "four lesser Crosses" seen around each Great Cross that hangs suspended in a white cloud. Kelley says of them: "These Crosses had on them, each of them ten, like men, their faces distinctly appearing on the four parts of the Crosse, all over" (Casaubon, p. 168).

Since each lesser, or Sephirothic, Cross on the Great Table is composed of ten cells with ten letters inside, we must assume that each letter is itself an angel. The letters in the column of each lesser cross, reading down, form the six-letter name of the angel by which the spirits of that lesser angle, or sub-quadrant, of the Great Table are to be summoned forth. The letters in the arm, or crossbar of each lesser cross, reading from left to right, form the five-letter name of the angel by which the spirits of that lesser angle, having been first summoned by the name on the column, are commanded. Thus it can be seen that each higher level of the mandalas is a level of authority over those levels below it.

The fourth level of each Watchtower mandala is formed of a large, elevated cross that fills the center of the mandala, its arms like four broad avenues. It is equivalent in Kelley's vision to the great rainbow cross that appears upon a white cloud, and in each Watchtower on the Great Table it is represented by the Great Cross which divides the Watchtower into four sub-quadrants. Ave informed Dee that this cross represents the Holy Trinity. The twin columns of the vertical arm represent God the Father when taken together as a single pillar, but the Father and the Son when divided by a vertical line. The horizontal arm of the Great Cross is the *linea Spiritus Sancti*, the line of the Holy Ghost.

Extracted from the letters upon each Great Cross are the names of the six Seniors of Kelley's vision, "six ancient men, with white beards and staves in their hands" (Casaubon, p. 168). Ave tells Dee that the twenty-four old men of Kelley's vision are "the twenty-four Seniors, that St. John remembreth" (Casaubon, p. 170). The reference is to the Revelation of St. John the Divine in the New Testament, verse 4:4.

In the exact center of each Watchtower mandala, at the highest, fifth level, is a hexagram. This should be visualized as a low stone dais or altar made of stone. It is the place of union for the masculine and feminine spiritual energies, called *Shiva* and *Shakti* in Hindu Tantric texts. The union of male and female is symbolized by the interlocking triangles of the hexagram. This fifth level is the highest attainment and ultimate goal of the Watchtowers. In Kelley's vision, it is the king that issues from the door of each Watchtower, who is described by Kelley as "a comely man, with very much Apparel on his back, his Robe having a long train" (Casaubon, p. 168).

Bear in mind that Kelley was describing the vision with the eyes of an Elizabethan, whose ideal of dignity and power was the sovereign of an Earthly nation. This limited perspective (and all human perspectives are limited) has cast a very stately, medieval gloss over his vision. Ave himself, in expounding the vision and giving the title "Prince" to this figure (elsewhere calling him "King"), says to Dee: "these names I must use for your instruction" (Casaubon, p. 170), meaning that he had to employ terms with which Dee and Kelley were familiar. The Schuelers have recognized the arbitrary gender of this spirit, and have instructed women using the mandalas to invoke the form of a goddess rather than that of a king.

On the Great Table, this fifth level is represented by the names of the kings of the Watchtowers, which are extracted by reading the letters that lie around the intersection of the central cross of each Watchtower in a spiral pattern. For example, on the Watchtower of the east, the name of the king is BATAIVAH. The king of each Watchtower rules over all the lesser spirits of that Watchtower. In fact, it is scarcely possible to distinguish the king from the Watchtower itself. Expounding on Kelley's vision, Ave says: "The four houses, are the four Angels of the Earth, which are the four Overseers, and Watch-towers, that the eternal God in his providence hath placed, against the usurping blasphemy, misuse, and stealth of the wicked and great enemy, the Devil" (Casaubon, p. 170).

The Angels' Message to Humanity

Each of the five levels of the Watchtowers is ascended by assuming the god-form of a spirit of that level, except for the fifth and highest, which is really an extension of the fourth. Thus to trace a path from an outer gate to the hexagram at the center, it is necessary to successively assume the identities and forms of four angels. Although all paths lead to the center, this goal can be reached in various ways. First, it is possible to enter the lowest level by any one of the four outer double gates, allowing eight possible entries. You may ascend to the second level of the Kerubic Squares by any of eight stairs. Access is to be gained to the third level of the Sephirothic Crosses from any one of the eight platforms of the second level. Finally, you may attain the fourth level of the Great Cross from any one of the four Sephirothic Crosses that constitute the third level.

Choices made limit future options. Once entry is made through either the left or right side of one of the double outer gates, there are two possible stairs to the second-level of that particular quarter of the mandala, and both second-level platforms lead to the same third-level Sephirothic Cross, which leads to the fourth-level Great Cross. In fact, there are sixteen distinct possible paths from outside the gates to the center of each Watchtower mandala, and because each path involves the assumption of different spirit identities, or god-forms, each path is a unique experience. To fully take advantage of these differences it is necessary to appreciate the natures of all the spirits involved as completely as possible.

Those familiar with the Sephirothic Tree of the Kabbalah and the technique of path-working to ascend the channels of the Tree, from Malkuth, the lowest Sephirah, to Kether, the highest (although practically speaking, Chesed, the fourth Sephirah, is the highest attainable), will at once understand that this innovative work of the Schuelers represents a viable method for path-working upon the Great Table of Enochian magic. Each Watchtower transforms from a flat letter square into a three-dimensional ritual space that can be entered in the astral body. The Enochian spirits, which probably remain little more than awkwardly-pronounced names for most ritualists, become living beings when their forms must be assumed and understood in order to complete the paths.

Although I have some reservations about the occult correspondences used in the Golden Dawn system of Enochian magic, the concept of transforming the letter squares of the Watchtowers into actual ritual spaces, and the brilliant idea of using these mandalas for initiatory path-working, represent a quantum leap forward in Enochian magic. Prior to this innovation by the Schuelers, Enochian magic was largely limited to the use of the Enochian language in the Keys and the names of spirits. Now it can be expanded into a visual and sensory realm. With the increasing popularity of computer-generated virtual reality environments, the idea that a mentally constructed place can be entered and interacted with will seem more natural to a growing number of individuals, who will be less likely to dismiss the whole concept as airy fantasy.

UNION OF SHIVA AND SHAKTI

A few words must be said about the union of Shiva and Shakti, male and female, at the center of each mandala. This book is at its heart Tantric in nature. By this I mean that it involves what is known as the "short path" of sensual experience to the attainment of enlightenment. Tantra differs from other mystical philosophies in that it advocates the

Foreword

use, rather than the avoidance, of the senses to produce altered states of consciousness. It thus lends itself very well to Western magic.

The most intense sensual experience is the sexual experience. The Tantrist refuses to allow his (or her) soul to be dragged down from its god state by the weight of fleshy allurements and experiences. Instead, the Tantrist takes on the form and identity of divinity and elevates the sexual experience to the level of spiritual initiation. Through the union of opposites diversity is annihilated and oneness achieved. The primal duality of the universe is sexual.

The male ritualist, having ascended one of the paths to the hexagram at the center of a Watchtower mandala in the form of the king of that Watchtower, receives the sexual embrace of the goddess-form of the Watchtower (i.e., the goddess-form of the element to which the Watchtower is related). This may be either a human partner who has assumed the god-form of the goddess of the Watchtower, or the goddess herself as a spirit, which the ritualist experiences with full sensory awareness.

Since the ritualist in effect *becomes* the king of the Watchtower during this sexual experience, his thoughts and feelings are noble and elevated. It is both his wish and his duty to honor his partner, the goddess, by heightening her sensation to the maximum and prolonging it as much as possible. Similarly, the female ritualist, having assumed the god-form of the goddess, thinks and feels with the thoughts and feelings of a divine being, and responds to her partner, whether human or spirit, with the dignity and devotion due to a sovereign ruler.

It may be argued that it is impossible to have a full sexual union with a spiritual being. This objection can only be raised by those who lack a direct experience of Tantra. It is indeed possible to share a complete sexual ecstasy with a spirit, or angel, involving all the senses to a magnified and extended degree. In fact, I will go so far as to say that a true Tantric union, where transcendence of self is attained, is much easier with a spiritual partner than a human partner. There is no fantasy involved in this love-making—or if there is, it is being incorrectly carried out. Arousal and climax do not need to be provoked manually, and the caresses of the spirit are felt physically both upon the skin and within the body.

Some readers may be offended by the idea of consummating each path-working with a sexual experience. Although a full sexual experience is undoubtedly the highest goal of each path initiation, I do not myself regard it as essential to the use of the paths. It is enough to merely embrace the king or goddess who forms your partner with love in your heart to realize a portion of the fulfillment of the path. Sexual climax is not essential.

PATH-WORKING

In using the mandalas for Enochian path-working, it is necessary to build up very real and complete sensory impressions of them as actual spaces that can be entered. This can be accomplished over time, with successive attempts to follow the paths. Each detail gained adds to the impressions that came before it, until a fully real space is created on the astral plane.

It will help if you have another person working with you, ideally a partner of the opposite sex who understands the spiritual significance of the work. You and your partner can then provide each other with details of touch and sight and sound and smell and taste, thereby reinforcing each other's astral mandalas until they come into perfect harmony and become a single ritual space.

In discussions with the authors on the present work, I formed my own personal impression of the mandalas, which, although it is only one of innumerable possible ritual structures that can be erected upon the mandalas, I will present here to give the reader a clear idea of what is entailed in making the mandalas real. In this example I will adhere to the Golden Dawn associations which are used in the present work.

I visualize each mandala as a walled citadel in a flat expanse of desert. The outer fortification wall is constructed of large stone blocks colored in harmony with the elemental association of each mandala. For example, using the Golden Dawn elemental colors, the mandala of Earth is made of black stones, the mandala of Water of blue stones, that of Air from mustard-colored stones, and the mandala of Fire from dark red stones. Each mandala is absolutely alone on the plain, since each occupies its own dimension (or plain) of reality. The walls of the enclosure are windowless and face the four directions: east, south, west, north.

In the exact center of each wall is an open archway leading into a small alcove or foyer with an arched stone roof. On the rear wall of this entrance hangs a circular stone plaque carved with the image of the Kerubic beast that is linked with the point of the compass faced by the entrance. Thus, if I enter through the eastern gate, I see a plaque carved with the head of an angel in profile; if I enter through the southern gate, the plaque bears the image of a lion; if the western gate, an eagle; if the northern gate, a bull.

In the walls of this alcove, to the left and right of the open entrance arch, are heavy doors of dark wood studded with iron nails. A spirit stands guard before each door. In order to pass through the door it is first necessary to assume the god-form of its sentinel. This I do by embracing the spirit and absorbing its substance into my own body. I follow the same practice in taking on the god-forms of all the other spirits encountered upon the paths.

The gate opens. Within is a walled garden that occupies the sub-quadrant of the mandala. The lawn is crossed with gravel paths, the gravel the same color as the element of the mandala, and along the paths are planted flowers of the mandala's elemental color. Various Earth spirits are visible, hiding among the trees and shrubs that grow in the garden. I cross the open lawn, following the path to the foot of the low stair that leads up to one of the raised plazas of the second Kerubic level. There are two of these plazas in each sub-quadrant. After assuming the god-form of the spirit who stands sentinel at the base of the stair, I climb the steps.

The second level is composed of a rectangular plaza with a row of ornamental trees growing along each side. Most of the plaza, which is paved around its edges with slate, is occupied by a long reflecting pool. A series of stepping stones leads across the pool to the far end of the plaza. I can make out the dim shapes of spirits as they swim to and fro beneath the surface of the water, occasionally approaching the surface. I cross the pool on the stepping stones to the foot of another low stair. This leads up to the door of a long hall with two narrow wings—the Sephirothic Cross of that sub-quadrant of the Great Table. After assuming the god-form of the guardian spirit at the door, I enter.

Foreword

The hall has a medieval appearance, with exposed oaken beams and a high, peaked ceiling. In each wall of the wide central aisle are many tall, open windows through which a gentle breeze constantly blows, lifting the silk curtains that hang at the windows and causing them to billow across the center of the hall. In each of the branching side aisles, spirits seated in church-like pews chant in low voices. I walk down the central aisle to the far end. Here there is another flight of stairs leading up to a small door with a Gothic arch. Climbing the steps, I assume the god-form of the guardian of the stair, the king of the mandala, and open the door upon the fourth level of Fire.

The door opens upon a flat rooftop in the shape of a great cross. The edge of the roof, which is paved with red brick, is bordered by a stone parapet that rises about six feet from the level of the roof itself. The sun beams down warmly from a clear blue sky. Along the parapet iron braziers smoulder with frankincense. At the far end of the opposite arm of the Cross stands a beautiful female figure, naked even as I am naked in the god-form of the king. I make my way between two rows of spirits who stand on either side with flaming torches in their hands toward the center of the Great Cross. At the same time, the female figure also begins to approach the center.

At the intersection of the Great Cross is a raised platform or low altar, very much like a stage, in the shape of a hexagram. Six elderly men with white beards and long robes, holding staves in their hands, stand guard around the hexagram facing outward. As I step up onto the hexagram wearing the god-form of the king, the female figure, who is the goddess, also steps into the hexagram on the opposite side. We embrace and make love, merging together in our union upon the sun-warmed stones of the altar.

When we separate, we turn from each other and leave the hexagram at the same moment. I leave the mandala by retracing the path by which I entered. As I pass from level to level, the various layers of god-forms I have assumed while ascending fall from my body like layers of clothing, so that when I exit the outer gate, I do so in my own identity.

This is a brief description of my own concept of the mandalas. Yours may vary in many details. The important thing is that your astral mandala be finely detailed and perfectly real to you when you enter it. Remember, the mandala exists within your imagination after you have constructed it, not before. The images of the mandalas on the pages of this book are no more than architectural blueprints of the mandalas that you must build yourself upon the astral plane. Also remember that the mandalas are not sterile, empty places, but inhabited with countless spirits. There is nothing to prevent you from pausing on your path to interact with these spiritual beings when this seems to be in your interest. Detours off the paths, however, should only be attempted after the paths themselves have been fully experienced.

THE ENOCHIAN CUBE

In closing, I would like to make a few remarks about the nature of the Enochian cube. When I first saw the Schuelers' drawing of the complete Enochian mandala, composed of the four mandalas of the Watchtowers and the fifth mandala of the Tablet of Union arranged in a cross pattern, it immediately struck me that this same structure might be represented by a cube in which the four Watchtowers formed the sides and the Tablet of Union the top.

Of course, this necessitated the creation of a mirror-opposite Tablet of Chaos to occupy the remaining face of the cube opposite the Tablet of Union. This was created by inverting the spirit names on the Tablet of Union. The practice of inverting the name of a good (or constructive) spirit to create an evil or destructive spirit is almost universal in magic, and in fact frequently occurs in Dee's magical diary.

For example, speaking about the final letter in the name of one of the geographical spirits whose sigil appears on one of the Watchtowers, Ave told Kelley: "This *p* may stand backward, or forward." Kelley responded: "What is the reason of that diverse setting?" Ave answered: "For beginning there it will make the name of a wicked spirit" (Casaubon, p. 176). In other words, the name of any Enochian angel written in reverse is the name of its evil twin, its mirror-opposite, in which all motivations and responses are inverted. A little farther on in the record, Ave in speaking of an evil spirit told Dee: "When thou callest him, call him by the name of god, backward," (Casaubon, p. 180).

The Tablet of Chaos is the arrangement of letters that results when the Tablet of Union is reflected in a mirror. Thus the Tablet of Chaos seen in a mirror reveals the Tablet of Union. However, it is not merely a single side of the cube that is inverted. The entire Enochian cube is reflected in the mirror surface of the waters of creation, so that effectively, when the Tablet of Union is underneath and the Tablet of Chaos uppermost, the entire cube — that is, the entire universe — is chaotic. Just as the Tablet of Union ties together and sustains an orderly universe of natural laws, so does the Tablet of Chaos support and tie together a disorderly universe of random chance and destruction.

The world of matter that the human race inhabits can be considered to reside inside the cube. In Kelley's vision, the castles or Watchtowers stand at the four extremities of the world, and are analogous to the four pillars of Egyptian mythology that hold up the firmament and keep it separate, yet forever bound, to the Earth. On the cube the Watchtowers form the four walls of the universe, and the mandala of the Tablet of Union the vault of the heavens. Each Watchtower occupies a separate dimension of reality, symbolized by the separate planes of the cube, but opposite Watchtowers are more distinctly divided from each other since their planes are not congruent.

In order to travel from the material world in the center of the cube to one of the dimensions of the Watchtowers, we must exit our reality through the points at the corners of the cube and move along the edges until we reach the gates. Travel from one dimension to another is always made through a point expanded by means of a spiral vortex into a doorway. Progress can then be made along a line, or ray. The edges of the cube are the locations of the gates of entry to the mandalas.

At the beginning of the ritual of path-working, face the appropriate direction to confront the gate you wish to enter, standing or sitting in that quarter of the circle that accords with the element and direction of the particular mandala you are working with (for the Tablet of Union or the Tablet of Chaos, you would stand in the center of the circle). Then fix a point in space by inscribing a standing cross of equal arms in the direction you are facing. The intersection of the arms of the cross locates the point you will use as a doorway. By inscribing a counterclockwise outward spiral that begins at the point and expands into a large circle, you open the point doorway. You may visualize the ray that leads to the gate of the mandala you wish to enter as a straight road or path crossing the desert, with the wall of the mandala in the distance on the horizon. It is then a simple matter to mentally move along that ray, or road, to the gate.

To travel from one mandala to another it is necessary to pass from its plane of being through a right angle of space into the plane of being occupied by an adjacent mandala. This passage through a right angle is a way of representing geometrically the passage from one dimension of reality to another.

A way to visualize this transition from one plane on the cube to an adjacent plane is to picture a road leading to the horizon of the flat desert when you stand in the gateway of the mandala preparing to exit it after completing one of its paths. If you were to return to your normal self within your ritual circle, you would move along this road until you saw the open dimensional doorway leading back to your normal physical world. But if you chose to travel directly from one mandala to an adjacent mandala, as you travelled along the road, the horizon would gradually reveal the stone wall of the second mandala in the distance. In this way you can move from a gateway of a mandala to any adjacent gateway on another congruent mandala. Since you are moving in the astral, these journeys along the ray between gateways can be accomplished in a matter of a few moments.

On the model of the cube, all six sides can be rotated about a central pivot point, allowing passage from any of the four gates of a mandala into any gate of an adjacent mandala, but not directly to the mandala on the opposite face of the cube. To pass from one face of the cube to its opposite face requires passage through an intermediary mandala connecting the two dimensions. Thus, passage from the Tablet of Union (heaven) cannot be made directly into the Tablet of Chaos (hell) without traversing one of the Watchtowers (the material world). Although the structure of the cube would seem to imply that entry into the mandalas of Union or Chaos can be made directly from the ritual circle, in my opinion, entry into either the Tablet of Union mandala or the opposite Tablet of Chaos mandala should only be made by first passing through one of the four mandalas of the Watchtowers. By traveling first through one of the Watchtowers, you avoid the need to open a vortex doorway directly between the mandala of Union or of Chaos (which is more dangerous) and our everyday material world.

The Tablet of Union represents the throne of God in the vision of St. John the Divine, even as the entire Great Table of the Watchtowers represents the city of new Jerusalem. The Tablet of Union is the central intersection of the four extremities of reality. About the throne are seated the twenty-four elders (Revelation 4:4), and in Kelley's vision these old men were explicitly said by the spirit Ave to be the same as the elders of the Apocalypse. In Kelley's vision, Ave says of the Seniors: "The twenty-four Senators meet: They seem to consult" (Casaubon, p. 171). In other words, the Seniors gathered together in a ring at the central point of intersection between the four Watchtowers. This is conclusive evidence that the Tablet of Union and the throne of God in the book of Revelation are one and the same.

It follows that the Tablet of Chaos must be the throne of Lucifer, Satan, or Samael, lord of the dark forces of disorder and destruction, who rules hell with his consort queen of many names—among them Proserpina, Hecate, and Lilith. The existence of gates in the four Watchtowers that guard our world from the Dark Lord (or as Ave puts it, "that

The Angels' Message to Humanity

the eternal God in his providence hath placed, against the usurping blasphemy, misuse, and stealth of the wicked and great enemy, the Devil" [Casaubon, p. 170]) raises an obvious question: If the spirits of order can be called into the world by Enochian magic, might not the spirits of misrule also be summoned? The method of their summoning would be simply to invert the names and procedures of Enochian magic.

If, as Ave states, the four Watchtowers have been erected to guard our universe from the entry of hellish spirits, it is clear that these lower demons cannot force them open from the outside. Their locks must be opened by certain Keys from the inside, by those beings who already dwell in the universe of matter. Perhaps this is the origin of the old belief that a vampire cannot enter a house by force, but must first be invited in by its inhabitants. The universe is our house. The Watchtowers have been erected for our protection. We open their gates at our peril, and should never do so without observing all the safeguards.

This raises a disturbing question: Who, exactly, delivered the Enochian Keys to John Dee and Edward Kelley? The spirits assured Dee on many occasions that they were the angels of God. Kelley never completely believed them. He was well familiar with chthonian forces from his necromantic work. Can it be that he knew the spirits better than Dee? The spirits assured Dee that the Great Table and the Keys were delivered for his benefit, to grant him control over the sovereigns of the far nations of the Earth and to reveal to him arcane secrets. Dee believed them. But what if the spirits who delivered the Keys had their own agenda, an agenda they kept hidden from Dee and Kelley? What if they wanted the gates of the Watchtowers unlocked for their own purposes, which had nothing to do with the needs and desires of humanity?

These speculations follow naturally from the models of the Enochian cube and the Tablet of Chaos. I recommend that anyone seriously intent on using the mandalas for astral travel and path-working construct the model of the cube out of heavy cardboard or book board, since it is ideal for meditation and reveals many fascinating and hitherto hidden aspects of the Great Table. Forewarned is forearmed. Enochian magic is a very serious magic indeed, fraught with hazards which, until now, have been imperfectly understood by those who practiced the art. The cube provides a structural map of the Enochian universe, and is invaluable for finding the correct road.

—Donald Tyson

INTRODUCTION

This book presents a series of practical exercises. It consists of eighty-eight graduated rituals that can be conducted in a number of ways. Each ritual includes an encounter with one or more Angels, who will bestow upon you an initiation. Initiation is a process or path leading to a new viewpoint based on knowledge. It is a step beyond theory, into direct experience. As used here, it means encountering a new series of experiences. Each experience is pregnant with opportunities for your future growth and the accumulation of new knowledge. The series of eighty-eight magical initiations presented here are spiritual in nature. The most important goal of any spiritual initiation, and these are no exception, is the attainment of wisdom. The resultant knowledge that you will gain is the Angels' message to humanity. However, each exercise is also associated with more practical attainments, such as health, wealth, fame, love, luck, and so on. The exact result depends upon the Angel that you meet and your surroundings during the encounter. What you can expect to gain is given in the short introduction to each exercise.

Virtually all occult and mystery schools offer initiation ceremonies of some kind. In most, a candidate is brought into an entirely new dimension of supra-physical experience.[1] In self-initiation, you are given specific directions and general guidance. However, you must enter the experience, or series of experiences, by yourself. With self-initiation, you progress at your own pace.[2] These rituals are specially designed to provide you with a comprehensive set of self-initiation experiences.

You can use this book as your guide through a graduated series of eighty-eight magical initiatory experiences.[3] Each initiation is a pathworking exercise through the invisible worlds that surround our physical planet. These worlds are the Watchtowers and the Tablet of Union, as described in Enochian Magic (see our *Enochian Magic: A Practical Manual*, Llewellyn, St. Paul, 1990, orig. 1984). Until recently, these subtle regions of the magical universe were inaccessible except to a few. Today, techniques have been published with which anyone who sincerely tries can visit these areas, first reported by Dr. John Dee in a series of angelic messages that he received over 400 hundred years ago. The traditional methodolgies comprise either magic or yoga or a combination of both. As you work through these rituals, you can use either yoga, or magic, or any combination of the two. The rituals are especially written to allow you a wide latitude in just how you want to conduct them.

Using magic, you can wear colorful robes, speak strange words aloud, and move about in various directions! You can also use your magical imagination to visualize yourself and your surroundings as you move about, or you can create elaborate backdrops and props. To help with your visualizations and movements, you can use mandalas and mantras. Furthermore, you can conduct each ritual by yourself, or with others.

Using yoga, you can sit quietly and visualize your surroundings while moving and speaking in your subtle Body of Light (see our *Enochian Yoga: Uniting Humanity with Divinity*, Llewellyn, St. Paul, 1990). The Angels will appear as psychic archetypal projections, which you will encounter and assimilate as you move from the outside of each mandala to the center, and then return along the same path. Each ritual addresses a different section of what we have called the Enochian Mandala. In each, you will encounter at least one different Angel.

The Enochian Mandalas presented in this book will provide you with the necessary structure for each of your initiations.[4] The mantras will provide the necessary emotional and psychic atmosphere.[5] Although mandalas and mantras are Eastern terms, the ideas behind them are well known in Western occultism. Mandalas are special visualizations or images of the invisible worlds that surround us. Mantras are magic words or series of magic words that are slowly repeated or chanted like spells.

The basis of the mandala initiations or pathworking exercises described here are given in our *Enochian Magic*.[6] The Angels, Seniors, and Kings, are pictured and described in our *The Enochian Tarot*.[7] The first series of initiatory paths will take you into four special regions or invisible worlds of Enochian Magic called the Four Great Watchtowers. In the last series of initiations, you will enter a spiritual region called the Tablet of Union that links the Watchtowers together into a synthesis of the magical universe.[8] The magical universe, as defined here, is that which lies between the highest realms of divinity and our everyday physical world. It is the region that lies between spirit and matter and it shares in both.[9] To help you understand this magical universe, we have devised the Enochian Cube. The four sides of this cube contain a Watchtower, and the top contains the Tablet of Union that unites the Watchtowers together. The bottom is the obverse of the top, and contains the Tablet of Chaos, the reversed image of the Tablet of Union.

This book is your stand-alone guide. Although we have created the concepts, descriptions, and operations that describe what we call the Enochian Mandalas, the use of mandalas and mantras, to visit the Enochian watchtowers, represents a natural synthesis of Eastern yoga and Western magic. We have taken Dr. John Dee's concept of the Four Great Watchtowers and the Tablet of Union and converted them into mandalas that you can enter and experience in several different ways. Through this method, you can pathwork each of the five Holy Tablets of Enochian Magic. We use Enochian words, capitalized throughout for your convenience, for mantras. A knowledge of Enochian Magic, while helpful, is not necessary to practice and benefit from these exercises.

Introduction

You may wonder how magic and yoga can be blended together. The reason is that they both have the same goal: the mystical union of the human with the divine.[10] This series of eighty-eight separate self-initiations (sixty-four with the Watchtowers and twenty-four with the Tablet of Union), which are magical pathworking exercises, are designed to lead you toward this lofty goal. Buddhism teaches that yoga can control the three main components of every human being—body, speech, and mind. By sitting in a particular posture, we can transcend our body. By repeating a certain mantra, we can transcend our speech. And by directing our thinking toward one object to attain one-pointed concentration, we can transcend our mind. Thus yoga usually works in a quiet and still framework. Yoga employs the technique of meditation. Magic also addresses the body, speech, and mind. But rather than trying to suppress these components, as is the case with many yogas, magic channels or focuses them by making use of all three together. Magic employs the technique of ritual. The idea used here is to perform a ritual in which your body, speech, and mind all work together toward focusing consciousness on the goal of pathworking in a way that is similar to the techniques used in the Hindu and Buddhist Tantras. Magical rituals are not only dependent upon you doing things and saying things, but to be effective your mind must also employ imagery or visualization. All three components must be brought into play.

Anyone who is interested in learning more about Enochian Magic and its relation to Enochian Yoga will want to study this book. Those who seek direct knowledge of these invisible worlds and their inhabitants will want to conduct the rituals. The rituals present a logical extension of Enochian Yoga in a form that is suitable for the magical student. The 88 yogic pathworking rituals are graduated in difficulty to allow you to safely explore the Watchtowers and Tablet of Union of Enochian Magic. This can be done individually, using visualization in the manner described in our Enochian Yoga, or either alone or jointly with others as elaborate magical rituals in which a candidate becomes self-initiated into the knowledge and use of subtle forces and powers that surround us but usually remain unconscious and ineffective.

The Enochian Cube is introduced as a three-dimensional model of the magical universe of Enochian Magic suitable for pathworking exercises. It is intended to serve as a meditational device to help orient yourself as you undergo the rituals.

Each ritual, like Tantric rituals in the East, ends with the union of masculine and feminine forces to produce a holistic state of consciousness. This union can be either imaginary (uniting with the inner anima or animus of Jungian psychology) or with a partner (called a karmamudra, in Eastern Tantricism). The Watchtowers themselves tend toward a sexual bias as follows: The Watchtowers of Earth and Water are feminine, while the Watchtowers of Air and Fire are masculine. The Kings of each Watchtower tend to be the sexual complements of their domains (see Table 8 of our The Enochian Tarot). The ritualistic imagery used is the King in sexual union with his consort, but the magical effect is a merging and balancing of inner sexual forces into a blissful mystical experience (called samadhi in the East) in which the full initiatory energy of the ritual is allowed to flow through you for as long as possible. This occurs at the very center and highest area of the 3-dimensional mandalas, and thus at the center of the particular subtle region of the magical universe that is under consideration.

The Angels' Message to Humanity

You will probably want to repeat these rituals, getting more proficient each time you work through them. You can also try them as magical rituals and also as meditative pathworking exercises, to see which works better for you. While rituals work well for some, others may find yogic visualizations to be easier and more natural. We suggest that you use what works best for you. Results are what is important, and you should feel free to adopt these exercises to ways that you find the most comfortable and effective.

NOTES TO INTRODUCTION

1. The ancients taught a progression of seven initiations, or seven degrees of initiation. The four watchtower initiations that we present here are equivalent to the fourth initiation of the ancients. According to the theosophist, G. de Purucker:

   "In olden times there were seven—and even ten—degrees of initiation. Of these seven degrees, three consisted of teachings alone, which formed the preparation, the discipline, spiritual and mental and psychic and physical—what the Greeks called the catharses or cleansing. When the disciple was considered sufficiently cleansed, purified, disciplined, quiet mentally, tranquil spiritually, then he was taken into the fourth degree, which likewise consisted partly of teaching, but also in part of direct personal introduction by the old mystical processes into the structure and operations of the universe, by which means truth was gained by first-hand personal experience. In other words, to speak in plain terms, his spirit-soul, his individual consciousness, was assisted to pass into other planes and realms of being, and to know and to understand by the sheer process of becoming them." (*Occult Glossary*, Theosophical University Press, Pasadena, 1972 (orig. 1933), page 66).

2. The theory and practice of self-initiation is nothing new. Many excellent books are available. For magic, we recommend *Techniques of High Magic, A Manual of Self-Initiation* by Francis King and Stephen Skinner, Destiny Books, New York, 1976. For Tarot, we recommend *Tarot Spells* by Janina Renee, Llewellyn Publishing, St. Paul, 1990.

3. Traditionally, initiation into occult wisdom has been taught to require a Master. The maxim "when the student is ready, the Master will appear" until recently has been considered a sacred law. The idea of using a book for self-initiation is gaining ground in the West. Llewellyn Publishing states the following in the introduction to their series of books on High Magic:

   "In recent years there has been a change from the traditional thoughts regarding High Magick. The average intelligence today is vastly superior to that of four or five centuries ago... The Llewellyn High Magick Series has taken the place of the Mage, the Master Magician who would teach the apprentice."

4. For more information on mandalas, we recommend *The Theory and Practice of the Mandala* by Giuseppe Tucci, Samuel Weiser, Inc., New York, 1970 (orig. 1961), and *Mandala* by Jose and Miriam Arguelles, Shambala, Berkeley, 1972.

5. Probably one of the finest books available on the subject of mantras is *The Garland of Letters*, by Sir John Woodroffe, 5th Ed., Ganesh & Co. Madras, 1969.

6. *Enochian Magic: A Practical Manual*, Llewellyn, St. Paul, 1990 (orig. 1984). *The Angels' Message to Humanity* is not specifically a book on Enochian Magic. However, the Enochian magical universe is used as the structure for the initiations. For further reading on Enochian Magic, see our Llewellyn series which includes *Enochian Magic, a Practical Manual, An Advanced Guide to Enochian Magick, Enochian Physics, The Enochian Tarot, Enochian Yoga*, and *The Enochian Workbook*. Many books on Enochian Magic are available today by other authors as well.

7. Gerald and Betty Schueler, *The Enochian Tarot: A New System of Divination for a New Age*, Llewellyn, St. Paul, 1989. Each of the four Watchtowers is governed by a King and six Seniors. There are also Sephirothic Cross Angels, Kerubic Angels, Archangels, Ruling Angels, and Lesser Angels. The student is referred to pages 29-30 of our Tarot book which discusses the reality of these deities.

Introduction

8. The magical universe is a general name given to the invisible worlds that surround our Earth. Among other things, it contains cosmic planes in which the Four Watchtowers and the Tablet of Union are located. The Four Watchtower Tablets and the Tablet of Union were channeled by Dr. John Dee and Edmond (sometimes Edward) Kelly (sometimes this is spelled Kelley, but we prefer the spelling of Aleister Crowley, Geoffrey James, and others, with one *e*) during the latter part of 16th-century in England. The five Tablets consisted of rows of squares, each containing letters in what came to be known as Enochian, the Angelic Language. Dee and Kelly made numerous changes and revisions to the letters of the squares. The Tablets found their way into the magical Order of the Golden Dawn during the latter part of 19th century. The Golden Dawn kept all of the letters, rather than any single one. We prefer to use this approach, and so we have used the Golden Dawn Tablet arrangement in all of our Enochian Magic books. For purposes of the mandala initiations presented in this book, the exact letter arrangements on the Tablets are immaterial.

9. We have described this arrangement of the magical universe in great detail in our Enochian Physics where it is described in the Cosmic Planes and Elements Model (see Figure 12 on page 41 of our Enochian Physics).

10. Israel Regardie writes, "The inevitable end of Magic is identical to that conceived of in Mysticism, union with God-head." (The Art & Meaning of Magic, Sangreal Series No. 1, Sangreal Foundation Inc., Dallas, Helios Ltd., 1971). Furthermore, Aleister Crowley equates yoga and magic in his fourth lecture on yoga entitled "Yoga for Yellowbellies" in *Eight Lectures on Yoga*, Sangreal Foundation Inc., Dallas, 1969 (also Equinox Vol. III, No. 4).

Chapter 1

INVISIBLE WORLDS AND THE FIVE ELEMENTS

There are invisible worlds all around us. They range from realities just beyond our physical senses to realms of the highest spirituality. The ultimate source of all manifestation is divinity, which is beyond verbal description. Occultism teaches that between this and our everyday physical world exists a graduated series of worlds or cosmic planes. We call the series, in its totality, the *magical universe*.

Each world, or cosmic plane, is composed of cosmic elements[1], and there are seven in all.[2] The highest is divinity, and the lowest and most dense is the physical substance of our everyday world, matter. Between these two extremes are the five elements of Earth, Water, Air, Fire, and Spirit.

Most magical or occult schools view the elements and planes in slightly different ways. In this book we will define them as follows:

Cosmic Element	Cosmic Plane	Mandala
✸✸✸	Physical	✸✸✸
Earth	Etheric	Watchtower of Earth
Water	Astral	Watchtower of Water
Air	Mental	Watchtower of Air
Fire	Causal	Watchtower of Fire
Spirit	Spiritual	Tablet of Union
✸✸✸	Divine	✸✸✸

From this table we can see that the cosmic element Earth does not equate with physical matter; it is more subtle (i.e., less dense). We call it *etheric substance*, and it is too subtle to detect with our physical senses. Beyond the etheric lies a subtler plane, composed of what we call *astral substance*. Beyond the astral lies a still more subtle plane, composed of what we call *psychic substance*. Beyond this is *causal substance*, and beyond that, *spiritual substance*. Instead of saying "etheric substance," however, we usually simply say "Earth." Instead of saying "astral substance," we simply say "Water," and so on with all the elements.

1

The Angels' Message to Humanity

Each of the cosmic planes is composed of a cosmic element, and has a special structure. The structure of each plane can be symbolized by a mandala.³ For example, when we enter the Mandala of the Watchtower of Earth, we magically project our consciousness into the etheric plane. When we enter the Mandala of the Watchtower of Water, we magically project our consciousness into the astral plane. And thus, by proper use of the mandalas, we become initiated into the higher cosmic planes.⁴

NOTES TO CHAPTER ONE

1. The teaching of cosmic elements, in one form or another, is as ancient as it is pervasive. In Tibetan Buddhism, for example, these elements are personified as the Wisdom Dakinis (see *Magic Dance, The Display of the Self-Nature of the Five Wisdom Dakinis* by Thinley Norbu [New York: Jewel Publishing House, 1981 and 1985] for an excellent introduction). In Western occultism, they are often personified as the four elementals: gnomes, undines, sylphs, and salamanders. Exoteric tradition acknowledges four elements: Earth, Water, Air, and Fire. Esoteric tradition adds a fifth element, Spirit. Eastern occultism usually switches the positions of Air and Fire, but acknowledges five, the fifth being called *Space* or *Akasa*.

2. The number of elements differs among magical schools. The idea of seven cosmic elements is Theosophical; it includes four lower, or *rupa* (with form), and three higher, or *arupa* (without form). In our Enochian Magic books, we have pointed out that the Watchtower of Earth cannot refer to our physical planet. Rather, it refers to the etheric plane which surrounds our globe; thus the cosmic element Earth includes not only gross physical matter (in which solids, liquids, and gases are but the lowest three subplanes), but etheric substance as well.

3. In *The Theory and Practice of the Mandala*, Giuseppe Tucci says that at mandala "is, above all, a map of the cosmos. It is the whole universe in its essential plan, in the process of emanation and of reabsorption." (York Beach, ME: Samual Weiser, 1961, p. 23. Also London: Rider, 1960).

4. That the mandala has a strong psychological correlation was well known to the Swiss psychiatrist Carl Jung, who wrote: "The unconscious can be reached and expressed only by symbols, which is the reason why the process of individuation can never do without the symbol. The symbol is the primitive expression of the unconscious, but at the same time it is also an idea corresponding to the highest intuition produced by consciousness. The oldest mandala drawing known to me is a Paleolithic so-called 'sun wheel,' recently discovered in Rhodesia... Things reaching so far back in human history naturally touch upon the deepest layers of the unconscious and affect the latter where conscious speech shows itself to be quite impotent" (Commentary on *The Secret of the Golden Flower*, New York: Harcourt, Brace, & World, Inc, 1967). Jung's concept of individuation corresponds to what you can obtain after successfully undergoing our five mandala initiations. Speech, a mental process, is not enough for a successful initiation. Symbols must be used that will strike deeply into the unconscious and stir its secret contents, so they may float upward into the light of consciousness.

Chapter 2

THE FOUR GREAT WATCHTOWERS AND THE TABLET OF UNION

Working together, John Dee and Edward Kelly channeled five important Tablets.[1] These Tablets are cosmic maps of the invisible worlds that comprise the magical universe. The Hermetic Order of the Golden Dawn used Dee's Tablets in their magical operations.[2] The Four Great Watchtowers and Tablet of Union, as used by the Golden Dawn, are shown in Figures 1 through 5. Each Tablet is divided into a matrix of squares containing a letter of the Enochian alphabet. Each of the squares within the five Tablets (the four Watchtowers and Tablet of Union) represents a specific location, or subplane, in the planes of the magical universe.

As shown in Figures 1 through 4, each Watchtower is composed of twelve columns of squares in thirteen rows for a total of 156 squares (or sub-regions). The squares of all four Watchtowers total 624. The Tablet of Union, shown in Figure 5, has twenty squares.[3] The five Holy Tablets of Enochian Magic thus address 644 regions of the magical universe.

Each Watchtower is composed of four quadrants: Air in the upper left corner, Water in the upper right corner, Earth in the lower left, and Fire in the lower right for a total of sixteen quadrants (four quadrants in each of the four Watchtowers). Each quadrant contains a Sephirothic Cross of ten squares. Each Watchtower contains a Great Cross of

b	O	a	Z	a	R	o	p	h	a	R	a
u	N	n	a	x	o	P	S	o	n	d	n
a	i	g	r	a	n	o	o	m	a	g	g
o	r	p	m	n	i	n	g	b	e	a	l
r	s	O	n	i	z	i	r	l	e	m	u
i	z	i	n	r	K	z	i	a	M	h	l
M	O	r	d	i	a	l	h	K	t	G	a
R	o	a	n	k	h	i	i	a	o	o	m
A	r	b	i	z	m	i	l	l	p	i	z
O	p	a	n	a	l	a	m	S	m	a	T
d	O	l	o	P	l	n	i	a	n	b	a
r	x	p	a	o	k	s	i	z	i	x	p
a	x	t	i	r	V	a	s	t	r	i	m

Figure 1: Watchtower of Earth in the North

3

The Angels' Message to Humanity

T	a	o	A	d	u	p	t	D	n	i	m
a	a	b	k	o	o	r	o	m	e	b	b
T	o	g	k	o	n	x	i	a	l	G	m
n	h	o	d	D	i	a	i	a	a	o	k
p	a	t	A	x	i	v	V	s	P	x	n
S	a	a	i	z	a	a	r	V	r	L	i
m	p	h	a	r	s	l	g	a	i	o	l
M	a	m	g	l	o	i	n	L	i	r	x
o	l	a	a	D	n	g	a	T	a	p	a
p	a	L	k	o	i	d	x	P	a	k	n
n	d	a	z	N	z	i	V	a	a	s	a
r	i	d	P	o	n	s	d	A	s	p	i
x	r	i	n	h	t	a	r	n	d	i	L

Figure 2: Watchtower of Water in the West

r	Z	i	l	a	f	A	y	t	l	p	a
a	r	d	Z	a	i	d	p	a	L	a	m
K	z	o	n	s	a	r	o	Y	a	u	b
T	o	i	T	t	z	o	P	a	k	o	K
S	i	g	a	s	o	n	r	b	z	n	h
f	m	o	n	d	a	T	d	i	a	r	l
o	r	o	i	b	a	h	a	o	z	p	i
t	N	a	b	a	V	i	x	g	a	z	d
O	i	i	i	t	T	p	a	l	O	a	i
A	b	a	m	o	o	o	a	K	u	k	a
N	a	o	k	O	T	t	n	p	r	a	T
o	k	a	n	m	a	g	o	t	r	o	i
S	h	i	a	l	r	a	p	m	z	o	x

Figure 3: Watchtower of Air in the East

thirty-six squares. The Great Cross of each Tablet consists of the Tablet's central row together with its two central columns. This arrangement is shown in Figure 6 for the Watchtower of Air.[4] All four Watchtowers share this arrangement. The main components of each Watchtower are used to create the mandalas.

The Great Northern Watchtower of Earth (Figure 1) is the closest to our physical world. It is a region of strong formative forces that causes all material objects to manifest, but is not those objects itself. This Watchtower is said to begin at the surface of the Earth and continue upward in all directions until its highest subplane touches the surface of the Moon.

The Great Western Watchtower of Water[5] (Figure 2) reflects images upon our physical world. It is a region of strong life-creating forces, which brings about all living beings but is not life itself. It is said that this Watchtower begins at the surface of the Moon and continues upward in all directions until its highest subplane touches the surface of the planet Venus.

The Great Eastern Watchtower of Air (Figure 3) pours thoughts and ideas upon our physical world. It is a region of strong intelligent forces, which provides the power of logic and reason to all living beings. It is said that this Watchtower begins at the surface of the planet Venus, continuing upward in all directions until its highest subplane touches the surface of the planet Mercury.

The Great Southern Watchtower of Fire (Figure 4) causes constant change in our physical world. It is a region of strong creative and destructive forces, which makes the growth of all living things possible. It is said that this Watchtower begins at the surface of the planet Mercury and continues upward in all directions, until its highest subplane touches the surface of the Sun.[6]

Watchtowers and the Tablet of Union

d	o	n	p	a	T	d	a	n	V	a	a
a	l	o	a	G	e	o	o	b	a	u	a
O	P	a	m	n	o	v	G	m	d	n	m
a	p	l	s	T	e	k	e	k	a	o	P
s	k	m	i	o	a	n	A	m	l	o	x
V	a	r	s	G	d	L	b	r	i	a	p
o	i	P	t	e	a	a	p	D	o	k	e
P	s	u	a	k	n	r	Z	i	r	z	a
S	i	o	d	a	o	i	n	r	z	f	m
d	a	l	t	T	d	n	a	d	i	r	e
d	i	x	o	m	o	n	s	i	o	s	p
O	o	D	p	z	i	A	p	a	n	l	i
r	g	o	a	n	n	O	A	K	r	a	r

	Spirit	Air	Water	Earth	Fire	
	E	X	A	R	P	Air
	H	K	O	M	A	Water
	N	A	N	T	A	Earth
	B	I	T	O	M	Fire

Figure 4: Watchtower of Fire in the South   *Figure 5: The Tablet of Union*

After delivering the letters of the four Watchtower Tablets to John Dee, the Angel Ave listed several of their features. One of these was that they contain:

> The knowledge of all elemental Creatures, amongst you. How many kinds there are, and for what use they were created. Those that live in the air, by themselves. Those that live in the waters, by themselves. Those that dwell in the earth, by themselves. The property of the fire, which is the secret life of all things.[7]

The Tablet of Union (Figure 5) is the Great Tablet, that is the primary source of all manifestation, of all that exists upon our physical world. It is a region of strong causative forces that creates the entire universe of all living beings. It is said that this Tablet begins at the surface of the Sun and continues upward and outward in all directions until the highest subplane touches the farthest reaches of the solar system.

You should understand that the Watchtowers are not physically located throughout our solar system. They do not exist on the physical plane at all. However, the inner planets of our solar system (here the Moon and Sun are considered planets only in an occult sense) do exercise specific influences over the atmospheres of the Watchtowers. Each Watchtower is divided into subregions, as shown in Figure 6 (the Watchtower of Air), and these are used to form the Watchtower Mandalas, as shown in the first four color plates.

The Angel Gabriel once said to Dee and Kelly, "In these Keys which we deliver are the mysteries and secret beings and effects of all things moving, and moved within the world." This implies that the entire universe can be understood by a proper conception of Enochian Magic.[8]

You do not have to memorize these Tablets. They are presented here only to show you how the mandalas were derived. The components of the Enochian Watchtowers have corresponding components in the Watchtower Mandalas. In addition, each

The Angels' Message to Humanity

mandala contains the main ruling deities of the Watchtowers, and has corresponding atmospheres. Therefore, when you conduct the rituals of the sixty-four Watchtower mandala paths and twenty-four Tablet of Union mandala paths presented here, you will effectively be pathworking the Watchtowers and Tablet of Union themselves.

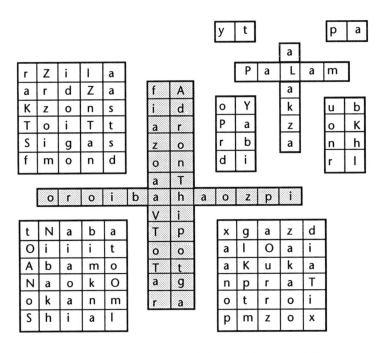

Figure 6: Primary Divisions of the Great Watchtower of Air

Watchtowers and the Tablet of Union

NOTES TO CHAPTER TWO

1. The origins of the Enochian magical system remain cloudy. Some say that Dee and Kelly invented the entire system. Dee himself recorded that the information was channeled by Angels. Some say that Dee and Kelly only channeled parts of a much more ancient system, which dates back to the lost continent of Atlantis. According to Israel Regardie, "Regardless of their origin, these Tablets and the whole Enochian system do represent realities of the inner planes." (*The Golden Dawn*, St. Paul: Llewellyn Publications, 1989, sixth ed., p. 626). See *The Enochian Magick of Dr. John Dee*, edited and translated by Geoffrey James (St Paul: Llewellyn Publications, 1994) for details on the Enochian Tablets. Although Dee and Kelly channeled many Tablets, five remain today as the most important: the four Watchtowers and the Tablet of Union.

2. See Book Nine, "The Angelic Tablets," in *The Golden Dawn*, edited by Israel Regardie (St. Paul: Llewellyn Publications, 1989). Pages 631 through 634 of the fifth edition show the four Watchtowers that we use here. The Tablet of Union is shown on p. 674 of *The Golden Dawn*. The original diaries of John Dee, which record the development of the Tablets, can be found in the Sloane Manuscripts (3189-3191) in the British Library.

3. For those readers who enjoy mathematical manipulations, we point out here that the squares of all five Tablets sum 644 (624+20=644), and 644 reduces to 5 (6+4+4=14 and 1+4=5), the number of Tablets. This reduction process is called Theosophic Reduction, or *Aiq Bkr*, and is simply an addition of each digit in the number.

4. The attributions given to the squares are not arbitrary, but carefully defined by a complex system worked out in great detail by the Golden Dawn. See the Golden Dawn's "Concourse of the Forces" in Regardie's *The Golden Dawn*. We have presented the same material in an easier-to-read format in *Enochian Magic, A Practical Manual*.

5. The Golden Dawn, following Dee's diary, placed the Watchtower of Water in the West. We consider this to be unfortunate. Water, the matrix of new life, would have best been placed in the East, the direction of the rising/new sun. With some reluctance, we follow this arrangement.

6. The assignment of the planetary influences of the Moon, Venus, Mercury, and Sun to the four Watchtowers is not found in Dee's original work, nor in that of the Golden Dawn, but is a logical extension of their Enochian magical system, first presented in our *Enochian Physics* (St. Paul: Llewellyn Publications, 1989).

7. Meric Casaubon, *A True & Faithful Relation of What Passed for Many Years between Dr. John Dee and Some Spirits* (1659). This book is considered an occult classic. Magickal Childe Publishing (New York) has a very fine 1992 edition of this book, which includes some of Dee's diary notes and letters. This quote is from page 179. All quotes from this work throughout this book refer to Magickal Childe's 1992 edition.

8. This quote is from Casaubon, p. 94.

Chapter 3

The Mandala

In *The Theory and Practice of the Mandala*, Giuseppe Tucci calls the mandala "A map of the cosmos."[1] Mandalas are often circular, and usually symmetrical. They are intended to be a symbolic representation or magical reflection of a particular world or universe. Often, as in the case of Black Elk[2], one is first seen in a dream or a vision, and only later given a physical reality on paper or other medium (such as sand). Another way of viewing the mandala is given by the Argüelles:

> A Mandala consists of a series of concentric forms, suggestive of a passage between different dimensions. In its essence, it pertains not only to the earth but to the macrocosm and microcosm, the largest structural processes as well as the smallest. It is the gatepost between the two.[3]

The center of the mandala represents the center, or height, of its corresponding realm. A mandala's symmetry is representative of the polarity or duality found in our everyday human world. Thus North is opposed to South, East faces West, high opposes low, and so on. The circular movement suggested by the mandala expresses those forces that tend toward unification of these dualities.

Mandalas have been used by virtually every civilization throughout the history of humankind. For this reason, Carl Jung attributed their existence to the collective unconscious. He wrote, "For quite in accord with the Eastern conception, the mandala symbol is not only a means of expression, but works an effect. It reacts upon its maker. Very ancient magical effects lie hidden in this symbol, for it derives originally from the 'enclosing circle,' the 'charmed circle,' the magic of which has been preserved in countless folk customs."[4]

In Verena Kast's *The Dynamics of Symbols: Fundamentals of Jungian Psychotherapy*, she calls the mandala "one of the best-known symbols expressing the structural aspect of the self-archetype ... " and writes: "The creation of such mandalas is a manifestation of psychic centering" (New York: Fromm International Publishing Corporation, 1992, pp. 108-9) — indicating that in Jungian psychology, the mandala is seen to have a therapeutic effect on the integration of consciousness.

The Angels' Message to Humanity

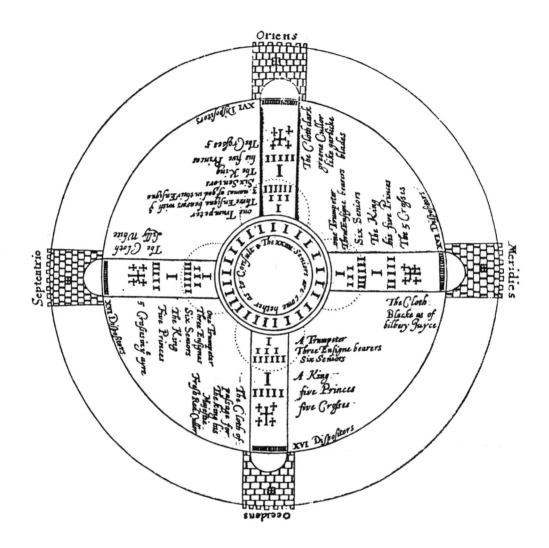

Figure 7: The Mandala of John Dee

Although John Dee had probably never heard the term *mandala*, we know he was nevertheless familiar with the concept, because he drew an Enochian Mandala in his diaries.[5] His mandala, a gold talisman, is shown in Figure 7. It is circular with four doors—each of which is one of the Four Watchtowers. Each Watchtower faces its associated direction in space, while the four spokes each contain one Trumpeter, three Ensign Bearers, six Seniors, one King, five Princes, five Crosses, and sixteen Dispositors. The spoke-like aisles link the Watchtowers with the center—an inner hub where the twenty-four Seniors come together to consult with the magician adept enough to communicate with them. Therefore, Dee's entire mandala is a graphic illustration of the Magical Universe of Enochian Magic.[6]

The Mandala

We will use the mandala in the sense given by the Argüelles, who stated that "... the Mandala is essentially a vehicle for concentrating the mind so that it may pass beyond its usual fetters."[7] The primary Enochian mandalas are each four-sided, just like the Holy Tablets. In this case, the number four implies both cosmos and world[8], because each mandala symbolizes a world.

NOTES TO CHAPTER THREE

1. Giuseppe Tucci, *The Theory and Practice of the Mandala* (York Beach, ME: Samuel Weiser, 1961).

2. The Oglala Sioux medicine man gave us perhaps the most famous Native American mandala. See *Black Elk Speaks*, by John G. Neihardt (Lincoln, NE: University of Nebraska Press, orig. 1932).

3. Jos and Miriam Argüelles, *Mandala* (Boston, MA: Shambhala Publications, Inc., 1995).

4. Carl G. Jung's *Commentary to The Secret of the Golden Flower* (trans. Richard Wilhelm, Orlando, FL: Harcourt, Brace & World; orig. 1931, trans. from the German by Cary F. Baynes). Jung was convinced that we all have access to mandalas through the collective unconscious of humankind.

5. See Casaubon. Dee's mandala is also shown on the page before the preface in *The Enochian Magick of Dr. John Dee* (ed. & trans. by Geoffrey James, St. Paul, MN: Llewellyn Publications, 1994).

6. On p. 168 of Casaubon, we read of Kelly's vision, written in Dee's hand on Wednesday, June 20, 1584. The vision is as follows:

> There appeared to him (Kelly) four very fair Castles, standing in the four parts of the world, out of which he heard the sound of a Trumpet. Then seemed out of every Castle a cloth to be thrown on the ground, of more than the breadth of a table-cloth. Out of that in the East, the cloth seemed to be red, which was cast. Out of that in the South, the cloth seemed white. Out of that in the West, the cloth seemed green, with great knops on it. Out of that in the North, spread, or thrown out from the Gate under foot, the cloth seemed to be very black. Out of every Gate then issued one Trumpeter, whose Trumpets were of strange form, wreathing, and growing bigger and bigger toward the end. After the Trumpeter followed three Ensign bearers. After them six ancient men, with white beards and staves in their hands. Then followed a comely man, with very much Apparel on his back, his Robe having a long train. After him came five men, carrying up of his train. Then followed one Great Cross, and about that four Lesser Crosses. These Crosses had on them, each of them ten, like men, their faces distinctly appearing on the four parts of the Cross, all over. After the Crosses followed sixteen white Creatures. And after them, an infinite number seemed to issue, and to spread themselves orderly in a compass, almost before the four forsaid Castles.

> Later that same day, the Angel Ave explained the vision, saying that the Castles were the four Watchtowers, and "In each of these Houses, the chief Watchman is a mighty Prince, a mighty Angel of the Lord, which has under him 5 Princes." The twenty-four old men are the twenty-four Seniors, and "Out of these Crosses come the Angels of all the Aires, which presently give obedience to the will of men, when they see them."

7. This quote is from *Mandala* by Jos and Miriam Argüelles (Boston, MA: Shambhala Publications Inc., 1995, p. 15).

8. See *The Occult Power of Numbers* by W. Wynn Westcott (North Hollywood, CA: Newcastle Publishing, 1984, p 52).

Chapter 4

THE PENTAGRAM
AND THE MAGIC CIRCLE

The following ten-step Ritual of the Pentagram is used to invoke Watchtower forces at the beginning of an initiation and to banish forces after its completion.[1] You can use either a Wand or the index finger of your right hand. Figure 8 shows the pentagram as used in Enochian Magic.[2] Each of its points corresponds to an element. Figure 9 shows how to trace invoking and banishing pentagrams during the ritual. You will trace the appropriate invoking pentagram at the beginning of each initiation and the corresponding banishing pentagram at its end. In every case, you should use the invoking and banishing pentagram corresponding to the Watchtower that you enter.

Always conduct the invoking pentagram ritual in a magic circle. You can either draw a physical circle around you on the floor, or a psychic one in your mind. Your circle can be as elaborate as you like. For our purposes, a simple circle about ten feet in diameter is probably sufficient.[3] For these five initiations, draw your circle in the

Figure 8: The Enochian Pentagram

Figure 9: The Invoking and Banishing Pentagrams

corresponding color of the Watchtower: black for the first initiation, blue for the second, yellow for the third, red for the fourth, and white for the fifth.

THE RITUAL

Step 1. Stand at the center of your circle. Touch your forehead and say, "**ZAH**" (pronounced either "zod-ah" or "zah"). This means "within is."

Step 2. Touch your left breast and say, "**ONDOH**" ("oh-en-doh"). This means "the kingdom."

The Pentagram and the Magic Circle

Step 3. Touch your right shoulder and say, "**MIH**" ("mee-heh"). This means "the power."

Step 4. Touch your left shoulder and say, "**BUZD**" ("booz-deh"). This means "the glory."

Step 5. Touch both hands together on your right breast and say, "**PAID**" ("pah-ee-deh"). This means "forever."

Step 6. Turn to the East, trace a yellow Pentagram of Air (see Figure 9) before you, and say, "**EXARP**" ("etz-ar-peh").

Step 7. Turn to the South, trace a red Pentagram of Fire (see Figure 9) before you, and say, "**BITOM**" ("bee-toh-meh").

Step 8. Turn to the West, trace a blue Pentagram of Water (see Figure 9) before you, and say, "**HKOMA**" ("heh-koh-mah").

Step 9. Turn to the North, trace a black Pentagram of Earth (see Figure 9) before you and say, "**NANTA**" ("nah-en-tah").

Step 10. Face the North, extend your arms outward to form a cross, and for invoking say,

> **Before me, IKZHIKAL** ("ee-keh-zeh-hee-kal")
> **Behind me, EDLPRNAA** ("eh-del-prah-nah-ah")
> **On my right, BATAIVAH** ("bah-tah-ee-vah-heh")
> **On my left, RAAGIOSL** ("rah-ah-gee-os-sel")
> **Behold, the four flaming pentagrams,**
> **And I alone in the midst.**

For banishing say,

> **Thank you, IKZHIKAL**
> **Thank you, EDLPRNAA**
> **Thank you, BATAIVAH**
> **Thank you, RAAGIOSL**
> **Behold, the four flaming pentagrams**
> **Separate me from the midst.**[4]

COMMENTS

With your imagination, see each of the four pentagrams shimmering clearly in their appropriate colors.[5] Figure 9 shows how to draw the pentagrams.[6]

The importance of proper pronunciation cannot be overstated. The Angel ATH once said to Dee and Kelly, "It is good to know my name; to see whether it agree with my Doctrine."[7] This reflects the occult teaching that the nature of all deities can be found in their names. This was also believed in ancient Egypt, where the goddess Isis attained the name of the Sun god, Ra (or Re), by pleading, "Consider, tell me your name, O Divine Father, for the life of a person is invested in his name."[8]

Notes to Chapter Four.

1. We first explained the Enochian Pentagram Ritual in *An Advanced Guide* (St. Paul, MN: Llewellyn Publications, 1992). It is a slight modification of the Golden Dawn's pentagram ritual. We prefer it to the Golden Dawn's ritual because it lends an Enochian flavor to the initiations.

2. According to Eliphas Levi, "The Pentagram signifies the dominion of the mind over the elements, and the demons of air, the spirits of fire, the phantoms of water, and ghosts of earth are enchained by this sign." (*Transcendental Magic*, York Beach, ME: Samuel Weiser, first published in 1896). In the same work the author says, "Now, if Magic be a reality, if occult science be really the true law of the three worlds, this absolute sign, this sign ancient as history and more ancient, should and does exercise an incalculable influence upon spirits set free from their material envelope." Levi's view of the importance of the pentagram has been adopted by Western occult tradition.

3. We describe how to make a psychic circle in our *Enochian Yoga* (St. Paul, MN: Llewellyn Publications, 1990, pp. 96-7). Figure 14 of that book shows a double-lined circle with Enochian words for the four elements written within. However, for these initiations, we suggest a simpler figure, such as a single-lined circle in the color of the appropriate Watchtower.

4. The Enochian words here are the names of the four Kings of the Watchtowers. IKZHIKAL is the King of the Watchtower of Earth, EDLPRNAA that of Water, BATAIVAH of Air, and RAAGIOSL of Fire. See chapter 11.

5. As far as we know, imagination is strictly a human trait. Its power in magic and yoga has been well known for centuries. Levi wrote, "What is called the imagination within us is only the soul's inherent faculty of assimilating the images and reflections contained in the living light, being the Great Magnetic Agent." (*Transcendental Magic*, York Beach, ME: Samuel Weiser, p. 63). Lama Anagarika Govinda, discussing Tibetan Tantra, wrote:

   > This power of creative imagination is not merely content with observing the world as it is, accepting a given reality, but is capable of creating a new reality by transforming the inner as well as the outer world. This is the very heart of the Tantric teaching and experience, which adds a new dimension to the practice of meditation and spiritual discipline." (Creative Meditation and Multi-Dimensional Consciousness, Quest Books, Wheaton, IL: Theosophical Publishing House, 1990, 4th printing, p. 42). Carl Jung recognized a similar process, which he called "active imagination": "These experiences and reflections lead me to believe that there are certain collective unconscious conditions which act as regulators and stimulators of creative fantasy activity and call forth corresponding formations by availing themselves of the existing conscious material. They behave exactly like the motive forces of dreams, for which reason active imagination, as I have called this method, to some extent takes the place of dreams. The existence of these unconscious regulators—I sometimes refer to them as "dominants" because of their mode of functioning—seemed to me so important that I based upon it my hypothesis of an impersonal collective unconscious (*On the Nature of the Psyche—Collected Works of C. G. Jung, Vol. 8*, Bollingen Series XX).

   Jung's method of "active imagination" was developed to put consciousness in tune with one or more unconscious archetypes, without losing consciousness.

6. When invoking, the first line drawn is the line towards the point that corresponds to the element of the operation (the operation or element is shown in Figure 8). When banishing, the tracing begins at the corresponding point, and the first line is drawn away from that point. Figure 9 shows this by using arrows at the point where you are to begin tracing. If done properly, the invoking ritual will give you a sense of being at the heart of the magical universe, while the banishing ritual will break any psychic linkages that may have been established with the deities.

7. See Casaubon, p. 8.

8. This quote is from our *Coming Into the Light* (retitled *Egyptian Magick*, St. Paul, MN: Llewellyn Publications, 1994, p. 45).

Chapter 5

ASSUMING THE GOD-FORM

Only deities can enter the mandalas[1]; therefore, the ability to assume the form of a god or goddess is critical to success in these pathworking initiations. In short, you must temporarily *become* a god or goddess. Because we are using an Enochian structure, you will assume the god-form of an Enochian deity, through the magical and psychological process of *invocation*.[2]

Every living person has an *aura* (also called the Body of Light), a subtle energy field that surrounds and permeates the physical body.[3] The Body of Light is elastic; it usually takes the physical body's form, but you can consciously re-shape it to temporarily assume any form—which allows you to "become" a god while traveling in the magical universe.[4]

To prepare yourself for assumption of a god-form, begin by imagining an astral image of the chosen deity.[5] The specific deity will be determined by the paths you decide to take inside a mandala. As you move upward through the four levels of the Watchtower Mandalas, for example, you will assume four god-forms, one for each level.[6]

To assume a god-form, begin by imagining your body to be completely empty, like a balloon. Visualize your outer skin as elastic or rubber that can easily be molded. Then shape your Body of Light in the form of the deity you want to become.[7]

See yourself as the deity. Assume his or her countenance and stature.[8] If the deity holds objects, then you should hold them too. If the deity is (or wears clothes of) a certain color, see yourself doing the same. If the deity has magical powers, then see yourself with those powers. To assume a god-form properly, you must *become* (at least in your imagination) that deity.[9] If done properly, you will not have to pretend that you are a deity—a deity will actually be invoked within you.

Each initiatory path has its own series of deities, described for you in the instructions for the ritual. For example, each Watchtower Mandala contains sixteen paths, with eight Angels who stand guard at the entrance gates and eight Kerubic Angels standing guard at the stairways.

Read over each deity's description before attempting to follow a path, in order to familiarize yourself with the deity. Some are masculine, some feminine, and others almost androgynous. Each has a color, and each holds an instrument with magical power.[10]

The Angels' Message to Humanity

NOTES TO CHAPTER FIVE

1. Obviously, your physical body cannot enter a mandala. The mandalas given here are intended to serve as psychic images of the magical universe. You must enter them with your Body of Light, or aura.
   As long as your sense of identity is completely focused on the human personality or ego, you will not be able to enter fully into any of the mandalas, and your attempts at self-initiation will be unsuccessful. You must learn to shift this sense of identity. The magical technique for doing so is called *the assumption of a god-form* (and here, "god" can mean either a god or a goddess).

2. According to King and Skinner's *Techniques of High Magick*, "Invocation is the process by which the trained magician 'calls down' into himself a particular force from the cosmos personified by usage as a god." (New York: Destiny, 1976, p. 158). When you invoke an Enochian god or goddess during the five initiations, you will be temporarily filled and strengthened by a powerful force or emotion. (Although questions about the nature of the deities' existence always surface at some point, the rituals can only be conducted successfully if we first assume the deities are externally real rather than psychological projections.)

3. C.W. Leadbeater's *Man Visible and Invisible*, a classic on the subtle bodies, is highly recommended (Quest Books, Wheaton, IL: Theosophical Publishing House, 1987).

4. An excellent guide to magical projection of the subtle body can be found in *Astral Projection, Magic and Alchemy* (ed. Francis King, New York: Samuel Weiser, 1972). This book contains important Golden Dawn texts called "flying rolls." We also recommend the (rather difficult) classic, *Liber O*, by Aleister Crowley (in *Magicak: Liber ABA, Book Four* [York Beach, ME: Samual Weiser, 1994]). Some easy techniques can also be found in *The Llewellyn Guide to Astral Projection* by Melita Denning and Osborne Phillips (St. Paul, MN: Llewellyn Publishing, 1995).

5. Most Enochian deities remain obscure to the general public. Because of this, each initiation briefly lists key elements of the deities to be invoked. Detailed images of Enochian Kings and Seniors can be found in our Enochian tarot deck (St. Paul, MN: Llewellyn Publishing, 1989). For a guide to the standard Hebrew and Egyptian god-forms, see *The Book of Celestial Images* by A. C. Highfield (Wedingborough, Great Britian: Aquarian Press, 1984). Wallis Budge's *The Gods of the Egyptians* (New York: Dover Publications, Inc., 1969) has been used as the standard reference for Egyptian god-forms for many years.

6. Each Watchtower Mandala has sixteen possible paths. Although you need only invoke four deities per initiation, you do have a choice in some of them.

7. This technique is widely acknowledged in magic circles, having been taught and practiced by the Golden Dawn. It is also well known in the East (in Tibetan Buddhism it is known as deity yoga). For reference, we highly recommend *Deity Yoga in Action and Performance Tantras*, by H. H. the Dali Lama, Tsong-ka-pa and Jeffrey Hopkins (New York: Snow Lion Publications, 1981).

8. An Angel once said to John Dee, "Angels, I say, of themselves, neither are man nor woman; Therefore they do take forms not according to any proportion in imagination, but according to the discreet and applicable will both of him, and of the thing wherein they are Administrators." (See Dee's *Liber Mysteriorum [& Sancti] parallelus Novalisque*, as found on p. 13 of Casaubon.)

9. Correct assumption of a god-form is an important magical and yogic technique. The more you know about the deity in question, the better. The method used here is to visualize your own body as if it were the deity's while slowly repeating the deity's name slowly, like a mantra. This invokes the deity into your body. If you are successful, the deity will temporarily influence you by its presence.

10. The characteristics of the deities we give here are not arbitrary. They have been derived from the deities' names, through a technique called *gematria*, which employs the numeric value associated with each letter of the Enochian alphabet. In gematria, by adding together the values of each letter in a word or name, we arrive at a numeric (and thus symbolic) value for that name. This process shows words, names, and phrases with equal number values to have occult or hidden similarities, and allows us to reliably determine the qualities of the Enochian deities.
    Gematria values for the Enochian alphabet can be found in Table III of our *An Advanced Guide to Enochian Magick* (St. Paul, MN: Llewellyn Publishing, 1992). Although the referenced table

Assuming the God-Form

shows four different gematria schemes, we prefer the one given by Aleister Crowley in *The Vision and the Voice* (Dallas, TX: Sangreal Foundation, 1972, also in *Gems from the Equinox*, St Paul: Llewellyn, 1974) (Crowley's values are in the last column of Table III on p. 26 of *An Advanced Guide*). His gematria scheme was used to derive a numerical value for each deity name in our mandalas. Then this number was reduced by a magical technique called *theosophic reduction* (or *magical addition*). The technique simply adds up the individual digits in a number to get a reduced value. For example, the number 237 reduces to 12, because 2+3+7=12. If we like, we can continue the reduction process until a number between 1 and 9 is obtained. In our example, we would obtain 3, because 12 reduces to 3 (1+2=3).

After we determined the reduced numerical value for a deity's name, we turned to Crowley's *Liber 777* (in *777 and Other Qabalistic Writings of Aleister Crowley*, New York: Samuel Weiser, 1973) and found a corresponding color (Column XV), stone (Column XL), plant (Column XXXIX), magical power (Column XLV), and so on. We also used Scott Cunningham's *Encyclopedia of Crystal, Gem & Metal Magic* and *Encyclopedia of Magical Herbs* (both St. Paul, MN: Llewellyn Publishing, 1995) to determine additional associations (mainly to avoid duplication while remaining magically correct). Other features include gender, fierceness, beauty, heaviness, and darkness. These correspondences, and the presence or absence of wings, are derived from the letters in the deity's name, using the table of Enochian letter correspondences for telesmatic figures. You can find these in Table IX (p. 293) of *An Advanced Guide*, or Table 11 (p. 42) of our *Enochian Yoga* (St. Paul, MN: Llewellyn Publications, 1990).

On Saturday, April 21, 1584, the Angel GABRIEL delivered an interesting message concerning the use of numbers for Enochian letters to John Dee (Casaubon, p. 92). Part of that message was as follows:

> Every letter signifies the number of the substance whereof it speaks. Every word signifies the quiddity of the substance. The letters are separated, and in confusion, and therefore, are by numbers gathered together; which also gathered signifies a number, for as every greater contains his letter, so are the secret and unknown forms of things knit up in their parents, where being known in number, they are easily distinguished, so that herein we teach places to be numbered, letters to be elected from the numbered, and proper words from the letters, signifying substantially the same thing that is spoken of in the center of his Creator, whereby even as the mind of man moves at an ordered speech, and is easily persuaded in things that are true, so are the creatures of God stirred up in themselves, when they hear the words wherewith they were nursed and brought forth. For nothing moves that is not persuaded, neither can any thing be persuaded that is unknown.

Chapter 6

THE SIX ENOCHIAN MANDALAS

A mandala is a symbolic representation of a sacred region or sacred concept. It is usually circular, but can also be square or rectangular. If used properly, a mandala will induce a liberating psychological experience—an initiation. A mandala acts as a map of the higher cosmic planes and forces. As we use the term here, it represents a world or a discrete portion of the magical universe.[1] Because mandalas are maps, we can use them for pathworking the realms of Enochian Magic.

The first four color plates show the four Watchtower Mandalas that you will use. The Earth Mandala is black, the Water Mandala is blue, the Air Mandala is yellow, and the Fire Mandala is red. Each of these color plates shows the locations of regions within that mandala: the first or bottom level, called the Earth-Tiers, is to be visualized as black (although it is necessarily shown in the plates as white). The second level, called the Water-Tiers, is shown as blue. The third level, called the Air-Tiers, is yellow, and the highest, or fourth level, called the Fire-Tiers, is red. These regions, together with the other components of the four Watchtower Mandalas, are shown in Figure 10. A comparison between Figures 6 (see page 5) and 10 will illustrate how the Watchtower Mandalas are derived from the four Watchtower Tablets presented by Dee and Kelly.

Each path through a Watchtower Mandala begins at a gate. At the center of each side of the mandala is a large opening which contains two gates, one at each side of the opening, making eight gates in all. After entering a gate, you travel across the Earth-Tier (the Lesser Squares). The path splits, and you can go up one of two stairways to a blue Water-Tier (the Kerubic Squares). The two paths then merge as you go up a second stairway to the yellow Air-Tier (the Sephirothic Cross Squares). This leads up a third stairway to the cross-shaped Fire-Tier (the Great Cross Squares). Each path ends at a white circle within a central hexagram in the center of the mandala.

Figure 11 shows the basic Tablet of Union Mandala. Essentially, this mandala consists of a truncated pyramid with a central pentagram.[2] Figure 12 shows the mandala as it is normally used for pathworking the Tablet of Union, which is itself on the spiritual plane. There are two steps shown on each side of the pyramid, each of which contains a letter. These are the Enochian letters for A (on the first step) and D (on

The Angels' Message to Humanity

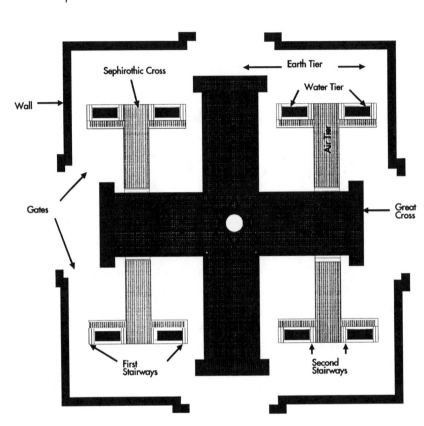

Figure 10: Components of an Enochian Mandala

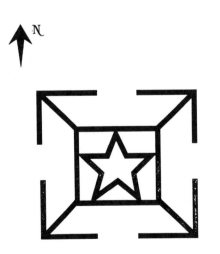

Figure 11: The Tablet of Union Mandala

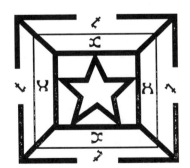

Figure 12: The Tablet of Union Mandala Showing Steps and Letters

The Six Enochian Mandalas

Figure 13: The Tablet of Chaos Mandala *Figure 14: The Tablet of Chaos Mandala Showing Steps and Letters*

the second step), letters associated with the Brow Center (chakra) according to Enochian Yoga.[3] Figure 13 shows the basic Tablet of Chaos Mandala, symbolic of the lowest sphere of the magical universe ruled by the forces of chaos (which are actually directed by karma). It consists of a truncated pyramid with a central vortex of three and one half counterclockwise turns (according to Kundalini yoga, the goddess Kundalini has the form of a snake with three and one half coils located in the root center or *muladhara* chakra). Figure 14 shows this mandala as used for pathworking (which we do not address in this book owing to the inherent dangers associated with pathworking chaotic/demonic realms). Like the Tablet of Union, it also has two steps with Enochian letters. The letters are Enochian for E and L, which spell the word *EL*, meaning "first" or "primal." These letters emphasize that cosmos and chaos are the most fundamental duality in our universe.[4]

You should practice the eighty-eight initiatory paths in the order that we present them in this book:

    Paths 1-16: Paths through the Watchtower of Earth.
    Paths 17-32: Paths through the Watchtower of Water.
    Paths 33-48: Path through the Watchtower of Air.
    Paths 48-64: Paths through the Watchtower of Fire.
    Paths 65-88: Paths through the Tablet of Union.

The four Watchtower Mandalas are similar. The only differences are colors, atmospheres, and deities[5] as follows:

a. **Colors**: The walls and steps are black for Earth, blue for Water, yellow for Air, and red for Fire.[6]

The Angels' Message to Humanity

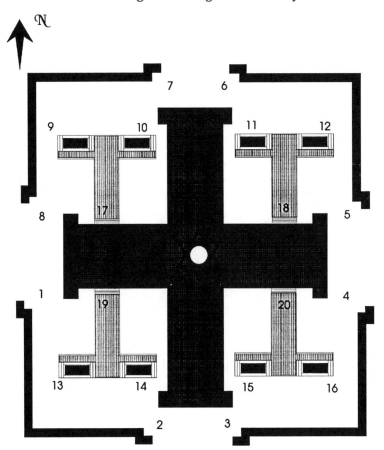

Figure 15: The Earth Mandala Showing Position Numbers

b. **Atmosphere**: Each Watchtower Mandala is as follows:

Earth—nourishment, sustenance, permanence
Water—creation, desire, renewal, manifestation
Air—motion, intelligence, relationships
Fire—destruction, change, transformation

c. **Deities**. The deities are different in each mandala.[7] Actually, each Watchtower has a host of deities, but you will only need to become familiar with twenty-two for each Watchtower. For each of the first sixty-four initiatory paths, you will assume the god-form of four deities: one for each level of the mandala. You will be an Angel, a Kerubic Angel, a Sephirothic Cross Angel, and a King or Goddess. The possible stations of each deity are shown in the corresponding Figures for each Watchtower mandala. For example, Figure 15 shows position numbers 1 through 21 as follows:

1-8: Angel positions
9-16: Kerubic Angel positions
17-20: Sephirothic Cross Angel positions
21: King (if you are male) or Goddess (if you are female)

The Six Enochian Mandalas

For the last twenty-four initiatory paths, using the Tablet of Union Mandala, you will assume the god-form of three deities: an Angel, a Senior, and the God or Goddess of the Tablet of Union.

Now let's look at the first four color plates. Each Watchtower Mandala is divided into four main parts or quadrants, with two entrances into each quadrant. To enter one of the four Watchtower Mandalas, you assume the god-form of an Angel (a Ruling Angel) standing guard at one of the eight entrances. When you enter the mandala through one of the eight entrances, you will be on the first floor or Earth-Tier. The Earth-Tier contains all the Lesser Squares of the Watchtower (see Figure 6, which shows the Lesser Squares for the Watchtower of Air).[8]

In each quadrant is a yellow cross. Above the two arms of each cross are eight blue rectangular areas that can each be entered by climbing a flight of stairs.[9] These eight blue areas comprise the second floor or Water-Tier, and consist of the Kerubic Squares (see Figure 6). To enter a Water-Tier, you assume the god-form of a Kerubic Angel (numbers 9 through 16 in Figure 15).

In each of the eight divisions of the blue Water-Tier, a flight of stairs leads upward to the third floor, the yellow Air-Tier. There are four Air-Tiers in each mandala representing Sephirothic Crosses. These are the four Sephirothic Crosses shown in Figure 6. To enter these areas, you assume the god-form of a Sephirothic Cross Angel (numbers 17 through 20 in Figure 15).

A stairway leads from each Sephirothic Cross upward to the fourth floor, the red Fire-Tier. The Fire-Tier represents the Great Cross that divides each Watchtower into four quadrants (see Figure 6). There is one Fire-Tier in each mandala. To enter this cross-shaped area, you assume the god-form of the King of the Watchtower, if you are a male. You assume the god-form of the Goddess of the Watchtower, if you are female.[10]

Each Watchtower Mandala allows for sixteen separate paths that you can take to reach the center of the Fire-Tier. The primary differences in which path you select are the god-forms that you assume along the way and the stairways and gates through which you must pass. In each Watchtower Mandala path you will assume the same King or Goddess form, but you will encounter differences in the other deities depending upon the path that you take. There are eight Angels, eight Kerubic Angels, and four Sephirothic Cross Angels.[11]

During each of the twenty-four Tablet of Union Initiatory paths, you will assume three separate god-forms. First you assume the god-form of an Angel to pass through a Watchtower. You will have a choice between twenty-four Angels, six per Watchtower (these are the same as given in the Watchtower paths). Your choice of Watchtower to pass through will limit your choice of Senior to one of the six Seniors who govern that Watchtower. Then you will rise up to the top of the mandala and assume the god-form of EHNB, the God of the Tablet of Union.[12]

The eighty-eight initiatory paths are arranged in order of difficulty, with the first being the easiest.

NOTES TO CHAPTER SIX

1. Contrary to popular opinion, mandalas are not only found in the East. Many Native Americans, for example, make beautiful religious mandalas with sand. For reference, we recommend *Tapestries in Sand: The Spirit of Indian Sandpainting*, by David Villasenor (NatureGraph Company, California, 1963 and 1966). Perhaps the best-known mandala in magical schools today is the Qabalistic Tree of Life, which shows ten spheres or Sephiroth connected by twenty-two paths (see Regardie's *The Golden Dawn*).

2. As we said in *An Advanced Guide to Enochian Magic* (Llewellyn, first edition 1987), a pyramid "represents the magical universe as a graduated expression in time, space, and form of BEING, from the highest spiritual spheres to the lowest material globes." (p. 42).

3. See Table 19 in our *Enochian Yoga*.

4. See card 4 of our Enochian tarot card deck, as well as p. 63 of our *Enochian Tarot*.

5. The structure of the four Watchtowers is the same as shown in Figures 1-4. Therefore, one mandala can be used for all four, but during the pathworking exercises you must use visualization to differentiate between the four mandalas in terms of deities, forces or atmospheres, and colors. The four color plates are provided to assist you.

6. These are the standard Golden Dawn colors for the Watchtowers. For a full description of the Tablets and colors, as well as Golden Dawn weapons and an entire Golden Dawn temple, see *The Secret Temple* by Robert Wang (New York: Samuel Weiser, 1980).

7. The names of the deities who govern specific regions of each Watchtower are derived from the letters in the squares. Observant students will probably notice that in some cases different authors use different spellings for the same deity. This is because some of the Watchtower squares contain multiple letters, owing to revisions made by Dee and Kelly, which allows for a choice of spellings. See our *An Advanced Guide to Enochian Magic* (Llewellyn), pp. 46-47.

8. The Lesser Squares are so-called because they are the lowest regions, which is to say the closest within the Watchtower to the physical plane (represented by the Chaos Mandala), and thus the most material. The Golden Dawn attributes Egyptian deities and sphinxes to these regions. The Lesser Squares also contain Demons, the demonic forces of the Watchtowers.

9. The number of steps of each stairway is determined from the name of the Kerubic Angel guarding it. In each case, the numeric value of the name is found from Crowley's gematria and reduced by magical addition to the number of steps.

10. Until this point, gender is not considered a factor in the mandala pathworking exercises. Although Enochian Magic teaches that all Watchtower deities are masculine, we have pointed out in our *Enochian Tarot* that about half have masculine characteristics while the other half have feminine characteristics. The Watchtowers contain both masculine and feminine forces that sweep through various regions like rivers and are called sexual currents. At the point of the Fire-Tier, these sexual currents become too strong to ignore and must be assimilated. It should be noted here that the phrases "if you are male" and "if you are female" refer more to your sexual preference than your physical body.

11. Choices can be made in the lower tiers, but not in the Fire-Tier. The highest region of a Watchtower is the Great Cross, where all differences must come together in a synthesis of conscious energies. The fact that the lower forces of a Watchtower are assimilated into a oneness at the highest region results in using the symbol of a pyramid for each square—each square is represented by a truncated pyramid similar to the one used here in the Tablet of Union Mandala.

12. The name EHNB is found by using the first letter of the Enochian name for each of the four cosmic elements. It is the first file (or column) of the Tablet of Union (see Figure 5). EHNB is sometimes considered to be the Enochian word for the fifth element, Spirit. Here, we use it as the name of the supreme God of the Enochian magical universe. The supreme Goddess is BABALON (the names of the four Watchtower Goddesses are anagrams of BABALON, and thus they are aspects of her).

Chapter 7

THE MANTRAS

In addition to mandalas, the pathworking exercises also use mantras. Like the word *mandala*, the word *mantra* comes to us from the East.[1] As a mandala is visual, so is a mantra verbal. Mantras are to be spoken aloud. As you pass through the levels or tiers of each Watchtower, you will say a special mantra, a magical word that will aid your overall visualization of the process.

Before entering each Watchtower, you are to say the Threefold Secret (or Holy) Word for that Watchtower. This word has twelve letters, and is "threefold" because it includes three words, the first made of three letters, the second of four, and the third of five.[2] Thus MORDIALHKTGA, the holy word for the Watchtower of Earth, can be written MOR-DIAL-HKTGA to show its threefold nature. The purpose of saying the threefold mantra is for protection against the demonic forces that lurk on the lowest level of each Watchtower.[3]

All of the mantras used are in Enochian, the Angelic language. The rules for pronouncing Enochian are:

Most consonants are followed by "eh" (*i.e.*, B is "beh," D is "deh").
Most vowels are followed by "h" (i.e., A is "ah," O is "oh").
In general, each letter forms a syllable.
The letters Y and I are interchangeable, as are V and U, and S and Z.
Z can be pronounced "zode" (traditional) or "zeh" (modern).[4]
S is pronounced either "ess" or "seh."
R can be either "reh," "rah," or "ar."
I is pronounced "ee" (TI is "teh-ee" or just "tee").

Suggested pronunciations of all Enochian words are given in the Preparations (see chapter 8 below) or the first time the word is used in the initiation itself.[5] Compare the pronunciations we suggest with the rules shown above. Try to pronounce each of the mantras correctly before actually beginning an initiation. Pronunciation should be practiced as part of your preparation exercises. Each word or name should be spoken aloud, like a magic spell.[6]

NOTES TO CHAPTER SEVEN

1. Probably the best book available on Eastern mantras is *The Garland of Letters*, by Sir John Woodroffe (Madras: Ganesh & Co., 1969, distributed by Vedanta Press, Hollywood, CA). This classic tantric work on words and sounds is a bit hard-going for the novice, but well worth the effort of deep study. Unlike modern writers, Woodroffe keeps the original Sanskrit words, which makes the reading difficult, but adds a magical flavor lacking in most modern Tantric translations. Woodroffe presents the Tantric teaching of sound in very great detail. The basic theory is very similar to that of Western magical tradition. We also recommend *Mantras, Sacred Words of Power*, by John Blofeld (New York: Dutton Paperbacks, 1977).

2. The middle row of a Watchtower is called the *Linea Spiritus Sancti*. Because each Watchtower has twelve columns, each secret holy word has twelve letters. If you look at Figures 1-4, you will see each holy word along the middle row.

3. His Holiness, the Dali Lama, says love is the real protection in these matters: "As much as love increases in your mind, so much do harmful forces not affect you. Since this is the case, the actual method for protecting against harm is the cultivation of love" (Tengin Guatso [14th Dali Lama, and H. H. The Dali Lama, Jeffrey Hopkins [ed. and trans.] *Kalachakra Tantra Rite of Initiation*, Londom, Wisdom Publications, 1989 [first published in 1985] p. 193). We agree with this sound advice. When you assume the god-form of an Angel and move through the Earth-Tier of one of the Watchtower Mandalas, you open yourself up to demonic influences. The best protection is sincere love and compassion.

4. The pronunciation of Z as "zode" (with a long o as in toad) comes from the Golden Dawn. However, many people today use "zeh" with good results. We agree that "zeh" has a better flow, and use it throughout this book, but you can use the more traditional "zode" if you prefer.

5. Throughout this book, all Enochian words are in capital letters.

6. The Western idea of casting a magic spell is similar to the Eastern idea of chanting a mantra. See *Spells and How They Work* by Janet and Stewart Farrar (Custer, WA: Phoenix Publishing Co., 1990) for an interesting look at how spells work in modern Witchcraft.

Chapter 8

SEX AND BLISS

One of the results of pathworking the Enochian Mandalas is the generation of *bliss*, or *ecstasy*.[1] Sexual union with a consort, real or imagined, is one technique used to assist in this process.[2] The meditation rituals in this book make use of sex and sexual forces to generate various degrees of bliss. Generally, five levels are recognized: bliss, enhanced bliss, supreme bliss, special bliss, and innate or natural bliss.[3]

We inevitably encounter the extremely pleasurable sensation of bliss in a high spiritual state of consciousness. Our highest subtle body, the spiritual body, is sometimes called the *Body of Bliss*, because its vibrations are so high that whenever we become conscious of it, our physical body is filled with a blissful sensation (similar to that reached in orgasm, but much more acute). In the East, the Body of Bliss is called the *ananda-maya-kosha*.[4]

An abyss exists between spiritual consciousness, which is formless, and normal human consciousness, which has forms.[5] In rituals, we arrange our bodies in special positions or postures, say certain words, and/or visualize in certain ways to narrow the gap, and thus shift consciousness from a normal, human state to one that is exalted, formless, spiritual. Sexual union with a consort can be used to align orgasmic bliss with the ecstasy of spiritual consciousness.[6]

To understand the use of sex here, it is essential to understand the *doctrine of dualities*. A duality implies any twofold force or two-sided expression; it most often appears to us as two separate concepts or forces. "Large" and "small," for example, are two sides of a duality. We usually think of "large" as very different from "small," but they actually only exist in relation to each other. "Large" is only meaningful when something small is compared to it. For example, a mouse is small when compared to an elephant, but large when compared to a grain of sand. A man is small when compared to the universe of planets and stars, but large when compared to the world of molecules and atoms. The concept of "up" is similarly meaningless without that of "down." When you think of "up," you usually think of what is over your head or above you. However, to people on the other side of the world, your "up" is their "down," and vice-versa.

Relativity is an important element of duality. The modern doctrine of relativity, described mathematically by Einstein, says that everything exists relative to something else: nothing has absolute existence. This doctrine is very similar to the ancient Buddhist doctrine of *dependent arising*, which asserts that the existence of every object in the universe depends on the existence of something else: nothing has independent existence.

The term *duality* refers to any force or expression with two sides, either of which is meaningless without the other. When you see a person and think in terms of ugly or beautiful, you are using a duality to compare that person with others. If only one man existed, he could be neither ugly nor beautiful, because the duality of beauty and ugliness would not exist.

It is impossible to become aware of one side of a duality without awareness of the other. The nature of duality is that we become aware of both sides simultaneously, and can only eliminate one side at the expense of the other. Likewise, we can only keep hold of one side of a duality by clinging (in some cases unconsciously) to the other. Awareness of this concept is extremely important for a full understanding of Enochian Magic.[7]

As an Enochian magical tool, sex is used to eliminate the duality of masculinity and femininity. In the mandala initiations, it is used to combine the masculine (subjective or inward) and feminine (objective or outward) forces that exist in the Watchtowers. Each pathworking ritual culminates in visualized sexual union with a deity (and in every case, the deity is a ruler of one of the four Watchtowers or the Tablet of Union). In psychological terms, this means union with the inner man or woman—the *anima* or *animus* of Carl Jung. Because of this, such a union has psychological benefits as well.[8]

The union can also involve a physical partner. If so, your consort should enter the mandala by the opposite gate, and ascend to the fourth level of the Great Cross on the opposite side, to maintain a magical balance of forces. In this case, the ritual would be a combined or joint pathworking. Each partner can alternately recite the appropriate verses over the opposite gates, and assume the appropriate god-forms, in their simultaneous progress towards the center of the mandala.

The four Watchtowers contain *sexual currents* where either masculinity or femininity is especially strong. The sexual currents of the cosmic planes of manifestation are a natural result of duality. Subjectivity is separate from objectivity, and this division forms the basic polarity of existence. The initial dualistic split into masculinity and femininity lead to sexuality and the sexual currents.[9]

The masculine current is characterized by consciousness; the feminine current is characterized by love. As manifestation proceeds deeper into time and space (i.e., downward from the Tablet of Union through the Watchtowers), the masculine current precipitates the mind, and the feminine consciousness precipitates the emotions. The masculine current is hot and dry. It is stern, unyielding, continuous. The feminine current is warm and wet. It is soft, yielding, and periodically changing.

The highest manifestation of the masculine current in our solar system is the sun; the highest manifestation of the feminine current in our solar system is the moon. The magical symbol of sun and moon conjoined symbolizes the union of masculinity and femininity, and of yourself with your consort. Again, your consort can be a physical person with whom you sexually unite, or a magical partner—a visualization with whom you merge.

All eighty-eight paths can be conducted as rituals in which you actually wear robes of the appropriate color, climb stairways, and so on. This will, of course, require you to prepare physical props beforehand. The rituals can also be conducted in a yogic sense, however, by intense visualization while within a magic circle. In either case, your partner can be either another person acting as your ritual consort or an imaginary figure.

NOTES TO CHAPTER EIGHT

1. Bliss is called *ananda* in the East, and is generated to varying degrees. Many excellent books are available for the study of Buddhist Tantric methods for generation of bliss. We recommend *Teachings of Tibetan Yoga* by Garma C. C. Chang (New Hyde Park, NY: University Books, 1963), *The Tantric View of Life* by Herbert V. Guenther (Boston, MA: Shambhala Publications, Inc., 1972), and *Highest Yoga Tantra* by Daniel Cozort (Ithaca, NY: Snow Lion Publications, 1986).

2. Tibetan Tantra recognizes two separate types of sex magic: (1) *Karmamudra*, sex with a physical partner, and (2) *Jnanamudra*, sex with an imaginary partner. *Karmamudra* means "action seal"; *Jnanamudra* means "wisdom seal." One or the other is considered indispensable to generating bliss. The deities of Tibetan Tantra are often shown in sexual embrace with their consorts (Egyptian deities had consorts as well, but these were never shown in sexual embrace). The so-called left-hand path of Tantra was never considered evil. It was called left-handed because when sex was physical, the woman sat on the left side of the man during the ceremony; when sex was imagined, the woman sat on the right side of the man. See *Tantra for Westerners: A Practical Guide to the Way of Action*, by Francis King (Rochester, VT: Destiny Books, 1995).

3. The student should not become bogged down by these names. The idea here is that each initiation generates a slightly higher and more intense degree of bliss.

4. Curiously, the idea of a Body of Bliss has never taken hold in Western magic, except perhaps in a few marginal schools of sexual magic. However, the idea of ecstasy accompanying exalted states of consciousness is widely acknowledged in Western mysticism, as the writings of the Christian mystics show.

5. As above so below—just as the Great Outer Abyss is said to exist in the magical universe between the planes of manifestation and the planes of formless spirit, so an Abyss exists within every person.

6. This can be with either a physical or imaginary consort. Most schools teach that you must begin with a physical consort, and progress to an imaginary one. We suggest that you use an imaginary consort in these initiations unless you have a consort with whom you share an enduring relationship. Our rationale for this is that any sexual union with a physical partner subjects both parties to karmic entanglement. In an enduring relationship, the karmic entanglement already exists. With a temporary relationship, however, you may subject yourself to unknown and unnecessary karmic burdens, and it is quite possible that the costs will outweigh the benefits.

7. The following three laws of duality are from our *Enochian Physics* (St. Paul, MN: Llewellyn Publications, 1989, pp. 26-27):

Duality Law 1. When one side of a duality is created, the other side comes into existence simultaneously.

Duality Law 2. When one side of a duality is eliminated, the other side ceases to exist simultaneously.

Duality Law 3. Everything that exists is one side of a duality, even existence itself.

The Angels' Message to Humanity

8. Although we say that your partner is "imaginary," he or she will, nonetheless, be real. You must remember that during the initiation, you will no longer be you—you will be a deity. Your consort will be as real as you are, no more and no less. The god and goddess of each Watchtower are real beings. The sexual union is a merging of their subtle bodies and, therefore, of themselves. When your god and goddess merge, it will feel like it is actually happening to you. The result is that you will merge with your consort and become a completed being.

9. The following five laws that govern the sexual currents are from our *Enochian Physics*:

    Sexual Current Law 1: Opposite currents will attract while like currents will repulse.

    Comments: In general, male magicians will find the feminine current to be sexually stimulating, attractive, and alluring. The masculine current will not seem sexually charged at all. Female magicians will be sexually aroused by the masculine current but not by the feminine current.

    Sexual Current Law 2: A sexual current will be induced by a magician whenever s/he moves through a field/plane.

    Comments: A magician who enters a region such as an Aethyr or Watchtower square will not automatically encounter a sexual current. Sexual currents can only be encountered while "moving about" in such regions. Here "moving" does not mean motion through space-time, but rather an acceleration of consciousness. It can be viewed as an increase or decrease in the vibratory rate of the magician's aura (Body of Light).

    Sexual Current Law 3: The type of sexual current induced is such as to oppose the sexuality of the magician.

    Comments: A male magician will induce the feminine current. A female magician will induce the masculine current.

    Sexual Current Law 4: As a sexual current can influence a magician, so a magician can influence a sexual current.

    Comments: Any sexual current can be bent to the will of the trained magician. Sexual currents are used in many magical operations as energy sources, much like a battery is used as a source of electrical energy.

    Sexual Current Law 5: A magician who induces a sexual current over a given region can influence any other being within that region.

    Comments: Two people within the same sexual current can easily influence each other, whether conscious or unconscious of that current. A strong thought in the mind of one can cause that thought to be shared by the other. In other words, the power of telepathy increases in a sexual current.

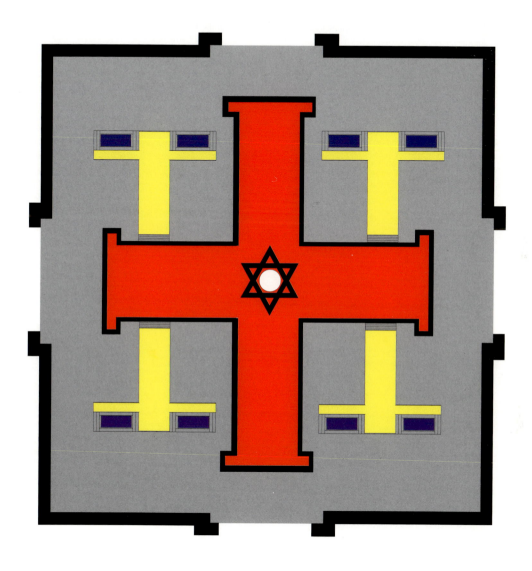

I
THE EARTH MANDALA

II
THE WATER MANDALA

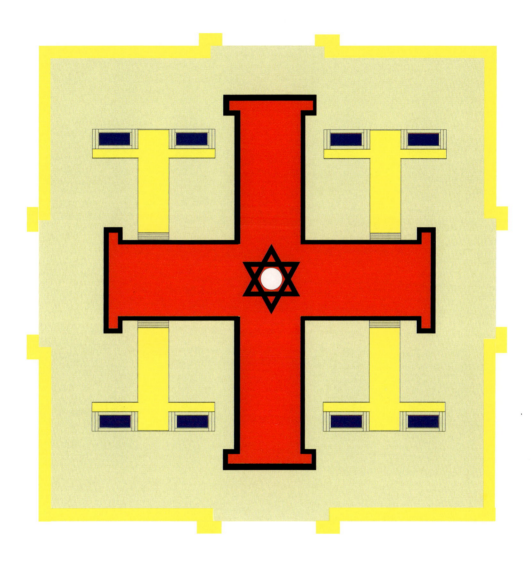

III
THE AIR MANDALA

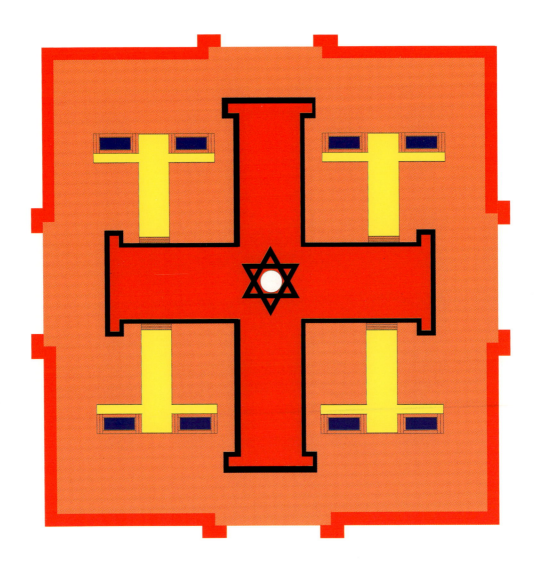

IV

THE FIRE MANDALA

V
THE COMPLETE DIRECTIONAL ENOCHIAN MANDALA

VI
THE SIX MANDALAS OF THE DIRECTIONAL ENOCHIAN CUBE

VII
THE SIX MANDALAS OF THE SERIAL ENOCHIAN CUBE

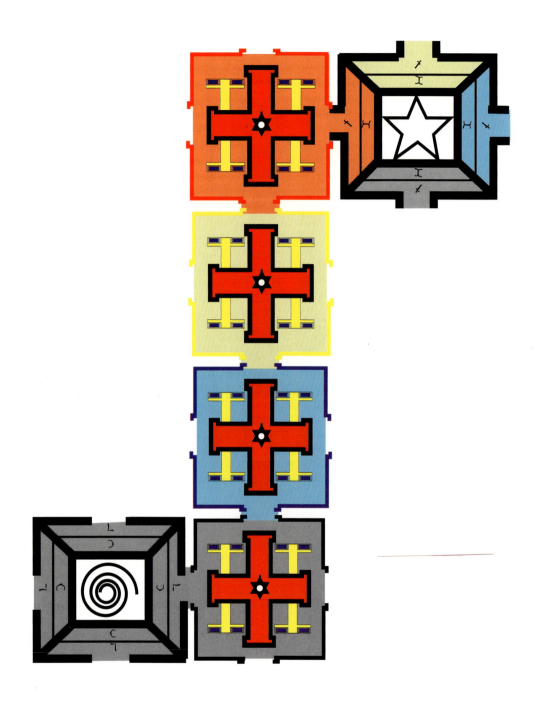

VIII
Pathworking Foldout of the Serial
Enochian Cube

Chapter 9

THE PREPARATION

To complete our series of ritual initiations successfully, begin with Path 1, entering the Watchtower of Earth, and continue through Path 16. Work your way, one path at a time, up to the Tablet of Union, which contains the last twenty-four paths.[1]

In each case, read the entire pathworking ritual carefully. As part of your preparation exercise, make sure that you understand each step, know how to make a circle, do the pentagram ritual, and pronounce the magic words (mantras).[2] Choose your path in advance so you know which god-forms you will assume. The god-forms are given for each path. However, only a few characteristics are given. You will be told (1) a name, (2) a color, (3) whether the deity has wings or not (and if so, whether they are small or large), and (4) a magical instrument. In some cases, you will be provided other qualities, such as whether the deity is heavy or thin, attractive or fierce in appearance, etc. Let your magical imagination fill in details around these general guidelines, to develop as specific a god-form as possible.

The following four lists of correspondences will help you visualize the composition and atmosphere of each of the four Watchtowers. Use as many of these correspondences as you can during the initiations. These lists also contain pronunciations of the Enochian words and names to be spoken aloud during the initiations.

THE WATCHTOWER OF EARTH

Element: Earth (NANTA, pronounced "nah-en-tah").
Symbol: ▽
Cosmic Plane: Etheric
Planet: Moon
Properties: Cold and dry. Objects/form. Body.
Quadrant: Northern
Color: Black
Enochian Letters: P, T, X, Z (Ω, ✓, Γ, P,)
Sense: Smell

Body: Etheric body
Chakra: Root (*Muladhara*)
Power: Healing
Holy Name: MOR-DIAL-HKTGA (pronounced "moh-ar-dee-al-heh-keh-teh-gah").
King: IKZHIKAL (pronounced "ee-keh-zeh-hee-kal").
Goddess: ORABALN (pronounced "oh-rah-bah-el-en").
Magic Words: XUM and AH (pronounced "etz-oom" and "ah-heh").
Seniors:
> LAIDROM, a Son of Mars from the Secret Mountains. (Pronounced "el-ahee-dar-oh-em.")
>
> AKZINOR, a Son of Jupiter from the Dark Mountains. (Pronounced "ah-keh-zee-noh-rah.")
>
> LZINOPO, a Son of the Moon from the High Mountains. (Pronounced "el-zee-noh-poh.")
>
> ALHKTGA, a Son of Venus from the Mountains of Spirit. (Pronounced "ah-leh-hek-teh-gah.")
>
> AHMLLKV, a Son of Mercury from the Ancient Mountains. (Pronounced "ah-mel-el-keh-veh.")
>
> LIIANSA, a Son of Saturn from the Mountains of Truth. (Pronounced "elee-ee-ah-ness-ah.")

THE WATCHTOWER OF WATER

Element: Water (HKOMA, pronounced "heh-koh-mah").
Symbol: ▽
Cosmic Plane: Astral
Planet: Venus
Properties: Cold and wet. Sound. Speech.
Quadrant: Western
Color: Blue
Enochian Letters: M, N, Q, R, V (Ɛ, Ɔ, ⊔, Ɛ, ∂)
Sense: Taste
Body: Astral body
Chakra: Navel (*Manipura*)
Power: Creation
Holy Name: MPH-ARSL-GAIOL (pronounced "em-peh-heh-ar-ess-el-gah-ee-oh-leh").
King: RAAGIOSL (pronounced "rah-ah-gee-oh-sel").
Goddess: LOBABAN (pronounced "el-oh-bah-bah-en").
Magic Words: QUM and TRAM (pronounced "que-m" and "teh-rah-meh").
Seniors:
> LSRAHPM, a Son of Mars from the Waters of Slaughter. (Pronounced "less-rah-pem.")
>
> SAIINOV, a Son of Jupiter from the Waters of the Temple. (Pronounced "sah-ee-ee-noh-veh.")
>
> LAVAXRP, a Son of the Moon from the Waters of Arrogance. (Pronounced "el-

The Preparation

ah-vahtz-ar-peh.")

SLGAIOL, a Son of Venus from the Waters of Spirit. (Pronounced "sel-gah-ee-oh-leh.")

SOAIZNT, a Son of Mercury from the Saving Waters. (Pronounced "soh-ahee-zen-teh.")

LIGDISA, a Son of Saturn from the Headless Waters. (Pronounced "elee-geh-dee-sah.")

THE WATCHTOWER OF AIR

Element: Air (EXARP, pronounced "etz-ar-peh").
Symbol: △
Cosmic Plane: Mental
Planet: Mercury
Properties: Hot and wet. Thoughts. Mind.
Quadrant: Eastern
Color: Yellow
Enochian Letters: E, G, H, I, L, O, S (⊓, Ꮟ, ⑪, Ꮑ, ⊂, ᒪ, ⊓)
Sense: Sight
Body: Mental body
Chakra: Heart (*Anahata*)
Power: Telepathy
Holy Name: ORO-IBAH-AOZPI (pronounced "oh-roh-ee-beh-ah-oh-zeh-pee").
King: BATAIVAH (pronounced "bah-tah-ee-vah-heh").
Goddess: ALOBABN (pronounced "ah-loh-bah-ben").
Magic Words: HUM and MUM (pronounced "hoom" and "moom").
Seniors:

HABIORO, a Son of Mars from the Low Winds. (Pronounced "hah-bee-oh-roh.")

AAOZAIF, a Son of Jupiter from the Frequent Winds. (Pronounced "ah-ah-oh-zah-ee-feh.")

HTNORDA, a Son of the Moon from the Offspring Winds. (Pronounced "heh-teh-noh-rah-dah.")

AHAOZPI, a Son of Venus from the Contented Winds. (Pronounced "aha-oh-zeh-pee.")

AVTOTAR, a Son of Mercury from the Listening Winds. (Pronounced "ah-veh-toh-tah-rah.")

HIPOTGA, a Son of Saturn from the Unique Winds. (Pronounced "hee-poh-teh-gah.")

THE WATCHTOWER OF FIRE

Element: Fire (BITOM, pronounced "bee-toh-meh").
Symbol: △
Cosmic Plane: Spiritual

The Angels' Message to Humanity

Planet: Sun
Properties: Hot and dry. Bliss.
Quadrant: Southern
Color: Red
Enochian Letters: B, F, K (Ʋ, ✗, ꓭ)
Sense: Touch
Body: Causal body
Chakra: Throat (*Vishuddha*)
Power: Destruction
Holy Name: OIP-TEAA-PDOKE (pronounced "oh-ee-peh-teh-ah-ah-peh-doh-keh").
King: EDLPRNAA (pronounced "eh-del-par-nah-ah").
Goddess: BALOBAN (pronounced "bah-loh-bah-neh").
Magic Words: KUM and RI (pronounced "koom" and "ar-ee").
Seniors:

AAETPIO, a Son of Mars from the Seeking Fires. (Pronounced "ah-ah-eteh-pee-oh.")

ADAEOET, a Son of Jupiter from the Singing Fires. (Pronounced "ah-dah-eh-oh-eteh.")

ALNKVOD, a Son of the Moon from the Serving Fires. (Pronounced "ah-len-keh-voh-deh.")

AAPDOKE, a Son of Venus from the Remaining Fires. (Pronounced "ah-ah-ped-oh-keh.")

ANODOIN, a Son of Mercury from the Opening Fires. (Pronounced "ah-noh-doh-ee-neh.")

ARINNAP, a Son of Saturn from the Protecting Fires. (Pronounced "ah-ree-neh-nah-peh.")

You may either use visualization alone or with props, or work solely with props to effect the proper god-form. Props would include robes of the proper color and simulated magical instruments to be held. The four ruling Kings and four Goddesses of the Watchtowers, and EHNB and BABALON in the Tablet of Union, are naked. When assuming their forms, you can either visualize yourself as naked or remove your robe. You can also arrange four stations inside your magic circle to represent the four levels or tiers of each Watchtower.[3] The important thing is to be able to see yourself as a god or goddess actually entering each Watchtower.[4]

At the beginning of each of the eighty-eight initiatory paths, you will say a short prayer in the Enochian language called the Centering Spell. Our Enochian Centering Spell is as follows:

OL ELONUSAHE OIADA IA-I-DON ELAZAPE KOMESALAHE MIKAELAZO MADA DAS APILA LU IPAMIS, ELA GO-A-AL PE-RIPESOL KAOSAGO OD FAOREGITA ORESA OD TOFAGILO DAS KAHISA DO-NO POAMALA DAS LARASADA DO-ANANAEL TOFAG-ILO DO-ORESA SA-DO-LUKIFTIASA.

This powerful spell can be translated:

I am exalted in the Power of God, [I am] the All-Powerful, [I am] the Center of the Circle, [I am the] powerful God who lives on and whose end cannot be,

The Preparation

the only creator of heaven, earth, and the Dwelling of Darkness and all that is in their places, who disposes in Secret Wisdom of all things in darkness and in light.[5]

NOTES TO CHAPTER NINE

1. The eighty-eight initiatory paths are very similar outwardly. But inwardly, there is a great deal of difference among them, because they take place on different cosmic subplanes, have slightly different deities, and so on. The safest way to complete these exercises is to begin with Path 1 and continue, one at a time, to Path 88. After experiencing the paths in this way, you can then safely skip around and conduct those exercises that you need to gain or enhance specific abilities.

2. The rules for pronunciation of Enochian are in chapter 6. As a rule of thumb, the pronunciation should be sonorous and flow easily, almost musically. Variations in the rules given above for pronunciation of letters allow for several possible ways to say most Enochian words and names. There is no right or wrong way, so long as the general rules are obeyed.

3. There are no hard and fast rules. If you have experience with yogic meditation and visualization, you probably won't need physical props. If you don't, props may be helpful, since they tend to make the initiatory paths feel more like rituals. If a hall can be arranged like the mandala, and an appropriate partner is present to play the role of the consort, the ritual would result in *Karmamudra* (sex with a physical partner). If you prefer yoga, visualize the mandala and culminate the initiation with *Jnanamudra* (sex with a magical partner).

4. His Holiness, the Dali Lama, says, "When practicing Mantra in a mandala, it is necessary to have clear appearance of yourself as a deity and the pride [or conception] of yourself as a deity. The chief of these two is the pride of being a deity for which it is necessary to have clear appearance of yourself as a deity." (*Kalachakra Tantra*, London: Wisdom, 1985, p. 219)

5. This prayer is a slight modification of a section of Aleister Crowley's Enochian rendering of the Goetia. See *The Book of the Goetia of Solomon the King* (New York: Magickal Childe Publishing, 1989, p. 62). An alternate centering spell, written by Donald Tyson, is as follows:

   OL LANSH OIADA,
   (I am) (in power exalted) (of God, the Just One)

   IAIDON, OVOARS COMSELHA, MICALZO
   (the All-powerful) (the center) (of the circle) (mighty)

   MAD DS APILA LU SOBA ULS IPAMIS, EL
   (God) (who) (lives) (nor) (whose) (end) (cannot be) (one)

   QADAH PERIPSOL CAOSGA OD FAORGT
   (creator of) (heaven) (of Earth) (and) (the dwelling-place)

   ORSA OD TOFGLO DS CHISA PRIAZ
   (of darkness) (and) (all things) (which) (are in) (those)

   PI, DS LRASD LAIADA ANANAEL TOFGLO
   (places) (who) (disposes) (in secret) (wisdom) (all things)

   ORSA OD LUCIFTIAS.
   (in darkness) (and) (in brightness)

Chapter 10

Pathworking the Watchtower of Earth

This chapter contains the first sixteen initiatory paths. In these paths, you will use the Watchtower Mandala of Earth, as shown in color plate I. The critical twenty-one positions within the mandala are shown in Figure 15, the names of the entrance gates and first stairways are shown in Figure 16, and the names and positions of the twenty-two deities of the Mandala of Earth are shown in Figure 17. Figures 18 through 33 show the sixteen paths you will take through the Earth Mandala.

The Earth Quadrant of the Earth Mandala

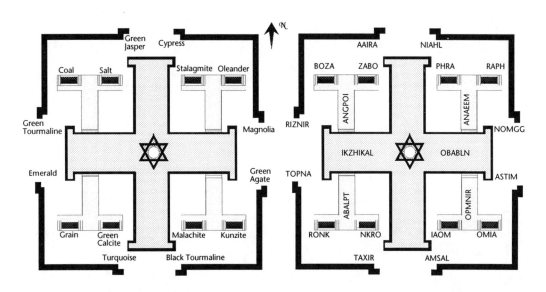

Figure 16: The Earth Mandala Showing Gates and Stairways

Figure 17: The Earth Mandala Showing Deities

Path One

The Path of Inoculation leads through the four positions 1-13-19-21, as shown in Figure 18. It contains the specific atmospheres of karma, protection, healing, and sustenance. It is the First Path of Beauty. Use this path for protection from physical disease or sickness of any kind.

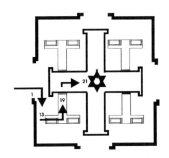

Step 1. Make a circle and conduct the invoking pentagram ritual.

Figure 18: Path 1, The Path of Innoculation

Step 2. Face the East, and imagine the Mandala of the Watchtower of Earth clearly before you.[1] You are facing its Western wall. Imagine the walls and floors to be black. Recite the Centering Spell.[2] Then say:

> May I enter and safely pass through this black Watchtower of Earth.
> May I obtain success in this, the first of my initiations.
> In the threefold secret and holy name of MORDIALHKTGA
> I make this request. ORERI KALAZ KORESA TAZA SAGE DO
> HOMILA IPAME KAOSAGO[3]

Step 3. Visualize the closed Emerald Gate. say:

> O TOPNA I invoke thee. Come unto me from the Watchtower of Earth.

Visualize TOPNA before you. Approach the Angel unafraid; open your arms and embrace him. Feel his body melt into your own and become a part of you. Assume the god-form of the Angel TOPNA, who guards the Emerald Gate (position 1), as follows:

The god-form of TOPNA: See page 243 for the god-form of TOPNA.

There are special words written above the Emerald Gate to be spoken before entering.[4] Say:

> The sinner knocketh and is heard; but he that is just entereth.

Step 4. Visualize the gate opening at these words. Step within the Emerald Gate.[5] Face the Earth-Tier. In the god-form of TOPNA, say:

> I am the Angel of Earth. I am the Angel TOPNA.
> I am the Guardian of the Emerald Gate. I enter into the Watchtower of Earth.

While slowly repeating the Threefold Holy Word, enter into the Watchtower of Earth and move across the Earth-Tier to the bottom of the Grain Stairway leading up to the Water-Tier. The Threefold Word that you recite will protect you from the Demons who reside on the Earth-Tier.

Step 5. Face the Grain Stairway. Visualize the Kerubic Angel RONK before you. Approach the Angel unafraid; open your arms and embrace him. Feel his body melt into your own and become a part of you. Assume the god-form of RONK, who guards the Grain Stairway, as follows:[6]

Pathworking the Watchtower of Earth

The god-form of RONK: see page 242 for the god-form of RONK.

Recite the words written over the Grain Stairway:[7]

> **Come O you that have sucked of the breasts, wherein the judgments and secret will of the Lord is hid, and of Necessity to come.**

Step 6. In the god-form of the Kerubic Angel RONK, while slowly repeating the magic word XUM[8], climb the twelve steps of the Grain Stairway to the Water-Tier. Then say:

> **I am a Kerubic Angel of Earth. I am Kerubic Angel RONK.**
> **I am the Guardian of the Grain Stairway.**
> **I rise up through the Watchtower of Earth.**
> **Throughout eternity I manifest myself from Earth to Water within Earth.**

Step 7. Slowly repeat the magic word XUM as you move across the Water-Tier. Approach the Stairway to the Air-Tier. Before entering the Second Stairway, say:

> **Human policy cannot prevail here. As many as are not faithful in these regions, shall die a most miserable death, and shall drink of sleep everlasting.**[9]

Climb the Second Stairway, which has seven steps, to the Air-Tier. Visualize Sephirothic Cross Angel ABALPT before you. Approach the Angel unafraid; open your arms and embrace him. Feel his body melt into your own and become a part of you. Assume the god-form of ABALPT ("ah-bah-leh-peh-teh"), who guards the Air-Tier and Third Stairway (position 19), as follows:

The god-form of ABALPT: See page 235 for the god-form of ABALPT.

The Third Stairway is black and smells of musk. This Stairway is also dry and cold. It has four steps. Each step has a letter written in white and blazing to look upon. The letter P is on the first step, the letter T is on the second, the letter X is on the third, and the letter Z is on the fourth.[10] Recite the words written above the Third Stairway before ascending:[11]

> **Behold, there are which rise, and have lost their bodies, and there are also which rise, and they rise in body.**

Step 8. In the god-form of the Sephirothic Cross Angel, slowly repeat the magic word AH[12] as you climb. Climb up to the top of the Third Stairway and say:

> **I am a Sephirothic Cross Angel of Earth.**
> **I am Sephirothic Cross Angel ABALPT.**
> **I bear the Cross of Earth from Water to Air within Earth.**

Step 9. As ABALPT, slowly repeat the word AH and at the top of the Stairway, turn toward the center of the Fire-Tier. If you are male, assume the naked god-form of the King of Earth, IKZHIKAL ("ee-keh-zeh-hee-kal"). If you are female, assume the naked god-form of the Goddess of Earth, ORABALN ("oh-rah-bah-el- en").[13]

The god-form of IKZHIKAL: See page 239 for the god-form of IKZHIKAL.

The god-form of ORABALN: See page 241 for the god-form of ORABALN.[14]

The Angels' Message to Humanity

Step 10. Slowly repeat the name of your consort (either ORABALN or IKZHIKAL) while walking along the Fire-Tier, the Great Cross of the Watchtower, toward the center of the mandala. Face the large hexagram made of black stone with a white circle at its center. You are now facing the center of the mandala. If you are male, visualize your consort, ORABALN, standing naked at the center of the black hexagram (position 21 in Figure 15) waiting for you. If you are female, visualize your consort, IKZHIKAL, standing naked at the center of the hexagram (position 21 in Figure 15) waiting for you.[15]

Step 11. Stand just outside of the hexagram, face your consort (who is naked and very beautiful) before you[16], and say:

> **I am the good Angel of man. I am the external Center of the Soul, and I do carry with me the internal Character of that thing whereof one seeks to be a Dignifier, within which lies a great secret: the conjunction and separation of the proportion of their times, between the soul and body of man. Happy, therefore, is that soul who beholds the glory of his dignification, and is partaker with him that is his keeper. May this be known unto men, so that the thickness of the earth cannot hinder their speeches; neither can the darkness of the lowest air obscure, or make dark, the sharpness of their eyes. May this Character be made manifest in me.[17]**

While you face each other, enter the stone hexagram. See yourselves clearly at the center of the Earth Mandala. Then smile at each other as if in love. Slowly move together and embrace. While saying the word NANTA, merge God/King and Goddess of Earth together while holding a detailed awareness of the Watchtower around you.[18] Remain this way for as long as you can, and then say:

> **Thus has Truth vanquished Darkness. Even so shall I vanquish the World in the name of the Spirit of Power and Truth. Thus am I sworn. But I cease for days to come; for they are days delivered. Let them be therefore to me as Days of Repentance. For the end of forty days must come. And this doctrine shall be written to all nations, even to the end of the World. The grain is yet in the Earth, and has newly consented with the Earth. But when it springs, and bears seed, the number shall be the last.[19]**

Step 12. Turn from your consort and step outside the black hexagram. Leave by the same path that you entered.[20] After leaving the mandala, conduct the banishing pentagram ritual. This completes the first initiatory path.

PATH TWO

The Path of Wealth leads through the four positions 1-14-19-21, as shown in Figure 19. It contains the specific atmospheres of karma, protection, knowledge, and prosperity. It is the Second Path of Beauty. Use this path for physical wealth.

Step 1. Make a circle and conduct the invoking pentagram ritual.

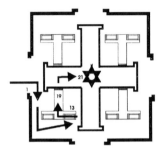

Figure 19: Path 2, The Path of Wealth

Pathworking the Watchtower of Earth

Step 2. Face the East, and imagine the Mandala of the Watchtower of Earth clearly before you. You are facing its Western wall. Imagine the walls and floors to be black. Recite the Centering Spell. Then say:

> May I enter and safely pass through this black Watchtower of Earth.
> May I obtain success in this, the second of my initiations.
> In the threefold secret and holy name of MORDIALHKTGA I make this request. ORERI KALAZ KORESA TAZA SAGE
> DO HOMILA IPAME KAOSAGO

Step 3. Visualize the closed Emerald Gate. say:

> O TOPNA I invoke thee. Come unto me from the Watchtower of Earth.

Visualize TOPNA before you. Approach the Angel unafraid; open your arms and embrace him. Feel his body melt into your own and become a part of you. Assume the god-form of the Angel TOPNA, who guards the Emerald Gate (position 1), as follows:

The god-form of TOPNA: See page 243 for the god-form of TOPNA.

There are special words written above the Emerald Gate to be spoken before entering. Say:

> The sinner knocketh and is heard; but he that is just entereth.

Step 4. Visualize the gate opening at these words. Step within the Emerald Gate. Face the Earth-Tier. In the god-form of TOPNA, say:

> I am the Angel of Earth. I am the Angel TOPNA.
> I am the Guardian of the Emerald Gate. I enter into the Watchtower of Earth.

While slowly repeating the Threefold Holy Word, enter into the Watchtower of Earth and move across the Earth-Tier to the bottom of the Green Calcite Stairway leading up to the Water-Tier. The Threefold Word that you recite will protect you from the Demons who reside on the Earth-Tier.

Step 5. Face the Green Calcite Stairway. Visualize the Kerubic Angel NKRO before you. Approach the Angel unafraid; open your arms and embrace him. Feel his body melt into your own and become a part of you. Assume the god-form of NKRO ("en-keh-roh"), who guards the Green Calcite Stairway, as follows:

The god-form of NKRO: See page 241 for the god-form of NKRO.

Recite the words written over the Green Calcite Stairway:

> You number without number, wherefore shew you not yourselves?

Step 6. In the god-form of the Kerubic Angel NKRO, while slowly repeating the magic word XUM, climb the twelve steps of the Green Calcite Stairway to the Water-Tier. Then say:

> I am a Kerubic Angel of Earth. I am Kerubic Angel NKRO.
> I am the Guardian of the Green Calcite Stairway.

The Angels' Message to Humanity

**I rise up through the Watchtower of Earth.
Throughout eternity I manifest myself from Earth to Water within Earth.**

Step 7. Slowly repeat the magic word XUM as you move across the Water-Tier. Approach the Stairway to the Air-Tier. Before entering the Second Stairway, say:

Human policy cannot prevail here. As many as are not faithful in these regions, shall die a most miserable death, and shall drink of sleep everlasting.

Climb the Second Stairway, which has seven steps, to the Air-Tier. Visualize the Sephirothic Cross Angel ABALPT before you. Approach the Angel unafraid; open your arms and embrace him. Feel his body melt into your own and become a part of you. Assume the god-form of ABALPT, who guards the Air-Tier and Third Stairway (position 19), as follows:

The god-form of ABALPT: See page 235 for the god-form of ABALPT.

The Third Stairway is black and smells of musk. This Stairway is also dry and cold. It has four steps. Each step has a letter written in white and blazing to look upon. The letter P is on the first step, the letter T is on the second, the letter X is on the third, and the letter Z is on the fourth. Recite the words written above the Third Stairway before ascending:

**Behold, there are which rise, and have lost their bodies,
and there are also which rise, and they rise in body.**

Step 8. In the god-form of the Sephirothic Cross Angel, slowly repeat the magic word AH as you climb. Climb up to the top of the Third Stairway and say:

**I am a Sephirothic Cross Angel of Earth.
I am Sephirothic Cross Angel ABALPT.
I bear the Cross of Earth from Water to Air within Earth.**

Step 9. As ABALPT, slowly repeat the word AH and at the top of the Stairway, turn toward the center of the Fire-Tier. If you are male, assume the naked god-form of the King of Earth, IKZHIKAL. If you are female, assume the naked god-form of the Goddess of Earth, ORABALN.

Step 10. Same as Step 10 in Path 1.[21]

Step 11. Same as Step 11 in Path 1.

Step 12. Turn from your consort and step outside the black hexagram. Leave by the same path that you entered. After leaving the mandala, conduct the banishing pentagram ritual. This completes the second initiatory path.

Pathworking the Watchtower of Earth

PATH THREE

The Path of Physical Sustenance leads through the four positions 2-13-19-21, as shown in Figure 20. It contains the specific atmospheres of strength, protection, healing, and sustenance. It is the Third Path of Beauty. Use this path to increase physical strength.

Step 1. Make a circle and conduct the invoking pentagram ritual.

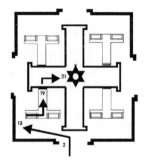

Figure 20: Path 3, The Path of Physical Sustenance

Step 2. Face the North, and imagine the Mandala of the Watchtower of Earth clearly before you. You are facing its Southern wall. Imagine the walls and floors to be black. Recite the Centering Spell. Then say:

> May I enter and safely pass through this black Watchtower of Earth.
> May I obtain success in this, the third of my initiations.
> In the threefold secret and holy name of MORDIALHKTGA
> I make this request. ORERI KALAZ KORESA TAZA
> SAGE DO HOMILA IPAME KAOSAGO

Step 3. Visualize the closed Turquoise Gate. say:

> O TAXIR I invoke thee. Come unto me from the Watchtower of Earth.

Visualize TAXIR before you. Approach the Angel unafraid; open your arms and embrace him. Feel his body melt into your own and become a part of you. Assume the god-form of the Angel TAXIR, who guards the Turquoise Gate (position 2), as follows:

The god-form of TAXIR: See page 243 for the god-form of TAXIR.

There are special words written above the Turquoise Gate to be spoken before entering. Say:

> **Wonderful and great are the secrets and judgments of God's determinations to come, which are already leased and gathered into your bosom.**

Step 4. Visualize the gate opening at these words. Step within the Turquoise Gate. Face the Earth-Tier. In the god-form of TAXIR, say:

> O TAXIR I invoke thee. Come unto me from the Watchtower of Earth.
> I am the Angel of Earth. I am the Angel TAXIR.
> I am the Guardian of the Turquoise Gate.
> I enter into the Watchtower of Earth.

While slowly repeating the Threefold Holy Word, enter into the Watchtower of Earth and move across the Earth-Tier to the bottom of the Grain Stairway (position 13) leading up to the Water-Tier. The Threefold Word that you recite will protect you from the Demons who reside on the Earth-Tier.

Step 5. Face the Grain Stairway. Visualize the Kerubic Angel RONK before you. Approach the Angel unafraid; open your arms and embrace him. Feel his body melt into your own and become a part of you. Assume the god-form of RONK, who guards the Grain Stairway, as follows:

The god-form of RONK: See page 242 for the god-form of RONK.

Recite the words written over the Grain Stairway:

**Come O you that have sucked of the breasts,
wherein the judgments and secret will of the Lord is hid,
and of Necessity to come.**

Step 6. In the god-form of the Kerubic Angel RONK, while slowly repeating the magic word XUM, climb the twelve steps of the Grain Stairway to the Water-Tier. Then say:

**I am a Kerubic Angel of Earth. I am Kerubic Angel RONK.
I am the Guardian of the Grain Stairway.
I rise up through the Watchtower of Earth.
Throughout eternity I manifest myself from Earth to Water within Earth.**

Step 7. Slowly repeat the magic word XUM as you move across the Water-Tier. Approach the Stairway to the Air-Tier. Before entering the Second Stairway, say:

Human policy cannot prevail here. As many as are not faithful in these regions, shall die a most miserable death, and shall drink of sleep everlasting.

Climb the Second Stairway, which has seven steps, to the Air-Tier. Visualize the Sephirothic Cross Angel ABALPT before you. Approach the Angel unafraid; open your arms and embrace him. Feel his body melt into your own and become a part of you.

Assume the god-form of ABALPT, who guards the Air-Tier and Third Stairway (position 19), as follows:

The god-form of ABALPT: See page 235 for the god-form of ABALPT.

The Third Stairway is black and smells of musk. It is also dry and cold. It has four steps, each of which bears a letter written in white and blazing to look upon. The letter P is on the first step, the letter T is on the second, the letter X on the third, and the letter Z on the fourth. Recite the words written above the Third Stairway before ascending:

**Behold, there are which rise, and have lost their bodies,
and there are also which rise, and they rise in body.**

Step 8. In the god-form of the Sephirothic Cross Angel, slowly repeat the magic word AH as you climb. Climb up to the top of the Third Stairway and say:

I am a Sephirothic Cross Angel of Earth. I am Sephirothic Cross Angel ABALPT. I bear the Cross of Earth from Water to Air within Earth.

Step 9. As ABALPT, slowly repeat the word AH and at the top of the Stairway, turn toward the center of the Fire-Tier. If you are male, assume the naked god-form of the King of Earth, IKZHIKAL. If you are female, assume the naked god-form of the Goddess of Earth, ORABALN.

Step 10. Same as Step 10 in Path 1.

Pathworking the Watchtower of Earth

Step 11. Same as Step 11 in Path 1.

Step 12. Turn from your consort and step outside the black hexagram. Leave by the same path that you entered. After leaving the mandala, conduct the banishing pentagram ritual. This completes the third initiatory path.

PATH FOUR

The Path of Physical Security leads through the four positions 2-14-19-21, as shown in Figure 21. It contains the specific atmospheres of strength, protection, knowledge, and prosperity. It is the Fourth Path of Beauty. Use this path for physical safety and security.

Step 1. Make a circle and conduct the invoking pentagram ritual.

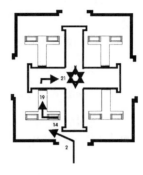

Figure 21: Path 4, The Path of Physical Security

Step 2. Face the North, and imagine the Mandala of the Watchtower of Earth clearly before you. You are facing its Southern wall. Imagine the walls and floors to be black. Recite the Centering Spell. Then say:

> May I enter and safely pass through this black Watchtower of Earth.
> May I obtain success in this, the fourth of my initiations.
> In the threefold secret and holy name of MORDIALHKTGA
> I make this request. ORERI KALAZ KORESA TAZA
> SAGE DO HOMILA IPAME KAOSAGO

Step 3. Visualize the closed Turquoise Gate. say:

> O TAXIR I invoke thee. Come unto me from the Watchtower of Earth.

Visualize TAXIR before you. Approach the Angel unafraid; open your arms and embrace him. Feel his body melt into your own and become a part of you. Assume the god-form of the Angel TAXIR, who guards the Turquoise Gate (position 2), as follows:

> **The god-form of TAXIR:** See page 243 for the god-form of TAXIR.

There are special words written above the Turquoise Gate to be spoken before entering. Say:

> **Wonderful and great are the secrets and judgments of God's determinations to come, which are already leased and gathered into your bosom.**

Step 4. Visualize the gate opening at these words. Step within the Turquoise Gate. Face the Earth-Tier. In the god-form of TAXIR, say:

> O TAXIR I invoke thee. Come unto me from the Watchtower of Earth.
> I am the Angel of Earth. I am the Angel TAXIR. I am the Guardian
> of the Turquoise Gate. I enter into the Watchtower of Earth.

While slowly repeating the Threefold Holy Word, enter into the Watchtower of Earth and move across the Earth-Tier to the bottom of the Green Calcite Stairway

The Angels' Message to Humanity

(position 14) leading up to the Water-Tier. The Threefold Word that you recite will protect you from the Demons who reside on the Earth-Tier.

Step 5. Face the Green Calcite Stairway. Visualize the Kerubic Angel NKRO before you. Approach the Angel unafraid; open your arms and embrace him. Feel his body melt into your own and become a part of you. Assume the god-form of NKRO, who guards the Green Calcite Stairway, as follows:

The god-form of NKRO: See page 241 for the god-form of NKRO.

Recite the words written over the Green Calcite Stairway:

You number without number, wherefore shew you not yourselves?

Step 6. In the god-form of the Kerubic Angel NKRO, while slowly repeating the magic word XUM, climb the twelve steps of the Green Calcite Stairway to the Water-Tier. Then say:

**I am a Kerubic Angel of Earth. I am Kerubic Angel NKRO.
I am the Guardian of the Green Calcite Stairway. I rise up through the Watchtower of Earth. Throughout eternity
I manifest myself from Earth to Water within Earth.**

Step 7. Slowly repeat the magic word XUM as you move across the Water-Tier. Approach the Stairway to the Air-Tier. Before entering the Second Stairway, say:

Human policy cannot prevail here. As many as are not faithful in these regions, shall die a most miserable death, and shall drink of sleep everlasting.

Climb the Second Stairway, which has seven steps, to the Air-Tier. Visualize the Sephirothic Cross Angel ABALPT before you. Approach the Angel unafraid; open your arms and embrace him. Feel his body melt into your own and become a part of you. Assume the god-form of ABALPT, who guards the Air-Tier and Third Stairway (position 19), as follows:

The god-form of ABALPT: See page 235 for the god-form of ABALPT.

The Third Stairway is black and smells of musk. It is also dry and cold. It has four steps, each of which bears a letter written in white and blazing to look upon. The letter P is on the first step, the letter T is on the second, the letter X is on the third, and the letter Z is on the fourth. Recite the words written above the Third Stairway before ascending:

**Behold, there are which rise, and have lost their bodies,
and there are also which rise, and they rise in body.**

Step 8. In the god-form of the Sephirothic Cross Angel, slowly repeat the magic word AH as you climb. Climb up to the top of the Third Stairway and say:

**I am a Sephirothic Cross Angel of Earth.
I am Sephirothic Cross Angel ABALPT.
I bear the Cross of Earth from Water to Air within Earth.**

Pathworking the Watchtower of Earth

Step 9. As ABALPT, slowly repeat the word AH and at the top of the Stairway, turn toward the center of the Fire-Tier. If you are male, assume the naked god-form of the King of Earth, IKZHIKAL. If you are female, assume the naked god-form of the Goddess of Earth, ORABALN.

Step 10. Same as Step 10 in Path 1.

Step 11. Same as Step 11 in Path 1.

Step 12. Turn from your consort and step outside the black hexagram. Leave by the same path that you entered. After leaving the mandala, conduct the banishing pentagram ritual. This completes the fourth initiatory path.

THE WATER QUADRANT OF THE EARTH MANDALA

PATH FIVE

The Path of Physical Love leads through the four positions 5-12-18-21, as shown in Figure 22. It contains the specific atmospheres of consecration, peace, truth, and love. It is the First Path of Obedience. Use this path for love.

Step 1. Make a circle and conduct the invoking pentagram ritual.

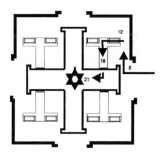

Figure 22: Path 5, The Path of Physical Love

Step 2. Face the West, and imagine the Mandala of the Watchtower of Earth clearly before you. You are facing its Eastern wall. Imagine the walls and floors to be black. Recite the Centering Spell. Then say:

> May I enter and safely pass through this black Watchtower of Earth.
> May I obtain success in this, the fifth of my initiations.
> In the threefold secret and holy name of MORDIALHKTGA
> I make this request. ORERI KALAZ KORESA TAZA
> SAGE DO HOMILA IPAME KAOSAGO

Step 3. Visualize the closed Magnolia Gate. say:

> O NOMGG I invoke thee. Come unto me from the Watchtower of Earth.

Visualize NOMGG before you. Approach the Angel unafraid; open your arms and embrace her. Feel her body melt into your own and become a part of you. Assume the god-form of the Angel NOMGG ("no-meh-geh-geh"), who guards the Magnolia Gate (position 5), as follows:

The god-form of NOMGG: See page 241 for the god-form of NOMGG.

There are special words written above the Magnolia Gate to be spoken before entering. Say:

The Angels' Message to Humanity

Woe be unto the seeds of the earth, and unto the seed within her, for she is touched with fire from on high.

Step 4. Visualize the gate opening at these words. Step within the Magnolia Gate. Face the Earth-Tier. In the god-form of NOMGG, say:

**I am the Angel of Earth. I am the Angel NOMGG.
I am the Guardian of the Magnolia Gate.
I enter into the Watchtower of Earth.**

While slowly repeating the Threefold Holy Word, enter into the Watchtower of Earth and move across the Earth-Tier to the bottom of the Oleander Stairway leading up to the Water-Tier (position 12). The Threefold Word that you recite will protect you from the Demons who reside on the Earth-Tier.

Step 5. Face the Oleander Stairway. Visualize the Kerubic Angel RAPH before you. Approach the Angel unafraid; open your arms and embrace him. Feel his body melt into your own and become a part of you. Assume the god-form of RAPH ("rah-peh-heh"), who guards the Oleander Stairway, as follows:

The god-form of RAPH: See page 242 for the god-form of RAPH.

Recite the words written over the Oleander Stairway:

**And it shall be a Garden for you, wherein you shall not borrow
of the World, but of the Gift of God.**

Step 6. In the god-form of the Kerubic Angel RAPH, while slowly repeating the magic word XUM, climb the eight steps of the Oleander Stairway to the Water-Tier. Then say:

**I am a Kerubic Angel of Earth. I am Kerubic Angel RAPH. I am the
Guardian of the Oleander Stairway. I rise up through the Watchtower of
Earth. Throughout eternity I manifest myself from Earth to Water
within Earth.**

Step 7. Slowly repeat the magic word XUM as you move across the Water-Tier. Approach the Stairway to the Air-Tier. Before entering the Second Stairway, say:

**Human policy cannot prevail here. As many as are not faithful in these
regions, shall die a most miserable death, and shall drink of sleep everlasting.**

Climb the Second Stairway, which has ten steps, to the Air-Tier. Visualize the Sephirothic Cross Angel ANAEEM before you. Approach the Angel unafraid; open your arms and embrace him. Feel his body melt into your own and become a part of you. Assume the god-form of ANAEEM ("ah-nah-eh-eh-meh"), who guards the Air-Tier and Third Stairway, as follows:

The god-form of ANAEEM: See page 237 for the god-form of ANAEEM.

The Third Stairway is black and smells of musk. It is also dry and cold. It has four steps, each of which bears a letter written in white and blazing to look upon. The letter P is on the first step, the letter T is on the second, the letter X on the third,

Pathworking the Watchtower of Earth

and the letter Z on the fourth. Recite the words written above the Third Stairway before ascending:

> Cast pride away and be humble,
> for he that hath a humble spirit knoweth much.

Step 8. In the god-form of the Sephirothic Cross Angel, slowly repeat the magic word AH as you climb. Climb up to the top of the Third Stairway and say:

> I am a Sephirothic Cross Angel of Earth.
> I am Sephirothic Cross Angel ANAEEM.
> I bear the Cross of Earth from Water to Air within Earth.

Step 9. As ANAEEM, slowly repeat the word AH and at the top of the Stairway, turn toward the center of the Fire-Tier. If you are male, assume the naked god-form of the King of Earth, IKZHIKAL. If you are female, assume the naked god-form of the Goddess of Earth, ORABALN.

Step 10. Same as Step 10 in Path 1.

Step 11. Same as Step 11 in Path 1.

Step 12. Turn from your consort and step outside the black hexagram. Leave by the same path that you entered. After leaving the mandala, conduct the banishing pentagram ritual. This completes the fifth initiatory path.

PATH SIX

The Path of Fertility leads through the four positions 5-11-18-21, as shown in Figure 23. It contains the specific atmospheres of consecration, peace, visions, and fertility. It is the Second Path of Obedience. Use this path to increase fertility.

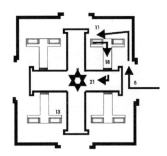

Figure 23: Path 6, The Path of Fertility

Step 1. Make a circle and conduct the invoking pentagram ritual.

Step 2. Face the West, and imagine the Mandala of the Watchtower of Earth clearly before you. You are facing its Eastern wall. Imagine the walls and floors to be black. Recite the Centering Spell. Then say:

> May I enter and safely pass through this black Watchtower of Earth.
> May I obtain success in this, the sixth of my initiations.
> In the threefold secret and holy name of MORDIALHKTGA
> I make this request. ORERI KALAZ KORESA TAZA
> SAGE DO HOMILA IPAME KAOSAGO

Step 3. Visualize the closed Magnolia Gate. say:

> O NOMGG I invoke thee. Come unto me from the Watchtower of Earth.

Visualize NOMGG before you. Approach the Angel unafraid; open your arms and embrace her. Feel her body melt into your own and become a part of you. Assume the god-form of the Angel NOMGG, who guards the Magnolia Gate (position 5), as follows:

The god-form of NOMGG: See page 241 for the god-form of NOMGG.

There are special words written above the Magnolia Gate to be spoken before entering. Say:

Woe be unto the seeds of the earth, and unto the seed within her, for she is touched with fire from on high.

Step 4. Visualize the gate opening at these words. Step within the Magnolia Gate. Face the Earth-Tier. In the god-form of NOMGG, say:

**I am the Angel of Earth. I am the Angel NOMGG.
I am the Guardian of the Magnolia Gate.
I enter into the Watchtower of Earth.**

While slowly repeating the Threefold Holy Word, enter into the Watchtower of Earth and move across the Earth-Tier to the bottom of the Stalagmite Stairway leading up to the Water-Tier (position 11). The Threefold Word that you recite will protect you from the Demons who reside on the Earth-Tier.

Step 5. Face the Stalagmite Stairway. Visualize the Kerubic Angel PHRA before you. Approach the Angel unafraid; open your arms and embrace him. Feel his body melt into your own and become a part of you. Assume the god-form of PHRA ("peh-har-ah"), who guards the Stalagmite Stairway, as follows:

The god-form of PHRA: See page 242 for the god-form of PHRA.

Recite the words written over the Stalagmite Stairway:

The same way thou camest, the same way thou shalt also return.

Step 6. In the god-form of the Kerubic Angel PHRA, while slowly repeating the magic word XUM, climb the eight steps of the Stalagmite Stairway to the Water-Tier. Then say:

**I am a Kerubic Angel of Earth. I am Kerubic Angel PHRA.
I am the Guardian of the Stalagmite Stairway.
I rise up through the Watchtower of Earth.
Throughout eternity I manifest myself from Earth to Water within Earth.**

Step 7. Slowly repeat the magic word XUM as you move across the Water-Tier. Approach the Stairway to the Air-Tier. Before entering the Second Stairway, say:

Human policy cannot prevail here. As many as are not faithful in these regions, shall die a most miserable death, and shall drink of sleep everlasting.

Climb the Second Stairway, which has ten steps, to the Air-Tier. Visualize the Sephirothic Cross Angel ANAEEM before you. Approach the Sephirothic Cross

Pathworking the Watchtower of Earth

Angel unafraid; open your arms and embrace him. Feel his body melt into your own and become a part of you. Assume the god-form of ANAEEM, who guards the Air-Tier and Third Stairway (position 18), as follows:

The god-form of ANAEEM: See page 237 for god-form of ANAEEM.

The Third Stairway is black and smells of musk. It is also dry and cold. It has four steps, each of which bears a letter written in white and blazing to look upon. The letter P is on the first step, the letter T is on the second, the letter X on the third, and the letter Z on the fourth. Recite the words written above the Third Stairway before ascending:

**Cast pride away and be humble,
for he that hath a humble spirit knoweth much.**

Step 8. In the god-form of the Sephirothic Cross Angel, slowly repeat the magic word AH as you climb. Climb up to the top of the Third Stairway and say:

**I am a Sephirothic Cross Angel of Earth.
I am Sephirothic Cross Angel ANAEEM.
I bear the Cross of Earth from Water to Air within Earth.**

Step 9. As ANAEEM, slowly repeat the word AH and at the top of the Stairway, turn toward the center of the Fire-Tier. If you are male, assume the naked god-form of the King of Earth, IKZHIKAL. If you are female, assume the naked god-form of the Goddess of Earth, ORABALN.

Step 10. Same as Step 10 in Path 1.

Step 11. Same as Step 11 in Path 1.

Step 12. Turn from your consort and step outside the black hexagram. Leave by the same path that you entered. After leaving the mandala, conduct the banishing pentagram ritual. This completes the sixth initiatory path.

PATH SEVEN

The Path of True Vision leads through the four positions 6-12-18-21, as shown in Figure 24. It contains the specific atmospheres of visions, death, truth, and love. It is the Third Path of Obedience. Use this path for truthful visions.

Step 1. Make a circle and conduct the invoking pentagram ritual.

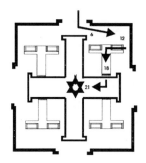

Figure 24: Path 7, The Path of True Vision

Step 2. Face the South, and imagine the Mandala of the Watchtower of Earth clearly before you. You are facing its Northern wall. Imagine the walls and floors to be black. Recite the Centering Spell. Then say:

The Angels' Message to Humanity

> May I enter and safely pass through this black Watchtower of Earth.
> May I obtain success in this, the seventh of my initiations.
> In the threefold secret and holy name of MORDIALHKTGA
> I make this request. ORERI KALAZ KORESA TAZA SAGE
> DO HOMILA IPAME KAOSAGO

Step 3. Visualize the closed Cypress Gate. say:

> O NIAHL I invoke thee. Come unto me from the Watchtower of Earth.

Visualize NIAHL before you. Approach the Angel unafraid; open your arms and embrace her. Feel her body melt into your own and become a part of you. Assume the god-form of the Angel NIAHL ("nee-ah-hel"), who guards the Cypress Gate (position 6), as follows:

The god-form of NIAHL: See page 240 for the god-form of NIAHL.

There are special words written above the Cypress Gate to be spoken before entering. Say:

> There is a battle proclaimed in Heaven, and the God of Hosts hath put
> on his armour, and is become a Fire of Wrath.

Step 4. Visualize the gate opening at these words. Step within the Cypress Gate. Face the Earth-Tier. In the god-form of NIAHL, say:

> I am the Angel of Earth. I am the Angel NIAHL.
> I am the Guardian of the Cypress Gate.
> I enter into the Watchtower of Earth.

While slowly repeating the Threefold Holy Word, enter into the Watchtower of Earth and move across the Earth-Tier to the bottom of the Oleander Stairway leading up to the Water-Tier (position 12). The Threefold Word that you recite will protect you from the Demons who reside on the Earth-Tier.

Step 5. Face the Oleander Stairway. Visualize the Kerubic Angel RAPH before you. Approach the Angel unafraid; open your arms and embrace him. Feel his body melt into your own and become a part of you. Assume the god-form of RAPH, who guards the Oleander Stairway, as follows:

The god-form of RAPH: See page 242 for the god-form of RAPH.

Recite the words written over the Oleander Stairway:

> And it shall be a Garden for you,
> wherein you shall not borrow of the World, but of the Gift of God.

Step 6. In the god-form of the Kerubic Angel RAPH, while slowly repeating the magic word XUM, climb the eight steps of the Oleander Stairway to the Water-Tier. Then say:

> I am a Kerubic Angel of Earth. I am Kerubic Angel RAPH.
> I am the Guardian of the Oleander Stairway. I rise up

Pathworking the Watchtower of Earth

through the Watchtower of Earth. Throughout eternity
I manifest myself from Earth to Water within Earth.

Step 7. Slowly repeat the magic word XUM as you move across the Water-Tier. Approach the Stairway to the Air-Tier. Before entering the Second Stairway, say:

Human policy cannot prevail here. As many as are not faithful in these regions, shall die a most miserable death, and shall drink of sleep everlasting.

Climb the Second Stairway, which has ten steps, to the Air-Tier. Visualize the Sephirothic Cross Angel ANAEEM before you. Approach the Angel unafraid; open your arms and embrace him. Feel his body melt into your own and become a part of you. Assume the god-form of ANAEEM, who guards the Air-Tier and Third Stairway (position 18), as follows:

The god-form of ANAEEM: See page 237 for the god-form of ANAEEM.

The Third Stairway is black and smells of musk. It is also dry and cold. It has four steps, each of which bears a letter written in white and blazing to look upon. The letter P is on the first step, the letter T is on the second, the letter X on the third, and the letter Z on the fourth. Recite the words written above the Third Stairway before ascending:

**Cast pride away and be humble,
for he that hath a humble spirit knoweth much.**

Step 8. In the god-form of the Sephirothic Cross Angel, slowly repeat the magic word AH as you climb. Climb up to the top of the Third Stairway and say:

**I am a Sephirothic Cross Angel of Earth.
I am Sephirothic Cross Angel ANAEEM.
I bear the Cross of Earth from Water to Air within Earth.**

Step 9. As ANAEEM, slowly repeat the word AH and at the top of the Stairway, turn toward the center of the Fire-Tier. If you are male, assume the naked god-form of the King of Earth, IKZHIKAL. If you are female, assume the naked god-form of the Goddess of Earth, ORABALN.

Step 10. Same as Step 10 in Path 1.

Step 11. Same as Step 11 in Path 1.

Step 12. Turn from your consort and step outside the black hexagram. Leave by the same path that you entered. After leaving the mandala, conduct the banishing pentagram ritual. This completes the seventh initiatory path.

The Angels' Message to Humanity

Path Eight

The Path of Births and Deaths leads through the four positions 6-11-18-21, as shown in Figure 25. It contains the specific atmospheres of visions, death, and fertility. It is the Fourth Path of Obedience. Use this path for visions of births and deaths.

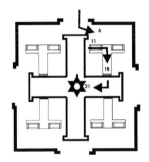

Figure 25: Path 8, The Path of Births and Deaths

Step 1. Make a circle and conduct the invoking pentagram ritual.

Step 2. Face the South, and imagine the Mandala of the Watchtower of Earth clearly before you. You are facing its Northern wall. Imagine the walls and floors to be black. Recite the Centering Spell. Then say:

May I enter and safely pass through this black Watchtower of Earth.
May I obtain success in this, the eighth of my initiations.
In the threefold secret and holy name of MORDIALHKTGA
I make this request. ORERI KALAZ KORESA TAZA SAGE
DO HOMILA IPAME KAOSAGO

Step 3. Visualize the closed Cypress Gate. say:

O NIAHL I invoke thee. Come unto me from the Watchtower of Earth.

Visualize NIAHL before you. Approach the Angel unafraid; open your arms and embrace her. Feel her body melt into your own and become a part of you. Assume the god-form of the Angel NIAHL, who guards the Cypress Gate (position 6), as follows:

The god-form of NIAHL: See page 240 for the goe-form of NIAHL.

There are special words written above the Cypress Gate to be spoken before entering. Say:

There is a battle proclaimed in Heaven, and the God of Hosts
hath put on his armour, and is become a Fire of Wrath.

Step 4. Visualize the gate opening at these words. Step within the Cypress Gate. Face the Earth-Tier. In the god-form of NIAHL, say:

I am the Angel of Earth. I am the Angel NIAHL.
I am the Guardian of the Cypress Gate.
I enter into the Watchtower of Earth.

While slowly repeating the Threefold Holy Word, enter into the Watchtower of Earth and move across the Earth-Tier to the bottom of the Stalagmite Stairway leading up to the Water-Tier (position 11). The Threefold Word that you recite will protect you from the Demons who reside on the Earth-Tier.

Step 5. Face the Stalagmite Stairway. Visualize the Kerubic Angel PHRA before you. Approach the Angel unafraid; open your arms and embrace him. Feel his body melt into your own and become a part of you. Assume the god-form of PHRA, who guards the Stalagmite Stairway, as follows:

Pathworking the Watchtower of Earth

The god-form of PHRA: See page 242 for the god-form of PHRA.

Recite the words written over the Stalagmite Stairway:

The same way thou camest, the same way thou shalt also return.

Step 6. In the god-form of the Kerubic Angel PHRA, while slowly repeating the magic word XUM, climb the eight steps of the Stalagmite Stairway to the Water-Tier. Then say:

I am a Kerubic Angel of Earth. I am Kerubic Angel PHRA. I am the Guardian of the Stalagmite Stairway. I rise up through the Watchtower of Earth. Throughout eternity I manifest myself from Earth to Water within Earth.

Step 7. Slowly repeat the magic word XUM as you move across the Water-Tier. Approach the Stairway to the Air-Tier. Before entering the Second Stairway, say:

Human policy cannot prevail here. As many as are not faithful in these regions, shall die a most miserable death, and shall drink of sleep everlasting.

Climb the Second Stairway, which has ten steps, to the Air-Tier. Visualize the Sephirothic Cross Angel ANAEEM before you. Approach the Angel unafraid; open your arms and embrace him. Feel his body melt into your own and become a part of you. Assume the god-form of ANAEEM, who guards the Air-Tier and Third Stairway (position 18), as follows:

The god-form of ANAEEM: See page 237 for the god-form of ANAEEM.

The Third Stairway is black and smells of musk. It is also dry and cold. It has four steps, each of which bears a letter written in white and blazing to look upon. The letter *P* is on the first step, the letter *T* is on the second, the letter *X* on the third, and the letter *Z* on the fourth. Recite the words written above the Third Stairway before ascending:

**Cast pride away and be humble,
for he that hath a humble spirit knoweth much.**

Step 8. In the god-form of the Sephirothic Cross Angel, slowly repeat the magic word AH as you climb. Climb up to the top of the Third Stairway and say:

**I am a Sephirothic Cross Angel of Earth.
I am Sephirothic Cross Angel ANAEEM.
I bear the Cross of Earth from Water to Air within Earth.**

Step 9. As ANAEEM, slowly repeat the word AH and at the top of the Stairway, turn toward the center of the Fire-Tier. If you are male, assume the naked god-form of the King of Earth, IKZHIKAL. If you are female, assume the naked god-form of the Goddess of Earth, ORABALN.

Step 10. Same as Step 10 in Path 1.

Step 11. Same as Step 11 in Path 1.

Step 12. Turn from your consort and step outside the black hexagram. Leave by the same path that you entered. After leaving the mandala, conduct the banishing pentagram ritual. This completes the eighth initiatory path.

THE AIR QUADRANT OF THE EARTH MANDALA

PATH NINE

The Path of Physical Magic leads through the four positions 7-9-17-21, as shown in Figure 26. It contains the specific atmospheres of purification, healing, magical power, and good karma. It is the First Path of Logic and Reason. Use this path to increase magical ability.

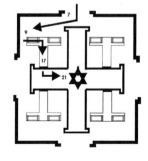

Figure 26: Path 9, The Path of Physical Magic

Step 1. Make a circle and conduct the invoking pentagram ritual.

Step 2. Face the South, and imagine the Mandala of the Watchtower of Earth clearly before you. You are facing its Northern wall. Imagine the walls and floors to be black. Recite the Centering Spell. Then say:

> **May I enter and safely pass through this black Watchtower of Earth.**
> **May I obtain success in this, the ninth of my initiations.**
> **In the threefold secret and holy name of MORDIALHKTGA**
> **I make this request. ORERI KALAZ KORESA TAZA SAGE**
> **DO HOMILA IPAME KAOSAGO**

Step 3. Visualize the closed Green Jasper Gate. say:

> **O AAIRA I invoke thee. Come unto me from the Watchtower of Earth.**

Visualize AAIRA before you. Approach the Angel unafraid; open your arms and embrace him. Feel his body melt into your own and become a part of you. Assume the god-form of the Angel AAIRA ("ah-ah-ee-rah"), who guards the Green Jasper Gate (position 7), as follows:

The god-form of AAIRA: See page 235 for the god-form of AAIRA.

There are special words written above the Green Jasper Gate to be spoken before entering. Say:

> **Great sorrow is at hand unto all flesh.**

Step 4. Visualize the gate opening at these words. Step within the Green Jasper Gate. Face the Earth-Tier. In the god-form of AAIRA, say:

> **I am the Angel of Earth. I am the Angel AAIRA.**
> **I am the Guardian of the Green Jasper Gate.**
> **I enter into the Watchtower of Earth.**

Pathworking the Watchtower of Earth

While slowly repeating the Threefold Holy Word, enter into the Watchtower of Earth and move across the Earth-Tier to the bottom of the Coal Stairway leading up to the Water-Tier (position 9). The Threefold Word that you recite will protect you from the Demons who reside on the Earth-Tier.

Step 5. Face the Coal Stairway. Visualize the Kerubic Angel BOZA before you. Approach the Angel unafraid; open your arms and embrace him. Feel his body melt into your own and become a part of you. Assume the god-form of BOZA ("boh-zah"), who guards the Coal Stairway, as follows:

The god-form of BOZA. See page 238 for the god-form of BOZA.

Recite the words written over the Coal Stairway:

**He that committeth himself unto me, and heareth my voice,
I will write his Name in the Book of Life.**

Step 6. In the god-form of the Kerubic Angel BOZA, while slowly repeating the magic word XUM, climb the five steps of the Coal Stairway to the Water-Tier. Then say:

**I am a Kerubic Angel of Earth. I am Kerubic Angel BOZA.
I am the Guardian of the Coal Stairway.
I rise up through the Watchtower of Earth.
Throughout eternity I manifest myself from Earth to Water within Earth.**

Step 7. Slowly repeat the magic word XUM as you move across the Water-Tier. Approach the Stairway to the Air-Tier. Before entering the Second Stairway, say:

Human policy cannot prevail here. As many as are not faithful in these regions, shall die a most miserable death, and shall drink of sleep everlasting.

Climb the Second Stairway, which has ten steps, to the Air-Tier. Visualize the Sephirothic Cross Angel ANGPOI before you. Approach the Angel unafraid; open your arms and embrace him. Feel his body melt into your own and become a part of you. Assume the god-form of ANGPOI ("ah-neh-geh-poh-ee"), who guards the Air-Tier and Third Stairway, as follows:

The god-form of ANGPOI: See page 237 for the god-form of ANGPOI.

The Third Stairway is black and smells of musk. It is also dry and cold. It has four steps, each of which bears a letter written in white and blazing to look upon. The letter *P* is on the first step, the letter *T* is on the second, the letter *X* on the third, and the letter *Z* on the fourth. Recite the words written above the Third Stairway before ascending:

As your sight is, so shall you see me.

Step 8. In the god-form of the Sephirothic Cross Angel, slowly repeat the magic word AH as you climb. Climb up to the top of the Third Stairway and say:

I am a Sephirothic Cross Angel of Earth. I am Sephirothic Cross Angel ANGPOI. I bear the Cross of Earth from Water to Air within Earth.

Step 9. As ANGPOI, slowly repeat the word AH and at the top of the Stairway, turn toward the center of the Fire-Tier. If you are male, assume the naked god-form of the King of Earth, IKZHIKAL. If you are female, assume the naked god-form of the Goddess of Earth, ORABALN.

Step 10. Same as Step 10 in Path 1.

Step 11. Same as Step 11 in Path 1.

Step 12. Turn from your consort and step outside the black hexagram. Leave by the same path that you entered. After leaving the mandala, conduct the banishing pentagram ritual. This completes the ninth initiatory path.

Path Ten

The Path of Physical Healing leads through the four positions 7-10-17-21, as shown in Figure 27. It contains the specific atmospheres of purification, healing, creative energy, and purity. It is the Second Path of Logic and Reason. Use this path to increase healing energy.

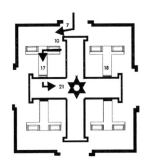

Step 1. Make a circle and conduct the invoking pentagram ritual.

Figure 27: Path 10, The Path of Physical Healing

Step 2. Face the South, and imagine the Mandala of the Watchtower of Earth clearly before you. You are facing its Northern wall. Imagine the walls and floors to be black. Recite the Centering Spell. Then say:

> **May I enter and safely pass through this black Watchtower of Earth.**
> **May I obtain success in this, the tenth of my initiations.**
> **In the threefold secret and holy name of MORDIALHKTGA**
> **I make this request. ORERI KALAZ KORESA TAZA SAGE**
> **DO HOMILA IPAME KAOSAGO**

Step 3. Visualize the closed Green Jasper Gate. say:

> **O AAIRA I invoke thee. Come unto me from the Watchtower of Earth.**

Visualize AAIRA before you. Approach the Angel unafraid; open your arms and embrace him. Feel his body melt into your own and become a part of you. Assume the god-form of the Angel AAIRA, who guards the Green Jasper Gate (position 7), as follows:

The god-form of AAIRA: See page 235 for the god-form of AAIRA.

There are special words written above the Green Jasper Gate to be spoken before entering. Say:

> **Great sorrow is at hand unto all flesh.**

Pathworking the Watchtower of Earth

Step 4. Visualize the gate opening at these words. Step within the Green Jasper Gate. Face the Earth-Tier. In the god-form of AAIRA, say:

I am the Angel of Earth. I am the Angel AAIRA. I am the Guardian of the Green Jasper Gate. I enter into the Watchtower of Earth.

While slowly repeating the Threefold Holy Word, enter into the Watchtower of Earth and move across the Earth-Tier to the bottom of the Salt Stairway leading up to the Water-Tier (position 10). The Threefold Word that you recite will protect you from the Demons who reside on the Earth-Tier.

Step 5. Face the Salt Stairway. Visualize the Kerubic Angel ZABO before you. Approach the Angel unafraid; open your arms and embrace him. Feel his body melt into your own and become a part of you. Assume the god-form of ZABO ("zah-boh"), who guards the Salt Stairway, as follows:

The god-form of ZABO: See page 00 for the god-form of ZABO.

Recite the words written over the Salt Stairway:

Excuse yourselves with men, and gird up your Garments to the travail.

Step 6. In the god-form of the Kerubic Angel ZABO, while slowly repeating the magic word XUM, climb the five steps of the Salt Stairway to the Water-Tier. Then say:

I am a Kerubic Angel of Earth. I am Kerubic Angel ZABO. I am the Guardian of the Salt Stairway. I rise up through the Watchtower of Earth. Throughout eternity I manifest myself from Earth to Water within Earth.

Step 7. Slowly repeat the magic word XUM as you move across the Water-Tier. Approach the Stairway to the Air-Tier. Before entering the Second Stairway, say:

Human policy cannot prevail here. As many as are not faithful in these regions, shall die a most miserable death, and shall drink of sleep everlasting.

Climb the Second Stairway, which has ten steps, to the Air-Tier. Visualize the Sephirothic Cross Angel ANGPOI before you. Approach the Angel unafraid; open your arms and embrace him. Feel his body melt into your own and become a part of you. Assume the god-form of ANGPOI, who guards the Air-Tier and Third Stairway, as follows:

The god-form of ANGPOI: See page 237 for the god-form of ANGPOI.

The Third Stairway is black and smells of musk. It is also dry and cold. It has four steps, each of which bears a letter written in white and blazing to look upon. The letter *P* is on the first step, the letter *T* is on the second, the letter *X* on the third, and the letter *Z* on the fourth. Recite the words written above the Third Stairway before ascending:

As your sight is, so shall you see me.

The Angels' Message to Humanity

Step 8. In the god-form of the Sephirothic Cross Angel, slowly repeat the magic word AH as you climb. Climb up to the top of the Third Stairway and say:

I am a Sephirothic Cross Angel of Earth. I am Sephirothic Cross Angel ANGPOI. I bear the Cross of Earth from Water to Air within Earth.

Step 9. As ANGPOI, slowly repeat the word AH and at the top of the Stairway, turn toward the center of the Fire-Tier. If you are male, assume the naked god-form of the King of Earth, IKZHIKAL. If you are female, assume the naked god-form of the Goddess of Earth, ORABALN.

Step 10. Same as Step 10 in Path 1.

Step 11. Same as Step 11 in Path 1.

Step 12. Turn from your consort and step outside the black hexagram. Leave by the same path that you entered. After leaving the mandala, conduct the banishing pentagram ritual. This completes the tenth initiatory path.

PATH ELEVEN

The Path of Magical Knowledge leads through the four positions 8-9-17-21, as shown in Figure 28. It contains the specific atmospheres of foreknowledge, creativity, magical power, and good karma. It is the Third Path of Logic and Reason. Use this path to increase foreknowledge.

Step 1. Make a circle and conduct the invoking pentagram ritual.

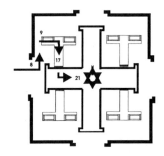

Figure 28: Path 11, The Path of Magical Knowledge

Step 2. Face the East, and imagine the Mandala of the Watchtower of Earth clearly before you. You are facing its Western wall. Imagine the walls and floors to be black. Recite the Centering Spell. Then say:

May I enter and safely pass through this black Watchtower of Earth. May I obtain success in this, the eleventh of my initiations. In the threefold secret and holy name of MORDIALHKTGA I make this request. ORERI KALAZ KORESA TAZA SAGE DO HOMILA IPAME KAOSAGO

Step 3. Visualize the closed Green Tourmaline Gate. say:

O RIZNR I invoke thee. Come unto me from the Watchtower of Earth.

Visualize RIZNR before you. Approach the Angel unafraid; open your arms and embrace him. Feel his body melt into your own and become a part of you. Assume the god-form of the Angel RIZNR ("ree-zen-ar"), who guards the Green Tourmaline Gate (position 8), as follows:

The god-form of RIZNR: See page 242 for the god-form of RIZNAR.

Pathworking the Watchtower of Earth

There are special words written above the Green Tourmaline Gate to be spoken before entering. Say:

> **Who is he that girdeth his sword unto him,
> or what is he that is ready for the battle?**

Step 4. Visualize the gate opening at these words. Step within the Green Tourmaline Gate. Face the Earth-Tier. In the god-form of RIZNR, say:

> **I am the Angel of Earth. I am the Angel RIZNR. I am the Guardian of the Green Tourmaline Gate. I enter into the Watchtower of Earth.**

While slowly repeating the Threefold Holy Word, enter into the Watchtower of Earth and move across the Earth-Tier to the bottom of the Coal Stairway leading up to the Water-Tier (position 9). The Threefold Word that you recite will protect you from the Demons who reside on the Earth-Tier.

Step 5. Face the Coal Stairway. Visualize the Kerubic Angel BOZA before you. Approach the Angel unafraid; open your arms and embrace him. Feel his body melt into your own and become a part of you. Assume the god-form of BOZA, who guards the Coal Stairway, as follows:

> **The god-form of BOZA:** See page 238 for the god-form of BOZA.

Recite the words written over the Coal Stairway:

> **He that committeth himself unto me, and heareth my voice,
> I will write his Name in the Book of Life.**

Step 6. In the god-form of the Kerubic Angel BOZA, while slowly repeating the magic word XUM, climb the five steps of the Coal Stairway to the Water-Tier. Then say:

> **I am a Kerubic Angel of Earth. I am Kerubic Angel BOZA.
> I am the Guardian of the Coal Stairway. I rise up
> through the Watchtower of Earth. Throughout eternity
> I manifest myself from Earth to Water within Earth.**

Step 7. Slowly repeat the magic word XUM as you move across the Water-Tier. Approach the Stairway to the Air-Tier. Before entering the Second Stairway, say:

> **Human policy cannot prevail here. As many as are not faithful in these regions, shall die a most miserable death, and shall drink of sleep everlasting.**

Climb the Second Stairway, which has ten steps, to the Air-Tier. Visualize the Sephirothic Cross Angel ANGPOI before you. Approach the Angel unafraid; open your arms and embrace him. Feel his body melt into your own and become a part of you. Assume the god-form of ANGPOI, who guards the Air-Tier and Third Stairway (position 17), as follows:

> **The god-form of ANGPOI:** See page 237 for the god-form of ANGPOI.

The Third Stairway is black and smells of musk. It is also dry and cold. It has four steps, each of which bears a letter written in white and blazing to look upon. The

The Angels' Message to Humanity

letter *P* is on the first step, the letter *T* is on the second, the letter *X* on the third, and the letter *Z* on the fourth. Recite the words written above the Third Stairway before ascending:

> **As your sight is, so shall you see me.** Step 8. In the god-form of the Sephirothic Cross Angel, slowly repeat the magic word AH as you climb. Climb up to the top of the Third Stairway and say:

> **I am a Sephirothic Cross Angel of Earth. I am Sephirothic Cross Angel ANGPOI. I bear the Cross of Earth from Water to Air within Earth.** Step 9. As ANGPOI, slowly repeat the word AH and at the top of the Stairway, turn toward the center of the Fire-Tier. If you are male, assume the naked god-form of the King of Earth, IKZHIKAL. If you are female, assume the naked god-form of the Goddess of Earth, ORABALN.

Step 10. Same as Step 10 in Path 1.

Step 11. Same as Step 11 in Path 1.

Step 12. Turn from your consort and step outside the black hexagram. Leave by the same path that you entered. After leaving the mandala, conduct the banishing pentagram ritual. This completes the eleventh initiatory path.

Path Twelve

The Path of Physical Creativity leads through the four positions 8-10-17-21, as shown in Figure 29. It contains the specific atmospheres of foreknowledge, creativity, creative energy, and purity. It is the Fourth Path of Logic and Reason. Use this path to increase your creativity.

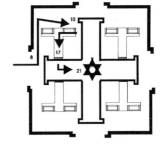

Figure 29: Path 12, The Path of Physical Creativity

Step 1. Make a circle and conduct the invoking pentagram ritual.

Step 2. Face the East, and imagine the Mandala of the Watchtower of Earth clearly before you. You are facing its Western wall. Imagine the walls and floors to be black. Recite the Centering Spell. Then say:

> **May I enter and safely pass through this black Watchtower of Earth.**
> **May I obtain success in this, the twelfth of my initiations.**
> **In the threefold secret and holy name of MORDIALHKTGA**
> **I make this request. ORERI KALAZ KORESA TAZA SAGE**
> **DO HOMILA IPAME KAOSAGO.**

Step 3. Visualize the closed Green Tourmaline Gate. say:

> **O RIZNR I invoke thee. Come unto me from the Watchtower of Earth.**

Visualize RIZNR before you. Approach the Angel unafraid; open your arms and embrace him. Feel his body melt into your own and become a part of you. Assume

Pathworking the Watchtower of Earth

the god-form of the Angel RIZNR, who guards the Green Tourmaline Gate (position 8), as follows:

The god-form of RIZNR: See page 242 for the god-form of RIZNAR.

There are special words written above the Green Tourmaline Gate to be spoken before entering. Say:

**Who is he that girdeth his sword unto him,
or what is he that is ready for the battle?**

Step 4. Visualize the gate opening at these words. Step within the Green Tourmaline Gate. Face the Earth-Tier. In the god-form of RIZNR, say:

**I am the Angel of Earth. I am the Angel RIZNR. I am the Guardian
of the Green Tourmaline Gate. I enter into the Watchtower of Earth.**

While slowly repeating the Threefold Holy Word, enter into the Watchtower of Earth and move across the Earth-Tier to the bottom of the Salt Stairway leading up to the Water-Tier (position 10). The Threefold Word that you recite will protect you from the Demons who reside on the Earth-Tier.

Step 5. Face the Salt Stairway. Visualize the Kerubic Angel ZABO before you. Approach the Angel unafraid; open your arms and embrace him. Feel his body melt into your own and become a part of you. Assume the god-form of ZABO, who guards the Salt Stairway, as follows:

The god-form of ZABO: See page 243 for the god-form of ZABO.

Recite the words written over the Salt Stairway:

Excuse yourselves with men, and gird up your Garments to the travail.

Step 6. In the god-form of the Kerubic Angel ZABO, while slowly repeating the magic word XUM, climb the five steps of the Salt Stairway to the Water-Tier. Then say:

**I am a Kerubic Angel of Earth. I am Kerubic Angel ZABO.
I am the Guardian of the Salt Stairway. I rise up through
the Watchtower of Earth. Throughout eternity
I manifest myself from Earth to Water within Earth.**

Step 7. Slowly repeat the magic word XUM as you move across the Water-Tier. Approach the Stairway to the Air-Tier. Before entering the Second Stairway, say:

**Human policy cannot prevail here. As many as are not faithful in these
regions, shall die a most miserable death, and shall drink of sleep everlasting.**

Climb the Second Stairway, which has ten steps, to the Air-Tier. Visualize the Sephirothic Cross Angel ANGPOI before you. Approach the Angel unafraid; open your arms and embrace him. Feel his body melt into your own and become a part of you. Assume the god-form of ANGPOI, who guards the Air-Tier and Third Stairway (position 17), as follows:

The Angels' Message to Humanity

The god-form of ANGPOI: See page 237 for the god-form of ANGPOI.

The Third Stairway is black and smells of musk. It is also dry and cold. It has four steps, each of which bears a letter written in white and blazing to look upon. The letter *P* is on the first step, the letter *T* is on the second, the letter *X* on the third, and the letter *Z* on the fourth. Recite the words written above the Third Stairway before ascending:

As your sight is, so shall you see me.

Step 8. In the god-form of the Sephirothic Cross Angel, slowly repeat the magic word AH as you climb. Climb up to the top of the Third Stairway and say:

I am a Sephirothic Cross Angel of Earth. I am Sephirothic Cross Angel ANGPOI. I bear the Cross of Earth from Water to Air within Earth.

Step 9. As ANGPOI, slowly repeat the word AH and at the top of the Stairway, turn toward the center of the Fire-Tier. If you are male, assume the naked god-form of the King of Earth, IKZHIKAL. If you are female, assume the naked god-form of the Goddess of Earth, ORABALN.

Step 10. Same as Step 10 in Path 1.

Step 11. Same as Step 11 in Path 1.

Step 12. Turn from your consort and step outside the black hexagram. Leave by the same path that you entered. After leaving the mandala, conduct the banishing pentagram ritual. This completes the twelfth initiatory path.

THE FIRE QUADRANT OF THE EARTH MANDALA

PATH THIRTEEN

The Path of Grounding leads through the four positions 3-16-20-21, as shown in Figure 30. It contains the specific atmospheres of knowledge, protection, and purification. It is the First Path of Harmony. Use this path for physical protection.

Step 1. Make a circle and conduct the invoking pentagram ritual.

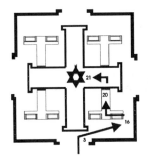

Figure 30: Path 13, The Path of Grounding

Step 2. Face the North, and imagine the Mandala of the Watchtower of Earth clearly before you. You are facing its Southern wall. Imagine the walls and floors to be black. Recite the Centering Spell. Then say:

**May I enter and safely pass through this black Watchtower of Earth.
May I obtain success in this, the thirteenth of my initiations.
In the threefold secret and holy name of MORDIALHKTGA**

Pathworking the Watchtower of Earth

> **I make this request. ORERI KALAZ KORESA TAZA SAGE DO HOMILA IPAME KAOSAGO**

Step 3. Visualize the closed Black Tourmaline Gate. say:

> **O AMSAL I invoke thee. Come unto me from the Watchtower of Earth.**

Visualize AMSAL before you. Approach the Angel unafraid; open your arms and embrace him. Feel his body melt into your own and become a part of you. Assume the god-form of the Angel AMSAL ("ah-meh-sah-leh"), who guards the Black Tourmaline Gate (position 3), as follows:

The god-form of AMSAL: See page 237 for the god-form of AMSAL.

There are special words written above the Black Tourmaline Gate to be spoken before entering. Say:

> **Woe be unto the World, for she hath appeared before the Lord unpure.**

Step 4. Visualize the gate opening at these words. Step within the Black Tourmaline Gate. Face the Earth-Tier. In the god-form of AMSAL, say:

> **I am the Angel of Earth. I am the Angel AMSAL. I am the Guardian of the Black Tourmaline Gate. I enter into the Watchtower of Earth.**

While slowly repeating the Threefold Holy Word, enter into the Watchtower of Earth and move across the Earth-Tier to the bottom of the Kunzite Stairway leading up to the Water-Tier (position 15). The Threefold Word that you recite will protect you from the Demons who reside on the Earth-Tier.

Step 5. Face the Kunzite Stairway. Visualize the Kerubic Angel OMIA before you. Approach the Angel unafraid; open your arms and embrace him. Feel his body melt into your own and become a part of you. Assume the god-form of OMIA ("oh-mee- ah"), who guards the Kunzite Stairway, as follows:

The god-form of OMIA: See page 241 for the god-form of OMIA.

Recite the words written over the Kunzite Stairway:

> **And hitherto I will deal with thee, that the least thing which thou hast bestowed in obedience toward me, shall not be forgotten.**

Step 6. In the god-form of the Kerubic Angel OMIA, while slowly repeating the magic word XUM, climb the six steps of the Kunzite Stairway to the Water-Tier. Then say:

> **I am a Kerubic Angel of Earth. I am Kerubic Angel OMIA.**
> **I am the Guardian of the Kunzite Stairway.**
> **I rise up through the Watchtower of Earth. Throughout eternity**
> **I manifest myself from Earth to Water within Earth.**

Step 7. Slowly repeat the magic word XUM as you move across the Water-Tier. Approach the Stairway to the Air-Tier. Before entering the Second Stairway, say:

> **Human policy cannot prevail here. As many as are not faithful in these regions, shall die a most miserable death, and shall drink of sleep everlasting.**

The Angels' Message to Humanity

Climb the Second Stairway, which has six steps, to the Air-Tier. Visualize the Sephirothic Cross Angel OPMNIR before you. Approach the Angel unafraid; open your arms and embrace him. Feel his body melt into your own and become a part of you. Assume the god-form of OPMNIR ("oh-pem-nee-ar"), who guards the Air-Tier and Third Stairway (position 20), as follows:

The god-form of OPMNIR: See page 241 for the god-form of OPMNIR.

The Third Stairway is black and smells of musk. It is also dry and cold. It has four steps, each of which bears a letter written in white and blazing to look upon. The letter P is on the first step, the letter T is on the second, the letter X on the third, and the letter Z on the fourth. Recite the words written above the Third Stairway before ascending:

Lift up yourselves, and behold the heavens, and look upon the earth, and muse at her wonders. And let not the lesser part carry away the greater.

Step 8. In the god-form of the Sephirothic Cross Angel, slowly repeat the magic word AH as you climb. Climb up to the top of the Third Stairway and say:

I am a Sephirothic Cross Angel of Earth. I am Sephirothic Cross Angel OPMNIR. I bear the Cross of Earth from Water to Air within Earth.

Step 9. As OPMNIR. slowly repeat the word AH and at the top of the Stairway, turn toward the center of the Fire-Tier. If you are male, assume the naked god-form of the King of Earth, IKZHIKAL. If you are female, assume the naked god-form of the Goddess of Earth, ORABALN.

Step 10. Same as Step 10 in Path 1.

Step 11. Same as Step 11 in Path 1.

Step 12. Turn from your consort and step outside the black hexagram. Leave by the same path that you entered. After leaving the mandala, conduct the banishing pentagram ritual. This completes the thirteenth initiatory path.

Path Fourteen

The Path of Physical Harmony leads through the four positions 3-15-20-21, as shown in Figure 31. It contains the specific atmospheres of knowledge, protection, peace, and harmony. It is the Second Path of Harmony. Use this path to generate or enhance harmony.

Step 1. Make a circle and conduct the invoking pentagram ritual.

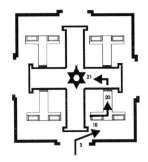

Figure 31: Path 14, The Path of Physical Harmony

Step 2. Face the North, and imagine the Mandala of the Watchtower of Earth clearly before you. You are facing its Southern wall. Imagine the walls and floors to be

Pathworking the Watchtower of Earth

black. Recite the Centering Spell. Then say:

> May I enter and safely pass through this black Watchtower of Earth.
> May I obtain success in this, the fourteenth of my initiations.
> In the threefold secret and holy name of MORDIALHKTGA
> I make this request. ORERI KALAZ KORESA TAZA SAGE
> DO HOMILA IPAME KAOSAGO

Step 3. Visualize the closed Black Tourmaline Gate. say:

> **O AMSAL I invoke thee. Come unto me from the Watchtower of Earth.**

Visualize AMSAL before you. Approach the Angel unafraid; open your arms and embrace him. Feel his body melt into your own and become a part of you. Assume the god-form of the Angel AMSAL, who guards the Black Tourmaline Gate (position 3), as follows:

The god-form of AMSAL: See page 237 for the god-form of AMSAL.

There are special words written above the Black Tourmaline Gate to be spoken before entering. Say:

> **Woe be unto the World, for she hath appeared before the Lord unpure.**

Step 4. Visualize the gate opening at these words. Step within the Black Tourmaline Gate. Face the Earth-Tier. In the god-form of AMSAL, say:

> **I am the Angel of Earth. I am the Angel AMSAL. I am the Guardian of the Black Tourmaline Gate. I enter into the Watchtower of Earth.**

While slowly repeating the Threefold Holy Word, enter into the Watchtower of Earth and move across the Earth-Tier to the bottom of the Malachite Stairway leading up to the Water-Tier (position 16). The Threefold Word that you recite will protect you from the Demons who reside on the Earth-Tier.

Step 5. Face the Malachite Stairway. Visualize the Kerubic Angel IAOM before you. Approach the Angel unafraid; open your arms and embrace him. Feel his body melt into your own and become a part of you. Assume the god-form of IAOM ("ee-ah-oh-meh"), who guards the Malachite Stairway, as follows:

The god-form of IAOM: See page 239 for the god-form of IAOM.

Recite the words written over the Malachite Stairway:

> **This may seem unto you, a strange and stumbling Doctrine.**
> **I have laid the Basis.**

Step 6. In the god-form of the Kerubic Angel IAOM, while slowly repeating the magic word XUM, climb the six steps of the Malachite Stairway to the Water-Tier. Then say:

> **I am a Kerubic Angel of Earth. I am Kerubic Angel IAOM.**
> **I am the Guardian of the Malachite Stairway. I rise up**
> **through the Watchtower of Earth. Throughout eternity**
> **I manifest myself from Earth to Water within Earth.**

Step 7. Slowly repeat the magic word XUM as you move across the Water-Tier. Approach the Stairway to the Air-Tier. Before entering the Second Stairway, say:

Human policy cannot prevail here. As many as are not faithful in these regions, shall die a most miserable death, and shall drink of sleep everlasting.

Climb the Second Stairway, which has six steps, to the Air-Tier. Visualize the Sephirothic Cross Angel OPMNIR before you. Approach the Angel unafraid; open your arms and embrace him. Feel his body melt into your own and become a part of you. Assume the god-form of OPMNIR, who guards the Air-Tier and Third Stairway (position 20), as follows:

The god-form of OPMNIR: See page 241 for the god-form of OPMNIR.

The Third Stairway is black and smells of musk. It is also dry and cold. It has four steps, each of which bears a letter written in white and blazing to look upon. The letter P is on the first step, the letter T is on the second, the letter X on the third, and the letter Z on the fourth. Recite the words written above the Third Stairway before ascending:

Lift up yourselves, and behold the heavens, and look upon the earth, and muse at her wonders. And let not the lesser part carry away the greater.

Step 8. In the god-form of the Sephirothic Cross Angel, slowly repeat the magic word AH as you climb. Climb up to the top of the Third Stairway and say:

I am a Sephirothic Cross Angel of Earth. I am Sephirothic Cross Angel OPMNIR. I bear the Cross of Earth from Water to Air within Earth.

Step 9. As OPMNIR, slowly repeat the word AH and at the top of the Stairway, turn toward the center of the Fire-Tier. If you are male, assume the naked god-form of the King of Earth, IKZHIKAL. If you are female, assume the naked god-form of the Goddess of Earth, ORABALN.

Step 10. Same as Step 10 in Path 1.

Step 11. Same as Step 11 in Path 1.

Step 12. Turn from your consort and step outside the black hexagram. Leave by the same path that you entered. After leaving the mandala, conduct the banishing pentagram ritual. This completes the fourteenth initiatory path.

Pathworking the Watchtower of Earth

PATH FIFTEEN

The Path of Physical Health leads through the four positions 4-16-20-21, as shown in Figure 32. It contains the specific atmospheres of insight, health, purification, and protection. It is the Third Path of Harmony. Use this path for good physical health.

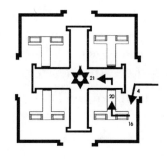

Figure 32: Path 15, The Path of Physical Health

Step 1. Make a circle and conduct the invoking pentagram ritual.

Step 2. Face the West, and imagine the Mandala of the Watchtower of Earth clearly before you. You are facing its Eastern wall. Imagine the walls and floors to be black. Recite the Centering Spell. Then say:

> May I enter and safely pass through this black Watchtower of Earth.
> May I obtain success in this, the fifteenth of my initiations.
> In the threefold secret and holy name of MORDIALHKTGA
> I make this request. ORERI KALAZ KORESA TAZA SAGE
> DO HOMILA IPAME KAOSAGO

Step 3. Visualize the closed Green Agate Gate. say:

> O ASTIM I invoke thee. Come unto me from the Watchtower of Earth.

Visualize ASTIM before you. Approach the Angel unafraid; open your arms and embrace him. Feel his body melt into your own and become a part of you. Assume the god-form of the Angel ASTIM ("ah-seh-tee-meh"), who guards the Green Agate Gate (position 4), as follows:

The god-form of ASTIM: See page 237 for the god-form of ASTIM.

There are special words written above the Green Agate Gate to be spoken before entering. Say:

> Woe be unto the Sons of Men, for they are the dwelling places of the beast.

Step 4. Visualize the gate opening at these words. Step within the Green Agate Gate. Face the Earth-Tier. In the god-form of ASTIM, say:

> I am the Angel of Earth. I am the Archangel ASTIM. I am the Guardian of the Green Agate Gate. I enter into the Watchtower of Earth.

While slowly repeating the Threefold Holy Word, enter into the Watchtower of Earth and move across the Earth-Tier to the bottom of the Kunzite Stairway leading up to the Water-Tier (position 15). The Threefold Word that you recite will protect you from the Demons who reside on the Earth-Tier.

Step 5. Face the Kunzite Stairway. Visualize the Kerubic Angel OMIA before you. Approach the Angel unafraid; open your arms and embrace him. Feel his body melt into your own and become a part of you. Assume the god-form of OMIA, who guards the Kunzite Stairway, as follows:

The god-form of OMIA: See page 241 for the god-form of OMIA.

Recite the words written over the Kunzite Stairway:

And hitherto I will deal with thee, that the least thing which thou hast bestowed in obedience toward me, shall not be forgotten.

Step 6. In the god-form of the Kerubic Angel OMIA, while slowly repeating the magic word X̣UM, climb the six steps of the Kunzite Stairway to the Water-Tier. Then say:

**I am a Kerubic Angel of Earth. I am Kerubic Angel OMIA.
I am the Guardian of the Kunzite Stairway. I rise up through
the Watchtower of Earth. Throughout eternity
I manifest myself from Earth to Water within Earth.**

Step 7. Slowly repeat the magic word XUM as you move across the Water-Tier. Approach the Stairway to the Air-Tier. Before entering the Second Stairway, say:

Human policy cannot prevail here. As many as are not faithful in these regions, shall die a most miserable death, and shall drink of sleep everlasting.

Climb the Second Stairway, which has six steps, to the Air-Tier. Visualize the Sephirothic Cross Angel OPMNIR before you. Approach the Angel unafraid; open your arms and embrace him. Feel his body melt into your own and become a part of you. Assume the god-form of OPMNIR, who guards the Air-Tier and Third Stairway (position 20), as follows:

The god-form of OPMNIR: See page 241 for the god-form of OPMNIR.

The Third Stairway is black and smells of musk. It is also dry and cold. It has four steps, each of which bears a letter written in white and blazing to look upon. The letter P is on the first step, the letter T is on the second, the letter X on the third, and the letter Z on the fourth. Recite the words written above the Third Stairway before ascending:

Lift up yourselves, and behold the heavens, and look upon the earth, and muse at her wonders. And let not the lesser part carry away the greater.

Step 8. In the god-form of the Sephirothic Cross Angel, slowly repeat the magic word AH as you climb. Climb up to the top of the Third Stairway and say:

I am a Sephirothic Cross Angel of Earth. I am Sephirothic Cross Angel OPMNIR. I bear the Cross of Earth from Water to Air within Earth.

Step 9. As OPMNIR, slowly repeat the word AH and at the top of the Stairway, turn toward the center of the Fire-Tier. If you are male, assume the naked god-form of the King of Earth, IKZHIKAL. If you are female, assume the naked god-form of the Goddess of Earth, ORABALN.

Step 10. Same as Step 10 in Path 1.

Pathworking the Watchtower of Earth

Step 11. Same as Step 11 in Path 1.

Step 12. Turn from your consort and step outside the black hexagram. Leave by the same path that you entered. After leaving the mandala, conduct the banishing pentagram ritual. This completes the fifteenth initiatory path.

Path Sixteen

The Path of Physical Insight leads through the four positions 11-15-20-21, as shown in Figure 33. It contains the specific atmospheres of insight, health, peace, and harmony. It is the Fourth Path of Harmony. Use this path for insight into physical matters.

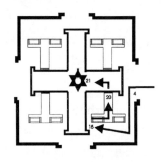

Figure 33: Path 16, The Path of Physical Insight

Step 1. Make a circle and conduct the invoking pentagram ritual.

Step 2. Face the West, and imagine the Mandala of the Watchtower of Earth clearly before you. You are facing its Eastern wall. Imagine the walls and floors to be black. Recite the Centering Spell. Then say:

> May I enter and safely pass through this black Watchtower of Earth.
> May I obtain success in this, the sixteenth of my initiations.
> In the threefold secret and holy name of MORDIALHKTGA
> I make this request. ORERI KALAZ KORESA TAZA SAGE
> DO HOMILA IPAME KAOSAGO

Step 3. Visualize the closed Green Agate Gate. say:

> O ASTIM I invoke thee. Come unto me from the Watchtower of Earth.

Visualize ASTIM before you. Approach the Angel unafraid; open your arms and embrace him. Feel his body melt into your own and become a part of you. Assume the god-form of the Archangel ASTIM, who guards the Green Agate Gate (position 4), as follows:

The god-form of ASTIM: See page 237 for the god-form of ASTIM.

There are special words written above the Green Agate Gate to be spoken before entering. Say: Woe be unto the Sons of Men, for they are the dwelling places of the beast.

Step 4. Visualize the gate opening at these words. Step within the Green Agate Gate. Face the Earth-Tier. In the god-form of ASTIM, say:

> I am the Archangel of Earth. I am the Archangel ASTIM. I am the Guardian of the Green Agate Gate. I enter into the Watchtower of Earth.

While slowly repeating the Threefold Holy Word, enter into the Watchtower of Earth and move across the Earth-Tier to the bottom of the Malachite Stairway leading up to the Water-Tier (position 15). The Threefold Word that you recite will protect you from the Demons who reside on the Earth-Tier.

Step 5. Face the Malachite Stairway. Visualize the Kerubic Angel IAOM before you. Approach the Angel unafraid; open your arms and embrace him. Feel his body melt into your own and become a part of you. Assume the god-form of IAOM, who guards the Grain Stairway, as follows:

The god-form of IAOM: See page 239 for the god-form of IAOM.

Recite the words written over the Malachite Stairway:

> **This may seem unto you, a strange and stumbling Doctrine.
> I have laid the Basis.**

Step 6. In the god-form of the Kerubic Angel IAOM, while slowly repeating the magic word XUM, climb the six steps of the Malachite Stairway to the Water-Tier. Then say:

> **I am a Kerubic Angel of Earth. I am Kerubic Angel IAOM.
> I am the Guardian of the Malachite Stairway. I rise up through
> the Watchtower of Earth. Throughout eternity
> I manifest myself from Earth to Water within Earth.**

Step 7. Slowly repeat the magic word XUM as you move across the Water-Tier. Approach the Stairway to the Air-Tier. Before entering the Second Stairway, say:

> **Human policy cannot prevail here. As many as are not faithful in these regions, shall die a most miserable death, and shall drink of sleep everlasting.**

Climb the Second Stairway, which has six steps, to the Air-Tier. Visualize the Sephirothic Cross Angel OPMNIR before you. Approach the Angel unafraid; open your arms and embrace him. Feel his body melt into your own and become a part of you. Assume the god-form of OPMNIR, who guards the Air-Tier and Third Stairway (position 20), as follows:

The god-form of OPMNIR: See page 241 for the god-form of OPMNIR.

The Third Stairway is black and smells of musk. It is also dry and cold. It has four steps, each of which bears a letter written in white and blazing to look upon. The letter P is on the first step, the letter T is on the second, the letter X on the third, and the letter Z on the fourth. Recite the words written above the Third Stairway before ascending:

> **Lift up yourselves, and behold the heavens, and look upon the earth, and muse at her wonders. And let not the lesser part carry away the greater.**

Step 8. In the god-form of the Sephirothic Cross Angel, slowly repeat the magic word AH as you climb. Climb up to the top of the Third Stairway and say:

> **I am a Sephirothic Cross Angel of Earth. I am Sephirothic Cross Angel OPMNIR. I bear the Cross of Earth from Water to Air within Earth.**

Pathworking the Watchtower of Earth

Step 9. As OPMNIR, slowly repeat the word AH and at the top of the Stairway, turn toward the center of the Fire-Tier. Continue as in Step 9 in Path 1.

Step 10. Same as Step 10 in Path 1.

Step 11. Same as Step 11 in Path 1.

Step 12. Turn from your consort and step outside the black hexagram. Leave by the same path that you entered. After leaving the mandala, conduct the banishing pentagram ritual. This completes the sixteenth initiatory path.

Notes to Chapter Ten

1. You must visualize each mandala in its proper color, especially the walls and the stairs. The Earth Mandala is black.

2. The Centering Spell should be spoken aloud in Enochian. The words are given at the end of chapter 9, "The Preparation."

3. The last two lines of this speech contain a magical spell that is to be spoken aloud in the Enochian language. These words mean, "The stones from the Firmament of Wrath are in the Ages of Time at the beginning of the Earth." Using gematria, the letters of the spell add up to 1,934, which reduces to 8 (1+9+3+4=17= 1+7=8).

4. Each of the words over the Earth-Tier Gates in this mandala were words spoken to John Dee by Angels. They are all found on p. 374 of Casaubon.

5. Movement through each Watchtower can be made either by visualization alone, or by actually walking a few steps. If you take a few steps, keep within your circle. Ideally, you would construct a hall with three stairways and physically move through the structure. In practice, however, it is easier (and cheaper) to imagine the mandala structure within your magic circle.

6. If you use an actual robe and magical instrument, change them at this point to assume the new god-form.

7. For all sixteen paths, the writings to be recited at each First Stairway (the First Stairway leads from the Earth-Tier to the Water-Tier) are taken from Dee's diary (see Casaubon, pp. 380-383).

8. The magical word XUM corresponds to the Root Center (the *muladhara chakra* of Kundalini yoga), as shown in *Enochian Yoga* (St. Paul, MN: Llewellyn Publications, 1990).

9. These words were spoken by the Angel MADIMI to Dee (see Casaubon, p. 29).

10. The letters on the steps correspond to the letters of the Root Center as given in our Enochian Yoga (St. Paul, MN: Llewellyn Publications, 1990). For best results, these letters should be visualized in Enochian as follows:

    P = Ω   T = ✓   X = Γ   Z = P

11. For all sixteen paths, the writings to be recited at each Third Stairway (from the Air-Tier to the Fire-Tier) are taken from Dee's diary (see Casaubon, pp. 375 or 376).

12. The magical word AH corresponds with the Root Center (the Muladhara chakra of Kundalini yoga), as shown in our *Enochian Yoga* (St. Paul, MN: Llewellyn Publications, 1990).

13. This is the fourth assumption of a god-form, and the highest within a Watchtower. This god-form depends upon your gender. Males should assume a male form (the King of the Watchtower), while females should assume a female form (a reflex of BABALON). The god-forms

of these deities are in the next step of the ritual. These god-forms are naked, so either visualize yourself as naked, or take off your robe.

14. The god-forms of the Kings are taken from our *Enochian Tarot*. Both god-forms can be found on p. 169 of *Enochian Yoga* (St. Paul, MN: Llewellyn Publications, 1990).

15. The reason for your sexual god-form is now obvious. The central deity of each Watchtower Mandala is the complementary god or goddess to your god-form, and represents everything that you lack in order to be perfect and complete. This deity is also the embodiment of the Watchtower itself. The names of the primary god and goddess of the Watchtower of Earth are from Table 21 of *Enochian Yoga* (St. Paul, MN: Llewellyn Publications, 1990).

16. Sex is well known in magical schools for its ability to generate magic power. See *Lust for Enlightenment: Buddhism and Sex* by John Stevens (Boston, MA: Shambhala Publications, Inc., 1990) for an informative look at sex in the East. See *Sexual Life in Ancient Egypt*, by Lise Manniche (KPI, distributed by Routledge & Kegan Paul, 1987), for a sexual look at ancient Egypt. We also recommend almost anything by Aleister Crowley, especially his *Energized Enthusiasm* (*Gems from the Equinox*, St. Paul: Llewellyn), for a look at contemporary Western sex magic.

17. These words were spoken to Dee by the Angel MADIMI (see p. 29 of Casaubon).

18. This is the fourfold climax to the initiation. The stages are looking, smiling, touching, and merging (sexual union), and they culminate in the generation of bliss. Try to keep the four stages separate and distinct. The merging of god-forms should be slow and sensual. As you merge into one complete being, you will take on the qualities and characteristics of your consort. The net effect is that you will embody the entire Watchtower of Earth.

19. This quote is from p. 57 of Casaubon.

20. You can leave each mandala quickly, without recitations or god-forms. Simply visualize your path in reversed order, clearly and without error (do not, for example, forget to descend each Stairway that you climbed). This technique, together with the banishing ritual, is provided to help sever you from any psychic or karmic effects of the initiation that could otherwise cause you problems at some point after the exercise.

21. Steps 10 and 11 are identical for each of the exercises in the Watchtower of Earth. To conserve space, we refer you to those steps given fully in Path 1 rather than repeat them throughout.

Chapter 11

PATHWORKING THE WATCHTOWER OF WATER

This chapter contains the second set of initiatory paths, paths 17 through 32. In these paths you will use the Watchtower Mandala of Water, as shown in color plate II. The critical twenty-one positions within the mandala are shown in Figure 34. The names of the entrance gates and first stairways are shown in Figure 35. The names and positions of the twenty-two deities of the Mandala of Water are shown in Figure 36. Figures 37 through 52 show the sixteen paths that you will take through the Water Mandala.

THE EARTH QUADRANT OF THE WATER MANDALA

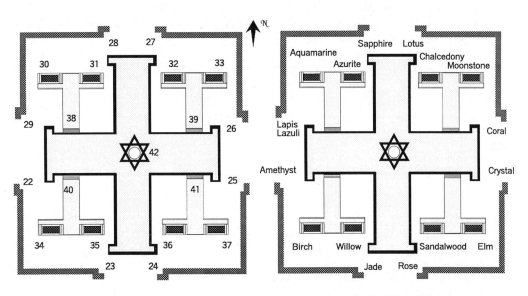

Figure 34: The Water Mandala Showing Positions

Figure 35: The Water Mandala Showing Gates and Stairways

The Angels' Message to Humanity

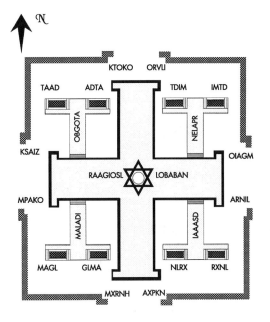

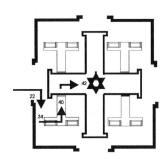

Figure 36: The Water Mandala Showing Deities   *Figure 37: Path 17, The Path of Dream Control*

Path Seventeen

The Path of Dream Control leads through the four positions 22-34-40-42, as shown in Figure 37. It contains the specific atmospheres of knowledge, dreams, love, and protection. It is the First Path of Feeling. Use this path to help control your dreams.

Step 1. Make a circle and conduct the invoking pentagram ritual.[1]

Step 2. Face the East, and imagine the Mandala of the Watchtower of Water clearly before you. You are facing the Western wall. Imagine the walls and floors to be blue. Recite the Centering Spell. Say:

> May I enter and safely pass through this blue Watchtower of Water.
> May I obtain success in this, the seventeenth of my initiations.
> In the threefold secret and holy name of MPHARSLGAIOL
> I make this request. TOFAGILO ZIN ASA TA KANILA.[2]

Step 3. Visualize the closed Amethyst Gate. Say:

> O MPAKO I invoke thee. Come unto me from the Watchtower of Water.

Visualize MPAKO before you. Approach the Angel unafraid; open your arms and embrace him. Feel his body melt into your own and become a part of you. Assume the god-form of the Angel MPAKO ("em-pah-koh"), who guards the Amethyst Gate (position 22), as follows:

The god-form of MPAKO: See page 240 for the god-form of MPAKO.

There are special words written above the Amethyst Gate to be spoken before entering.[3] Say:

Pathworking the Watchtower of Water

> As in one root there are many divisions,
> so in the stem and branches are many separations.

Step 4. Visualize the gate opening at these words. Step within the Amethyst Gate. Face the Earth-Tier. In the god-form of MPAKO, say:

> **I am the Angel of Water. I am the Angel MPAKO. I am the Guardian of the Amethyst Gate. I enter into the Watchtower of Water.**

While slowly repeating the Threefold Holy Word, enter the Watchtower of Water and move across the Earth-Tier, to the bottom of the Birch Stairway leading up to the Water-Tier (position 34). The Threefold Word that you recite protects you from the demons who reside on the Earth-Tier.

Step 5. Face the Birch Stairway. Visualize the Kerubic Angel MAGL before you. Approach the Angel unafraid; open your arms and embrace her. Feel her body melt into your own and become a part of you. Assume the god-form of MAGL ("mah-geh-el"), who guards the Water-Tier Stairway, as follows:

The god-form of MAGL: See page 240 for the god-form of MAGL.

Recite the words written over the Birch Stairway:[4]

> **This is he that sealeth up the Second Hell, with the Second Death.**

Step 6. In the god-form of the Kerubic Angel of Water, MAGL, while slowly repeating the magic word QUM[5], climb the four steps of the Birch Stairway to the Water-Tier. Then say:

> **I am a Kerubic Angel of Water. I am Kerubic Angel MAGL.**
> **I am the Guardian of the Birch Stairway. I rise up through**
> **the Watchtower of Water. Throughout eternity**
> **I renew myself from Earth to Water within Water.**

Step 7. Slowly repeat the magic word QUM as you move across the Water-Tier. Approach the Second Stairway leading up to the Air-Tier. Before entering the Second Stairway, say:

> **The spirit that speaks to you is she that has a Tower to build, a strong Tower and a mighty Tower. Yea, such a one as has not been from the beginning. No, not from the beginning. Great is the foundation thereof, for it is of Iron. But greater are her walls, for they are of Diamond. Most great are her Turrets, for they are the seven heads that behold, judge, and gather. And they are made of Truth, the Spirit of Eternity. Unto the laying of every stone, are you made privy, and for this Tower you are provided.**[6]

Climb the Second Stairway, which has twelve steps, to the Air-Tier. Visualize the Sephirothic Cross Angel MALADI before you. Approach the Angel unafraid; open your arms and embrace her. Feel her body melt into your own and become a part of you. Assume the god-form for MALADI ("mah-lah-dee"), who guards the Air-Tier and Third Stairway (position 40), as follows:

The Angels' Message to Humanity

The god-form of MALADI: See page 240 for the god-form of MALADI.

The Third Stairway is blue and smells of myrrh. It is also wet and cold. There are five steps, each of which bears a letter written in yellow that is blazing to look upon. The letter *M* is on the first step, *N* is on the second, *Q* is on the third, *R* on the fourth, and *V* on the fifth.[7] Recite the words written above the Third Stairway before ascending:

> **Lift up yourselves, as the Servants of God, and help to bring stones unto the building of this great City, that you may be openers of the Gates, and that the White Horse may enter, and that he that enters may reward you with honor.**[8]

As you climb the Stairway, recite the following magic words that are written, one each, on the steps of each Third Stairway as you ascend.[9]

First Step: **SUDSAMNA**

Second Step: **AFLAFBEN**

Third Step: **BAMASAN**

Fourth Step: **KORSAX**

Fifth Step: **TOHOMAPHALA**

Step 8. In the god-form of a Sephirotic Cross Angel of Water, slowly recite the magic word TRAM.[10] Move to the top of the Third Stairway and say:

> **I am a Sephirotic Cross Angel of Water. I am Sephirotic Cross Angel MALADI. I bear the Cross of Water from Water to Air within Water.**

Step 9. As MALADI, repeat the word TRAM and at the top of the Stairway, turn toward the center of the Fire-Tier. If you are male, assume the naked god-form of the King of Water, RAAGIOSL (pronounced "rah-ah-gee-oh-sel"). If you are female, assume the naked god-form of the Goddess of Water, LOBABAN ("el-oh-bah-bah-en").[11]

The god-form of RAAGIOSL:. See page 242 for the god-form of RAAGIOSL.

The god-form of LOBABAN: See page 240 for the god-form of LOBABAN.[12]

Step 10. Slowly repeat the name of your consort (either RAAGIOSL or LOBABAN) while walking along the Fire-Tier, the Great Cross of the Watchtower, toward the center of the mandala. Face the large, watery, blue hexagram with a white circle at its center. If you are male, visualize your consort, LOBABAN, standing naked in the center of the blue hexagram (position 42) waiting for you. If you are female, visualize your consort, RAAGIOSL, standing naked in the center of the hexagram (position 42) waiting for you.

Step 11. Stand just outside of the hexagram, face your consort (who is naked and very beautiful) before you, and say:

Pathworking the Watchtower of Water

> Let the Daughters of Light take up their garments, let them open
> the windows of their Secret Chambers. Show yourselves to be gods;
> Yea, perform that which you have already promised. Gather
> your vestures together, for those who are sick have need of help.
> You are the Children of Pity and in the Loins of Compassion do you dwell.
> Come gather up your garments, for the cankers are ripe,
> and the biting-worm seeks to gnaw into the lily.[13]

While you face each other, enter into the watery, blue hexagram. See yourself clearly at the center of the Water Mandala. Smile at each other as if in love; then move together and hold each other. While saying the name HKOMA, merge God/King and Goddess of Water together while holding a detailed awareness of the Watchtower around you. Remain this way for as long as you can, and then say:

> The works of the Spirit quicken. The doings of the Flesh
> lead unto distraction. May I have understanding, and cast away pride.
> By true understanding may I learn, first to know myself, what I am,
> of whom I am, and to what end I am. This understanding
> causes no self-love, but a spiritual self-love. This understanding teaches
> no blasphemy. This understanding teaches no fury. May it teach me
> to be angry, but not wrathful. For I may be angry, and not offend,
> but wrath is to damnation. Is God a God of Justice? May I be therefore,
> a just servant. No man inherits the Kingdom of Eternity, without he
> conquer in this World. No man can challenge justly a reward, without he
> be a Conqueror, or do the Works of Justice. Does the World
> not like me? It is for two causes: either for that I live well and not
> as a worldling, or else because my wickedness is such as that
> the World wonders at it. If I am in the first, I will rejoice, for blessed
> are those whom the World hates; when they laugh at my godliness,
> I will be sorry and grieve at their sinfulness. My Garland is Godliness,
> my Breastplate is Humility, and upon my back I wear Patience.[14]

Step 12. Turn from your consort and step out of the hexagram. Leave by the same path you entered. After leaving the mandala, conduct the banishing pentagram ritual. This completes the seventeenth initiatory path.

PATH EIGHTEEN

The Path of Sexual Attraction leads through the four positions 22-35-40-42, as shown in Figure 38. It contains the specific atmospheres of knowledge, dreams, sexual love, and love. It is the Second Path of Feeling. Use this path to develop or enhance sexual attraction.

Step 1. Make a circle and conduct the invoking pentagram ritual.

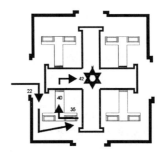

Figure 38: Path 18, The Path of Sexual Attraction

Step 2. Face the East, and imagine the Mandala of the Watchtower of Water clearly before you. You are facing the Western wall. Imagine the walls and floors to be blue. Recite the Centering Spell. Say:

**May I enter and safely pass through this blue Watchtower of Water.
May I obtain success in this, the eighteenth of my initiations.
In the threefold secret and holy name of MPHARSLGAIOL
I make this request. TOFAGILO ZIN ASA TA KANILA**

Step 3. Visualize the closed Amethyst Gate. Say:

O MPAKO I invoke thee. Come unto me from the Watchtower of Water.

Visualize MPAKO before you. Approach the Angel unafraid; open your arms and embrace him. Feel his body melt into your own and become a part of you. Assume the god-form of the Angel MPAKO, who guards the Amethyst Gate (position 22), as follows:

The god-form of MPAKO: See page 240 for the god-form of MPAKO.

There are special words written above the Amethyst Gate to be spoken before entering. Say:

**As in one root there are many divisions,
so in the stem and branches are many separations.**

Step 4. Visualize the gate opening at these words. Step within the Amethyst Gate. Face the Earth-Tier. In the god-form of MPAKO, say:

I am the Angel of Water. I am the Angel MPAKO. I am the Guardian of the Amethyst Gate. May I enter into the Watchtower of Water.

While slowly repeating the Threefold Holy Word, enter the Watchtower of Water and move across the Earth-Tier to the bottom of the Willow Stairway (position 35) leading up to the Water-Tier. The Threefold Word that you recite protects you from the demons who reside on the Earth-Tier.

Step 5. Face the Willow Stairway. Visualize the Kerubic Angel GLMA before you. Approach the Angel unafraid; open your arms and embrace her. Feel her body melt into your own and become a part of you. Assume the god-form of GLMA ("geh-leh-mah"), who guards the Water-Tier Stairway, as follows:

The god-form of GLMA: See page 238 for the god-form of GLMA.

Recite the words written over the Willow Stairway:

Are you not afraid of the unspeakable flames and fire-brands of Hell, which were prepared for the wicked?

Step 6. In the god-form of the Kerubic Angel of Water, GLMA, while slowly repeating the magic word QUM, climb the four steps of the Willow Stairway to the Water-Tier. Then say:

Pathworking the Watchtower of Water

> I am a Kerubic Angel of Water. I am Kerubic Angel GLMA. I am
> the Guardian of the Willow Stairway. I rise up
> through the Watchtower of Water. Throughout eternity
> I renew myself from Earth to Water within Water.

Step 7. Slowly repeat the magic word QUM as you move across the Water-Tier. Approach the Second Stairway leading up to the Air-Tier. Before entering the Second Stairway, say:

> **The spirit that speaks to you is he that has a Tower to build, a strong Tower and a mighty Tower. Yea, such a one as has not been from the beginning. No, not from the beginning. Great is the foundation thereof, for it is of Iron. But greater are her walls, for they are of Diamond. Most great are her Turrets, for they are the seven heads that behold, judge, and gather. And they are made of Truth, the Spirit of Eternity. Unto the laying of every stone, are you made privy, and for this Tower you are provided.**

Climb the Second Stairway, which has twelve steps, to the Air-Tier. Visualize the Sephirothic Cross Angel MALADI before you. Approach the Angel unafraid; open your arms and embrace her. Feel her body melt into your own and become a part of you. Assume the god-form for MALADI, who guards the Air-Tier and Third Stairway (position 40), as follows:

The god-form of MALADI: See page 240 for the god-form of MALADI.

The Third Stairway is blue and smells of myrrh. It is also wet and cold. There are five steps, each of which bears a letter written in yellow that is blazing to look upon. The letter *M* is on the first step, *N* is on the second, *Q* is on the third, *R* on the fourth, and *V* on the fifth.[7] Recite the words written above the Third Stairway before ascending:

> **Lift up yourselves, as the Servants of God, and help to bring stones
> unto the building of this great City, that you may be openers
> of the Gates, and that the White Horse may enter,
> and that he that enters may reward you with honor.**

As you climb the Stairway, recite the following magic words that are written, one each, on the steps of each Third Stairway as you ascend.

First Step: **SUDSAMNA**

Second Step: **AFLAFBEN**

Third Step: **BAMASAN**

Fourth Step: **KORSAX**

Fifth Step: **TOHOMAPHALA**

Step 8. In the god-form of a Sephirothic Cross Angel of Water, slowly recite the magic word TRAM. Move to the top of the Third Stairway and say:

The Angels' Message to Humanity

I am a Sephirothic Cross Angel of Water. I am Sephirothic Cross Angel MALADI. I bear the Cross of Water from Water to Air within Water.

Step 9. As MALADI, repeat the word TRAM and at the top of the Stairway, turn toward the center of the Fire-Tier. If you are male, assume the naked god-form of the King of Water, RAAGIOSL. If you are female, assume the naked god-form of the Goddess of Water, LOBABAN.

Step 10. Same as Step 10 of Path 17.[15]

Step 11. Same as Step 11 of Path 17.

Step 12. Turn from your consort and step out of the hexagram. Leave by the same path that you entered. After leaving the mandala, conduct the banishing pentagram ritual. This completes the eighteenth initiatory path.

Path Nineteen

The Path of Emotional Protection leads through the four positions 23-34-40-42, as shown in Figure 39. It contains the specific atmospheres of divination, love, and protection. It is the Third Path of Feeling. Use this path to develop love as a protective shield.

Step 1. Make a circle and conduct the invoking pentagram ritual.

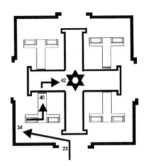

Figure 39: Path 19, The Path of Emotional Protection

Step 2. Face the North, and imagine the Mandala of the Watchtower of Water clearly before you. You are facing the Southern wall. Imagine the walls and floors to be blue. Recite the Centering Spell. Say:

> **May I enter and safely pass through this blue Watchtower of Water.**
> **May I obtain success in this, the nineteenth of my initiations.**
> **In the threefold secret and holy name of MPHARSLGAIOL**
> **I make this request. TOFAGILO ZIN ASA TA KANILA**

Step 3. Visualize the closed Jade Gate. Say:

> **O MXRNH I invoke thee. Come unto me from the Watchtower of Water.**

Visualize MXRNH before you. Approach the Angel unafraid; open your arms and embrace him. Feel his body melt into your own and become a part of you. Assume the god-form of the Angel MXRNH ("metz-ar-en-heh"), who guards the Jade Gate (position 23), as follows:

The god-form of MXRNH: See page 240 for the god-form of MXRNH.

There are special words written above the Jade Gate to be spoken before entering. Say:

> **The Fire that kindles All wherein I live is One, forming them**
> **according to the substance whereupon they are grounded. So by the less,**

Pathworking the Watchtower of Water

>is proved the greater. That as the particular,
>so likewise generally—all emanations are from the One.

Step 4. Visualize the gate opening at these words. Step within the Jade Gate. Face the Earth-Tier. In the god-form of MXRNH, say:

>I am the Angel of Water. I am the Angel MXRNH. I am the Guardian of the Jade Gate. May I enter into the Watchtower of Water.

While slowly repeating the Threefold Holy Word, enter the Watchtower of Water and move across the Earth-Tier to the bottom of the Birch Stairway (position 34) leading up to the Water-Tier. The Threefold Word that you recite protects you from the demons who reside on the Earth-Tier.

Step 5. Face the Birch Stairway. Visualize the Kerubic Angel MAGL before you. Approach the Angel unafraid; open your arms and embrace her. Feel her body melt into your own and become a part of you. Assume the god-form of MAGL, who guards the Water-Tier Stairway, as follows:

>**The god-form of MAGL:** See page 240 for the god-form of MAGL.

Recite the words written over the Birch Stairway:

>**This is she that sealeth up the Second Hell, with the Second Death.**

Step 6. In the god-form of the Kerubic Angel of Water, MAGL, while slowly repeating the magic word QUM, climb the four steps of the Birch Stairway to the Water-Tier. Then say:

>I am a Kerubic Angel of Water. I am Kerubic Angel MAGL.
>I am the Guardian of the Birch Stairway. I rise up through
>the Watchtower of Water. Throughout eternity
>I renew myself from Earth to Water within Water.

Step 7. Slowly repeat the magic word QUM as you move across the Water-Tier. Approach the Second Stairway leading up to the Air-Tier. Before entering the Second Stairway, say:

>The spirit that speaks to you is she that has a Tower to build, a strong Tower and a mighty Tower. Yea, such a one as has not been from the beginning. No, not from the beginning. Great is the foundation thereof, for it is of Iron. But greater are her walls, for they are of Diamond. Most great are her Turrets, for they are the seven heads that behold, judge, and gather. And they are made of Truth, the Spirit of Eternity. Unto the laying of every stone, are you made privy, and for this Tower you are provided.

Climb the Second Stairway, which has twelve steps, to the Air-Tier. Visualize the Sephirothic Cross Angel MALADI before you. Approach the Angel unafraid; open your arms and embrace her. Feel her body melt into your own and become a part of you. Assume the god-form for MALADI, who guards the Air-Tier and Third Stairway (position 40), as follows:

The Angels' Message to Humanity

The god-form of MALADI: See page 240 for the god-form of MALADI.

The Third Stairway is blue and smells of myrrh. It is also wet and cold. There are five steps, each of which bears a letter written in yellow that is blazing to look upon. The letter *M* is on the first step, *N* is on the second, *Q* is on the third, *R* on the fourth, and *V* on the fifth.[7] Recite the words written above the Third Stairway before ascending:

> **Lift up yourselves, as the Servants of God, and help to bring stones unto the building of this great City, that you may be openers of the Gates, and that the White Horse may enter, and that he that enters may reward you with honor.**

As you climb the Stairway, recite the following magic words that are written, one each, on the steps of each Third Stairway as you ascend.

First Step: **SUDSAMNA**

Second Step: **AFLAFBEN**

Third Step: **BAMASAN**

Fourth Step: **KORSAX**

Fifth Step: **TOHOMAPHALA**

Step 8. In the god-form of a Sephirothic Cross Angel of Water, slowly recite the magic word TRAM. Move to the top of the Third Stairway and say:

> **I am a Sephirothic Cross Angel of Water. I am Sephirothic Cross Angel MALADI. I bear the Cross of Water from Water to Air within Water.**

Step 9. As MALADI, repeat the word TRAM, and at the top of the Stairway, turn toward the center of the Fire-Tier. If you are male, assume the naked god-form of the King of Water, RAAGIOSL. If you are female, assume the naked god-form of the Goddess of Water, LOBABAN.

Step 10. Same as Step 10 of Path 17.

Step 11. Same as Step 11 of Path 17.

Step 12. Turn from your consort and step out of the hexagram. Leave by the same path that you entered. After leaving the mandala, conduct the banishing pentagram ritual. This completes the nineteenth initiatory path.

Pathworking the Watchtower of Water

PATH TWENTY

The Path of Sexual Desire leads through the four positions 23-35-40-42, as shown in Figure 40. It contains the specific atmospheres of divination, love, and sexual love. It is the Fourth Path of Feeling. Use this path to control lust or sexual desire.

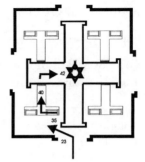

Figure 40: Path 20, The Path of Sexual Desire

Step 1. Make a circle and conduct the invoking pentagram ritual.

Step 2. Face the North, and imagine the Mandala of the Watchtower of Water clearly before you. You are facing the Southern wall. Imagine the walls and floors to be blue. Recite the Centering Spell. Say:

> **May I enter and safely pass through this blue Watchtower of Water.**
> **May I obtain success in this, the twentieth of my initiations.**
> **In the threefold secret and holy name of MPHARSLGAIOL**
> **I make this request. TOFAGILO ZIN ASA TA KANILA.**

Step 3. Visualize the closed Jade Gate. Say:

> **O MXRNH I invoke thee. Come unto me from the Watchtower of Water.**

Visualize MXRNH before you. Approach the Angel unafraid; open your arms and embrace him. Feel his body melt into your own and become a part of you. Assume the god-form of the Angel MXRNH, who guards the Jade Gate (position 23), as follows:

The god-form of MXRNH: See page 240 for the god-form of MXRNH.

There are special words written above the Jade Gate to be spoken before entering. Say:

> **The Fire that kindles All wherein I live is One, forming them**
> **according to the substance whereupon they are grounded.**
> **So by the less, is proved the greater. That as the particular,**
> **so likewise generally — all emanations are from the One.**

Step 4. Visualize the gate opening at these words. Step within the Jade Gate. Face the Earth-Tier. In the god-form of MXRNH, say:

> **I am the Angel of Water. I am the Angel MXRNH. I am the Guardian**
> **of the Jade Gate. I enter into the Watchtower of Water.**

While slowly repeating the Threefold Holy Word, enter the Watchtower of Water and move across the Earth-Tier to the bottom of the Willow Stairway (position 35) leading up to the Water-Tier. The Threefold Word that you recite protects you from the demons who reside on the Earth-Tier.

Step 5. Face the Willow Stairway. Visualize the Kerubic Angel GLMA before you. Approach the Angel unafraid; open your arms and embrace her. Feel her body melt into your own and become a part of you. Assume the god-form of GLMA, who guards the Water-Tier Stairway, as follows:

The Angels' Message to Humanity

The god-form of GLMA: See page 238 for the god-form of GLMA.

Recite the words written over the Willow Stairway:

> **Are you not afraid of the unspeakable flames and fire-brands of Hell, which were prepared for the wicked?**

Step 6. In the god-form of the Kerubic Angel of Water, GLMA, while slowly repeating the magic word QUM, climb the four steps of the Willow Stairway to the Water-Tier. Then say:

> **I am a Kerubic Angel of Water. I am Kerubic Angel GLMA.**
> **I am the Guardian of the Willow Stairway. I rise up through**
> **the Watchtower of Water. Throughout eternity**
> **I renew myself from Earth to Water within Water.**

Step 7. Slowly repeat the magic word QUM as you move across the Water-Tier. Approach the Second Stairway leading up to the Air-Tier. Before entering the Second Stairway, say:

> **The spirit that speaks to you is he that has a Tower to build, a strong Tower and a mighty Tower. Yea, such a one as has not been from the beginning. No, not from the beginning. Great is the foundation thereof, for it is of Iron. But greater are her walls, for they are of Diamond. Most great are her Turrets, for they are the seven heads that behold, judge, and gather. And they are made of Truth, the Spirit of Eternity. Unto the laying of every stone, are you made privy, and for this Tower you are provided.**

Climb the Second Stairway, which has twelve steps, to the Air-Tier. Visualize the Sephirothic Cross Angel MALADI before you. Approach the Angel unafraid; open your arms and embrace her. Feel her body melt into your own and become a part of you. Assume the god-form of MALADI, who guards the Air-Tier and Third Stairway (position 40), as follows:

The god-form of MALIDI: See page 240 for the god-form of MALIDI.

The Third Stairway is blue and smells of myrrh. It is also wet and cold. There are five steps, each of which bears a letter written in yellow that is blazing to look upon. The letter M is on the first step, N is on the second, Q is on the third, R on the fourth, and V on the fifth.[7] Recite the words written above the Third Stairway before ascending:

> **Lift up yourselves, as the Servants of God, and help to bring stones unto the building of this great City, that you may be openers of the Gates, and that the White Horse may enter, and that he that enters may reward you with honor.**

As you climb the Stairway, recite the following magic words that are written, one each, on the steps of each Third Stairway as you ascend.

First Step: **SUDSAMNA**

Second Step: **AFLAFBEN**

Pathworking the Watchtower of Water

Third Step: **BAMASAN**

Fourth Step: **KORSAX**

Fifth Step: **TOHOMAPHALA**

Step 8. In the god-form of a Sephirothic Cross Angel of Water, slowly recite the magic word TRAM. Move to the top of the Third Stairway and say:

> **I am a Sephirothic Cross Angel of Water. I am Sephirothic Cross Angel MALADI. I bear the Cross of Water from Water to Air within Water.**

Step 9. As MALADI, repeat the word TRAM and at the top of the Stairway, turn toward the center of the Fire-Tier. If you are male, assume the naked god-form of the King of Water, RAAGIOSL. If you are female, assume the naked god-form of the Goddess of Water, LOBABAN.

Step 10. Same as Step 10 of Path 17.

Step 11. Same as Step 11 of Path 17.

Step 12. Turn from your consort and step out of the hexagram. Leave by the same path that you entered. After leaving the mandala, conduct the banishing pentagram ritual. This completes the twentieth initiatory path.

THE WATER QUADRANT OF THE WATER MANDALA

PATH TWENTY-ONE

The Path of Mystical Love leads through the four positions 26-33-39-42, as shown in Figure 41. It contains the specific atmospheres of love, healing, and mysticism. It is the First Path of Love. Use this path to understand and control the mysteries of love.

Step 1. Make a circle and conduct the invoking pentagram ritual.

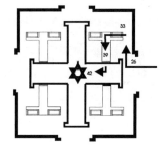

Figure 41: Path 21, The Path of Mystical Love

Step 2. Face the West, and imagine the Mandala of the Watchtower of Water clearly before you. You are facing the Eastern wall. Imagine the walls and floors to be blue. Recite the Centering Spell. Say:

> **May I enter and safely pass through this blue Watchtower of Water.**
> **May I obtain success in this, the twenty-first of my initiations.**
> **In the threefold secret and holy name of MPHARSLGAIOL**
> **I make this request. TOFAGILO ZIN ASA TA KANILA**

Step 3. Visualize the closed Coral Gate. Say:

The Angels' Message to Humanity

O OIAGM I invoke thee. Come unto me from the Watchtower of Water.

Visualize OIAGM before you. Approach the Angel unafraid; open your arms and embrace her. Feel her body melt into your own and become a part of you. Assume the god-form of the Angel OIAGM ("oh-ee-ah-gem"), who guards the Coral Gate (position 26), as follows:

The god-form of OIAGM: See page 241 for the god-form of OIAGM.

There are special words written above the Coral Gate to be spoken before entering. Say:

It is sealed, and therefore it has an end.

Step 4. Visualize the gate opening at these words. Step within the Coral Gate. Face the Earth-Tier. In the god-form of OIAGM, say:

I am the Angel of Water. I am the Angel OIAGM. I am the Guardian of the Coral Gate. I enter into the Watchtower of Water.

While slowly repeating the Threefold Holy Word, enter the Watchtower of Water and move across the Earth-Tier to the bottom of the Moonstone Stairway (position 33) leading up to the Water-Tier. The Threefold Word that you recite protects you from the demons who reside on the Earth-Tier.

Step 5. Face the Moonstone Stairway. Visualize the Kerubic Angel IMTD before you. Approach the Angel unafraid; open your arms and embrace her. Feel her body melt into your own and become a part of you. Assume the god-form of IMTD ("ee-meh-teh-deh"), who guards the Water-Tier Stairway, as follows:

The god-form of IMTD: See page 239 for the god-form of IMTD.

Recite the words written over the Moonstone Stairway:

Joy and Perseverence. Whereof the greatest is Perseverence.

Step 6. In the god-form of the Kerubic Angel of Water, IMTD, while slowly repeating the magic word QUM, climb the ten steps of the Moonstone Stairway to the Water-Tier. Then say:

I am a Kerubic Angel of Water. I am Kerubic Angel IMTD. I am the Guardian of the Moonstone Stairway. I rise up through the Watchtower of Water. Throughout eternity I renew myself from Earth to Water within Water.

Step 7. Slowly repeat the magic word QUM as you move across the Water-Tier. Approach the Second Stairway leading up to the Air-Tier. Before entering the Second Stairway, say:

The spirit that speaks to you is he that has a Tower to build, a strong Tower and a mighty Tower. Yea, such a one as has not been from the beginning. No, not from the beginning. Great is the foundation thereof, for it is of Iron. But greater are her walls, for they are of Diamond. Most great are

Pathworking the Watchtower of Water

her Turrets, for they are the seven heads that behold, judge, and gather. And they are made of Truth, the Spirit of Eternity. Unto the laying of every stone, are you made privy, and for this Tower you are provided.

Climb the Second Stairway, which has twelve steps, to the Air-Tier. Visualize the Sephirothic Cross Angel NELAPR before you. Approach the Angel unafraid; open your arms and embrace him. Feel his body melt into your own and become a part of you. Assume the god-form for NELAPR ("neh-lah-par"), who guards the Air-Tier and Third Stairway (position 40), as follows:

The god-form of NELAPR: See page 240 for the god-form of NELAPR.

The Third Stairway is blue and smells of myrrh. It is also wet and cold. There are five steps, each of which bears a letter written in yellow that is blazing to look upon. The letter *M* is on the first step, *N* is on the second, *Q* is on the third, *R* on the fourth, and *V* on the fifth.[7] Recite the words written above the Third Stairway before ascending:

Behold, the work is great, the labor is also equal unto it.

As you climb the Stairway, recite the following magic words that are written, one each, on the steps of each Third Stairway as you ascend.

First Step: **SUDSAMNA**

Second Step: **AFLAFBEN**

Third Step: **BAMASAN**

Fourth Step: **KORSAX**

Fifth Step: **TOHOMAPHALA**

Step 8. In the god-form of a Sephirothic Cross Angel of Water, slowly recite the magic word TRAM. Move to the top of the Third Stairway and say:

I am a Sephirothic Cross Angel of Water. I am Sephirothic Cross Angel NELAPR. I bear the Cross of Water from Water to Air within Water.

Step 9. As NELAPR, repeat the word TRAM and at the top of the Stairway, turn toward the center of the Fire-Tier. If you are male, assume the naked god-form of the King of Water, RAAGIOSL. If you are female, assume the naked god-form of the Goddess of Water, LOBABAN.

Step 10. Same as Step 10 of Path 17.

Step 11. Same as Step 11 of Path 17.

Step 12. Turn from your consort and step out of the hexagram. Leave by the same path that you entered. After leaving the mandala, conduct the banishing pentagram ritual. This completes the twenty-first initiatory path.

Path Twenty-Two

The Path of the Power of Love leads through the four positions 26-32-39-42, as shown in Figure 42. It contains the specific atmospheres of love, healing, divinity, and peace. It is the Second Path of Love. Use this path to develop the healing power of love.

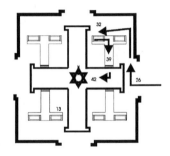

Step 1. Make a circle and conduct the invoking pentagram ritual.

Figure 42: Path 22, The Path of the Power of Love

Step 2. Face the West, and imagine the Mandala of the Watchtower of Water clearly before you. You are facing the Eastern wall. Imagine the walls and floors to be blue. Recite the Centering Spell. Say:

> May I enter and safely pass through this blue Watchtower of Water.
> May I obtain success in this, the twenty-second of my initiations.
> In the threefold secret and holy name of MPHARSLGAIOL
> I make this request. TOFAGILO ZIN ASA TA KANILA

Step 3. Visualize the closed Coral Gate. Say:

> O OIAGM I invoke thee. Come unto me from the Watchtower of Water.

Visualize OIAGM before you. Approach the Angel unafraid; open your arms and embrace her. Feel her body melt into your own and become a part of you. Assume the god-form of the Angel OIAGM, who guards the Coral Gate (position 26), as follows:

The god-form of OIAGM: See page 241 for the god-form of OIAGM.

There are special words written above the Coral Gate to be spoken before entering. Say:

> It is sealed, and therefore it has an end.

Step 4. Visualize the gate opening at these words. Step within the Coral Gate. Face the Earth-Tier. In the god-form of OIAGM, say:

> I am the Angel of Water. I am the Angel OIAGM. I am the Guardian of the Coral Gate. I enter into the Watchtower of Water.

While slowly repeating the Threefold Holy Word, enter the Watchtower of Water and move across the Earth-Tier to the bottom of the Chalcedony Stairway (position 32) leading up to the Water-Tier. The Threefold Word that you recite protects you from the demons who reside on the Earth-Tier.

Step 5. Face the Chalcedony Stairway. Visualize the Kerubic Angel TDIM before you. Approach the Angel unafraid; open your arms and embrace her. Feel her body melt into your own and become a part of you. Assume the god-form of TDIM ("teh-dee-meh"), who guards the Water-Tier Stairway, as follows:

Pathworking the Watchtower of Water

The god-form of TDIM: See page 243 for the god-form of TDIM.

Recite the words written over the Chalcedony Stairway:

Behold, no man is penitent, but he useth Prayer. No man satisfieth, but he useth Prayer. No man taketh part with the Church, but in Prayer, for Prayer is the Key.

Step 6. In the god-form of the Kerubic Angel of Water, TDIM, while slowly repeating the magic word QUM, climb the ten steps of the Chalcedony Stairway to the Water-Tier. Then say:

I am a Kerubic Angel of Water. I am Kerubic Angel TDIM. I am the Guardian of the Chalcedony Stairway. I rise up through the Watchtower of Water. Throughout eternity I renew myself from Earth to Water within Water.

Step 7. Slowly repeat the magic word QUM as you move across the Water-Tier. Approach the Second Stairway leading up to the Air-Tier. Before entering the Second Stairway, say:

The spirit that speaks to you is he that has a Tower to build, a strong Tower and a mighty Tower. Yea, such a one as has not been from the beginning. No, not from the beginning. Great is the foundation thereof, for it is of Iron. But greater are her walls, for they are of Diamond. Most great are her Turrets, for they are the seven heads that behold, judge, and gather. And they are made of Truth, the Spirit of Eternity. Unto the laying of every stone, are you made privy, and for this Tower you are provided.

Climb the Second Stairway, which has twelve steps, to the Air-Tier. Visualize the Sephirothic Cross Angel NELAPR before you. Approach the Angel unafraid; open your arms and embrace him. Feel his body melt into your own and become a part of you. Assume the god-form for NELAPR, who guards the Air-Tier and Third Stairway (position 40), as follows:

The god-form of NELAPR: See page 240 for the god-form of NELAPR.

The Third Stairway is blue and smells of myrrh. It is also wet and cold. There are five steps, each of which bears a letter written in yellow that is blazing to look upon. The letter *M* is on the first step, *N* is on the second, *Q* is on the third, *R* on the fourth, and *V* on the fifth.[7] Recite the words written above the Third Stairway before ascending:

Behold, the work is great, the labor is also equal unto it.

As you climb the Stairway, recite the following magic words that are written, one each, on the steps of each Third Stairway as you ascend.

First Step: **SUDSAMNA**

Second Step: **AFLAFBEN**

The Angels' Message to Humanity

Third Step: **BAMASAN**

Fourth Step: **KORSAX**

Fifth Step: **TOHOMAPHALA**

Step 8. In the god-form of a Sephirothic Cross Angel of Water, slowly recite the magic word TRAM. Move to the top of the Third Stairway and say:

> **I am a Sephirothic Cross Angel of Water. I am Sephirothic Cross Angel NELAPR. I bear the Cross of Water from Water to Air within Water.**

Step 9. As NELAPR, repeat the word TRAM, and at the top of the Stairway turn toward the center of the Fire-Tier. If you are male, assume the naked god-form of the King of Water, RAAGIOSL. If you are female, assume the naked god-form of the Goddess of Water, LOBABAN.

Step 10. Same as Step 10 of Path 17.

Step 11. Same as Step 11 of Path 17.

Step 12. Turn from your consort and step out of the hexagram. Leave by the same path that you entered. After leaving the mandala, conduct the banishing pentagram ritual. This completes the twenty-second initiatory path.

PATH TWENTY-THREE

The Path of Love leads through the four positions 27-33-39-42, as shown in Figure 43. It contains the specific atmospheres of strength, protection, mysticism, and love. It is the Third Path of Love. Use this path to strengthen love.

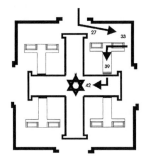

Figure 43: Path 23, The Path of Love

Step 1. Make a circle and conduct the invoking pentagram ritual.

Step 2. Face the South, and imagine the Mandala of the Watchtower of Water clearly before you. You are facing the Northern wall. Imagine the walls and floors to be blue. Recite the Centering Spell. Say:

> **May I enter and safely pass through this blue Watchtower of Water.**
> **May I obtain success in this, the twenty-third of my initiations.**
> **In the threefold secret and holy name of MPHARSLGAIOL**
> **I make this request. TOFAGILO ZIN ASA TA KANILA.**

Step 3. Visualize the closed Lotus Gate. Say:

> **O ORVLI I invoke thee. Come unto me from the Watchtower of Water.**

Visualize ORVLI before you. Approach the Angel unafraid; open your arms and embrace him. Feel his body melt into your own and become a part of you. Assume

Pathworking the Watchtower of Water

the god-form of the Angel ORVLI ("oh-rah-veh-lee"), who guards the Lotus Gate (position 27), as follows:

The god-form of ORVLI: See page 241 for the god-form of ORVLI.

There are special words written above the Lotus Gate to be spoken before entering. Say:

The Sun, through the Circles and Body Mass, is the Heart of the Body, the intelligence in the inward man.

Step 4. Visualize the gate opening at these words. Step within the Lotus Gate. Face the Earth-Tier. In the god-form of ORVLI, say:

I am the Angel of Water. I am the Angel ORVLI. I am the Guardian of the Lotus Gate. I enter into the Watchtower of Water.

While slowly repeating the Threefold Holy Word, enter the Watchtower of Water and move across the Earth-Tier to the bottom of the Moonstone Stairway (position 33) leading up to the Water-Tier. The Threefold Word that you recite protects you from the demons who reside on the Earth-Tier.

Step 5. Face the Moonstone Stairway. Visualize the Kerubic Angel IMTD before you. Approach the Angel unafraid; open your arms and embrace her. Feel her body melt into your own and become a part of you. Assume the god-form of IMTD, who guards the Water-Tier Stairway, as follows:

The god-form of IMTD: See page 239 for the god-form of IMTD.

Recite the words written over the Moonstone Stairway:

Joy and Perseverence. Whereof the greatest is Perseverence.

Step 6. In the god-form of the Kerubic Angel of Water, IMTD, while slowly repeating the magic word QUM, climb the ten steps of the Moonstone Stairway to the Water-Tier. Then say:

**I am a Kerubic Angel of Water. I am Kerubic Angel IMTD.
I am the Guardian of the Moonstone Stairway. I rise up
through the Watchtower of Water.
Throughout eternity I renew myself from Earth to Water within Water.**

Step 7. Slowly repeat the magic word QUM as you move across the Water-Tier. Approach the Second Stairway leading up to the Air-Tier. Before entering the Second Stairway, say:

The spirit that speaks to you is he that has a Tower to build, a strong Tower and a mighty Tower. Yea, such a one as has not been from the beginning. No, not from the beginning. Great is the foundation thereof, for it is of Iron. But greater are her walls, for they are of Diamond. Most great are her Turrets, for they are the seven heads that behold, judge, and gather. And they are made of Truth, the Spirit of Eternity. Unto the laying of every stone, are you made privy, and for this Tower you are provided.

Climb the Second Stairway, which has twelve steps, to the Air-Tier. Visualize the Sephirothic Cross Angel NELAPR before you. Approach the Angel unafraid; open your arms and embrace him. Feel his body melt into your own and become a part of you. Assume the god-form for NELAPR, who guards the Air-Tier and Third Stairway (position 40), as follows:

The god-form of NELAPR: See page 240 for the god-form of NELAPR.

The Third Stairway is blue and smells of myrrh. It is also wet and cold. There are five steps, each of which bears a letter written in yellow that is blazing to look upon. The letter *M* is on the first step, *N* is on the second, *Q* is on the third, *R* on the fourth, and *V* on the fifth.[7] Recite the words written above the Third Stairway before ascending:

Behold, the work is great, the labor is also equal unto it.

As you climb the Stairway, recite the following magic words that are written, one each, on the steps of each Third Stairway as you ascend.

First Step: **SUDSAMNA**

Second Step: **AFLAFBEN**

Third Step: **BAMASAN**

Fourth Step: **KORSAX**

Fifth Step: **TOHOMAPHALA**

Step 8. In the god-form of a Sephirothic Cross Angel of Water, slowly recite the magic word TRAM. Move to the top of the Third Stairway and say:

I am a Sephirothic Cross Angel of Water. I am Sephirothic Cross Angel NELAPR. I bear the Cross of Water from Water to Air within Water.

Step 9. As NELAPR, repeat the word TRAM, and at the top of the Stairway turn toward the center of the Fire-Tier. If you are male, assume the naked god-form of the King of Water, RAAGIOSL. If you are female, assume the naked god-form of the Goddess of Water, LOBABAN.

Step 10. Same as Step 10 of Path 17.

Step 11. Same as Step 11 of Path 17.

Step 12. Turn from your consort and step out of the hexagram. Leave by the same path that you entered. After leaving the mandala, conduct the banishing pentagram ritual. This completes the twenty-third initiatory path.

Pathworking the Watchtower of Water

PATH TWENTY-FOUR

The Path of Peace leads through the four positions 27-32-39-42, as shown in Figure 44. It contains the specific atmospheres of strength, protection, divinity, and peace. It is the Fourth Path of Love. Use this path to strengthen peace.

Step 1. Make a circle and conduct the invoking pentagram ritual.

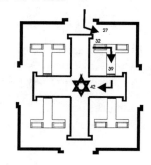

Figure 44: Path 24, The Path of Peace

Step 2. Face the South, and imagine the Mandala of the Watchtower of Water clearly before you. You are facing the Northern wall. Imagine the walls and floors to be blue. Recite the Centering Spell. Say:

> **May I enter and safely pass through this blue Watchtower of Water.**
> **May I obtain success in this, the twenty-fourth of my initiations.**
> **In the threefold secret and holy name of MPHARSLGAIOL**
> **I make this request. TOFAGILO ZIN ASA TA KANILA**

Step 3. Visualize the closed Lotus Gate. Say:

> **O ORVLI I invoke thee. Come unto me from the Watchtower of Water.**

Visualize ORVLI before you. Approach the Angel unafraid; open your arms and embrace him. Feel his body melt into your own and become a part of you. Assume the god-form of the Angel ORVLI, who guards the Lotus Gate (position 27), as follows:

The god-form of ORVLI: See page 241 for the god-form of ORVLI.

There are special words written above the Lotus Gate to be spoken before entering. Say:

> **The Sun, through the Circles and Body Mass, is the Heart of the Body, the intelligence in the inward man.**

Step 4. Visualize the gate opening at these words. Step within the Lotus Gate. Face the Earth-Tier. In the god-form of ORVLI, say:

> **I am the Angel of Water. I am the Angel ORVLI. I am the Guardian of the Lotus Gate. I enter into the Watchtower of Water.**

While slowly repeating the Threefold Holy Word, enter the Watchtower of Water and move across the Earth-Tier to the bottom of the Chalcedony Stairway (position 32) leading up to the Water-Tier. The Threefold Word that you recite protects you from the demons who reside on the Earth-Tier.

Step 5. Face the Chalcedony Stairway. Visualize the Kerubic Angel TDIM before you. Approach the Angel unafraid; open your arms and embrace her. Feel her body melt into your own and become a part of you. Assume the god-form of TDIM, who guards the Water-Tier Stairway, as follows:

The god-form of TDIM: See page 243 for the god-form of TDIM.

The Angels' Message to Humanity

Recite the words written over the Chalcedony Stairway:

> **Behold, no man is penitent, but he useth Prayer. No man satisfieth, but he useth Prayer. No man taketh part with the Church, but in Prayer, for Prayer is the Key.**

Step 6. In the god-form of the Kerubic Angel of Water, TDIM, while slowly repeating the magic word QUM, climb the ten steps of the Chalcedony Stairway to the Water-Tier. Then say:

> **I am a Kerubic Angel of Water. I am Kerubic Angel TDIM. I am the Guardian of the Chalcedony Stairway. I rise up through the Watchtower of Water. Throughout eternity I renew myself from Earth to Water within Water.**

Step 7. Slowly repeat the magic word QUM as you move across the Water-Tier. Approach the Second Stairway leading up to the Air-Tier. Before entering the Second Stairway, say:

> **The spirit that speaks to you is he that has a Tower to build, a strong Tower and a mighty Tower. Yea, such a one as has not been from the beginning. No, not from the beginning. Great is the foundation thereof, for it is of Iron. But greater are her walls, for they are of Diamond. Most great are her Turrets, for they are the seven heads that behold, judge, and gather. And they are made of Truth, the Spirit of Eternity. Unto the laying of every stone, are you made privy, and for this Tower you are provided.**

Climb the Second Stairway, which has twelve steps, to the Air-Tier. Visualize the Sephirothic Cross Angel NELAPR before you. Approach the Angel unafraid; open your arms and embrace him. Feel his body melt into your own and become a part of you. Assume the god-form for NELAPR, who guards the Air-Tier and Third Stairway (position 40), as follows:

The god-form of NELAPR: See page 240 for the god-form of NELAPR.

The Third Stairway is blue and smells of myrrh. It is also wet and cold. There are five steps, each of which bears a letter written in yellow that is blazing to look upon. The letter M is on the first step, N is on the second, Q is on the third, R on the fourth, and V on the fifth.[7] Recite the words written above the Third Stairway before ascending:

> **Behold, the work is great, the labor is also equal unto it.**

As you climb the Stairway, recite the following magic words that are written, one each, on the steps of each Third Stairway as you ascend.

First Step: **SUDSAMNA**

Second Step: **AFLAFBEN**

Third Step: **BAMASAN**

Pathworking the Watchtower of Water

Fourth Step: **KORSAX**

Fifth Step: **TOHOMAPHALA**

Step 8. In the god-form of a Sephirothic Cross Angel of Water, slowly recite the magic word TRAM. Move to the top of the Third Stairway and say:

> I am a Sephirothic Cross Angel of Water. I am Sephirothic Cross Angel NELAPR. I bear the Cross of Water from Water to Air within Water.

Step 9. As NELAPR, repeat the word TRAM, and at the top of the Stairway turn toward the center of the Fire-Tier. If you are male, assume the naked god-form of the King of Water, RAAGIOSL. If you are female, assume the naked god-form of the Goddess of Water, LOBABAN.

Step 10. Same as Step 10 of Path 17.

Step 11. Same as Step 11 of Path 17.

Step 12. Turn from your consort and step out of the hexagram. Leave by the same path that you entered. After leaving the mandala, conduct the banishing pentagram ritual. This completes the twenty-fourth initiatory path.

The Air Quadrant of the Water Mandala

Path Twenty-Five

The Path of Universal Love leads through the four positions 28-30-38-42, as shown in Figure 45. It contains the specific atmospheres of fame, love, and psychic power. It is the First Path of Inner Strength. Use this path to develop universal unconditional love.

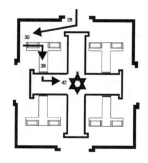

Figure 45: Path 25, The Path of Universal Love

Step 1. Make a circle and conduct the invoking pentagram ritual.

Step 2. Face the South, and imagine the Mandala of the Watchtower of Water clearly before you. You are facing the Northern wall. Imagine the walls and floors to be blue. Recite the Centering Spell. Say:

> May I enter and safely pass through this blue Watchtower of Water.
> May I obtain success in this, the twenty-fifth of my initiations.
> In the threefold secret and holy name of MPHARSLGAIOL
> I make this request. TOFAGILO ZIN ASA TA KANILA

Step 3. Visualize the closed Sapphire Gate. Say:

> O KTOKO I invoke thee. Come unto me from the Watchtower of Water.

The Angels' Message to Humanity

Visualize KTOKO before you. Approach the Angel unafraid; open your arms and embrace him. Feel his body melt into your own and become a part of you. Assume the god-form of the Angel KTOKO ("keh-toh-koh"), who guards the Sapphire Gate (position 28), as follows:

The god-form of KTOKO: See page 239 for the god-form of KTOKO.

There are special words written above the Sapphire Gate to be spoken before entering. Say:

> **Over the Sapphire Gate is written: The Sun, from its own Center, spreads out the beams of its limited virtue. The heart has a dual life, and yet it is the center of life to the whole body.**

Step 4. Visualize the gate opening at these words. Step within the Sapphire Gate. Face the Earth-Tier. In the god-form of KTOKO, say:

> **I am the Angel of Water. I am the Angel KTOKO. I am the Guardian of the Sapphire Gate. I enter into the Watchtower of Water.**

While slowly repeating the Threefold Holy Word, enter the Watchtower of Water and move across the Earth-Tier to the bottom of the Aquamarine Stairway (position 30) leading up to the Water-Tier. The Threefold Word that you recite protects you from the demons who reside on the Earth-Tier.

Step 5. Face the Aquamarine Stairway. Visualize the Kerubic Angel TAAD before you. Approach the Angel unafraid; open your arms and embrace him. Feel his body melt into your own and become a part of you. Assume the god-form of TAAD ("tah-ah-deh"), who guards the Water-Tier Stairway as follows:

The god-form of TAAD: See page 243 for the god-form of TAAD.

Recite the words written over the Aquamarine Stairway:

> **Happy are those that are elected. But happy, happier are those that persevere in their election.**

Step 6. In the god-form of the Kerubic Angel of Water, TAAD, while slowly repeating the magic word QUM, climb the seven steps of the Aquamarine Stairway to the Water-Tier. Then say:

> **I am a Kerubic Angel of Water. I am Kerubic Angel TAAD.**
> **I am the Guardian of the Aquamarine Stairway. I rise up**
> **through the Watchtower of Water. Throughout eternity**
> **I renew myself from Earth to Water within Water.**

Step 7. Slowly repeat the magic word QUM as you move across the Water-Tier. Approach the Second Stairway leading up to the Air-Tier. Before entering the Second Stairway, say:

> **The spirit that speaks to you is he that has a Tower to build, a strong Tower and a mighty Tower. Yea, such a one as has not been from the beginning.**

Pathworking the Watchtower of Water

> **No, not from the beginning. Great is the foundation thereof, for it is of Iron. But greater are her walls, for they are of Diamond. Most great are her Turrets, for they are the seven heads that behold, judge, and gather. And they are made of Truth, the Spirit of Eternity. Unto the laying of every stone, are you made privy, and for this Tower you are provided.**

Climb the Second Stairway, which has seven steps, to the Air-Tier. Visualize the Sephirothic Cross Angel OBGOTA before you. Approach the Angel unafraid; open your arms and embrace him. Feel his body melt into your own and become a part of you. Assume the god-form for OBGOTA ("oh-beh-goh-tah"), who guards the Air-Tier and Third Stairway (position 40), as follows:

The god-form of OBGOTA: See page 241 for the god-form of OBGOTA.

The Third Stairway is blue and smells of myrrh. It is also wet and cold. There are five steps, each of which bears a letter written in yellow that is blazing to look upon. The letter M is on the first step, N is on the second, Q is on the third, R on the fourth, and V on the fifth.[7] Recite the words written above the Third Stairway before ascending:

> **Have you any Law sweeter then the pure illumination, and sweet dewlike comforts, the voices and presence of the holy angels?**

As you climb the Stairway, recite the following magic words that are written, one each, on the steps of each Third Stairway as you ascend.

First Step: **SUDSAMNA**

Second Step: **AFLAFBEN**

Third Step: **BAMASAN**

Fourth Step: **KORSAX**

Fifth Step: **TOHOMAPHALA**

Step 8. In the god-form of a Sephirothic Cross Angel of Water, slowly recite the magic word TRAM. Move to the top of the Third Stairway and say:

> **I am a Sephirothic Cross Angel of Water. I am Sephirothic Cross Angel OBGOTA. I bear the Cross of Water from Water to Air within Water.**

Step 9. As OBGOTA, repeat the word TRAM, and at the top of the Stairway turn toward the center of the Fire-Tier. If you are male, assume the naked god-form of the King of Water, RAAGIOSL. If you are female, assume the naked god-form of the Goddess of Water, LOBABAN.

Step 10. Same as Step 10 of Path 17.

Step 11. Same as Step 11 of Path 17.

Step 12. Turn from your consort and step out of the hexagram. Leave by the same path that you entered. After leaving the mandala, conduct the banishing pentagram ritual. This completes the twenty-fifth initiatory path.

Path Twenty-Six

The Path of Psychic Power leads through the four positions 28-31-38-42, as shown in Figure 46. It contains the specific atmospheres of fame, love, transmutation, and psychic power. It is the Second Path of Inner Strength. Use this path to develop psychic powers.

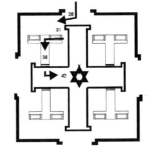

Figure 46: Path 26, The Path of Psychic Power

Step 1. Make a circle and conduct the invoking pentagram ritual.

Step 2. Face the South, and imagine the Mandala of the Watchtower of Water clearly before you. You are facing the Northern wall. Imagine the walls and floors to be blue. Recite the Centering Spell. Say:

> May I enter and safely pass through this blue Watchtower of Water.
> May I obtain success in this, the twenty-sixth of my initiations.
> In the threefold secret and holy name of MPHARSLGAIOL
> I make this request. TOFAGILO ZIN ASA TA KANILA.

Step 3. Visualize the closed Sapphire Gate. Say:

> O KTOKO I invoke thee. Come unto me from the Watchtower of Water.

Visualize KTOKO before you. Approach the Angel unafraid; open your arms and embrace him. Feel his body melt into your own and become a part of you. Assume the god-form of the Angel KTOKO, who guards the Sapphire Gate (position 28), as follows:

The god-form of KTOKO: See page 239 for the god-form of KTOKO.

There are special words written above the Sapphire Gate to be spoken before entering. Say:

> Over the Sapphire Gate is written: The Sun, from its own Center,
> spreads out the beams of its limited virtue. The heart has a dual life,
> and yet it is the center of life to the whole body.

Step 4. Visualize the gate opening at these words. Step within the Sapphire Gate. Face the Earth-Tier. In the god-form of KTOKO, say:

> I am the Angel of Water. I am the Angel KTOKO. I am the Guardian
> of the Sapphire Gate. I enter into the Watchtower of Water.

While slowly repeating the Threefold Holy Word, enter the Watchtower of Water and move across the Earth-Tier to the bottom of the Azurite Stairway (position 31) leading up to the Water-Tier. The Threefold Word that you recite protects you from the demons who reside on the Earth-Tier.

Step 5. Face the Azurite Stairway. Visualize the Kerubic Angel ADTA before you. Approach the Angel unafraid; open your arms and embrace him. Feel his body

Pathworking the Watchtower of Water

melt into your own and become a part of you. Assume the god-form of ADTA ("ah-peh-tah"), who guards the Water-Tier Stairway, as follows:

The god-form of ADTA: See page 236 for the god-form of ADTA.

Recite the words written over the Azurite Stairway:

**All things come on, and keep their course,
even as they are led, by the Image of justice. Man only excepted.**

Step 6. In the god-form of the Kerubic Angel of Water, ADTA, while slowly repeating the magic word QUM, climb the Azurite Stairway to the Water-Tier. Then say:

**I am a Kerubic Angel of Water. I am Kerubic Angel ADTA.
I am the Guardian of the Azurite Stairway. I rise up through
the Watchtower of Water. Throughout eternity
I renew myself from Earth to Water within Water.**

Step 7. Slowly repeat the magic word QUM as you move across the Water-Tier. Approach the Second Stairway leading up to the Air-Tier. Before entering the Second Stairway, say:

The spirit that speaks to you is he that has a Tower to build, a strong Tower and a mighty. Yea, such a one as has not been from the beginning. No, not from the beginning. Great is the foundation thereof, for it is of Iron. But greater are her walls, for they are of Diamond. Most great are her Turrets, for they are the seven heads that behold, judge, and gather. And they are made of Truth, the Spirit of Eternity. Unto the laying of every stone, are you made privy, and for this Tower you are provided.

Climb the Second Stairway, which has seven steps, to the Air-Tier. Visualize the Sephirotic Cross Angel OBGOTA before you. Approach the Angel unafraid; open your arms and embrace him. Feel his body melt into your own and become a part of you. Assume the god-form for OBGOTA, who guards the Air-Tier and Third Stairway (position 40), as follows:

The god-form of OBGOTA: See page 241 for the god-form of OBGOTA.

The Third Stairway is blue and smells of myrrh. It is also wet and cold. There are five steps, each of which bears a letter written in yellow that is blazing to look upon. The letter *M* is on the first step, *N* is on the second, *Q* is on the third, *R* on the fourth, and *V* on the fifth.[7] Recite the words written above the Third Stairway before ascending:

**Have you any Law sweeter then the pure illumination, and sweet
dewlike comforts, the voices and presence of the holy angels?**

As you climb the Stairway, recite the following magic words that are written, one each, on the steps of each Third Stairway as you ascend.

First Step: **SUDSAMNA**

Second Step: **AFLAFBEN**

The Angels' Message to Humanity

Third Step: **BAMASAN**

Fourth Step: **KORSAX**

Fifth Step: **TOHOMAPHALA**

Step 8. In the god-form of a Sephirothic Cross Angel of Water, slowly recite the magic word TRAM. Move to the top of the Third Stairway and say:

> I am a Sephirothic Cross Angel of Water. I am Sephirothic Cross Angel OBGOTA. I bear the Cross of Water from Water to Air within Water.

Step 9. As OBGOTA, repeat the word TRAM, and at the top of the Stairway turn toward the center of the Fire-Tier. If you are male, assume the naked god-form of the King of Water, RAAGIOSL. If you are female, assume the naked god-form of the Goddess of Water, LOBABAN.

Step 10. Same as Step 10 of Path 17.

Step 11. Same as Step 11 of Path 17.

Step 12. Turn from your consort and step out of the hexagram. Leave by the same path that you entered. After leaving the mandala, conduct the banishing pentagram ritual. This completes the twenty-sixth initiatory path.

Path Twenty-Seven

The Path of Love Magic leads through the four positions 29-30-38-42, as shown in Figure 47. It contains the specific atmospheres of divination, love, and psychic power. It is the Third Path of Inner Strength. Use this path for any form of love magic.

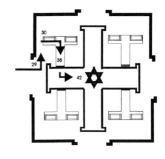

Figure 47: Path 27, The Path of Love Magic

Step 1. Make a circle and conduct the invoking pentagram ritual.

Step 2. Face the East, and imagine the Mandala of the Watchtower of Water clearly before you. You are facing the Western wall. Imagine the walls and floors to be blue. Recite the Centering Spell. Say:

> May I enter and safely pass through this blue Watchtower of Water.
> May I obtain success in this, the twenty-seventh of my initiations.
> In the threefold secret and holy name of MPHARSLGAIOL
> I make this request. TOFAGILO ZIN ASA TA KANILA.

Step 3. Visualize the closed Lapis Lazuli Gate. Say:

> O KSAIZ I invoke thee. Come unto me from the Watchtower of Water.

Visualize KSAIZ before you. Approach the Angel unafraid; open your arms and embrace him. Feel his body melt into your own and become a part of you. Assume

Pathworking the Watchtower of Water

the god-form of the Angel KSAIZ ("keh-sah-ee-zeh"), who guards the Lapis Lazuli Gate (position 29), as follows:

The god-form of KSAIZ: See page 239 for the god-form of KSAIZ.

There are special words written above the Lapis Lazuli Gate to be spoken before entering. Say:

> **It follows therefore that every thing has a center: From the which the circumfluent beams of my proper power do proceed. When these are perfectly known, then are things seen in their true kind.**

Step 4. Visualize the gate opening at these words. Step within the Lapis Lazuli Gate. Face the Earth-Tier. In the god-form of KSAIZ, say:

> **I am the Angel of Water. I am the Angel KSAIZ. I am the Guardian of the Lapis Lazuli Gate. I enter into the Watchtower of Water.**

While slowly repeating the Threefold Holy Word, enter the Watchtower of Water and move across the Earth-Tier to the bottom of the Aquamarine Stairway (position 30) leading up to the Water-Tier. The Threefold Word that you recite protects you from the demons who reside on the Earth-Tier.

Step 5. Face the Aquamarine Stairway. Visualize the Kerubic Angel TAAD before you. Approach the Angel unafraid; open your arms and embrace him. Feel his body melt into your own and become a part of you. Assume the god-form of TAAD, who guards the Water-Tier Stairway as follows:

The god-form of TAAD: See page 243 for the god-form of TAAD.

Recite the words written over the Aquamarine Stairway:

> **Happy are those that are elected. But happy, happier are those that persevere in their election.**

Step 6. In the god-form of the Kerubic Angel of Water, TAAD, while slowly repeating the magic word QUM, climb the seven steps of the Aquamarine Stairway to the Water-Tier. Then say:

> **I am a Kerubic Angel of Water. I am Kerubic Angel TAAD.
> I am the Guardian of the Aquamarine Stairway. I rise up through
> the Watchtower of Water. Throughout eternity
> I renew myself from Earth to Water within Water.**

Step 7. Slowly repeat the magic word QUM as you move across the Water-Tier. Approach the Second Stairway leading up to the Air-Tier. Before entering the Second Stairway, say:

> **The spirit that speaks to you is he that has a Tower to build, a strong Tower and a mighty Tower. Yea, such a one as has not been from the beginning. No, not from the beginning. Great is the foundation thereof, for it is of Iron. But greater are her walls, for they are of Diamond. Most great are her Turrets, for they are the seven heads that behold, judge, and gather.**

The Angels' Message to Humanity

And they are made of Truth, the Spirit of Eternity. Unto the laying of every stone, are you made privy, and for this Tower you are provided.

Climb the Second Stairway, which has seven steps, to the Air-Tier. Visualize the Sephirothic Cross Angel OBGOTA before you. Approach the Angel unafraid; open your arms and embrace him. Feel his body melt into your own and become a part of you. Assume the god-form for OBGOTA, who guards the Air-Tier and Third Stairway (position 40), as follows:

The god-form of OBGOTA: See page 241 for the god-form of OBGOTA.

The Third Stairway is blue and smells of myrrh. It is also wet and cold. There are five steps, each of which bears a letter written in yellow that is blazing to look upon. The letter *M* is on the first step, *N* is on the second, *Q* is on the third, *R* on the fourth, and *V* on the fifth.[7] Recite the words written above the Third Stairway before ascending:

Have you any Law sweeter then the pure illumination, and sweet dewlike comforts, the voices and presence of the holy angels?

As you climb the Stairway, recite the following magic words that are written, one each, on the steps of each Third Stairway as you ascend.

First Step: **SUDSAMNA**

Second Step: **AFLAFBEN**

Third Step: **BAMASAN**

Fourth Step: **KORSAX**

Fifth Step: **TOHOMAPHALA**

Step 8. In the god-form of a Sephirothic Cross Angel of Water, slowly recite the magic word TRAM. Move to the top of the Third Stairway and say:

I am a Sephirothic Cross Angel of Water. I am Sephirothic Cross Angel OBGOTA. I bear the Cross of Water from Water to Air within Water.

Step 9. As OBGOTA, repeat the word TRAM, and at the top of the Stairway turn toward the center of the Fire-Tier. If you are male, assume the naked god-form of the King of Water, RAAGIOSL. If you are female, assume the naked god-form of the Goddess of Water, LOBABAN.

Step 10. Same as Step 10 of Path 17.

Step 11. Same as Step 11 of Path 17.

Step 12. Turn from your consort and step out of the hexagram. Leave by the same path that you entered. After leaving the mandala, conduct the banishing pentagram ritual. This completes the twenty-seventh initiatory path.

Pathworking the Watchtower of Water

PATH TWENTY-EIGHT

The Path of Transmutation leads through the four positions 29-31-38-42, as shown in Figure 48. It contains the specific atmospheres of divination, love, transmutation, and psychic power. It is the Fourth Path of Inner Strength. Use this path to turn hatred into love.

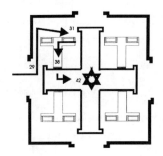

Figure 48: Path 28, The Path of Transmutation

Step 1. Make a circle and conduct the invoking pentagram ritual.

Step 2. Face the East, and imagine the Mandala of the Watchtower of Water clearly before you. You are facing the Western wall. Imagine the walls and floors to be blue. Recite the Centering Spell. Say:

> May I enter and safely pass through this blue Watchtower of Water.
> May I obtain success in this, the twenty-eighth of my initiations.
> In the threefold secret and holy name of MPHARSLGAIOL
> I make this request. TOFAGILO ZIN ASA TA KANILA

Step 3. Visualize the closed Lapis Lazuli Gate. Say:

> O KSAIZ I invoke thee. Come unto me from the Watchtower of Water.

Visualize KSAIZ before you. Approach the Angel unafraid; open your arms and embrace him. Feel his body melt into your own and become a part of you. Assume the god-form of the Angel KSAIZ, who guards the Lapis Lazuli Gate (position 29), as follows:

The god-form of KSAIZ: See page 239 for the god-form of KSAIZ.

There are special words written above the Lapis Lazuli Gate to be spoken before entering. Say:

> It follows therefore that every thing has a center: From the which the circumfluent beams of my proper power do proceed. When these are perfectly known, then are things seen in their true kind.

Step 4. Visualize the gate opening at these words. Step within the Lapis Lazuli Gate. Face the Earth-Tier. In the god-form of KSAIZ, say:

> I am the Angel of Water. I am the Angel KSAIZ. I am the Guardian of the Lapis Lazuli Gate. I enter into the Watchtower of Water.

While slowly repeating the Threefold Holy Word, enter the Watchtower of Water and move across the Earth-Tier to the bottom of the Azurite Stairway (position 31) leading up to the Water-Tier. The Threefold Word that you recite protects you from the demons who reside on the Earth-Tier.

Step 5. Face the Azurite Stairway. Visualize the Kerubic Angel ADTA before you. Approach the Angel unafraid; open your arms and embrace him. Feel his body melt into your own and become a part of you. Assume the god-form of ADTA, who guards the Water-Tier Stairway, as follows:

The god-form of ADTA: See page 236 for the god-form of ADTA.

Recite the words written over the Azurite Stairway:

All things come on, and keep their course, even as they are led, by the Image of justice. Man only excepted.

Step 6. In the god-form of the Kerubic Angel of Water, ADTA, while slowly repeating the magic word QUM, climb the seven steps of the Azurite Stairway to the Water-Tier. Then say:

**I am a Kerubic Angel of Water. I am Kerubic Angel ADTA.
I am the Guardian of the Azurite Stairway. I rise up through
the Watchtower of Water. Throughout eternity
I renew myself from Earth to Water within Water.**

Step 7. Slowly repeat the magic word QUM as you move across the Water-Tier. Approach the Second Stairway leading up to the Air-Tier. Before entering the Second Stairway, say:

The spirit that speaks to you is he that has a Tower to build, a strong Tower and a mighty Tower. Yea, such a one as has not been from the beginning. No, not from the beginning. Great is the foundation thereof, for it is of Iron. But greater are her walls, for they are of Diamond. Most great are her Turrets, for they are the seven heads that behold, judge, and gather. And they are made of Truth, the Spirit of Eternity. Unto the laying of every stone, are you made privy, and for this Tower you are provided.

Climb the Second Stairway, which has seven steps, to the Air-Tier. Visualize the Sephirothic Cross Angel OBGOTA before you. Approach the Angel unafraid; open your arms and embrace him. Feel his body melt into your own and become a part of you. Assume the god-form for OBGOTA, who guards the Air-Tier and Third Stairway (position 40), as follows:

The god-form of OBGOTA: See page 241 for the god-form of OBGOTA.

The Third Stairway is blue and smells of myrrh. It is also wet and cold. There are five steps, each of which bears a letter written in yellow that is blazing to look upon. The letter M is on the first step, N is on the second, Q is on the third, R on the fourth, and V on the fifth.[7] Recite the words written above the Third Stairway before ascending:

Have you any Law sweeter then the pure illumination, and sweet dewlike comforts, the voices and presence of the holy angels?

As you climb the Stairway, recite the following magic words that are written, one each, on the steps of each Third Stairway as you ascend.

Pathworking the Watchtower of Water

First Step: **SUDSAMNA**

Second Step: **AFLAFBEN**

Third Step: **BAMASAN**

Fourth Step: **KORSAX**

Fifth Step: **TOHOMAPHALA**

Step 8. In the god-form of a Sephirothic Cross Angel of Water, slowly recite the magic word TRAM. Move to the top of the Third Stairway and say:

> I am a Sephirothic Cross Angel of Water. I am Sephirothic Cross Angel OBGOTA. I bear the Cross of Water from Water to Air within Water.

Step 9. As OBGOTA, repeat the word TRAM, and at the top of the Stairway turn toward the center of the Fire-Tier. If you are male, assume the naked god-form of the King of Water, RAAGIOSL. If you are female, assume the naked god-form of the Goddess of Water, LOBABAN.

Step 10. Same as Step 10 of Path 17.

Step 11. Same as Step 11 of Path 17.

Step 12. Turn from your consort and step out of the hexagram. Leave by the same path that you entered. After leaving the mandala, conduct the banishing pentagram ritual. This completes the twenty-eighth initiatory path.

THE FIRE QUADRANT OF THE WATER MANDALA

PATH TWENTY-NINE

The Path of Love Visions leads through the four positions 24-37-41-42, as shown in Figure 49. It contains the specific atmospheres of enchantment, love, and visions. It is the First Path of Reflective Knowledge. Use this path to develop true visions of love.

Step 1. Make a circle and conduct the invoking pentagram ritual.

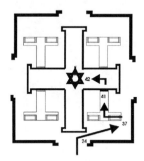

Figure 49: Path 29, The Path of Love Visions

Step 2. Face the North, and imagine the Mandala of the Watchtower of Water clearly before you. You are facing the Southern wall. Imagine the walls and floors to be blue. Recite the Centering Spell. Say:

> May I enter and safely pass through this blue Watchtower of Water.
> May I obtain success in this, the twenty-ninth of my initiations.
> In the threefold secret and holy name of MPHARSLGAIOL
> I make this request. TOFAGILO ZIN ASA TA KANILA

Step 3. Visualize the closed Rose Gate. Say:

O AXPKN I invoke thee. Come unto me from the Watchtower of Water.

Visualize AZPKN before you. Approach the Angel unafraid; open your arms and embrace him. Feel his body melt into your own and become a part of you. Assume the god-form of the Angel AXPKN ("ah-etz-peh-ken"), who guards the Rose Gate (position 24), as follows:

The god-form of AXPKN: See page 237 for the god-form of AXPKN.

There are special words written above the Rose Gate to be spoken before entering. Say:

In the First Workmanship lies the Secret of the Unknown.

Step 4. Visualize the gate opening at these words. Step within the Rose Gate. Face the Earth-Tier. In the god-form of AXPKN, say:

I am the Angel of Water. I am the Angel AXPKN. I am the Guardian of the Rose Gate. I enter into the Watchtower of Water.

While slowly repeating the Threefold Holy Word, enter the Watchtower of Water and move across the Earth-Tier to the bottom of the Elm Stairway (position 37) leading up to the Water-Tier. The Threefold Word that you recite protects you from the demons who reside on the Earth-Tier.

Step 5. Face the Elm Stairway. Visualize the Kerubic Angel RXNL before you. Approach the Angel unafraid; open your arms and embrace him. Feel his body melt into your own and become a part of you. Assume the god-form of RXNL ("rah-etz-en-el"), who guards the Water-Tier Stairway, as follows:

The god-form of RXNL: See page 242 for the god-form of RXNL.

Recite the words written over the Elm Stairway:

For though they believed not man, yet would they have believed an Angel.

Step 6. In the god-form of the Kerubic Angel of Water, RXNL, while slowly repeating the magic word QUM, climb the nine steps of the Elm Stairway to the Water-Tier. Then say:

**I am a Kerubic Angel of Water. I am Kerubic Angel RXNL.
I am the Guardian of the Elm Stairway. I rise up
through the Watchtower of Water. Throughout eternity
I renew myself from Earth to Water within Water.**

Step 7. Slowly repeat the magic word QUM as you move across the Water-Tier. Approach the Second Stairway leading up to the Air-Tier. Before entering the Second Stairway, say:

The spirit that speaks to you is he that has a Tower to build, a strong Tower and a mighty Tower. Yea, such a one as has not been from the beginning. No, not from the beginning. Great is the foundation thereof, for it is of

Pathworking the Watchtower of Water

Iron. But greater are her walls, for they are of Diamond. Most great are her Turrets, for they are the seven heads that behold, judge, and gather. And they are made of Truth, the Spirit of Eternity. Unto the laying of every stone, are you made privy, and for this Tower you are provided.

Climb the Second Stairway, which has eight steps, to the Air-Tier. Visualize the Sephirothic Cross Angel IAAASD before you. Approach the Angel unafraid; open your arms and embrace him. Feel his body melt into your own and become a part of you. Assume the god-form for IAAASD ("ee-ah-ah-ah-seh-deh"), who guards the Air-Tier and Third Stairway (position 40), as follows:

The god-form of IAAASD: See page 238 for the god-form of IAAASD.

The Third Stairway is blue and smells of myrrh. It is also wet and cold. There are five steps, each of which bears a letter written in yellow that is blazing to look upon. The letter *M* is on the first step, *N* is on the second, *Q* is on the third, *R* on the fourth, and *V* on the fifth.[7] Recite the words written above the Third Stairway before ascending:

There is horror and gnashing of teeth, there is misery and vengeance forever, there is horror and the Worm of Conscience.

As you climb the Stairway, recite the following magic words that are written, one each, on the steps of each Third Stairway as you ascend.

First Step: **SUDSAMNA**

Second Step: **AFLAFBEN**

Third Step: **BAMASAN**

Fourth Step: **KORSAX**

Fifth Step: **TOHOMAPHALA**

Step 8. In the god-form of a Sephirothic Cross Angel of Water, slowly recite the magic word TRAM. Move to the top of the Third Stairway and say:

I am a Sephirothic Cross Angel of Water. I am Sephirothic Cross Angel IAAASD. I bear the Cross of Water from Water to Air within Water.

Step 9. As IAAASD, repeat the word TRAM, and at the top of the Stairway turn toward the center of the Fire-Tier. If you are male, assume the naked god-form of the King of Water, RAAGIOSL. If you are female, assume the naked god-form of the Goddess of Water, LOBABAN.

Step 10. Same as Step 10 of Path 17.

Step 11. Same as Step 11 of Path 17.

Step 12. Turn from your consort and step out of the hexagram. Leave by the same path that you entered. After leaving the mandala, conduct the banishing pentagram ritual. This completes the twenty-ninth initiatory path.

The Angels' Message to Humanity

Path Thirty

The Path of Enchantment leads through the four positions 24-36-41-42, as shown in Figure 50. It contains the specific atmospheres of enchantment, love, and desire. It is the Second Path of Reflective Knowledge. Use this path to develop the power of enchantment.

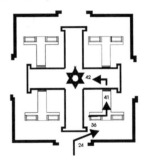

Figure 50: Path 30, The Path of Enchantment

Step 1. Make a circle and conduct the invoking pentagram ritual.

Step 2. Face the North, and imagine the Mandala of the Watchtower of Water clearly before you. You are facing the Southern wall. Imagine the walls and floors to be blue. Recite the Centering Spell. Say:

> **May I enter and safely pass through this blue Watchtower of Water.**
> **May I obtain success in this, the thirtieth of my initiations.**
> **In the threefold secret and holy name of MPHARSLGAIOL**
> **I make this request. TOFAGILO ZIN ASA TA KANILA**

Step 3. Visualize the closed Rose Gate. Say:

> **O AXPKN I invoke thee. Come unto me from the Watchtower of Water.**

Visualize AXPKN before you. Approach the Angel unafraid; open your arms and embrace him. Feel his body melt into your own and become a part of you. Assume the god-form of the Angel AXPKN, who guards the Rose Gate (position 24), as follows:

The god-form of AXPKN: See page 237 for the god-form of AXPKN.

There are special words written above the Rose Gate to be spoken before entering. Say:

> **In the First Workmanship lies the Secret of the Unknown.**

Step 4. Visualize the gate opening at these words. Step within the Rose Gate. Face the Earth-Tier. In the god-form of AXPKN, say:

> **I am the Angel of Water. I am the Angel AXPKN. I am**
> **the Guardian of the Rose Gate. I enter into the Watchtower of Water.**

While slowly repeating the Threefold Holy Word, enter the Watchtower of Water and move across the Earth-Tier to the bottom of the Sandalwood Stairway (position 36) leading up to the Water-Tier. The Threefold Word that you recite protects you from the demons who reside on the Earth-Tier.

Step 5. Face the Sandalwood Stairway. Visualize the Kerubic Angel NLRX before you. Approach the Angel unafraid; open your arms and embrace him. Feel his body melt into your own and become a part of you. Assume the god-form of NLRX ("nel-rah-etz"), who guards the Water-Tier Stairway as follows:

Pathworking the Watchtower of Water

The god-form of NLRX: See page 241 for the god-form of NLRX.

Recite the words written over the Sandalwood Stairway:

> **In respect of thy body and mind... thy body is which now had not been, and what thy mind seeth, cometh through the light that we leave with it.**

Step 6. In the god-form of the Kerubic Angel of Water, NLRX, while slowly repeating the magic word QUM, climb the nine steps of the Sandalwood Stairway to the Water-Tier. Then say:

> **I am a Kerubic Angel of Water. I am Kerubic Angel NLRX.
> I am the Guardian of the Sandalwood Stairway. I rise up
> through the Watchtower of Water. Throughout eternity
> I renew myself from Earth to Water within Water.**

Step 7. Slowly repeat the magic word QUM as you move across the Water-Tier. Approach the Second Stairway leading up to the Air-Tier. Before entering the Second Stairway, say:

> **The spirit that speaks to you is he that has a Tower to build, a strong Tower and a mighty Tower. Yea, such a one as has not been from the beginning. No, not from the beginning. Great is the foundation thereof, for it is of Iron. But greater are her walls, for they are of Diamond. Most great are her Turrets, for they are the seven heads that behold, judge, and gather. And they are made of Truth, the Spirit of Eternity. Unto the laying of every stone, are you made privy, and for this Tower you are provided.**

Climb the Second Stairway, which has eight steps, to the Air-Tier. Visualize the Sephirothic Cross Angel IAAASD before you. Approach the Angel unafraid; open your arms and embrace him. Feel his body melt into your own and become a part of you. Assume the god-form for IAAASD, who guards the Air-Tier and Third Stairway (position 40), as follows:

The god-form of IAAASD: See page 238 for the god-form of IAAASD.

The Third Stairway is blue and smells of myrrh. It is also wet and cold. There are five steps, each of which bears a letter written in yellow that is blazing to look upon. The letter *M* is on the first step, *N* is on the second, *Q* is on the third, *R* on the fourth, and *V* on the fifth.[7] Recite the words written above the Third Stairway before ascending:

> **There is horror and gnashing of teeth, there is misery
> and vengeance forever, there is horror and the Worm of Conscience.**

As you climb the Stairway, recite the following magic words that are written, one each, on the steps of each Third Stairway as you ascend.

First Step: **SUDSAMNA**

Second Step: **AFLAFBEN**

The Angels' Message to Humanity

Third Step: **BAMASAN**

Fourth Step: **KORSAX**

Fifth Step: **TOHOMAPHALA**

Step 8. In the god-form of a Sephirothic Cross Angel of Water, slowly recite the magic word TRAM. Move to the top of the Third Stairway and say:

I am a Sephirothic Cross Angel of Water. I am Sephirothic Cross Angel IAAASD. I bear the Cross of Water from Water to Air within Water.

Step 9. As IAAASD, repeat the word TRAM, and at the top of the Stairway turn toward the center of the Fire-Tier. If you are male, assume the naked god-form of the King of Water, RAAGIOSL. If you are female, assume the naked god-form of the Goddess of Water, LOBABAN.

Step 10. Same as Step 10 of Path 17.

Step 11. Same as Step 11 of Path 17.

Step 12. Turn from your consort and step out of the hexagram. Leave by the same path that you entered. After leaving the mandala, conduct the banishing pentagram ritual. This completes the thirtieth initiatory path.

Path Thirty-One

The Path of Visions leads through the four positions 25-37-41-42, as shown in Figure 51. It contains the specific atmospheres of visions, power, and love. It is the Third Path of Reflective Knowledge. Use this path to obtain prophetic visions.

Step 1. Make a circle and conduct the invoking pentagram ritual.

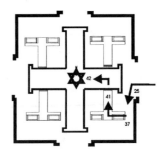

Figure 51: Path 31, The Path of Visions

Step 2. Face the West, and imagine the Mandala of the Watchtower of Water clearly before you. You are facing the Eastern wall. Imagine the walls and floors to be blue. Recite the Centering Spell. Say:

**May I enter and safely pass through this blue Watchtower of Water.
May I obtain success in this, the thirty-first of my initiations.
In the threefold secret and holy name of MPHARSLGAIOL
I make this request. TOFAGILO ZIN ASA TA KANILA**

Step 3. Visualize the closed Crystal Gate. Say:

O ARNIL I invoke thee. Come unto me from the Watchtower of Water.

Visualize ARNIL before you. Approach the Angel unafraid; open your arms and embrace him. Feel his body melt into your own and become a part of you. Assume

Pathworking the Watchtower of Water

the god-form of the Angel ARNIL ("ah-rah-nee-el"), who guards the Crystal Gate (position 25), as follows:

The god-form of ARNIL: See page 237 for the god-form of ARNIL.

There are special words written above the Crystal Gate to be spoken before entering. Say:

Understanding quickens the mind; that mind then puts on a fiery shape.

Step 4. Visualize the gate opening at these words. Step within the Crystal Gate. Face the Earth-Tier. In the god-form of ARNIL, say:

I am the Angel of Water. I am the Angel ARNIL. I am the Guardian of the Crystal Gate. I enter into the Watchtower of Water.

While slowly repeating the Threefold Holy Word, enter the Watchtower of Water and move across the Earth-Tier to the bottom of the Elm Stairway (position 37) leading up to the Water-Tier. The Threefold Word that you recite protects you from the demons who reside on the Earth-Tier.

Step 5. Face the Elm Stairway. Visualize the Kerubic Angel RXNL before you. Approach the Angel unafraid; open your arms and embrace him. Feel his body melt into your own and become a part of you. Assume the god-form of RXNL, who guards the Water-Tier Stairway, as follows:

The god-form of RXNL: See page 242 for the god-form of RXNL.

Recite the words written over the Elm Stairway:

For though they believed not man, yet would they have believed an Angel.

Step 6. In the god-form of the Kerubic Angel of Water, RXNL, while slowly repeating the magic word QUM, climb the nine steps of the Elm Stairway to the Water-Tier. Then say:

**I am a Kerubic Angel of Water. I am Kerubic Angel RXNL.
I am the Guardian of the Elm Stairway. I rise up
through the Watchtower of Water. Throughout eternity
I renew myself from Earth to Water within Water.**

Step 7. Slowly repeat the magic word QUM as you move across the Water-Tier. Approach the Second Stairway leading up to the Air-Tier. Before entering the Second Stairway, say:

The spirit that speaks to you is he that has a Tower to build, a strong Tower and a mighty Tower. Yea, such a one as has not been from the beginning. No, not from the beginning. Great is the foundation thereof, for it is of Iron. But greater are her walls, for they are of Diamond. Most great are her Turrets, for they are the seven heads that behold, judge, and gather. And they are made of Truth, the Spirit of Eternity. Unto the laying of every stone, are you made privy, and for this Tower you are provided.

The Angels' Message to Humanity

Climb the Second Stairway, which has eight steps, to the Air-Tier. Visualize the Sephirothic Cross Angel IAAASD before you. Approach the Angel unafraid; open your arms and embrace him. Feel his body melt into your own and become a part of you. Assume the god-form for IAAASD, who guards the Air-Tier and Third Stairway (position 40), as follows:

The god-form of IAAASD: See page 238 for the god-form of IAAASD.

The Third Stairway is blue and smells of myrrh. It is also wet and cold. There are five steps, each of which bears a letter written in yellow that is blazing to look upon. The letter *M* is on the first step, *N* is on the second, *Q* is on the third, *R* on the fourth, and *V* on the fifth.[7] Recite the words written above the Third Stairway before ascending:

There is horror and gnashing of teeth, there is misery and vengeance forever, there is horror and the Worm of Conscience.

As you climb the Stairway, recite the following magic words that are written, one each, on the steps of each Third Stairway as you ascend.

First Step: **SUDSAMNA**

Second Step: **AFLAFBEN**

Third Step: **BAMASAN**

Fourth Step: **KORSAX**

Fifth Step: **TOHOMAPHALA**

Step 8. In the god-form of a Sephirothic Cross Angel of Water, slowly recite the magic word TRAM. Move to the top of the Third Stairway and say:

I am a Sephirothic Cross Angel of Water. I am Sephirothic Cross Angel IAAASD. I bear the Cross of Water from Water to Air within Water.

Step 9. As IAAASD, repeat the word TRAM, and at the top of the Stairway turn toward the center of the Fire-Tier. If you are male, assume the naked god-form of the King of Water, RAAGIOSL. If you are female, assume the naked god-form of the Goddess of Water, LOBABAN.

Step 10. Same as Step 10 of Path 17.

Step 11. Same as Step 11 of Path 17.

Step 12. Turn from your consort and step out of the hexagram. Leave by the same path that you entered. After leaving the mandala, conduct the banishing pentagram ritual. This completes the thirty-first initiatory path.

Pathworking the Watchtower of Water

PATH THIRTY-TWO

The Path of Emotions leads through the four positions 25-36-41-42, as shown in Figure 52. It contains the specific atmospheres of visions, power, enchantment, and desire. It is the Fourth Path of Reflective Knowledge. Use this path to control emotions.

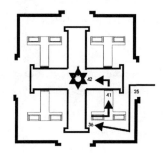

Step 1. Make a circle and conduct the invoking pentagram ritual.

Figure 52: Path 32, The Path of Emotions

Step 2. Face the West, and imagine the Mandala of the Watchtower of Water clearly before you. You are facing the Eastern wall. Imagine the walls and floors to be blue. Recite the Centering Spell. Say:

> May I enter and safely pass through this blue Watchtower of Water.
> May I obtain success in this, the thirty-second of my initiations.
> In the threefold secret and holy name of MPHARSLGAIOL
> I make this request. TOFAGILO ZIN ASA TA KANILA

Step 3. Visualize the closed Crystal Gate. Say:

> O ARNIL I invoke thee. Come unto me from the Watchtower of Water.

Visualize ARNIL before you. Approach the Angel unafraid; open your arms and embrace him. Feel his body melt into your own and become a part of you. Assume the god-form of the Angel ARNIL, who guards the Crystal Gate (position 25), as follows:

The god-form of ARNIL: See page 237 for the god-form of ARNIL.

There are special words written above the Crystal Gate to be spoken before entering. Say:

> Understanding quickens the mind; that mind then puts on a fiery shape.

Step 4. Visualize the gate opening at these words. Step within the Crystal Gate. Face the Earth-Tier. In the god-form of ARNIL, say:

> I am the Angel of Water. I am the Angel ARNIL. I am the Guardian of the Crystal Gate. I enter into the Watchtower of Water.

While slowly repeating the Threefold Holy Word, enter the Watchtower of Water and move across the Earth-Tier to the bottom of the Sandalwood Stairway (position 36) leading up to the Water-Tier. The Threefold Word that you recite protects you from the demons who reside on the Earth-Tier.

Step 5. Face the Sandalwood Stairway. Visualize the Kerubic Angel NLRX before you. Approach the Angel unafraid; open your arms and embrace him. Feel his body melt into your own and become a part of you. Assume the god-form of NLRX, who guards the Water-Tier Stairway, as follows:

The Angels' Message to Humanity

The god-form of NLRX: See page 241 for the god-form of NLRX

Recite the words written over the Sandalwood Stairway:

> **In respect of thy body and mind... thy body is which now had not been, and what thy mind seeth, cometh through the light that we leave with it.**

Step 6. In the god-form of the Kerubic Angel of Water, NLRX, while slowly repeating the magic word QUM, climb the nine steps of the Sandalwood Stairway to the Water-Tier. Then say:

> **I am a Kerubic Angel of Water. I am Kerubic Angel NLRX. I am the Guardian of the Sandalwood Stairway. I rise up through the Watchtower of Water. Throughout eternity I renew myself from Earth to Water within Water.**

Step 7. Slowly repeat the magic word QUM as you move across the Water-Tier. Approach the Second Stairway leading up to the Air-Tier. Before entering the Second Stairway, say:

> **The spirit that speaks to you is he that has a Tower to build, a strong Tower and a mighty Tower. Yea, such a one as has not been from the beginning. No, not from the beginning. Great is the foundation thereof, for it is of Iron. But greater are her walls, for they are of Diamond. Most great are her Turrets, for they are the seven heads that behold, judge, and gather. And they are made of Truth, the Spirit of Eternity. Unto the laying of every stone, are you made privy, and for this Tower you are provided.**

Climb the Second Stairway, which has eight steps, to the Air-Tier. Visualize the Sephirothic Cross Angel IAAASD before you. Approach the Angel unafraid; open your arms and embrace him. Feel his body melt into your own and become a part of you. Assume the god-form for IAAASD, who guards the Air-Tier and Third Stairway (position 40), as follows:

The god-form of IAAASD: See page 238 for the god-form of IAAASD.

The Third Stairway is blue and smells of myrrh. It is also wet and cold. There are five steps, each of which bears a letter written in yellow that is blazing to look upon. The letter M is on the first step, N is on the second, Q is on the third, R on the fourth, and V on the fifth.[7] Recite the words written above the Third Stairway before ascending:

> **There is horror and gnashing of teeth, there is misery and vengeance forever, there is horror and the Worm of Conscience.**

As you climb the Stairway, recite the following magic words that are written, one each, on the steps of each Third Stairway as you ascend.

First Step: **SUDSAMNA**

Second Step: **AFLAFBEN**

Third Step: **BAMASAN**

Pathworking the Watchtower of Water

Fourth Step: **KORSAX**

Fifth Step: **TOHOMAPHALA**

Step 8. In the god-form of a Sephirothic Cross Angel of Water, slowly recite the magic word TRAM. Move to the top of the Third Stairway and say:

I am a Sephirothic Cross Angel of Water. I am Sephirothic Cross Angel IAAASD. I bear the Cross of Water from Water to Air within Water.

Step 9. As IAAASD, repeat the word TRAM, and at the top of the Stairway turn toward the center of the Fire-Tier. If you are male, assume the naked god-form of the King of Water, RAAGIOSL. If you are female, assume the naked god-form of the Goddess of Water, LOBABAN.

Step 10. Same as Step 10 of Path 17.

Step 11. Same as Step 11 of Path 17.

Step 12. Turn from your consort and step out of the hexagram. Leave by the same path that you entered. After leaving the mandala, conduct the banishing pentagram ritual. This completes the thirty-second initiatory path.

NOTES TO CHAPTER ELEVEN

1. Most of the notes for the Earth Mandala initiatory paths in chapter 11 apply here as well. Only the deities, colors, and general atmospheres will change.

2. This last line contains a short magical spell to be spoken aloud in the Enochian language. The words mean, "All things of water are as blood." Using gematria, the letters add up to 737, which reduces to 8 (7+3+7=17=1+7=8).

3. The words above the Gates are all from Casaubon, p. 29. They were spoken to Dee by the Angel Madimi.

4. The words above the Stairways are all from Casaubon, pp. 384-386.

5. The magical word QUM is given in Table 21 of our Enochian Yoga (St. Paul, MN: Llewellyn Publications, 1990) as a special word associated with the navel center (the Manipura chakra of Kundalini yoga).

6. This passage is from Casaubon, p. 219.

7. The letters on the steps correspond to the letters of the navel center as given in our Enochian Yoga (St. Paul, MN: Llewellyn Publications, 1990). For best results, these letters should be visualized in Enochian as follows: M=Ɛ, N=Ǝ, Q=⊔, R=Ɛ, V=∂

8. These messages are from Casaubon, p. 393.

9. The five magic words above each of the five Third Stairways are from Casaubon, p. 224. They are (with gematria in parentheses): SUDSAMNA (240), AFLAFBEN (71), BAMASAN (170), KORSAX (843), and TOHOMAPHALA (196). These words were given to Dee by the Angel URIEL, who had them written in a magic book. Their gematric sum reduces to 8 (1520=1+5+2+0=8).

10. Like QUM, the magical word TRAM is also given in Table 21 of our Enochian Yoga (St. Paul, MN: Llewellyn Publications, 1990) as a special word associated with the navel center (the Manipura chakra of Kundalini yoga).

The Angels' Message to Humanity

11. The names of the primary god and goddess of the Watchtower of Water are from Table 21 of our Enochian Yoga (St. Paul, MN: Llewellyn Publications, 1990).

12. These god-forms are from p. 169 of our Enochian Yoga (St. Paul, MN: Llewellyn Publications, 1990).

13. This verse is an address to the Daughters of Light. It is found on p. 6 of Casaubon.

14. These words (except for our alteration of pronouns) were spoken by a Daughter of Light. See Casaubon, p. 7.

15. Steps 10 and 11 are identical for each of the exercises in the Watchtower of Water. To conserve space, we refer you to those steps given fully in path 17 rather than repeat them throughout.

Chapter 12

PATHWORKING THE WATCHTOWER OF AIR

This chapter contains the third set of initiatory paths, paths 33 through 48. In these paths, you will use the Watchtower Mandala of Air, as shown in color plate III. The critical twenty-one positions within the mandala are shown in Figure 53. The names of the entrance gates and first stairways are shown in Figure 54.

The names and positions of the twenty-two deities of the Mandala of Air are shown in Figure 55. Figures 56 through 71 show the sixteen paths you will take through the Air Mandala.

THE EARTH QUADRANT OF THE AIR MANDALA

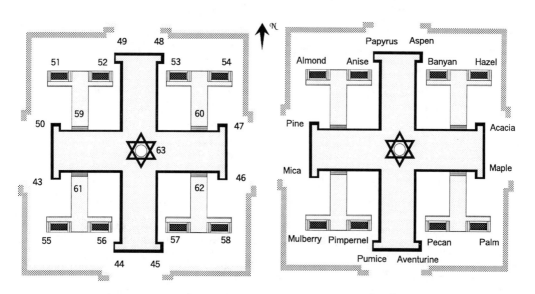

Figure 53: The Air Mandala Showing Position Numbers

Figure 54: The Air Mandala Showing Gates and Stairways

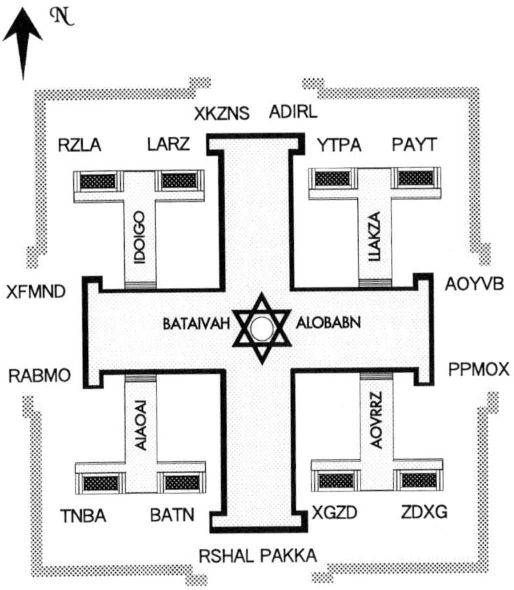

The Angels' Message to Humanity

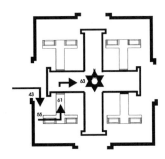

Figure 55: The Air Mandala Showing Deities

Figure 56: Path 33, The Path of Mental Stability

PATH THIRTY-THREE

The Path of Mental Stability leads through the four positions 43-55-61-63, as shown in Figure 56. It contains the specific atmospheres of harmony, protection, and sexual attraction. It is the First Path of Purification. Use this path for psychic protection and harmony.

Step 1. Make a circle and conduct the invoking pentagram ritual.

Step 2. Face the East, and imagine the Mandala of the Watchtower of Air clearly before you. You are facing the western wall of the mandala. Imagine the walls and floors to be yellow. Recite the Centering Spell. Then say:

> May I enter and safely pass through this yellow Watchtower of Air.
> May I obtain success in this, the thirty-third of my initiations.
> In the threefold secret and holy name of OROIBAHAOZPI
> I make this request. TOLTORGI-A GIGIPAHE ASAPATA
> OTAHILA SOBA OOAONA KAHISA RA-AS OD BOLANU.[1]

Step 3. Visualize the closed Mica Gate. say:

> O RABMO I invoke thee. Come unto me from the Watchtower of Water.

Visualize RABMO before you. Approach the Angel unafraid; open your arms and embrace him. Feel his body melt into your own and become a part of you. Assume the god-form of the Angel RABMO ("rah-beh-moh"), who guards the Mica Gate (position 43), as follows:

The god-form of RABMO: See page 242 for the god-form of RABMO.

There are special words written above the Mica Gate to be spoken before entering. say:

Pathworking the Watchtower of Air

> He that has his house inhemmed with a ditch, which is deep
> and swelled with water must needs make a bridge over,
> that he may be at liberty, else is he a prisoner unto the waters.[2]

Step 4. Visualize the gate opening at these words. Step within the Mica Gate. Face the Earth-Tier. In the god-form of RABMO, say:

> **I am the Angel of Air. I am the Angel RABMO. I am
> the Guardian of the Mica Gate. I enter into the Watchtower of Air.**

While slowly repeating the Threefold Holy Word, enter the Watchtower of Air and move across the Earth-Tier to the bottom of the Mulberry Stairway leading up to the Water-Tier (position 55). The Threefold Word that you recite will protect you from the demons who reside on the Earth-Tier.

Step 5. Face the Mulberry Stairway. Visualize the Kerubic Angel TNBA before you. Approach the Angel unafraid; open your arms and embrace him. Feel his body melt into your own and become a part of you. Assume the god-form of TNBA ("teh-neh-bah"), who guards the Mulberry Stairway, as follows:

The god-form of TNBA: See page 243 for the god-form of TBNA.

Recite the words written over the Mulberry Stairway:

> **I most humbly beseech you that I may have access
> into the Garden of Comfort.**[3]

Step 6. In the god-form of the Kerubic Angel of Air, TNBA, while slowly repeating the magic word HUM[4], climb the seven steps of the Mulberry Stairway to the Water-Tier. Then say:

> **I am a Kerubic Angel of Air. I am Kerubic Angel TNBA. I am
> the Guardian of the Mulberry Stairway. I rise up through
> the Watchtower of Air. Throughout eternity
> I move myself about from Earth to Water within Air.**

Step 7. Slowly repeat the magic word HUM as you move across the Water-Tier. Approach the Stairway to the Air-Tier. Before entering the Second Stairway, say:

> **Behold my brethren, God is ready to open his merciful star-houses and
> Gates of Understanding unto you. But he that liveth for himself, and for
> the end of this shadow, limiteth his wisdom with this number, and shall
> both have an end at once.**[5]

Climb the Second Stairway, which has six steps, to the Air-Tier. Visualize the Sephirothic Cross Angel AIAOAI before you. Approach the Angel unafraid; open your arms and embrace him. Feel his body melt into your own and become a part of you. Assume the god-form of AIAOAI ("ah-ee-ah-oh-ah-ee"), who guards the Air-Tier and Third Stairway (position 61), as follows:

The god-form of AIAOAI: See page 236 for the god-form of TBNA.

The Angels' Message to Humanity

The Third Stairway is yellow and smells of mint. The Third Stairway is also wet and hot. There are seven steps, each of which bears a letter written in blue that is blazing to look upon. The letter *E* is on the first step, *G* is on the second, *H* is on the third, *I* is on the fourth, *L* on the fifth, *O* on the sixth, and *S* on the seventh.[6] Recite the words written above the Third Stairway before ascending:[7]

> **I will hold up my House with Pillars of Hiacinct, and my Chambers shall be fullof modesty and comfort. I will bring the east wind over me, as a Lady of Comfort, and she shall sit upon my Castle with triumph, and I shall sleep with joy.**

Step 8. In the god-form of a Sephirothic Cross Angel of Air, slowly repeat the magic word MUM[8] as you climb. Climb up to the top of the Third Stairway and say:

> **I am a Sephirothic Cross Angel of Air. I am the Sephirothic Cross Angel AIAOAI. I bear the Cross of Air from Water to Air within Air.**

Step 9. As AIAOAI, slowly repeat the magic word MUM and at the top of the Third Stairway, turn toward the center of the Fire-Tier, which is the center of the mandala. If you are male, assume the naked god-form of the King of Air, BATAIVAH ("bah-tah-ee-vah-heh"). If you are female, assume the naked god-form of the Goddess of Air, ALOBABN ("ah-loh-bah-ben").[9]

> **The god-form of BATAIVAH:** See page 238 for the god-form of BATAIVAH.

> **The god-form of ALOBABN:** See page 236 for the god-form of ALOBABN.

Step 10. Slowly repeat the name of your consort (either ALOBABN or BATAIVAH) while walking along the Fire-Tier, the Great Cross of the Watchtower, toward the center of the mandala, a large, yellow hexagram with air circulating around it like a mild tornado. Beneath the tornado is a white circle marking the center of the mandala. If you are male, visualize your consort, ALOBABN, standing naked at the center of the hexagram (position 63) waiting for you. If you are female, visualize your consort, BATAIVAH, standing naked at the center of the hexagram (position 63) waiting for you.[10]

Step 11. Stand just outside the yellow airy hexagram, face your consort (who is naked and very beautiful) before you, and say:

> **From the North shall come a Whirlwind, and the hills shall open their mouths. And there shall a Dragon fly out, such as never was. And I will be glorified. I shall have power and I shall be glorified. I will keep the Statutes that I have been taught. I will forget not the words. I will not look back, but rather shall continue to the end.**[11]

While you face each other, enter into the yellow hexagram. See yourself clearly at the center of the Air Mandala. Smile at each other as if in love; then move together and hold each other. While saying the word EXARP, merge God/King and Goddess of Air together while holding a detailed awareness of the Watchtower around you. Remain this way for as long as you can, and then say:

Pathworking the Watchtower of Air

> The soul of man is the Image of God, after its form. It keeps within itself the Power of its divinity in the heavenly Spirit, whereby it has Authority to consent with God in the workmanship of his Will and Creatures. This Power being sealed already, gives to man, as King of himself, to consent to his own salvation, conjoining and knitting himself together, either with perseverance in the assured hope of mercy, or, with willful drunkenness, to the reward of such as fail. Therefore, become Holy. For the soul beautifies when it is beautiful in itself.[12]

Step 12. Turn from your consort and step outside the yellow hexagram. Leave by the same path that you entered. After leaving the mandala, conduct the banishing pentagram ritual. This completes the thirty-third initiatory path.

PATH THIRTY-FOUR

The Path of the Psychic Shield leads through the four positions 43-56-61-63, as shown in Figure 57. It contains the specific atmospheres of harmony, protection, and love. It is the Second Path of Purification. Use this path for protection from evil.

Step 1. Make a circle and conduct the invoking pentagram ritual.

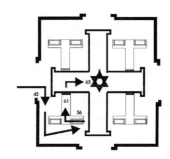

Figure 57: Path 34, The Path of the Psychic Shield

Step 2. Face the East, and imagine the Mandala of the Watchtower of Air clearly before you. You are facing the western wall of the mandala. Imagine the walls and floors to be yellow. Recite the Centering Spell. Then say:

> May I enter and safely pass through this yellow Watchtower of Air.
> May I obtain success in this, the thirty-fourth of my initiations.
> In the threefold secret and holy name of OROIBAHAOZPI
> I make this request. TOLTORGI-A GIGIPAHE ASAPATA
> OTAHILA SOBA OOAONA KAHISA RA-AS OD BOLANU.

Step 3. Visualize the closed Mica Gate. say: O RABMO I invoke thee. Come unto me from the Watchtower of Water. Visualize RABMO before you. Approach the Angel unafraid; open your arms and embrace him. Feel his body melt into your own and become a part of you. Assume the god-form of the Angel RABMO, who guards the Mica Gate (position 43), as follows:

The god-form of RABMO: See page 242 for the god-form of RABMO.

There are special words written above the Mica Gate to be spoken before entering. say:

> He that has his house inhemmed with a ditch, which is deep
> and swelled with water must needs make a bridge over,
> that he may be at liberty, else is he a prisoner unto the waters.

Step 4. Visualize the gate opening at these words. Step within the Mica Gate. Face the Earth-Tier. In the god-form of RABMO, say:

I am the Angel of Air. I am the Angel RABMO. I am the Guardian of the Mica Gate. I enter into the Watchtower of Air.

While slowly repeating the Threefold Holy Word, enter the Watchtower of Air and move across the Earth-Tier to the bottom of the Pimpernel Stairway leading up to the Water-Tier (position 56). The Threefold Word that you recite will protect you from the demons who reside on the Earth-Tier.

Step 5. Face the Pimpernel Stairway. Visualize the Kerubic Angel BATN before you. Approach the Angel unafraid; open your arms and embrace him. Feel his body melt into your own and become a part of you. Assume the god-form of BATN ("bah-teh-neh"), who guards the Pimpernel Stairway, as follows:

The god-form of BATN: See page 238 for the god-form of BATN.

Recite the words written over the Pimpernel Stairway:

You have received this Doctrine in chambers, and in secret places, but it shall stand in the Great City, and upon seven Hills, and shall establish herself in truth.

Step 6. In the god-form of the Kerubic Angel of Air, BATN, while slowly repeating the magic word HUM, climb the seven steps of the Pimpernel Stairway to the Water-Tier. Then say:

I am a Kerubic Angel of Air. I am Kerubic Angel BATN. I am the Guardian of the Pimpernel Stairway. I rise up through the Watchtower of Air. Throughout eternity I move myself about from Earth to Water within Air.

Step 7. Slowly repeat the magic word HUM as you move across the Water-Tier. Approach the Stairway to the Air-Tier. Before entering the Second Stairway, say:

Behold my brethren, God is ready to open his merciful star-houses and Gates of Understanding unto you. But he that liveth for himself, and for the end of this shadow, limiteth his wisdom with this number, and shall both have an end at once.

Climb the Second Stairway, which has six steps, to the Air-Tier. Visualize the Sephirothic Cross Angel AIAOAI before you. Approach the Angel unafraid; open your arms and embrace him. Feel his body melt into your own and become a part of you. Assume the god-form of AIAOAI, who guards the Air-Tier and Third Stairway (position 61), as follows:

The god-form of AIAOAI: See page 236 for the god-form of BATN.

The Third Stairway is yellow and smells of mint. The Third Stairway is also wet and hot. There are seven steps, each of which bears a letter written in blue that is blazing to look upon. The letter *E* is on the first step, *G* is on the second, *H* is on the third, *I* is on the fourth, *L* on the fifth, *O* on the sixth, and *S* on the seventh.[6] Recite the words written above the Third Stairway before ascending:

> **I will hold up my House with Pillars of Hiacinct, and my Chambers shall be full of modesty and comfort. I will bring the east wind over me, as a Lady of Comfort, and she shall sit upon my Castle with triumph, and I shall sleep with joy.**

Step 8. In the god-form of a Sephirothic Cross Angel of Air, slowly repeat the magic word MUM as you climb. Climb up to the top of the Third Stairway and say:

> **I am a Sephirothic Cross Angel of Air. I am the Sephirothic Cross Angel AIAOAI. I bear the Cross of Air from Water to Air within Air.**

Step 9. As AIAOAI, slowly repeat the magic word MUM, and at the top of the Third Stairway, turn toward the center of the Fire-Tier, which is the center of the mandala. If you are male, assume the naked god-form of the King of Air, BATAIVAH. If you are female, assume the naked god-form of the Goddess of Air, ALOBABN.

Step 10. Same as Step 9 of Path 33.

Step 11. Same as Step 10 of Path 33.

Step 12. Turn from your consort and step outside the yellow hexagram. Leave by the same path that you entered. After leaving the mandala, conduct the banishing pentagram ritual. This completes the thirty-fourth initiatory path.

PATH THIRTY-FIVE

The Path of Sexual Energy leads through the four positions 44-55-61-63, as shown in Figure 58. It contains the specific atmospheres of magical power, banishment, sexual attraction, and protection. It is the Third Path of Purification. Use this path to enhance sexual energy or to control sexual desire.

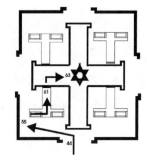

Figure 58: Path 35, The Path of Sexual Energy

Step 1. Make a circle and conduct the invoking pentagram ritual.

Step 2. Face the North, and imagine the Mandala of the Watchtower of Air clearly before you. You are facing the southern wall of the mandala. Imagine the walls and floors to be yellow. Recite the Centering Spell. Then say:

> **May I enter and safely pass through this yellow Watchtower of Air.**
> **May I obtain success in this, the thirty-fifth of my initiations.**
> **In the threefold secret and holy name of OROIBAHAOZPI**
> **I make this request. TOLTORGI-A GIGIPAHE ASAPATA**
> **OTAHILA SOBA OOAONA KAHISA RA-AS OD BOLANU.**

Step 3. Visualize the closed Pumice Gate. say: O RSHAL I invoke thee. Come unto me from the Watchtower of Water. Visualize RSHAL before you. Approach the Angel unafraid; open your arms and embrace him. Feel his body melt into your own and become a part of you. Assume the god-form of the Angel RSHAL ("rah-seh-hah-leh"), who guards the Pumice Gate (position 44), as follows:

The god-form of RSHAL: See page 242 for the god-form of RSHAL.

There are special words written above the Pumice Gate to be spoken before entering. say:

Behold, let thy house yield, and the covering of thy body give place to the necessity of hunger.

Step 4. Visualize the gate opening at these words. Step within the Pumice Gate. Face the Earth-Tier. In the god-form of RSHAL, say:

I am the Angel of Air. I am the Angel RSHAL. I am the Guardian of the Pumice Gate. I enter into the Watchtower of Air.

While slowly repeating the Threefold Holy Word, enter the Watchtower of Air and move across the Earth-Tier to the bottom of the Mulberry Stairway leading up to the Water-Tier (position 55). The Threefold Word that you recite will protect you from the demons who reside on the Earth-Tier.

Step 5. Face the Mulberry Stairway. Visualize the Kerubic Angel TNBA before you. Approach the Angel unafraid; open your arms and embrace him. Feel his body melt into your own and become a part of you. Assume the god-form of TNBA, who guards the Mulberry Stairway, as follows:

The god-form of TNBA: See page 243 for the god-form of TNBA.

Recite the words written over the Mulberry Stairway:

I most humbly beseech you that I may have access into the Garden of Comfort.

Step 6. In the god-form of the Kerubic Angel of Air, TNBA, while slowly repeating the magic word HUM, climb the seven steps of the Mulberry Stairway to the Water-Tier. Then say:

I am a Kerubic Angel of Air. I am Kerubic Angel TNBA. I am the Guardian of the Mulberry Stairway. I rise up through the Watchtower of Air. Throughout eternity I move myself about from Earth to Water within Air.

Step 7. Slowly repeat the magic word HUM as you move across the Water-Tier. Approach the Stairway to the Air-Tier. Before entering the Second Stairway, say:

Behold my brethren, God is ready to open his merciful star-houses and Gates of Understanding unto you. But he that liveth for himself, and for the end of this shadow, limiteth his wisdom with this number, and shall both have an end at once.

Pathworking the Watchtower of Air

Climb the Second Stairway, which has six steps, to the Air-Tier. Visualize the Sephirothic Cross Angel AIAOAI before you. Approach the Angel unafraid; open your arms and embrace him. Feel his body melt into your own and become a part of you. Assume the god-form of AIAOAI, who guards the Air-Tier and Third Stairway (position 61), as follows:

The god-form of AIAOAI: See page 236 for the god-form of AIAOAI

The Third Stairway is yellow and smells of mint. The Third Stairway is also wet and hot. There are seven steps, each of which bears a letter written in blue that is blazing to look upon. The letter *E* is on the first step, *G* is on the second, *H* is on the third, *I* is on the fourth, *L* on the fifth, *O* on the sixth, and *S* on the seventh.[6] Recite the words written above the Third Stairway before ascending:

> **I will hold up my House with Pillars of Hiacinct, and my Chambers shall be full of modesty and comfort. I will bring the east wind over me, as a Lady of Comfort, and she shall sit upon my Castle with triumph, and I shall sleep with joy.**

Step 8. In the god-form of a Sephirothic Cross Angel of Air, slowly repeat the magic word MUM as you climb. Climb up to the top of the Third Stairway and say:

> **I am a Sephirothic Cross Angel of Air. I am the Sephirothic Cross Angel AIAOAI. I bear the Cross of Air from Water to Air within Air.**

Step 9. As AIAOAI, slowly repeat the magic word MUM and at the top of the Third Stairway, turn toward the center of the Fire-Tier, which is the center of the mandala. If you are male, assume the naked god-form of the King of Air, BATAIVAH. If you are female, assume the naked god-form of the Goddess of Air, ALOBABN.

Step 10. Same as Step 9 of Path 33.[13]

Step 11. Same as Step 10 of Path 33.

Step 12. Turn from your consort and step outside the yellow hexagram. Leave by the same path that you entered. After leaving the mandala, conduct the banishing pentagram ritual. This completes the thirty-fifth initiatory path.

PATH THIRTY-SIX

The Path of Psychism leads through the four positions 44-56-61-63, as shown in Figure 59. It contains the specific atmospheres of magical power, banishment, love, and protection. It is the Fourth Path of Purification. Use this path to develop or enhance magical and psychic powers.

Step 1. Make a circle and conduct the invoking pentagram ritual.

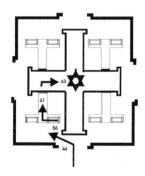

Figure 59: Path 36, The Path of Psychism

Step 2. Face the North, and imagine the Mandala of the Watchtower of Air clearly before you. You are facing the southern wall of the mandala. Imagine the walls and floors to be yellow. Recite the Centering Spell. Then say:

May I enter and safely pass through this yellow Watchtower of Air. May I obtain success in this, the thirty-sixth of my initiations. In the threefold secret and holy name of OROIBAHAOZPI I make this request. TOLTORGI-A GIGIPAHE ASAPATA OTAHILA SOBA OOAONA KAHISA RA-AS OD BOLANU.

Step 3. Visualize the closed Pumice Gate. say:

O RSHAL I invoke thee. Come unto me from the Watchtower of Water.

Visualize RSHAL before you. Approach the Angel unafraid; open your arms and embrace him. Feel his body melt into your own and become a part of you. Assume the god-form of the Angel RSHAL, who guards the Pumice Gate (position 44), as follows:

The god-form of RSHAL: See page 242 for the god-form of RSHAL.

There are special words written above the Pumice Gate to be spoken before entering. say:

**Behold, let thy house yield, and the covering of thy body
give place to the necessity of hunger.**

Step 4. Visualize the gate opening at these words. Step within the Pumice Gate. Face the Earth-Tier. In the god-form of RSHAL, say:

**I am the Angel of Air. I am the Angel RSHAL. I am
the Guardian of the Pumice Gate. I enter into the Watchtower of Air.**

While slowly repeating the Threefold Holy Word, enter the Watchtower of Air and move across the Earth-Tier to the bottom of the Mulberry Stairway leading up to the Water-Tier (position 55). The Threefold Word that you recite will protect you from the demons who reside on the Earth-Tier.

Step 5. Face the Pimpernel Stairway. Visualize the Kerubic Angel BATN before you. Approach the Angel unafraid; open your arms and embrace him. Feel his body melt into your own and become a part of you. Assume the god-form of BATN, who guards the Pimpernel Stairway, as follows:

The god-form of BATN: See page 238 for the god-form of BATN.

Recite the words written over the Pimpernel Stairway:

You have received this Doctrine in chambers, and in secret places, but it shall stand in the Great City, and upon seven Hills, and shall establish herself in truth.

Step 6. In the god-form of the Kerubic Angel of Air, BATN, while slowly repeating the magic word HUM, climb the seven steps of the Pimpernel Stairway to the Water-Tier. Then say:

Pathworking the Watchtower of Air

> I am a Kerubic Angel of Air. I am Kerubic Angel BATN. I am the Guardian of the Pimpernel Stairway. I rise up through the Watchtower of Air. Throughout eternity I move myself about from Earth to Water within Air.

Step 7. Slowly repeat the magic word HUM as you move across the Water-Tier. Approach the Stairway to the Air-Tier. Before entering the Second Stairway, say:

> Behold my brethren, God is ready to open his merciful star-houses and Gates of Understanding unto you. But he that liveth for himself, and for the end of this shadow, limiteth his wisdom with this number, and shall both have an end at once.

Climb the Second Stairway, which has six steps, to the Air-Tier. Visualize the Sephirothic Cross Angel AIAOAI before you. Approach the Angel unafraid; open your arms and embrace him. Feel his body melt into your own and become a part of you. Assume the god-form of AIAOAI, who guards the Air-Tier and Third Stairway (position 61), as follows:

The god-form of AIAOAI: See page 236 for the god-form of AIAOAI.

The Third Stairway is yellow and smells of mint. The Third Stairway is also wet and hot. There are seven steps, each of which bears a letter written in blue that is blazing to look upon. The letter *E* is on the first step, *G* is on the second, *H* is on the third, *I* is on the fourth, *L* on the fifth, *O* on the sixth, and *S* on the seventh.[6] Recite the words written above the Third Stairway before ascending:

> I will hold up my House with Pillars of Hiacinct, and my Chambers shall be full of modesty and comfort. I will bring the east wind over me, as a Lady of Comfort, and she shall sit upon my Castle with triumph, and I shall sleep with joy.

Step 8. In the god-form of a Sephirothic Cross Angel of Air, slowly repeat the magic word MUM as you climb. Climb up to the top of the Third Stairway and say:

> I am a Sephirothic Cross Angel of Air. I am the Sephirothic Cross Angel AIAOAI. I bear the Cross of Air from Water to Air within Air.

Step 9. As AIAOAI, slowly repeat the magic word MUM, and at the top of the Third Stairway, turn toward the center of the Fire-Tier, which is the center of the mandala. If you are male, assume the naked god-form of the King of Air, BATAIVAH. If you are female, assume the naked god-form of the Goddess of Air, ALOBABN.

Step 10. Same as Step 9 of Path 33.

Step 11. Same as Step 10 of Path 33.

Step 12. Turn from your consort and step outside the yellow hexagram. Leave by the same path that you entered. After leaving the mandala, conduct the banishing pentagram ritual. This completes the thirty-sixth initiatory path.

The Water Quadrant of the Air Mandala

Path Thirty-Seven

The Path of Prosperity leads through the four positions 47-54-60-63, as shown in Figure 60. It contains the specific atmospheres of love, psychic power, wealth, and fertility. It is the First Path of Insight. Use this path for the magical power of bestowing fertility or for general prosperity.

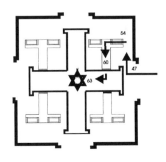

Figure 60: Path 37, The Path of Prosperity

Step 1. Make a circle and conduct the invoking pentagram ritual.

Step 2. Face the West, and imagine the Mandala of the Watchtower of Air clearly before you. You are facing the eastern wall of the mandala. Imagine the walls and floors to be yellow. Recite the Centering Spell. Then say:

> May I enter and safely pass through this yellow Watchtower of Air.
> May I obtain success in this, the thirty-seventh of my initiations.
> In the threefold secret and holy name of OROIBAHAOZPI
> I make this request. TOLTORGI-A GIGIPAHE ASAPATA
> OTAHILA SOBA OOAONA KAHISA RA-AS OD BOLANU.

Step 3. Visualize the closed Acacia Gate. say: O AOYVB I invoke thee. Come unto me from the Watchtower of Water. Visualize AOYVB before you. Approach the Angel unafraid; open your arms and embrace him. Feel his body melt into your own and become a part of you. Assume the god-form of the Angel AOYVB ("ah-oh-yeh-veh-beh"), who guards the Acacia Gate (position 47), as follows:

The god-form of AOYVB: See page 237 for the god-form of AOYVB.

There are special words written above the Acacia Gate to be spoken before entering. say:

> Wilt thou drown the World with waters, and root the wicked from the face of the Earth?

Step 4. Visualize the gate opening at these words. Step within the Acacia Gate. Face the Earth-Tier. In the god-form of AOYVB, say:

> I am the Angel of Air. I am the Angel AOYVB. I am the Guardian of the Acacia Gate. I enter into the Watchtower of Air.

While slowly repeating the Threefold Holy Word, enter the Watchtower of Air and move across the Earth-Tier to the bottom of the Hazel Stairway leading up to the Water-Tier (position 54). The Threefold Word that you recite will protect you from the demons who reside on the Earth-Tier.

Pathworking the Watchtower of Air

Step 5. Face the Hazel Stairway. Visualize the Kerubic Angel PAYT before you. Approach the Angel unafraid; open your arms and embrace him. Feel his body melt into your own and become a part of you. Assume the god-form of PAYT ("pah-yeh-teh"), who guards the Hazel Stairway, as follows:

The god-form of PAYT: See page 241 for the god-form of PAYT.

Recite the words written over the Hazel Stairway:

Dream not with the world, for the world shall perish, and all her adherents.

Step 6. In the god-form of the Kerubic Angel of Air, PAYT, while slowly repeating the magic word HUM, climb the twelve steps of the Hazel Stairway to the Water-Tier. Then say:

**I am a Kerubic Angel of Air. I am Kerubic Angel PAYT.
I am the Guardian of the Hazel Stairway. I rise up through
the Watchtower of Air. Throughout eternity
I move myself about from Earth to Water within Air.**

Step 7. Slowly repeat the magic word HUM as you move across the Water-Tier. Approach the Stairway to the Air-Tier. Before entering the Second Stairway, say:

Behold my brethren, God is ready to open his merciful star-houses and Gates of Understanding unto you. But he that liveth for himself, and for the end of this shadow, limiteth his wisdom with this number, and shall both have an end at once.

Climb the Second Stairway, which has thirteen steps, to the Air-Tier. Visualize the Sephirothic Cross Angel LLAKZA before you. Approach the Angel unafraid; open your arms and embrace him. Feel his body melt into your own and become a part of you. Assume the god-form of LLAKZA ("el-lah-keh-zah"), who guards the Air-Tier and Third Stairway (position 61), as follows:

The god-form of LLAKZA: See page 240 for the god-form of LLAKZA.

The Third Stairway is yellow and smells of mint. The Third Stairway is also wet and hot. There are seven steps, each of which bears a letter written in blue that is blazing to look upon. The letter E is on the first step, G is on the second, H is on the third, I is on the fourth, L on the fifth, O on the sixth, and S on the seventh.[6] Recite the words written above the Third Stairway before ascending:

Behold, let my spirit enter in, let there be separation made within the House of the North, that the Earth may be divided into her members. Cursed be that body that is not divided according to the proportion answering to the division. For she has yet not cast off the shape of darkness.

Step 8. In the god-form of a Sephirothic Cross Angel of Air, slowly repeat the magic word MUM as you climb. Climb up to the top of the Third Stairway and say:

I am a Sephirothic Cross Angel of Air. I am the Sephirothic Cross Angel LLAKZA. I bear the Cross of Air from Water to Air within Air.

The Angels' Message to Humanity

Step 9. As LLAKZA, slowly repeat the magic word MUM and at the top of the Third Stairway, turn toward the center of the Fire-Tier, which is the center of the mandala. If you are male, assume the naked god-form of the King of Air, BATAIVAH. If you are female, assume the naked god-form of the Goddess of Air, ALOBABN.

Step 10. Same as Step 9 of Path 33.

Step 11. Same as Step 10 of Path 33.

Step 12. Turn from your consort and step outside the yellow hexagram. Leave by the same path that you entered. After leaving the mandala, conduct the banishing pentagram ritual.

This completes the thirty-seventh initiatory path.

PATH THIRTY-EIGHT

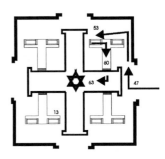

The Path of Fortune leads through the four positions 47-53-60-63, as shown in Figure 61. It contains the specific atmospheres of love, psychic power, magical power, and good luck. It is the Second Path of Insight. Use this path to promote or maintain good karma.

Step 1. Make a circle and conduct the invoking pentagram ritual.

Figure 61: Path 38, The Path of Fortune

Step 2. Face the West, and imagine the Mandala of the Watchtower of Air clearly before you. You are facing the eastern wall of the mandala. Imagine the walls and floors to be yellow. Recite the Centering Spell. Then say:

> **May I enter and safely pass through this yellow Watchtower of Air.**
> **May I obtain success in this, the thirty-eighth of my initiations.**
> **In the threefold secret and holy name of OROIBAHAOZPI**
> **I make this request. TOLTORGI-A GIGIPAHE ASAPATA**
> **OTAHILA SOBA OOAONA KAHISA RA-AS OD BOLANU.**

Step 3. Visualize the closed Acacia Gate. say: O AOYVB I invoke thee. Come unto me from the Watchtower of Water. Visualize AOYVB before you. Approach the Angel unafraid; open your arms and embrace him. Feel his body melt into your own and become a part of you. Assume the god-form of the Angel AOYVB, who guards the Acacia Gate (position 47), as follows:

The god-form of AOYVB: See page 237 for the god-form of AOYVB.

There are special words written above the Acacia Gate to be spoken before entering. say:

> **Wilt thou drown the World with waters,**
> **and root the wicked from the face of the Earth?**

Pathworking the Watchtower of Air

Step 4. Visualize the gate opening at these words. Step within the Acacia Gate. Face the Earth-Tier. In the god-form of AOYVB, say:

> **I am the Angel of Air. I am the Angel AOYVB. I am the Guardian of the Acacia Gate. I enter into the Watchtower of Air.**

While slowly repeating the Threefold Holy Word, enter the Watchtower of Air and move across the Earth-Tier to the bottom of the Banyan Stairway leading up to the Water-Tier (position 53). The Threefold Word that you recite will protect you from the demons who reside on the Earth-Tier.

Step 5. Face the Banyan Stairway. Visualize the Kerubic Angel YTPA before you. Approach the Angel unafraid; open your arms and embrace him. Feel his body melt into your own and become a part of you. Assume the god-form of YTPA ("yeh-teh- pah"), who guards the Banyan Stairway, as follows:

> **The god-form of YTPA:** See page 243 for the god-form of YTPA.

Recite the words written over the Banyan Stairway:

> **Woe be unto the world, for her light is taken away. Woe, woe be unto man, for the Eye of Light has forsaken him. Woe, woe be to the understanding of man, for it is led out, with a threefold spirit.**

Step 6. In the god-form of the Kerubic Angel of Air, YTPA, while slowly repeating the magic word HUM, climb the twelve steps of the Banyan Stairway to the Water-Tier. Then say:

> **I am a Kerubic Angel of Air. I am Kerubic Angel YTPA. I am the Guardian of the Banyan Stairway. I rise up through the Watchtower of Air. Throughout eternity I move myself about from Earth to Water within Air.**

Step 7. Slowly repeat the magic word HUM as you move across the Water-Tier. Approach the Stairway to the Air-Tier. Before entering the Second Stairway, say:

> **Behold my brethren, God is ready to open his merciful star-houses and Gates of Understanding unto you. But he that liveth for himself, and for the end of this shadow, limiteth his wisdom with this number, and shall both have an end at once.**

Climb the Second Stairway, which has thirteen steps, to the Air-Tier. Visualize the Sephirothic Cross Angel LLAKZA before you. Approach the Angel unafraid; open your arms and embrace him. Feel his body melt into your own and become a part of you. Assume the god-form of LLAKZA, who guards the Air-Tier and Third Stairway (position 61), as follows:

> **The god-form of LLAKZA:** See page 240 for the god-form of LLAKZA.

The Third Stairway is yellow and smells of mint. The Third Stairway is also wet and hot. There are seven steps, each of which bears a letter written in blue that is blazing to look upon. The letter *E* is on the first step, *G* is on the second, *H* is on the third, *I* is on the fourth, *L* on the fifth, *O* on the sixth, and *S* on the seventh.[6] Recite the words written above the Third Stairway before ascending:

> **Behold, let my spirit enter in, let there be separation madewithin the House of the North, that the Earth may be divided into her members. Cursed be that body that is not divided according to the proportion answering to the division. For she has yet not cast off the shape of darkness.**

Step 8. In the god-form of a Sephirothic Cross Angel of Air, slowly repeat the magic word MUM as you climb. Climb up to the top of the Third Stairway and say:

> **I am a Sephirothic Cross Angel of Air. I am the Sephirothic Cross Angel LLAKZA. I bear the Cross of Air from Water to Air within Air.**

Step 9. As LLAKZA, slowly repeat the magic word MUM, and at the top of the Third Stairway, turn toward the center of the Fire-Tier, which is the center of the mandala. If you are male, assume the naked god-form of the King of Air, BATAIVAH. If you are female, assume the naked god-form of the Goddess of Air, ALOBABN.

Step 10. Same as Step 9 of Path 33.

Step 11. Same as Step 10 of Path 33.

Step 12. Turn from your consort and step outside the yellow hexagram. Leave by the same path that you entered. After leaving the mandala, conduct the banishing pentagram ritual. This completes the thirty-eighth initiatory path.

Path Thirty-Nine

The Path of Eloquence leads through the four positions 48-54-60-63, as shown in Figure 62. It contains the specific atmospheres of protection, eloquence, wealth, and fertility. It is the Third Path of Insight. Use this path to obtain eloquence of speech.

Step 1. Make a circle and conduct the invoking pentagram ritual.

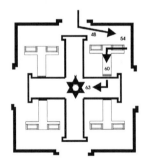

Figure 62: Path 39, The Path of Eloquence

Step 2. Face the South, and imagine the Mandala of the Watchtower of Air clearly before you. You are facing the north wall of the mandala. Imagine the walls and floors to be yellow. Recite the Centering Spell. Then say:

> **May I enter and safely pass through this yellow Watchtower of Air. May I obtain success in this, the thirty-ninth of my initiations. In the threefold secret and holy name of OROIBAHAOZPI I make this request. TOLTORGI-A GIGIPAHE ASAPATA OTAHILA SOBA OOAONA KAHISA RA-AS OD BOLANU.**

Pathworking the Watchtower of Air

Step 3. Visualize the closed Aspen Gate. say: O ADIRL I invoke thee. Come unto me from the Watchtower of Water. Visualize ADIRL before you. Approach the Angel unafraid; open your arms and embrace her. Feel her body melt into your own and become a part of you. Assume the god-form of the Angel ADIRL ("ah-dee-ar-el"), who guards the Aspen Gate (position 48), as follows:

The god-form of ADIRL: See page 236 for the god-form of ADIRL.

There are special words written above the Aspen Gate to be spoken before entering. say:

But such as I have, I will give thee, and it shall be sufficient, more then they vessels can hold, or thy days can thank me for.

Step 4. Visualize the gate opening at these words. Step within the Aspen Gate. Face the Earth-Tier. In the god-form of ADIRL, say:

I am the Angel of Air. I am the Angel ADIRL. I am the Guardian of the Aspen Gate. I enter into the Watchtower of Air.

While slowly repeating the Threefold Holy Word, enter the Watchtower of Air and move across the Earth-Tier to the bottom of the Hazel Stairway leading up to the Water-Tier (position 54). The Threefold Word that you recite will protect you from the demons who reside on the Earth-Tier.

Step 5. Face the Hazel Stairway. Visualize the Kerubic Angel PAYT before you. Approach the Angel unafraid; open your arms and embrace him. Feel his body melt into your own and become a part of you. Assume the god-form of the Kerubic Angel, PAYT, who guards the Hazel Stairway, as follows:

The god-form of PAYT: See page 241 for the god-form of PAYT.

Recite the words written over the Hazel Stairway:

Dream not with the world, for the world shall perish, and all her adherents.

Step 6. In the god-form of the Kerubic Angel of Air, PAYT, while slowly repeating the magic word HUM, climb the twelve steps of the Hazel Stairway to the Water-Tier. Then say:

I am a Kerubic Angel of Air. I am Kerubic Angel PAYT. I am the Guardian of the Hazel Stairway. I rise up through the Watchtower of Air. Throughout eternity I move myself about from Earth to Water within Air.

Step 7. Slowly repeat the magic word HUM as you move across the Water-Tier. Approach the Stairway to the Air-Tier. Before entering the Second Stairway, say:

Behold my brethren, God is ready to open his merciful star-houses and Gates of Understanding unto you. But he that liveth for himself, and for the end of this shadow, limiteth his wisdom with this number, and shall both have an end at once.

The Angels' Message to Humanity

Climb the Second Stairway, which has thirteen steps, to the Air-Tier. Visualize the Sephirothic Cross Angel LLAKZA before you. Approach the Angel unafraid; open your arms and embrace him. Feel his body melt into your own and become a part of you. Assume the god-form of LLAKZA, who guards the Air-Tier and Third Stairway (position 61), as follows:

The god-form of LLAKZA: See page 240 for the god-form of LLAKZA.

The Third Stairway is yellow and smells of mint. The Third Stairway is also wet and hot. There are seven steps, each of which bears a letter written in blue that is blazing to look upon. The letter *E* is on the first step, *G* is on the second, *H* is on the third, *I* is on the fourth, *L* on the fifth, *O* on the sixth, and *S* on the seventh.[6] Recite the words written above the Third Stairway before ascending:

Behold, let my spirit enter in, let there be separation made within the House of the North, that the Earth may be divided into her members. Cursed be that body that is not divided according to the proportion answering to the division. For she has yet not cast off the shape of darkness.

Step 8. In the god-form of a Sephirothic Cross Angel of Air, slowly repeat the magic word MUM as you climb. Climb up to the top of the Third Stairway and say:

I am a Sephirothic Cross Angel of Air. I am the Sephirothic Cross Angel LLAKZA. I bear the Cross of Air from Water to Air within Air.

Step 9. As LLAKZA, slowly repeat the magic word MUM and at the top of the Third Stairway, turn toward the center of the Fire-Tier, which is the center of the mandala. If you are male, assume the naked god-form of the King of Air, BATAIVAH. If you are female, assume the naked god-form of the Goddess of Air, ALOBABN.

Step 10. Same as Step 9 of Path 33.

Step 11. Same as Step 10 of Path 33.

Step 12. Turn from your consort and step outside the yellow hexagram. Leave by the same path that you entered. After leaving the mandala, conduct the banishing pentagram ritual. This completes the thirty-ninth initiatory path.

Path Forty

The Path of Communication leads through the four positions 48-53-60-63, as shown in Figure 63. It contains the specific atmospheres of protection, eloquence, magical power, and good luck. It is the Fourth Path of Insight. Use this path for the magical power of communication.

Step 1. Make a circle and conduct the invoking pentagram ritual.

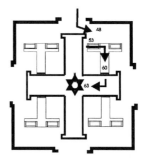

Figure 63: Path 40, The Path of Communication

Pathworking the Watchtower of Air

Step 2. Face the South, and imagine the Mandala of the Watchtower of Air clearly before you. You are facing the northern wall of the mandala. Imagine the walls and floors to be yellow. Recite the Centering Spell. Then say:

> May I enter and safely pass through this yellow Watchtower of Air.
> May I obtain success in this, the fortieth of my initiations.
> In the threefold secret and holy name of OROIBAHAOZPI
> I make this request. TOLTORGI-A GIGIPAHE ASAPATA
> OTAHILA SOBA OOAONA KAHISA RA-AS OD BOLANU.

Step 3. Visualize the closed Aspen Gate. say: O ADIRL I invoke thee. Come unto me from the Watchtower of Water. Visualize ADIRL before you. Approach the Angel unafraid; open your arms and embrace her. Feel her body melt into your own and become a part of you. Assume the god-form of the Angel ADIRL, who guards the Aspen Gate (position 48), as follows:

> **The god-form of ADIRL:** See page 236 for the god-form of ADIRL.

There are special words written above the Aspen Gate to be spoken before entering. say:

> But such as I have, I will give thee, and it shall be sufficient,
> more then they vessels can hold, or thy days can thank me for.

Step 4. Visualize the gate opening at these words. Step within the Aspen Gate. Face the Earth-Tier. In the god-form of ADIRL, say:

> I am the Angel of Air. I am the Angel ADIRL. I am
> the Guardian of the Aspen Gate. I enter into the Watchtower of Air.

While slowly repeating the Threefold Holy Word, enter the Watchtower of Air and move across the Earth-Tier to the bottom of the Banyan Stairway leading up to the Water-Tier (position 53). The Threefold Word that you recite will protect you from the demons who reside on the Earth-Tier.

Step 5. Face the Banyan Stairway. Visualize the Kerubic Angel YTPA before you. Approach the Angel unafraid; open your arms and embrace him. Feel his body melt into your own and become a part of you. Assume the god-form of the Kerubic Angel, YTPA, who guards the Banyan Stairway, as follows:

> **The god-form of YTPA:** See page 243 for the god-form of YTPA.

Recite the words written over the Banyan Stairway:

> Woe be unto the world, for her light is taken away. Woe, woe
> be unto man, for the Eye of Light has forsaken him. Woe, woe
> be to the understanding of man, for it is led out, with a threefold spirit.

Step 6. In the god-form of the Kerubic Angel of Air, YTPA, while slowly repeating the magic word HUM, climb the twelve steps of the Banyan Stairway to the Water-Tier. Then say:

> I am a Kerubic Angel of Air. I am Kerubic Angel YTPA.
> I am the Guardian of the Banyan Stairway. I rise up

through the Watchtower of Air. Throughout eternity
I move myself about from Earth to Water within Air.

Step 7. Slowly repeat the magic word HUM as you move across the Water-Tier. Approach the Stairway to the Air-Tier. Before entering the Second Stairway, say:

Behold my brethren, God is ready to open his merciful star-houses and Gates of Understanding unto you. But he that liveth for himself, and for the end of this shadow, limiteth his wisdom with this number, and shall both have an end at once.

Climb the Second Stairway, which has thirteen steps, to the Air-Tier. Visualize the Sephirothic Cross Angel LLAKZA before you. Approach the Angel unafraid; open your arms and embrace him. Feel his body melt into your own and become a part of you. Assume the god-form of the Sephirothic Cross Angel LLAKZA who guards the Air-Tier and Third Stairway (position 61), as follows:

The god-form of LLAKZA: See page 240 for the god-form of LLAKZA.

The Third Stairway is yellow and smells of mint. The Third Stairway is also wet and hot. There are seven steps, each of which bears a letter written in blue that is blazing to look upon. The letter *E* is on the first step, *G* is on the second, *H* is on the third, *I* is on the fourth, *L* on the fifth, *O* on the sixth, and *S* on the seventh.[6] Recite the words written above the Third Stairway before ascending:

Behold, let my spirit enter in, let there be separation made within the House of the North, that the Earth may be divided into her members. Cursed be that body that is not divided according to the proportion answering to the division. For she has yet not cast off the shape of darkness.

Step 8. In the god-form of a Sephirothic Cross Angel of Air, slowly repeat the magic word MUM as you climb. Climb up to the top of the Third Stairway and say:

I am a Sephirothic Cross Angel of Air. I am the Sephirothic Cross Angel LLAKZA. I bear the Cross of Air from Water to Air within Air.

Step 9. As LLAKZA, slowly repeat the magic word MUM, and at the top of the Third Stairway, turn toward the center of the Fire-Tier, which is the center of the mandala. If you are male, assume the naked god-form of the King of Air, BATAIVAH. If you are female, assume the naked god-form of the Goddess of Air, ALOBABN.

Step 10. Same as Step 9 of Path 33.

Step 11. Same as Step 10 of Path 33.

Step 12. Turn from your consort and step outside the yellow hexagram. Leave by the same path that you entered. After leaving the mandala, conduct the banishing pentagram ritual. This completes the fortieth initiatory path.

Pathworking the Watchtower of Air

THE AIR QUADRANT OF THE AIR MANDALA

PATH FORTY-ONE

The Path of Telepathy leads through the four positions 49-51-59-63, as shown in Figure 64. It contains the specific atmospheres of power, communication, protection, and prosperity. It is the First Path of Communication. Use this path for the magical power of telepathy.

Step 1. Make a circle and conduct the invoking pentagram ritual.

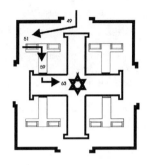

Figure 64: Path 41, The Path of Telepathy

Step 2. Face the South, and imagine the Mandala of the Watchtower of Air clearly before you. You are facing the northern wall of the mandala. Imagine the walls and floors to be yellow. Recite the Centering Spell. Then say:

> May I enter and safely pass through this yellow Watchtower of Air.
> May I obtain success in this, the forty-first of my initiations.
> In the threefold secret and holy name of OROIBAHAOZPI
> I make this request. TOLTORGI-A GIGIPAHE ASAPATA
> OTAHILA SOBA OOAONA KAHISA RA-AS OD BOLANU.

Step 3. Visualize the closed Papyrus Gate. say: O XKZNS I invoke thee. Come unto me from the Watchtower of Water. Visualize XKZNS before you. Approach the Angel unafraid; open your arms and embrace him. Feel his body melt into your own and become a part of you. Assume the god-form of the Angel XKZNS ("etz-keh-zen-ess"), who guards the Papyrus Gate (position 49), as follows:

> **The god-form of XKZNS:** A strong, dark, masculine Angel without wings wearing a greenish-yellow robe. He holds a cat's eye medallion that bestows power over all lower life forms, including animals and demons.

There are special words written above the Papyrus Gate to be spoken before entering. say:

> **If the Bridegroom invite thee himself, what needest thou his servant.**

Step 4. Visualize the gate opening at these words. Step within the Papyrus Gate. Face the Earth-Tier. In the god-form of XKZNS, say:

> I am the Angel of Air. I am the Angel XKZNS. I am the Guardian of the Papyrus Gate. I enter into the Watchtower of Air.

While slowly repeating the Threefold Holy Word, enter the Watchtower of Air and move across the Earth-Tier to the bottom of the Almond Stairway leading up to the Water-Tier (position 51). The Threefold Word that you recite will protect you from the demons who reside on the Earth-Tier.

The Angels' Message to Humanity

Step 5. Face the Almond Stairway. Visualize the Kerubic Angel RZLA before you. Approach the Angel unafraid; open your arms and embrace him. Feel his body melt into your own and become a part of you. Assume the god-form of RZLA ("rah-zeh-lah"), who guards the Almond Stairway, as follows:

The god-form of RZLA: See page 242 for the god-form RZLA.

Recite the words written over the Almond Stairway:

The King of Darkness wetteth his teeth against thee, and rampeth with great rage to overwhelm the world upon thee.

Step 6. In the god-form of the Kerubic Angel of Air, RZLA, while slowly repeating the magic word HUM, climb the six steps of the Almond Stairway to the Water-Tier. Then say:

I am a Kerubic Angel of Air. I am Kerubic Angel RZLA. I am the Guardian of the Almond Stairway. I rise up through the Watchtower of Air. Throughout eternity I move myself about from Earth to Water within Air.

Step 7. Slowly repeat the magic word HUM as you move across the Water-Tier. Approach the Stairway to the Air-Tier. Before entering the Second Stairway, say:

Behold my brethren, God is ready to open his merciful star-houses and Gates of Understanding unto you. But he that liveth for himself, and for the end of this shadow, limiteth his wisdom with this number, and shall both have an end at once.

Climb the Second Stairway, which has twelve steps, to the Air-Tier. Visualize the Sephirothic Cross Angel IDOIGO before you. Approach the Angel unafraid; open your arms and embrace her. Feel her body melt into your own and become a part of you. Assume the god-form of the Sephirothic Cross Angel IDOIGO ("ee-doh-ee-goh"), who guards the Air-Tier and Third Stairway (position 59), as follows:

The god-form of IDOIGO: See page 239 for the god-form of IDOIGO.

The Third Stairway is yellow and smells of mint. The Third Stairway is also wet and hot. There are seven steps, each of which bears a letter written in blue that is blazing to look upon. The letter E is on the first step, G is on the second, H is on the third, I is on the fourth, L on the fifth, O on the sixth, and S on the seventh.[6] Recite the words written above the Third Stairway before ascending:

I will bless all that thou takest in hand, and will cover thee with a Robe of Purple, that thou mayest understand that all is mine, and that I raise up whom I list.

Step 8. In the god-form of a Sephirothic Cross Angel of Air, slowly repeat the magic word MUM as you climb. Climb up to the top of the Third Stairway and say:

I am a Sephirothic Cross Angel of Air. I am the Sephirothic Cross Angel IDOIGO. I bear the Cross of Air from Water to Air within Air.

Pathworking the Watchtower of Air

Step 9. As IDOIGO, slowly repeat the magic word MUM, and at the top of the Third Stairway, turn toward the center of the Fire-Tier, which is the center of the mandala. If you are male, assume the naked god-form of the King of Air, BATAIVAH. If you are female, assume the naked god-form of the Goddess of Air, ALOBABN.

Step 10. Same as Step 9 of Path 33.

Step 11. Same as Step 10 of Path 33.

Step 12. Turn from your consort and step outside the yellow hexagram. Leave by the same path that you entered. After leaving the mandala, conduct the banishing pentagram ritual. This completes the forty-first initiatory path.

Path Forty-Two

The Path of Psychic Protection leads through the four positions 49-52-59-63, as shown in Figure 65. It contains the specific atmospheres of psychic power, communication, and protection. It is the Second Path of Communication. Use this path for protection against psychic attack.

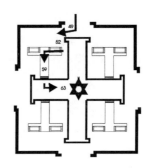

Figure 65: Path 42, The Path of Physic Protection

Step 1. Make a circle and conduct the invoking pentagram ritual.

Step 2. Face the South, and imagine the Mandala of the Watchtower of Air clearly before you. You are facing the northern wall of the mandala. Imagine the walls and floors to be yellow. Recite the Centering Spell. Then say:

> May I enter and safely pass through this yellow Watchtower of Air.
> May I obtain success in this, the forty-second of my initiations.
> In the threefold secret and holy name of OROIBAHAOZPI
> I make this request. TOLTORGI-A GIGIPAHE ASAPATA
> OTAHILA SOBA OOAONA KAHISA RA-AS OD BOLANU.

Step 3. Visualize the closed Papyrus Gate. say: O XKZNS I invoke thee. Come unto me from the Watchtower of Water. Visualize XKZNS before you. Approach the Angel unafraid; open your arms and embrace him. Feel his body melt into your own and become a part of you. Assume the god-form of the Angel XKZNS, who guards the Papyrus Gate (position 49), as follows:

The god-form of XKZNS: See page 243 for the god-form of XKZNS.

There are special words written above the Papyrus Gate to be spoken before entering. say:

> **If the Bridegroom invite thee himself, what needest thou his servant.**

Step 4. Visualize the gate opening at these words. Step within the Papyrus Gate. Face the Earth-Tier. In the god-form of XKZNS, say:

The Angels' Message to Humanity

I am the Angel of Air. I am the Angel XKZNS. I am the Guardian of the Papyrus Gate. I enter into the Watchtower of Air.

While slowly repeating the Threefold Holy Word, enter the Watchtower of Air and move across the Earth-Tier to the bottom of the Anise Stairway leading up to the Water-Tier (position 52). The Threefold Word that you recite will protect you from the demons who reside on the Earth-Tier.

Step 5. Face the Anise Stairway. Visualize the Kerubic Angel LARZ before you. Approach the Angel unafraid; open your arms and embrace him. Feel his body melt into your own and become a part of you. Assume the god-form of LARZ ("lah-rah- zeh"), who guards the Anise Stairway, as follows:

The god-form of LARZ: See page 239 for the god-form of LARZ.

Recite the words written over the Anise Stairway:

But his lips are sealed, and his claws made dull, that when he would bite he cannot, and where he scratches, the blood follows not.

Step 6. In the god-form of the Kerubic Angel of Air, LARZ, while slowly repeating the magic word HUM, climb the six steps of the Anise Stairway to the Water-Tier. Then say:

**I am a Kerubic Angel of Air. I am Kerubic Angel LARZ.
I am the Guardian of the Anise Stairway. I rise up
through the Watchtower of Air. Throughout eternity
I move myself about from Earth to Water within Air.**

Step 7. Slowly repeat the magic word HUM as you move across the Water-Tier. Approach the Stairway to the Air-Tier. Before entering the Second Stairway, say:

Behold my brethren, God is ready to open his merciful star-houses and Gates of Understanding unto you. But he that liveth for himself, and for the end of this shadow, limiteth his wisdom with this number, and shall both have an end at once.

Climb the Second Stairway, which has twelve steps, to the Air-Tier. Visualize the Sephirothic Cross Angel IDOIGO before you. Approach the Angel unafraid; open your arms and embrace her. Feel her body melt into your own and become a part of you. Assume the god-form of IDOIGO, who guards the Air-Tier and Third Stairway (position 59), as follows:

The god-form of IDOIGO: See page 239 for the god-form of IDOIGO.

The Third Stairway is yellow and smells of mint. The Third Stairway is also wet and hot. There are seven steps, each of which bears a letter written in blue that is blazing to look upon. The letter E is on the first step, G is on the second, H is on the third, I is on the fourth, L on the fifth, O on the sixth, and S on the seventh.[6] Recite the words written above the Third Stairway before ascending:

I will bless all that thou takest in hand, and will cover thee with a Robe of Purple, that thou mayest understand that all is mine, and that I raise up whom I list.

Pathworking the Watchtower of Air

Step 8. In the god-form of a Sephirothic Cross Angel of Air, slowly repeat the magic word MUM as you climb. Climb up to the top of the Third Stairway and say:

I am a Sephirothic Cross Angel of Air. I am the Sephirothic Cross Angel IDOIGO. I bear the Cross of Air from Water to Air within Air.

Step 9. As IDOIGO, slowly repeat the magic word MUM, and at the top of the Third Stairway, turn toward the center of the Fire-Tier, which is the center of the mandala. If you are male, assume the naked god-form of the King of Air, BATAIVAH. If you are female, assume the naked god-form of the Goddess of Air, ALOBABN.

Step 10. Same as Step 9 of Path 33.

Step 11. Same as Step 10 of Path 33.

Step 12. Turn from your consort and step outside the yellow hexagram. Leave by the same path that you entered. After leaving the mandala, conduct the banishing pentagram ritual. This completes the forty-second initiatory path.

PATH FORTY-THREE

The Path of Contentment leads through the four positions 50-51-59-63, as shown in Figure 66. It contains the specific atmospheres of protection and prosperity. It is the Third Path of Communication. Use this path for psychic health and contentment.

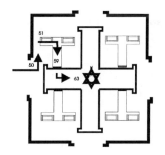

Figure 66: Path 43, The Path of Contentment

Step 1. Make a circle and conduct the invoking pentagram ritual.

Step 2. Face the East, and imagine the Mandala of the Watchtower of Air clearly before you. You are facing the western wall of the mandala. Imagine the walls and floors to be yellow. Recite the Centering Spell. Then say:

**May I enter and safely pass through this yellow Watchtower of Air.
May I obtain success in this, the forty-third of my initiations.
In the threefold secret and holy name of OROIBAHAOZPI
I make this request. TOLTORGI-A GIGIPAHE ASAPATA
OTAHILA SOBA OOAONA KAHISA RA-AS OD BOLANU.**

Step 3. Visualize the closed Pine Gate. say: O XFMND I invoke thee. Come unto me from the Watchtower of Water. Visualize XFMND before you. Approach the Angel unafraid; open your arms and embrace him. Feel his body melt into your own and become a part of you. Assume the god-form of the Angel XFMND ("etz-feh-men-deh"), who guards the Pine Gate (position 50), as follows:

The god-form of XFMND: See page 243 for the god-form of XFMND.

There are special words written above the Pine Gate to be spoken before entering. say:

The Angels' Message to Humanity

Cast away your murmuring, and sweep your houses, take heed of spiders, and of the whore rats.

Step 4. Visualize the gate opening at these words. Step within the Pine Gate. Face the Earth-Tier. In the god-form of XFMND, say:

**I am the Angel of Air. I am the Angel XFMND.
I am the Guardian of the Pine Gate. I enter into the Watchtower of Air.**

While slowly repeating the Threefold Holy Word, enter the Watchtower of Air and move across the Earth-Tier to the bottom of the Almond Stairway leading up to the Water-Tier (position 51). The Threefold Word that you recite will protect you from the demons who reside on the Earth-Tier.

Step 5. Face the Almond Stairway. Visualize the Kerubic Angel RZLA before you. Approach the Angel unafraid; open your arms and embrace him. Feel his body melt into your own and become a part of you. Assume the god-form of RZLA, who guards the Almond Stairway, as follows:

The god-form of RZLA: See page 242 for the god-form of RZLA.

Recite the words written over the Almond Stairway:

The King of Darkness wetteth his teeth against thee, and rampeth with great rage to overwhelm the world upon thee.

Step 6. In the god-form of the Kerubic Angel of Air, RZLA, while slowly repeating the magic word HUM, climb the six steps of the Almond Stairway to the Water-Tier. Then say:

**I am a Kerubic Angel of Air. I am Kerubic Angel RZLA.
I am the Guardian of the Almond Stairway. I rise up
through the Watchtower of Air. Throughout eternity
I move myself about from Earth to Water within Air.**

Step 7. Slowly repeat the magic word HUM as you move across the Water-Tier. Approach the Stairway to the Air-Tier. Before entering the Second Stairway, say:

Behold my brethren, God is ready to open his merciful star-houses and Gates of Understanding unto you. But he that liveth for himself, and for the end of this shadow, limiteth his wisdom with this number, and shall both have an end at once.

Climb the Second Stairway, which has twelve steps, to the Air-Tier. Visualize the Sephirothic Cross Angel IDOIGO before you. Approach the Angel unafraid; open your arms and embrace her. Feel her body melt into your own and become a part of you. Assume the god-form of the Sephirothic Cross Angel IDOIGO, who guards the Air-Tier and Third Stairway (position 59), as follows:

The god-form of IDOIGO: See page 239 for the god-form of IDOIGO.

The Third Stairway is yellow and smells of mint. The Third Stairway is also wet and hot. There are seven steps, each of which bears a letter written in blue that is

Pathworking the Watchtower of Air

blazing to look upon. The letter *E* is on the first step, *G* is on the second, *H* is on the third, *I* is on the fourth, *L* on the fifth, *O* on the sixth, and *S* on the seventh.[6] Recite the words written above the Third Stairway before ascending:

> I will bless all that thou takest in hand, and will cover thee with a Robe of Purple, that thou mayest understand that all is mine, and that I raise up whom I list.

Step 8. In the god-form of a Sephirothic Cross Angel of Air, slowly repeat the magic word MUM as you climb. Climb up to the top of the Third Stairway and say:

> I am a Sephirothic Cross Angel of Air. I am the Sephirothic Cross Angel IDOIGO. I bear the Cross of Air from Water to Air within Air.

Step 9. As IDOIGO, slowly repeat the magic word MUM, and at the top of the Third Stairway, turn toward the center of the Fire-Tier, which is the center of the mandala. If you are male, assume the naked god-form of the King of Air, BATAIVAH. If you are female, assume the naked god-form of the Goddess of Air, ALOBABN.

Step 10. Same as Step 9 of Path 33.

Step 11. Same as Step 10 of Path 33.

Step 12. Turn from your consort and step outside the yellow hexagram. Leave by the same path that you entered. After leaving the mandala, conduct the banishing pentagram ritual. This completes the forty-third initiatory path.

PATH FORTY-FOUR

The Path of Insulation leads through the four positions 50-52-59-63, as shown in Figure 67. It contains the specific atmospheres of protection and psychic power. It is the Fourth Path of Communication. Use this path for protection from psychic attack.

Step 1. Make a circle and conduct the invoking pentagram ritual.

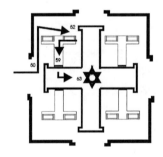

Figure 67: Path 44, The Path of Insulation

Step 2. Face the East, and imagine the Mandala of the Watchtower of Air clearly before you. You are facing the western wall of the mandala. Imagine the walls and floors to be yellow. Recite the Centering Spell. Then say:

> May I enter and safely pass through this yellow Watchtower of Air.
> May I obtain success in this, the forty-fourth of my initiations.
> In the threefold secret and holy name of OROIBAHAOZPI
> I make this request. TOLTORGI-A GIGIPAHE ASAPATA
> OTAHILA SOBA OOAONA KAHISA RA-AS OD BOLANU.

Step 3. Visualize the closed Pine Gate. say: O XFMND I invoke thee. Come unto me from the Watchtower of Water. Visualize XFMND before you. Approach the

The Angels' Message to Humanity

Angel unafraid; open your arms and embrace him. Feel his body melt into your own and become a part of you. Assume the god-form of the Angel XFMND, who guards the Pine Gate (position 50), as follows:

The god-form of XFMND: See page 243 for the god-form of XFMND.

There are special words written above the Pine Gate to be spoken before entering. say:

**Cast away your murmuring, and sweep your houses,
take heed of spiders, and of the whore rats.**

Step 4. Visualize the gate opening at these words. Step within the Pine Gate. Face the Earth-Tier. In the god-form of XFMND, say:

**I am the Angel of Air. I am the Angel XFMND. I am
the Guardian of the Pine Gate. I enter into the Watchtower of Air.**

While slowly repeating the Threefold Holy Word, enter the Watchtower of Air and move across the Earth-Tier to the bottom of the Anise Stairway leading up to the Water-Tier (position 51). The Threefold Word that you recite will protect you from the demons who reside on the Earth-Tier.

Step 5. Face the Anise Stairway. Visualize the Kerubic Angel LARZ before you. Approach the Angel unafraid; open your arms and embrace him. Feel his body melt into your own and become a part of you. Assume the god-form of LARZ, who guards the Anise Stairway, as follows:

The god-form of LARZ: See page 239 for the god-form of LARZ.

Recite the words written over the Anise Stairway:

**But his lips are sealed, and his claws made dull, that when he would bite
he cannot, and where he scratches, the blood follows not.**

Step 6. In the god-form of the Kerubic Angel of Air, LARZ, while slowly repeating the magic word HUM, climb the six steps of the Anise Stairway to the Water-Tier. Then say:

**I am a Kerubic Angel of Air. I am Kerubic Angel LARZ.
I am the Guardian of the Anise Stairway. I rise up
through the Watchtower of Air. Throughout eternity
I move myself about from Earth to Water within Air.**

Step 7. Slowly repeat the magic word HUM as you move across the Water-Tier. Approach the Stairway to the Air-Tier. Before entering the Second Stairway, say:

**Behold my brethren, God is ready to open his merciful star-houses and
Gates of Understanding unto you. But he that liveth for himself, and for
the end of this shadow, limiteth his wisdom with this number, and shall
both have an end at once. Climb the Second Stairway, which has twelve
steps, to the Air-Tier.**

Visualize the Sephirothic Cross Angel IDOIGO before you. Approach the Angel unafraid; open your arms and embrace her. Feel her body melt into your own and become a part of you. Assume the god-form of the Sephirothic Cross Angel IDOIGO, who guards the Air-Tier and Third Stairway (position 59), as follows:

The god-form of IDOIGO: See page 239 for the god-form of IDOIGO.

The Third Stairway is yellow and smells of mint. The Third Stairway is also wet and hot. There are seven steps, each of which bears a letter written in blue that is blazing to look upon. The letter *E* is on the first step, *G* is on the second, *H* is on the third, *I* is on the fourth, *L* on the fifth, *O* on the sixth, and *S* on the seventh.[6] Recite the words written above the Third Stairway before ascending:

I will bless all that thou takest in hand, and will cover thee with a Robe of Purple, that thou mayest understand that all is mine, and that I raise up whom I list.

Step 8. In the god-form of a Sephirothic Cross Angel of Air, slowly repeat the magic word MUM as you climb. Climb up to the top of the Third Stairway and say:

I am a Sephirothic Cross Angel of Air. I am the Sephirothic Cross Angel IDOIGO. I bear the Cross of Air from Water to Air within Air.

Step 9. As IDOIGO, slowly repeat the magic word MUM, and at the top of the Third Stairway, turn toward the center of the Fire-Tier, which is the center of the mandala. If you are male, assume the naked god-form of the King of Air, BATAIVAH. If you are female, assume the naked god-form of the Goddess of Air, ALOBABN.

Step 10. Same as Step 9 of Path 33.

Step 11. Same as Step 10 of Path 33.

Step 12. Turn from your consort and step outside the yellow hexagram. Leave by the same path that you entered. After leaving the mandala, conduct the banishing pentagram ritual. This completes the forty-fourth initiatory path.

THE FIRE QUADRANT OF THE AIR MANDALA

PATH FORTY-FIVE

The Path of Intelligence leads through the four positions 45-58-62-63, as shown in Figure 68. It contains the specific atmospheres of knowledge, intelligence, psychic power, and potency. It is the First Path of Karma. Use this path to enhance your intelligence and thinking ability.

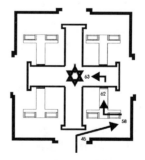

Figure 68: Path 45, The Path of Intelligence

Step 1. Make a circle and conduct the invoking pentagram ritual.

Step 2. Face the North, and imagine the Mandala of the Watchtower of Air clearly before you. You are facing the southern wall of the mandala. Imagine the walls and floors to be yellow. Recite the Centering Spell. Then say:

The Angels' Message to Humanity

May I enter and safely pass through this yellow Watchtower of Air. May I obtain success in this, the forty-fifth of my initiations. In the threefold secret and holy name of OROIBAHAOZPI I make this request. TOLTORGI-A GIGIPAHE ASAPATA OTAHILA SOBA OOAONA KAHISA RA-AS OD BOLANU.

Step 3. Visualize the closed Adventurine Gate. say: O PAKKA I invoke thee. Come unto me from the Watchtower of Water. Visualize PAKKA before you. Approach the Angel unafraid; open your arms and embrace him. Feel his body melt into your own and become a part of you. Assume the god-form of the Angel PAKKA ("pah-keh-kah"), who guards the Aventurine Gate (position 45), as follows:

The god-form of PAKKA: See page 241 for the god-form of PAKKA

There are special words written above the Aventurine Gate to be spoken before entering. say:

Behold, the Scourge is with you.

Step 4. Visualize the gate opening at these words. Step within the Aventurine Gate. Face the Earth-Tier. In the god-form of PAKKA, say:

I am the Angel of Air. I am the Angel PAKKA. I am the Guardian of the Aventurine Gate. I enter into the Watchtower of Air.

While slowly repeating the Threefold Holy Word, enter the Watchtower of Air and move across the Earth-Tier to the bottom of the Palm Stairway leading up to the Water-Tier (position 58). The Threefold Word that you recite will protect you from the demons who reside on the Earth-Tier.

Step 5. Face the Palm Stairway. Visualize the Kerubic Angel ZDXG before you. Approach the Angel unafraid; open your arms and embrace him. Feel his body melt into your own and become a part of you. Assume the god-form of ZDXG ("zeh-detz- geh"), who guards the Palm Stairway, as follows:

The god-form of ZDXG: See page 244 for the god-form of ZDXG.

Recite the words written over the Palm Stairway:

**But in the midst of his triumph he shall fall,
as a proud Tree doth, whose roots are uncertain.**

Step 6. In the god-form of the Kerubic Angel of Air, ZDXG, while slowly repeating the magic word HUM, climb the seven steps of the Palm Stairway to the Water-Tier. Then say:

I am a Kerubic Angel of Air. I am Kerubic Angel ZDXG. I am the Guardian of the Palm Stairway. I rise up through the Watchtower of Air. Throughout eternity I move myself about from Earth to Water within Air.

Step 7. Slowly repeat the magic word HUM as you move across the Water-Tier. Approach the Stairway to the Air-Tier. Before entering the Second Stairway, say:

Behold my brethren, God is ready to open his merciful star-houses and Gates of Understanding unto you. But he that liveth for himself, and for

Pathworking the Watchtower of Air

the end of this shadow, limiteth his wisdom with this number, and shall both have an end at once.

Climb the Second Stairway, which has nine steps, to the Air-Tier. Visualize the Sephirothic Cross Angel AOVRRZ before you. Approach the Angel unafraid; open your arms and embrace him. Feel his body melt into your own and become a part of you. Assume the god-form of AOVRRZ ("ah-oh-var-rah-zeh"), who guards the Air-Tier and Third Stairway (position 62), as follows:

The god-form of AOVRRZ: See page 237 for the god-form of AOVRRZ.

The Third Stairway is yellow and smells of mint. The Third Stairway is also wet and hot. There are seven steps, each of which bears a letter written in blue that is blazing to look upon. The letter *E* is on the first step, *G* is on the second, *H* is on the third, *I* is on the fourth, *L* on the fifth, *O* on the sixth, and *S* on the seventh.[6] Recite the words written above the Third Stairway before ascending:

For the root of number is one. And things that ascend are dignified by order. Out of this vessel go four vents ascending into that Rock, which is the Root, which is this building.

Step 8. In the god-form of a Sephirothic Cross Angel of Air, slowly repeat the magic word MUM as you climb. Climb up to the top of the Third Stairway and say:

I am a Sephirothic Cross Angel of Air. I am the Sephirothic Cross Angel IDOIGO. I bear the Cross of Air from Water to Air within Air.

Step 9. As IDOIGO, slowly repeat the magic word MUM, and at the top of the Third Stairway, turn toward the center of the Fire-Tier, which is the center of the mandala. If you are male, assume the naked god-form of the King of Air, BATAIVAH. If you are female, assume the naked god-form of the Goddess of Air, ALOBABN.

Step 10. Same as Step 9 of Path 33.

Step 11. Same as Step 10 of Path 33.

Step 12. Turn from your consort and step outside the yellow hexagram. Leave by the same path that you entered. After leaving the mandala, conduct the banishing pentagram ritual. This completes the forty-fifth initiatory path.

PATH FORTY-SIX

The Path of Psychic Knowledge leads through the four positions 45-57-62-63, as shown in Figure 69. It contains the specific atmospheres of knowledge, intelligence, love, and prosperity. It is the Second Path of Karma. Use this path to obtain knowledge of psychic realms.

Step 1. Make a circle and conduct the invoking pentagram ritual.

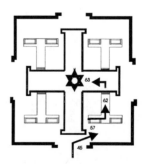

Figure 69: Path 46, The Path of Physical Knowledge

The Angels' Message to Humanity

Step 2. Face the North, and imagine the Mandala of the Watchtower of Air clearly before you. You are facing the southern wall of the mandala. Imagine the walls and floors to be yellow. Recite the Centering Spell. Then say:

> May I enter and safely pass through this yellow Watchtower of Air.
> May I obtain success in this, the forty-sixth of my initiations.
> In the threefold secret and holy name of OROIBAHAOZPI
> I make this request. TOLTORGI-A GIGIPAHE ASAPATA
> OTAHILA SOBA OOAONA KAHISA RA-AS OD BOLANU.

Step 3. Visualize the closed Adventurine Gate. say:

> O PAKKA I invoke thee. Come unto me from the Watchtower of Water.

Visualize PAKKA before you. Approach the Angel unafraid; open your arms and embrace him. Feel his body melt into your own and become a part of you. Assume the god-form of the Angel PAKKA, who guards the Aventurine Gate (position 45), as follows:

The god-form of PAKKA: See page 241 for the god-form of PAKKA.

There are special words written above the Aventurine Gate to be spoken before entering. say:

> **Behold, the Scourge is with you.**

Step 4. Visualize the gate opening at these words. Step within the Aventurine Gate. Face the Earth-Tier. In the god-form of PAKKA, say:

> I am the Angel of Air. I am the Angel PAKKA. I am the Guardian
> of the Aventurine Gate. I enter into the Watchtower of Air.

While slowly repeating the Threefold Holy Word, enter the Watchtower of Air and move across the Earth-Tier to the bottom of the Pecan Stairway leading up to the Water-Tier (position 57). The Threefold Word that you recite will protect you from the demons who reside on the Earth-Tier.

Step 5. Face the Pecan Stairway. Visualize the Kerubic Angel XGZD before you. Approach the Angel unafraid; open your arms and embrace him. Feel his body melt into your own and become a part of you. Assume the god-form of XGZD ("etz-geh- zeh-deh"), who guards the Pecan Stairway, as follows:

The god-form of XGZD: See page 243 for the god-form of XGZD.

Recite the words written over the Pecan Stairway:

> O thou whose look is more terrible unto thy Angels, than all the fires
> which thou hast created, either in the Bottomless Pit
> or in the life of all Elemental Creatures, or above in the heavens.

Step 6. In the god-form of the Kerubic Angel of Air, XGZD, while slowly repeating the magic word HUM, climb the seven steps of the Pecan Stairway to the Water-Tier. Then say:

Pathworking the Watchtower of Air

> I am a Kerubic Angel of Air. I am Kerubic Angel XGZD.
> I am the Guardian of the Pecan Stairway. I rise up
> through the Watchtower of Air. Throughout eternity
> I move myself about from Earth to Water within Air.

Step 7. Slowly repeat the magic word HUM as you move across the Water-Tier. Approach the Stairway to the Air-Tier. Before entering the Second Stairway, say:

> Behold my brethren, God is ready to open his merciful star-houses and Gates of Understanding unto you. But he that liveth for himself, and for the end of this shadow, limiteth his wisdom with this number, and shall both have an end at once.

Climb the Second Stairway, which has nine steps, to the Air-Tier. Visualize the Sephirothic Cross Angel AOVRRZ before you. Approach the Angel unafraid; open your arms and embrace him. Feel his body melt into your own and become a part of you. Assume the god-form of AOVRRZ, who guards the Air-Tier and Third Stairway (position 62), as follows:

The god-form of AOVRRZ: See page 237 for the god-form of AOVRRZ.

The Third Stairway is yellow and smells of mint. The Third Stairway is also wet and hot. There are seven steps, each of which bears a letter written in blue that is blazing to look upon. The letter *E* is on the first step, *G* is on the second, *H* is on the third, *I* is on the fourth, *L* on the fifth, *O* on the sixth, and *S* on the seventh.[6] Recite the words written above the Third Stairway before ascending:

> For the root of number is one. And things that ascend are dignified by order. Out of this vessel go four vents ascending into that Rock, which is the Root, which is this building.

Step 8. In the god-form of a Sephirothic Cross Angel of Air, slowly repeat the magic word MUM as you climb. Climb up to the top of the Third Stairway and say:

> I am a Sephirothic Cross Angel of Air. I am the Sephirothic Cross Angel IDOIGO. I bear the Cross of Air from Water to Air within Air.

Step 9. As IDOIGO, slowly repeat the magic word MUM, and at the top of the Third Stairway, turn toward the center of the Fire-Tier, which is the center of the mandala. If you are male, assume the naked god-form of the King of Air, BATAIVAH. If you are female, assume the naked god-form of the Goddess of Air, ALOBABN.

Step 10. Same as Step 9 of Path 33.

Step 11. Same as Step 10 of Path 33.

Step 12. Turn from your consort and step outside the yellow hexagram. Leave by the same path that you entered. After leaving the mandala, conduct the banishing pentagram ritual. This completes the forty-sixth initiatory path.

The Angels' Message to Humanity

PATH FORTY-SEVEN

The Path of Mental Health leads through the four positions 46-58-62-63, as shown in Figure 70. It contains the specific atmospheres of health, longevity, psychic power, and potency. It is the Third Path of Karma. Use this path for good mental health.

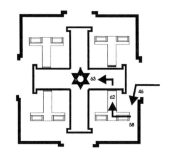

Step 1. Make a circle and conduct the invoking pentagram ritual.

Figure 70: Path 47, The Path of Mental Health

Step 2. Face the West, and imagine the Mandala of the Watchtower of Air clearly before you. You are facing the eastern wall of the mandala. Imagine the walls and floors to be yellow. Recite the Centering Spell. Then say:

> **May I enter and safely pass through this yellow Watchtower of Air.**
> **May I obtain success in this, the forty-seventh of my initiations.**
> **In the threefold secret and holy name of OROIBAHAOZPI**
> **I make this request. TOLTORGI-A GIGIPAHE ASAPATA**
> **OTAHILA SOBA OOAONA KAHISA RA-AS OD BOLANU.**

Step 3. Visualize the closed Maple Gate. say: O PPMOX I invoke thee. Come unto me from the Watchtower of Water. Visualize PPMOX before you. Approach the Angel unafraid; open your arms and embrace her. Feel her body melt into your own and become a part of you. Assume the god-form of the Angel PPMOX ("peh-peh-moh-etz"), who guards the Maple Gate (position 46), as follows:

> **The god-form of PPMOX:** See page 242 for the god-form of PPMOX.

There are special words written above the Maple Gate to be spoken before entering. say:

> **The Gate that you shall enter into, is a Fire of Fury, and of revenge.**

Step 4. Visualize the gate opening at these words. Step within the Maple Gate. Face the Earth-Tier. In the god-form of PPMOX, say:

> **I am the Angel of Air. I am the Angel PPMOX. I am the Guardian**
> **of the Maple Gate. I enter into the Watchtower of Air.**

While slowly repeating the Threefold Holy Word, enter the Watchtower of Air and move across the Earth-Tier to the bottom of the Palm Stairway leading up to the Water-Tier (position 58). The Threefold Word that you recite will protect you from the demons who reside on the Earth-Tier.

Step 5. Face the Palm Stairway. Visualize the Kerubic Angel ZDXG before you. Approach the Angel unafraid; open your arms and embrace him. Feel his body melt into your own and become a part of you. Assume the god-form of ZDXG, who guards the Palm Stairway, as follows:

> **The god-form of ZDXG:** See page 244 for the god-form of ZDXG.

Pathworking the Watchtower of Air

Recite the words written over the Palm Stairway, as follows:

> **But in the midst of his triumph he shall fall, as a proud Tree doth, whose roots are uncertain.**

Step 6. In the god-form of the Kerubic Angel of Air, ZDXG, while slowly repeating the magic word HUM, climb the seven steps of the Almond Stairway to the Water-Tier. Then say:

> **I am a Kerubic Angel of Air. I am Kerubic Angel ZDXG. I am the Guardian of the Palm Stairway. I rise up through the Watchtower of Air. Throughout eternity I move myself about from Earth to Water within Air.**

Step 7. Slowly repeat the magic word HUM as you move across the Water-Tier. Approach the Stairway to the Air-Tier. Before entering the Second Stairway, say:

> **Behold my brethren, God is ready to open his merciful star-houses and Gates of Understanding unto you. But he that liveth for himself, and for the end of this shadow, limiteth his wisdom with this number, and shall both have an end at once.**

Climb the Second Stairway, which has nine steps, to the Air-Tier. Visualize the Sephirothic Cross Angel AOVRRZ before you. Approach the Angel unafraid; open your arms and embrace him. Feel his body melt into your own and become a part of you. Assume the god-form of AOVRRZ, who guards the Air-Tier and Third Stairway (position 62), as follows:

> **The god-form of AOVRRZ:** See page 237 for the god-form of AOVRRZ.

The Third Stairway is yellow and smells of mint. The Third Stairway is also wet and hot. There are seven steps, each of which bears a letter written in blue that is blazing to look upon. The letter *E* is on the first step, *G* is on the second, *H* is on the third, *I* is on the fourth, *L* on the fifth, *O* on the sixth, and *S* on the seventh.[6] Recite the words written above the Third Stairway before ascending:

> **For the root of number is one. And things that ascend are dignified by order. Out of this vessel go four vents ascending into that Rock, which is the Root, which is this building.**

Step 8. In the god-form of a Sephirothic Cross Angel of Air, slowly repeat the magic word MUM as you climb. Climb up to the top of the Third Stairway and say:

> **I am a Sephirothic Cross Angel of Air. I am the Sephirothic Cross Angel IDOIGO. I bear the Cross of Air from Water to Air within Air.**

Step 9. As IDOIGO, slowly repeat the magic word MUM, and at the top of the Third Stairway, turn toward the center of the Fire-Tier, which is the center of the mandala. If you are male, assume the naked god-form of the King of Air, BATAIVAH. If you are female, assume the naked god-form of the Goddess of Air, ALOBABN.

Step 10. Same as Step 9 of Path 33.

Step 11. Same as Step 10 of Path 33.

The Angels' Message to Humanity

Step 12. Turn from your consort and step outside the yellow hexagram. Leave by the same path that you entered. After leaving the mandala, conduct the banishing pentagram ritual. This completes the forty-seventh initiatory path.

Path Forty-Eight

The Path of Longevity leads through the four positions 46-57-62-63, as shown in Figure 71. It contains the specific atmospheres of health, longevity, love, and prosperity. It is the Fourth Path of Karma. Use this path to ensure a long life.

Step 1. Make a circle and conduct the invoking pentagram ritual.

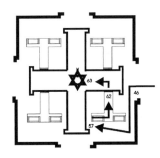

Figure 71: Path 48, The Path of Longevity

Step 2. Face the West, and imagine the Mandala of the Watchtower of Air clearly before you. You are facing the eastern wall of the mandala. Imagine the walls and floors to be yellow. Recite the Centering Spell. Then say:

> May I enter and safely pass through this yellow Watchtower of Air.
> May I obtain success in this, the forty-eighth of my initiations.
> In the threefold secret and holy name of OROIBAHAOZPI
> I make this request. TOLTORGI-A GIGIPAHE ASAPATA
> OTAHILA SOBA OOAONA KAHISA RA-AS OD BOLANU.

Step 3. Visualize the closed Maple Gate. say: O PPMOX I invoke thee. Come unto me from the Watchtower of Water. Visualize PPMOX before you. Approach the Angel unafraid; open your arms and embrace her. Feel her body melt into your own and become a part of you. Assume the god-form of the Angel PPMOX, who guards the Maple Gate (position 46), as follows:

The god-form of PPMOX: See page 242 for the god-form of PPMOX.

There are special words written above the Maple Gate to be spoken before entering. say:

The Gate that you shall enter into, is a Fire of Fury, and of revenge.

Step 4. Visualize the gate opening at these words. Step within the Maple Gate. Face the Earth-Tier. In the god-form of PPMOX, say:

> I am the Angel of Air. I am the Angel PPMOX. I am
> the Guardian of the Maple Gate. I enter into the Watchtower of Air.

While slowly repeating the Threefold Holy Word, enter the Watchtower of Air, and move across the Earth-Tier to the bottom of the Pecan Stairway leading up to the Water-Tier (position 58). The Threefold Word that you recite will protect you from the demons who reside on the Earth-Tier.

Pathworking the Watchtower of Air

Step 5. Face the Pecan Stairway. Visualize the Kerubic Angel XGZD before you. Approach the Angel unafraid; open your arms and embrace him. Feel his body melt into your own and become a part of you. Assume the god-form of XGZD, who guards the Pecan Stairway, as follows:

The god-form of XGZD: See page 243 for the god- form of XGZD.

Recite the words written over the Pecan Stairway:

> **O thou whose look is more terrible unto thy Angels, then all the fires which thou hast created, either in the Bottomless Pit or in the life of all Elemental Creatures, or above in the heavens.**

Step 6. In the god-form of the Kerubic Angel of Air, XGZD, while slowly repeating the magic word HUM, climb the seven steps of the Pecan Stairway to the Water-Tier. Then say:

> **I am a Kerubic Angel of Air. I am Kerubic Angel XGZD. I am the Guardian of the Pecan Stairway. I rise up through the Watchtower of Air. Throughout eternity I move myself about from Earth to Water within Air.**

Step 7. Slowly repeat the magic word HUM as you move across the Water-Tier. Approach the Stairway to the Air-Tier. Before entering the Second Stairway, say:

> **Behold my brethren, God is ready to open his merciful star-houses and Gates of Understanding unto you. But he that liveth for himself, and for the end of this shadow, limiteth his wisdom with this number, and shall both have an end at once.**

Climb the Second Stairway, which has nine steps, to the Air-Tier. Visualize the Sephirothic Cross Angel AOVRRZ before you. Approach the Angel unafraid; open your arms and embrace him. Feel his body melt into your own and become a part of you. Assume the god-form of AOVRRZ, who guards the Air-Tier and Third Stairway (position 62), as follows:

The god-form of AOVRRZ: See page 237 for the god-form of AOVRRZ.

The Third Stairway is yellow and smells of mint. The Third Stairway is also wet and hot. There are seven steps, each of which bears a letter written in blue that is blazing to look upon. The letter *E* is on the first step, *G* is on the second, *H* is on the third, *I* is on the fourth, *L* on the fifth, *O* on the sixth, and *S* on the seventh.[6] Recite the words written above the Third Stairway before ascending:

> **For the root of number is one. And things that ascend are dignified by order. Out of this vessel go four vents ascending into that Rock, which is the Root, which is this building.**

Step 8. In the god-form of a Sephirothic Cross Angel of Air, slowly repeat the magic word MUM as you climb. Climb up to the top of the Third Stairway and say:

The Angels' Message to Humanity

I am a Sephirothic Cross Angel of Air. I am the Sephirothic Cross Angel IDOIGO. I bear the Cross of Air from Water to Air within Air.

Step 9. As IDOIGO, slowly repeat the magic word MUM, and at the top of the Third Stairway, turn toward the center of the Fire-Tier, which is the center of the mandala. If you are male, assume the naked god-form of the King of Air, BATAIVAH. If you are female, assume the naked god-form of the Goddess of Air, ALOBABN.

Step 10. Same as Step 9 of Path 33.

Step 11. Same as Step 10 of Path 33.

Step 12. Turn from your consort and step outside the yellow hexagram. Leave by the same path that you entered. After leaving the mandala, conduct the banishing pentagram ritual. This completes the forty-eighth initiatory path.

NOTES TO CHAPTER TWELVE

1. The last two lines contain a magical spell. This short spell is to be spoken aloud in the Enochian language. The words mean, "There are creatures of living breath before the Throne, whose eyes are East and West." Using gematria, the letters add up to 1,493, which reduces to 8 (1+4+9+3=17=1+7=8).

2. The words on these eight Gates are from pp. 390 and 391 of Casaubon.

3. The words on the Second Stairways of Air are from pp. 216-221 of Casaubon.

4. The Enochian word HUM is given in Table 21 of our *Enochian Yoga* (St. Paul, MN: Llewellyn Publishing, 1990) as an Enochian magic word associated with the Heart Center (*Anahata* chakra).

5. These words were spoken by the Angel URIEL to Dee (see p. 224 of Casaubon).

6. The letters on the steps correspond to the letters of the Heart Center, as given in our *Enochian Yoga* (St. Paul, MN: Llewellyn Publishing, 1990). For best results, these letters should be visualized in Enochian as follows:

    E=⁊, G=ხ, H=ෆ, I=ℒ, L=C, O=ℒ, S=⁊

7. These words are from Casaubon, pp. 238 and 358.

8. The Enochian word MUM, like HUM, is given in Table 21 of our *Enochian Yoga* (St. Paul, MN: Llewellyn Publishing, 1990) as an Enochian magic word associated with the Heart Center (*Anahata* chakra).

9. The names of the primary god and goddess of the Air Mandala are found in Table 21 of our *Enochian Yoga* (St. Paul, MN: Llewellyn Publishing, 1990), where they are also associated with the Heart Center.

10. These god-forms are from our *Enochian Yoga* (St. Paul, MN: Llewellyn Publishing, 1990, p. 170, "The Heart Center").

11. This passage is taken from Casaubon, p. 43.

12. This message is taken from Casaubon, p. 58.

13. Steps 10 and 11 are identical for each of the exercises in the Watchtower of Air. To conserve space, we refer you to those steps given fully in path 33 rather than repeat them throughout.

Chapter 13

PATHWORKING THE WATCHTOWER OF FIRE

This chapter contains the fourth set of initiatory paths, paths 49 through 64. In these paths, you will use the Watchtower Mandala of Fire as shown in color plate IV. The critical 21 positions within the mandala are shown in Figure 72. The names of the entrance gates and first stairways are shown in Figure 73. The names and positions of the 22 deities of the Mandala of Fire are shown in Figure 74. Figures 75 through 90 show the 16 paths that you will take through the Fire Mandala.

THE EARTH QUADRANT OF THE FIRE MANDALA

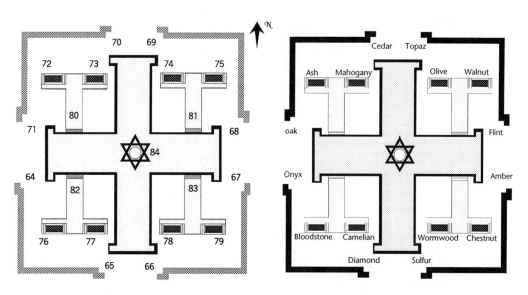

Figure 72: The Fire Mandala Showing Position Numbers

Figure 73: The Fire Mandala Showing Gates and Stairways

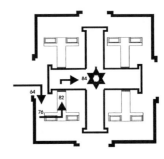

Figure 74: The Fire Mandala
Showing Deities

Figure 75: Path 49, The Path of Healing

PATH FORTY-NINE

The Path of Healing leads through the 4 positions 64-76-82-84 as shown in Figure 75. It contains the specific atmospheres of sexual energy, protection, knowledge, and healing. It is the First Path of Spiritualization. Use this path for any kind of healing.

Step 1. Make a circle and conduct the invoking pentagram ritual.

Step 2. Face the East, and imagine the Mandala of the Watchtower of Fire clearly before you. You are facing the western wall of the mandala. Imagine the walls and floors to be flame red. Recite the Centering Spell. Then say:

> May I enter and safely pass through this red Watchtower of Fire.
> May I obtain success in this, the forty-ninth of my initiations.
> In the threefold secret and holy name of OIPTEAAPDOKE
> I make this request. OEKARIMI NOTAHOA IALAPEREGI
> OD KA-KA-KOM DO-ZILODAREPE[1]

Step 3. Visualize the closed Onyx Gate. say:

> O ODATT I invoke thee. Come unto me from the Watchtower of Water.

Visualize ODATT materializing before you. Approach the Angel unafraid, open your arms and embrace him. Feel his body melt into your own body and become a part of you. Assume the god-form of the Angel ODATT (Oh-dah-teh-teh) who guards the Onyx Gate (position 64) as follows:

The god-form of ODATT: See page 241 for the god-form of ODATT.

There are special words written above the Onyx Gate to be spoken before entering. say:

Pathworking the Watchtower of Fire

No man that seeks the brightness of the Sun goes under the Earth. Neither creeps he into unknown Caves. The tigers seek not their prey upon Earth where the waters are not. Neither the eagles upon waters.[2]

Step 4. Visualize the gate opening at these words. Step within the Onyx Gate. Face the Earth-Tier. In the god-form of ODATT, say:

I am the Angel of Fire. I am the Angel ODATT. I am the Guardian of the Onyx Gate. I enter into the Watchtower of Fire.

While slowly repeating the Threefold Holy Word, enter into the Watchtower of Fire and move across the Earth-Tier to the bottom of the Bloodstone Stairway leading up to the Water-Tier (position 76). The Threefold Word that you recite will protect you from the Demons who reside on the Earth-Tier.

Step 5. Face the Bloodstone Stairway. Visualize the Kerubic Angel PSAK materializing before you. Approach the Angel unafraid, open your arms and embrace him. Feel his body melt into your own body and become a part of you. Assume the god-form of PSAK (Peh-sah-keh) who guards the Water-Tier Stairway as follows:

The god-form of PSAK: A strong masculine Kerubic Angel with small wings wearing an amber robe. He holds a red rose that bestows beauty.

Recite the words written over the Bloodstone Stairway:

I have attained unto the knowledge and secrets of the things in Nature.[3]

Step 6. In the god-form of the Kerubic Angel of Fire, PSAK, while slowly reciting the magic word KUM[4], climb the 7 steps of the Bloodstone Stairway to the Water-Tier. Then say:

I am a Kerubic Angel of Fire. I am Kerubic Angel PSAK. I am the Guardian of the Bloodstone Stairway. I rise up through the Watchtower of Fire. Throughout eternity I purify myself from Earth to Water within Fire.

Step 7. Slowly repeat the magic word KUM as you move across the Water-Tier. Approach the Stairway to the Air-Tier. Before entering the Second Stairway, say:

As the Sun deprives the Moon in respect of her end, which is to give light, but not of her self; so do the Angels and higher powers, drown and overshadow the soul in man when they are present.[5]

Climb the Second Stairway, which has 11 steps, to the Air-Tier. Visualize the Sephirothic Cross Angel VOLXDO materializing before you. Approach the Angel unafraid, open your arms and embrace him. Feel his body melt into your own body and become a part of you. Assume the god-form of VOLXDO (Voh-letz-doh) who guards the Air-Tier and Third Stairway (position 82) as follows:

The god-form of VOLXDO: See page 243 for the god-form of VOLXDO.

The Third Stairway is red and smells of cinnamon. The Third Stairway is also dry and hot. There are 3 steps. Each step has a letter written in green that is blazing to

The Angels' Message to Humanity

look upon. The letter *B* is on the first step, *F* is on the second, and *K* is on the third.[6] Recite the words written above the appropriate Third Stairway before ascending:

> **I came from the Fountain of Light, where there is no error or darkness, and I have Power, because it is given me from the Highest, which, Lo, is grown and become a mighty Rock.[7]**

Step 8. In the god-form of a Sephirothic Cross Angel of Fire, slowly repeat the magic word RI[8] (Ree) as you climb. Climb up to the top of the Third Stairway and say:

> **I am a Sephirothic Cross Angel of Fire. I am Sephirothic Cross Angel VOLXDO. I bear the Cross of Fire from Water to Air within Fire.**

Step 9. As VOLXDO, slowly repeat the word RI and at the top of the Stairway, turn toward the center of the Fire-Tier, which is also the center of the mandala. If you are male, assume the naked god-form of the King of Fire, EDLPRNAA (Eh-del-par-nah-ah). If you are female, assume the naked god-form of the Goddess of Fire, BALOBAN (Bah-loh-bah-neh).[9]

The god-form of EDLPRNAA: See page 238 for the god-form of EDLPRNAA.

The god-form of BALOBAN: See page 238 for the god-form of BALOBAN.[10]

Step 10. Slowly repeat the name of your consort (either EDLPRNAA or BALOBAN) while walking along the Fire-Tier, the Great Cross of the Watchtower, toward the center which is a large fiery red hexagram with flames dancing around the circumference. In the center of the hexagram is a white circle. If you are male, visualize your consort, BALOBAN, standing naked at the center of the red hexagram (position 84) waiting for you. If you are female, visualize your consort, EDLPRNAA, standing naked at the center of the hexagram (position 84) waiting for you.

Step 11. Stand just outside of the fiery red hexagram, face your consort who is naked and very beautiful before you, and say:

> **For it is written, Wisdom sits upon a Hill, and beholds the four Winds, and girds herself together as the Brightness of the Morning, for she is visited by a few, and dwells alone as though she were a Widow.[11]**

While you face each other, enter into the flaming hexagram. See yourself clearly at the center of the Fire Mandala. Then you smile at each other as if in love. Then you move together and hold each other. While saying the word BITOM, merge God/King and Goddess of Fire together while holding a detailed awareness of the Watchtower around you. Remain this way for as long as you can, and then say:

> **In this is the life of MOTION, in whom all tongues of the world are moved, for there is neither speech nor silence that was or shall be to the end of the world, but they are all as plain here, as in their own nakedness. Despise it not, therefore, for unto them that are hungry, it is bread, unto the thirsty drink, and unto the naked clothing. A Serpent it is of many heads invincible.[12]**

Pathworking the Watchtower of Fire

Step 12. Turn from your consort and step outside of the red hexagram. Leave by the same path that you entered. After leaving the Mandala, conduct the banishing pentagram ritual. This completes the forty-ninth initiatory path.

PATH FIFTY

The Path of Security leads through the 4 positions 64- 77-82-84 as shown in Figure 76. It contains the specific atmospheres of sexual energy and protection. It is the Second Path of Spiritualization. Use this path for protection against harm of any kind, but especially to prevent rape.

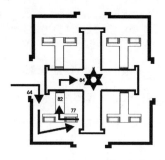

Figure 76: Path 50, The Path of Security

Step 1. Make a circle and conduct the invoking pentagram ritual.

Step 2. Face the East, and imagine the Mandala of the Watchtower of Fire clearly before you. You are facing the western wall of the mandala. Imagine the walls and floors to be flame red. Recite the Centering Spell. Then say:

> May I enter and safely pass through this red Watchtower of Fire.
> May I obtain success in this, the fiftieth of my initiations.
> In the threefold secret and holy name of OIPTEAAPDOKE
> I make this request. OEKARIMI NOTAHOA IALAPEREGI
> OD KA-KA-KOM DO-ZILODAREPE

Step 3. Visualize the closed Onyx Gate. say: O ODATT I invoke thee. Come unto me from the Watchtower of Water. Visualize ODATT materializing before you. Approach the Angel unafraid, open your arms and embrace him. Feel his body melt into your own body and become a part of you. Assume the god-form of the Angel ODATT who guards the Onyx Gate (position 64) as follows:

> **The god-form of ODATT:** See page 241 for the god-form of ODATT.

There are special words written above the Onyx Gate to be spoken before entering. say:

> No man that seeks the brightness of the Sun goes under the Earth.
> Neither creeps he into unknown Caves. The tigers seek not their prey
> upon Earth where the waters are not. Neither the eagles upon waters.[13]

Step 4. Visualize the gate opening at these words. Step within the Onyx Gate. Face the Earth-Tier. In the god-form of ODATT, say:

> I am the Angel of Fire. I am the Angel ODATT. I am the Guardian
> of the Onyx Gate. I enter into the Watchtower of Fire.

While slowly repeating the Threefold Holy Word, enter into the Watchtower of Fire and move across the Earth-Tier to the bottom of the Carnelian Stairway leading up to the Water-Tier (position 77). The Threefold Word that you recite will protect you from the Demons who reside on the Earth-Tier.

Step 5. Face the Carnelian Stairway. Visualize the Kerubic Angel AKPS materializing before you. Approach the Angel unafraid, open your arms and embrace him. Feel his body melt into your own body and become a part of you. Assume the god-form of AKPS (Ah-keh-pess) who guards the Water-Tier Stairway as follows:

The god-form of AKPS: See page 236 for the god-form of AKPS.

Recite the words written over the Carnelian Stairway:

Woe be unto the Earth, for it is corrupted. Woe be unto the Earth, for she is surrendered to her adversary. Woe be unto the Earth, she is delivered into the hands of her enemy. Yea, woe be unto the Sons of Men, for their vessels are poisoned. Yet will I be known in the wilderness, and will triumph in my weakness.[14]

Step 6. In the god-form of the Kerubic Angel of Fire, AKPS, while slowly reciting the magic word KUM, climb the 7 steps of the Carnelian Stairway to the Water-Tier. Then say:

I am a Kerubic Angel of Fire. I am Kerubic Angel AKPS. I am the Guardian of the Carnelian Stairway. I rise up through the Watchtower of Fire. Throughout eternity I purify myself from Earth to Water within Fire.

Step 7. Slowly repeat the magic word KUM as you move across the Water-Tier. Approach the Stairway to the Air-Tier. Before entering the Second Stairway, say:

As the Sun deprives the Moon in respect of her end, which is to give light, but not of her self; so do the Angels and higher powers, drown and overshadow the soul in man when they are present.

Climb the Second Stairway, which has 11 steps, to the Air-Tier. Visualize the Sephirothic Cross Angel VOLXDO materializing before you. Approach the Angel unafraid, open your arms and embrace him. Feel his body melt into your own body and become a part of you. Assume the god-form of VOLXDO who guards the Air-Tier and Third Stairway (position 82) as follows:

The god-form of VOLXDO: See page 243 for the god-form of VOLXDO.

The Third Stairway is red and smells of cinnamon. The Third Stairway is also dry and hot. There are 3 steps. Each step has a letter written in green that is blazing to look upon. The letter *B* is on the first step, *F* is on the second, and *K* is on the third. Recite the words written above the appropriate Third Stairway before ascending:

I came from the Fountain of Light, where there is no error or darkness, and I have Power, because it is given me from the Highest, which, Lo, is grown and become a mighty Rock.

Pathworking the Watchtower of Fire

Step 8. In the god-form of a Sephirothic Cross Angel of Fire, slowly repeat the magic word RI as you climb. Climb up to the top of the Third Stairway and say:

I am a Sephirothic Cross Angel of Fire. I am Sephirothic Cross Angel VOLXDO. I bear the Cross of Fire from Water to Air within Fire.

Step 9. As VOLXDO, slowly repeat the word RI and at the top of the Stairway, turn toward the center of the Fire-Tier, which is also the center of the mandala. If you are male, assume the naked god-form of the King of Fire, EDLPRNAA. If you are female, assume the naked god-form of the Goddess of Fire, BALOBAN.

Step 10. Same as Step 10 in Path 49.[15]

Step 11. Same as Step 11 in Path 49.

Step 12. Turn from your consort and step outside of the red hexagram. Leave by the same path that you entered. After leaving the Mandala, conduct the banishing pentagram ritual. This completes the fiftieth initiatory path.

PATH FIFTY-ONE

The Path of Regeneration leads through the 4 positions 65-76-82-84 as shown in Figure 77. It contains the specific atmospheres of sexual energy, spirituality, knowledge, and healing. It is the Third Path of Spiritualization. Use this path for any kind of regeneration or revitalization.

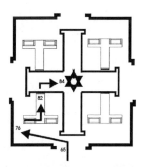

Figure 77: Path 51, The Path of Regeneration

Step 1. Make a circle and conduct the invoking pentagram ritual.

Step 2. Face the North, and imagine the Mandala of the Watchtower of Fire clearly before you. You are facing the southern wall of the mandala. Imagine the walls and floors to be flame red. Recite the Centering Spell. Then say:

**May I enter and safely pass through this red Watchtower of Fire.
May I obtain success in this, the fifty-first of my initiations.
In the threefold secret and holy name of OIPTEAAPDOKE
I make this request. OEKARIMI NOTAHOA IALAPEREGI
OD KA-KA-KOM DO-ZILODAREPE**

Step 3. Visualize the closed Diamond Gate. say: O ORGAN I invoke thee. Come unto me from the Watchtower of Water. Visualize ORGAN materializing before you. Approach the Angel unafraid, open your arms and embrace him. Feel his body melt into your own body and become a part of you. Assume the god-form of the Angel ORGAN (Oh-ra-gah-neh) who guards the Diamond Gate (position 65) as follows:

The god-form of ORGAN: See page 241 for the god-form of ORGAN.

The Angels' Message to Humanity

There are special words written above the Diamond Gate to be spoken before entering. say:

The Earth of itself brings forth nothing, for it is the lump and excrement of darkness, whose bowels are a burning lake. But where the heavens yield, and the Sun pours down his force, she opens herself, and becomes spongy, receving mixture to generation, and so is exalted above herself, and brings forth to the use of man.[16]

Step 4. Visualize the gate opening at these words. Step within the Diamond Gate. Face the Earth-Tier. In the god-form of ORGAN, say:

I am the Angel of Fire. I am the Angel ORGAN. I am the Guardian of the Diamond Gate. I enter into the Watchtower of Fire.

While slowly repeating the Threefold Holy Word, enter into the Watchtower of Fire and move across the Earth-Tier to the bottom of the Bloodstone Stairway leading up to the Water-Tier (position 76). The Threefold Word that you recite will protect you from the Demons who reside on the Earth-Tier.

Step 5. Face the Bloodstone Stairway. Visualize the Kerubic Angel PSAK materializing before you. Approach the Angel unafraid, open your arms and embrace him. Feel his body melt into your own body and become a part of you. Assume the god-form of PSAK who guards the Bloodstone Stairway as follows:

The god-form of PSAK: See page 242 for the god-form of PSAK.

Recite the words written over the Bloodstone Stairway:

I have attained unto the knowledge and secrets of the things in Nature.

Step 6. In the god-form of the Kerubic Angel of Fire, PSAK, while slowly reciting the magic word KUM, climb the 7 steps of the Bloodstone Stairway to the Water-Tier. Then say:

I am a Kerubic Angel of Fire. I am Kerubic Angel PSAK. I am the Guardian of the Bloodstone Stairway. I rise up through the Watchtower of Fire. Throughout eternity I purify myself from Earth to Water within Fire.

Step 7. Slowly repeat the magic word KUM as you move across the Water-Tier. Approach the Stairway to the Air-Tier. Before entering the Second Stairway, say:

As the Sun deprives the Moon in respect of her end, which is to give light, but not of her self; so do the Angels and higher powers, drown and overshadow the soul in man when they are present.

Climb the Second Stairway, which has 11 steps, to the Air-Tier. Visualize the Sephirothic Cross Angel VOLXDO materializing before you. Approach the Angel unafraid, open your arms and embrace him. Feel his body melt into your own body and become a part of you. Assume the god-form of VOLXDO who guards the Air-Tier and Third Stairway (position 82) as follows:

Pathworking the Watchtower of Fire

The god-form of VOLXDO: See page 243 for the god-form of VOLXDO.

The Third Stairway is red and smells of cinnamon. The Third Stairway is also dry and hot. There are 3 steps. Each step has a letter written in green that is blazing to look upon. The letter *B* is on the first step, *F* is on the second, and *K* is on the third. Recite the words written above the appropriate Third Stairway before ascending:

> **I came from the Fountain of Light, where there is no error or darkness, and I have Power, because it is given me from the Highest, which, Lo, is grown and become a mighty Rock.**

Step 8. In the god-form of a Sephirothic Cross Angel of Fire, slowly repeat the magic word RI as you climb. Climb up to the top of the Third Stairway and say:

> **I am a Sephirothic Cross Angel of Fire. I am Sephirothic Cross Angel VOLXDO. I bear the Cross of Fire from Water to Air within Fire.**

Step 9. As VOLXDO, slowly repeat the word RI and at the top of the Stairway, turn toward the center of the Fire-Tier, which is also the center of the mandala. If you are male, assume the naked god-form of the King of Fire, EDLPRNAA. If you are female, assume the naked god-form of the Goddess of Fire, BALOBAN.

Step 10. Same as Step 10 in Path 49.

Step 11. Same as Step 11 in Path 49.

Step 12. Turn from your consort and step outside of the red hexagram. Leave by the same path that you entered. After leaving the Mandala, conduct the banishing pentagram ritual. This completes the fifty-first initiatory path.

PATH FIFTY-TWO

The Path of Spirituality leads through the 4 positions 64-76-82-84 as shown in Figure 78. It contains the specific atmospheres of sexual energy, spirituality and protection. It is the Fouorth Path of Spiritualization. Use this path to enhance spirituality.

Step 1. Make a circle and conduct the invoking pentagram ritual.

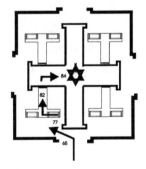

Figure 78: Path 52, The Path of Spirituality

Step 2. Face the North, and imagine the Mandala of the Watchtower of Fire clearly before you. You are facing the southern wall of the mandala. Imagine the walls and floors to be flame red. Recite the Centering Spell. Then say:

> **May I enter and safely pass through this red Watchtower of Fire.**
> **May I obtain success in this, the fifty-second of my initiations.**
> **In the threefold secret and holy name of OIPTEAAPDOKE**
> **I make this request. OEKARIMI NOTAHOA IALAPEREGI**
> **OD KA-KA-KOM DO-ZILODAREPE**

Step 3. Visualize the closed Diamond Gate. say: O ORGAN I invoke thee. Come unto me from the Watchtower of Water. Visualize ORGAN materializing before you. Approach the Angel unafraid, open your arms and embrace him. Feel his body melt into your own body and become a part of you. Assume the god-form of the Angel ORGAN who guards the Diamond Gate (position 65) as follows:

The god-form of ORGAN: See page 241 for the god-form of ORGAN.

There are special words written above the Diamond Gate to be spoken before entering. say:

The Earth of itself brings forth nothing, for it is the lump and excrement of darkness, whose bowles are a burning lake. But where the heavens yield, and the Sun pours down his force, she opens herself, and becomes spongy, receving mixture to generation, and so is exalted above herself, and brings forth to the use of man.

Step 4. Visualize the gate opening at these words. Step within the Diamond Gate. Face the Earth-Tier. In the god-form of ORGAN, say:

I am the Angel of Fire. I am the Angel ORGAN. I am the Guardian of the Diamond Gate. I enter into the Watchtower of Fire.

While slowly repeating the Threefold Holy Word, enter into the Watchtower of Fire and move across the Earth-Tier to the bottom of the Carnelian Stairway leading up to the Water-Tier (position 77). The Threefold Word that you recite will protect you from the Demons who reside on the Earth-Tier.

Step 5. Face the Carnelian Stairway. Visualize the Kerubic Angel AKPS materializing before you. Approach the Angel unafraid, open your arms and embrace him. Feel his body melt into your own body and become a part of you. Assume the god-form of AKPS who guards the Carnelian Stairway as follows:

The god-form of AKPS: See page 236 for the god-form of AKPS.

Recite the words written over the Carnelian Stairway:

Woe be unto the Earth, for it is corrupted. Woe be unto the Earth, for she is surrendered to her adversary. Woe be unto the Earth, she is delivered into the hands of her enemy. Yea, woe be unto the Sons of Men, for their vessels are poisoned. Yet will I be known in the wilderness, and will triumph in my weakness.

Step 6. In the god-form of the Kerubic Angel of Fire, AKPS, while slowly reciting the magic word KUM, climb the 7 steps of the Carnelian Stairway to the Water-Tier. Then say:

I am a Kerubic Angel of Fire. I am Kerubic Angel AKPS. I am the Guardian of the Carnelian Stairway. I rise up through the Watchtower of Fire. Throughout eternity I purify myself from Earth to Water within Fire.

Step 7. Slowly repeat the magic word KUM as you move across the Water-Tier. Approach the Stairway to the Air-Tier. Before entering the Second Stairway, say:

As the Sun deprives the Moon in respect of her end, which is to give light, but not of her self; so do the Angels and higher powers, drown and overshadow the soul in man when they are present.

Pathworking the Watchtower of Fire

Climb the Second Stairway, which has 11 steps, to the Air-Tier. Visualize the Sephirothic Cross Angel VOLXDO materializing before you. Approach the Angel unafraid, open your arms and embrace him. Feel his body melt into your own body and become a part of you. Assume the god-form of VOLXDO who guards the Air-Tier and Third Stairway (position 82) as follows:

The god-form of VOLXDO: See page 243 for the god-form of VOLXDO.

The Third Stairway is red and smells of cinnamon. The Third Stairway is also dry and hot. There are 3 steps. Each step has a letter written in green that is blazing to look upon. The letter *B* is on the first step, *F* is on the second, and *K* is on the third. Recite the words written above the appropriate Third Stairway before ascending:

I came from the Fountain of Light, where there is no error or darkness, and I have Power, because it is given me from the Highest, which, Lo, is grown and become a mighty Rock.

Step 8. In the god-form of a Sephirothic Cross Angel of Fire, slowly repeat the magic word RI as you climb. Climb up to the top of the Third Stairway and say:

I am a Sephirothic Cross Angel of Fire. I am Sephirothic Cross Angel VOLXDO. I bear the Cross of Fire from Water to Air within Fire.

Step 9. As VOLXDO, slowly repeat the word RI and at the top of the Stairway, turn toward the center of the Fire-Tier, which is also the center of the mandala. If you are male, assume the naked god-form of the King of Fire, EDLPRNAA. If you are female, assume the naked god-form of the Goddess of Fire, BALOBAN.

Step 10. Same as Step 10 in Path 49.

Step 11. Same as Step 11 in Path 49.

Step 12. Turn from your consort and step outside of the red hexagram. Leave by the same path that you entered. After leaving the Mandala, conduct the banishing pentagram ritual. This completes the fifty-second initiatory path.

THE WATER QUADRANT OF THE FIRE MANDALA

PATH FIFTY-THREE

The Path of Foreknowledge leads through the 4 positions 68-75-81-84 as shown in Figure 79. It contains the specific atmospheres of peace, protection, foreknowledge, and health. It is the First Path of Right Action. Use this path to develop the magical power of foreknowledge.

Step 1. Make a circle and conduct the invoking pentagram ritual.

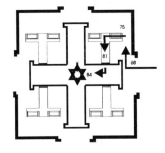

Figure 79: Path 53, The Path of Foreknowledge

Step 2. Face the West, and imagine the Mandala of the Watchtower of Fire clearly before you. You are facing the eastern wall of the mandala. Imagine the walls and floors to be flame red. Recite the Centering Spell. Then say:

> May I enter and safely pass through this red Watchtower of Fire.
> May I obtain success in this, the fifty-third of my initiations.
> In the threefold secret and holy name of OIPTEAAPDOKE
> I make this request. OEKARIMI NOTAHOA IALAPEREGI
> OD KA-KA-KOM DO-ZILODAREPE

Step 3. Visualize the closed Flint Gate. say:

> **O TGMNM I invoke thee. Come unto me from the Watchtower of Water.**

Visualize TGMNM materializing before you. Approach the Angel unafraid, open your arms and embrace him. Feel his body melt into your own body and become a part of you. Assume the god-form of the Angel TGMNM (Teh-geh-men-meh) who guards the Flint Gate (position 68) as follows:

> **The god-form of TGMNM:** See page 243 for the god-form of TGMNM.

There are special words written above the Flint Gate to be spoken before entering. Say:

> **If you now therefore be holy, put on the Garments of Innocency, and walk in righteousness. Then look to have the Reward of Children.**[17]

Step 4. Visualize the gate opening at these words. Step within the Flint Gate. Face the Earth-Tier. In the god-form of TGMNM, say:

> **I am the Angel of Fire. I am the Angel TGMNM. I am the Guardian of the Flint Gate. I enter into the Watchtower of Fire.**

While slowly repeating the Threefold Holy Word, enter into the Watchtower of Fire and move across the Earth-Tier to the bottom of the Walnut Stairway leading up to the Water-Tier (position 75). The Threefold Word that you recite will protect you from the Demons who reside on the Earth-Tier.

Step 5. Face the Walnut Stairway. Visualize the Kerubic Angel AAAN materializing before you. Approach the Angel unafraid, open your arms and embrace him. Feel his body melt into your own body and become a part of you. Assume the god-form of AAAN (Ah-ah-ah- neh) who guards the Walnut Stairway as follows:

> **The god-form of AAAN:** A dark masculine Kerubic Angel with very large wings wearing an emerald green robe. AAAN wears a magical ring with an emerald set in copper that bestows foreknowledge.

Recite the words written over the Walnut Stairway:

> **Behold, the Doors stand open before thee, why entereth thou not?**[18]

Step 6. In the god-form of the Kerubic Angel of Fire, AAAN, while slowly reciting the magic word KUM, climb the 14 steps of the Walnut Stairway to the Water-Tier. Then say:

> **I am a Kerubic Angel of Fire. I am Kerubic Angel AAAN. I am the Guardian of the Walnut Stairway. I rise up through the Watchtower of Fire. Throughout eternity I purify myself from Earth to Water within Fire.**

Step 7. Slowly repeat the magic word KUM as you move across the Water-Tier. Approach the Stairway to the Air-Tier. Before entering the Second Stairway, say:

Pathworking the Watchtower of Fire

As the Sun deprives the Moon in respect of her end, which is to give light, but not of her self; so do the Angels and higher powers, drown and overshadow the soul in man when they are present.

Climb the Second Stairway, which has 10 steps, to the Air-Tier. Visualize the Sephirothic Cross Angel VADALI materializing before you. Approach the Angel unafraid, open your arms and embrace him. Feel his body melt into your own body and become a part of you. Assume the god-form of VADALI (Vah-dah-lee) who guards the Air-Tier and Third Stairway (position 81) as follows:

The god-form of VADALI: See page 243 for the god-form of VADALI.

The Third Stairway is red and smells of cinnamon. The Third Stairway is also dry and hot. There are 3 steps. Each step has a letter written in green that is blazing to look upon. The letter *B* is on the first step, *F* is on the second, and *K* is on the third. Recite the words written above the appropriate Third Stairway before ascending:

The time shall come, that the oak that is beaten with every storm shall be a Dining Table in the Princes' Hall.[19]

Step 8. In the god-form of a Sephirothic Cross Angel of Fire, slowly repeat the magic word RI as you climb. Climb up to the top of the Third Stairway and say:

I am a Sephirothic Cross Angel of Fire. I am Sephirothic Cross Angel VADALI. I bear the Cross of Fire from Water to Air within Fire.

Step 9. As VADALI, slowly repeat the word RI and at the top of the Stairway, turn toward the center of the Fire-Tier, which is also the center of the mandala. If you are male, assume the naked god-form of the King of Fire, EDLPRNAA. If you are female, assume the naked god-form of the Goddess of Fire, BALOBAN.

Step 10. Same as Step 10 in Path 49.

Step 11. Same as Step 11 in Path 49.

Step 12. Turn from your consort and step outside of the red hexagram. Leave by the same path that you entered. After leaving the Mandala, conduct the banishing pentagram ritual. This completes the fifty-third initiatory path.

PATH FIFTY-FOUR

The Path of Spiritual Peace leads through the 4 positions 68-74-81-84 as shown in Figure 80. It contains the specific atmospheres of peace, protection, love, healing. It is the Second Path of Right Action. Use this path to obtain peace of spirit.

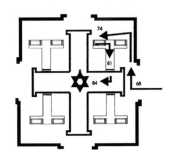

Figure 80: Path 54, The Path of Spiritual Peace

Step 1. Make a circle and conduct the invoking pentagram ritual.

Step 2. Face the West, and imagine the Mandala of the Watchtower of Fire clearly before you. You are facing the eastern wall of the mandala. Imagine the walls and floors to be flame red. Recite the Centering Spell. Then say:

> May I enter and safely pass through this red Watchtower of Fire.
> May I obtain success in this, the fifty-fourth of my initiations.
> In the threefold secret and holy name of OIPTEAAPDOKE
> I make this request. OEKARIMI NOTAHOA
> IALAPEREGI OD KA-KA-KOM DO-ZILODAREPE

Step 3. Visualize the closed Flint Gate. say:

> **O TGMNM I invoke thee. Come unto me from the Watchtower of Water.**

Visualize TGMNM materializing before you. Approach the Angel unafraid, open your arms and embrace him. Feel his body melt into your own body and become a part of you. Assume the god-form of the Angel TGMNM who guards the Flint Gate (position 68) as follows:

The god-form of TGMNM: See page 243 for the god-form of TGMNM.

There are special words written above the Flint Gate to be spoken before entering. say:

> **If you now therefore be holy, put on the Garments of Innocency, and walk in righteousness. Then look to have the Reward of Children.**

Step 4. Visualize the gate opening at these words. Step within the Flint Gate. Face the Earth-Tier. In the god-form of TGMNM, say:

> **I am the Angel of Fire. I am the Angel TGMNM. I am the Guardian of the Flint Gate. I enter into the Watchtower of Fire.**

While slowly repeating the Threefold Holy Word, enter into the Watchtower of Fire and move across the Earth-Tier to the bottom of the Olive Stairway leading up to the Water-Tier (position 75). The Threefold Word that you recite will protect you from the Demons who reside on the Earth-Tier.

Step 5. Face the Olive Stairway. Visualize the Kerubic Angel ANAA materializing before you. Approach the Angel unafraid, open your arms and embrace him. Feel his body melt into your own body and become a part of you. Assume the god-form of ANAA (Ah-nah- ah) who guards the Water-Tier Stairway as follows:

The god-form of ANAA: See page 237 for the god-form of ANAA.

Recite the words written over the Olive Stairway:

> **Love therefore one another, and comfort one another, for he that comforts his brother, comforts himself.**[20]

Step 6. In the god-form of the Kerubic Angel of Fire, ANAA, while slowly reciting the magic word KUM, climb the 14 steps of the Olive Stairway to the Water-Tier. Then say:

> **I am a Kerubic Angel of Fire. I am Kerubic Angel ANAA. I am the Guardian of the Olive Stairway. I rise up through the Watchtower of Fire. Throughout eternity I purify myself from Earth to Water within Fire.**

Step 7. Slowly repeat the magic word KUM as you move across the Water-Tier.

Pathworking the Watchtower of Fire

Approach the Stairway to the Air-Tier. Before entering the Second Stairway, say:

As the Sun deprives the Moon in respect of her end, which is to give light, but not of her self; so do the Angels and higher powers, drown and overshadow the soul in man when they are present.

Climb the Second Stairway, which has 10 steps, to the Air-Tier. Visualize the Sephirothic Cross Angel VADALI materializing before you. Approach the Angel unafraid, open your arms and embrace him. Feel his body melt into your own body and become a part of you. Assume the god-form of VADALI who guards the Air-Tier and Third Stairway (position 81) as follows:

The god-form of VADALI: See page 243 for the god-form of VADALI.

The Third Stairway is red and smells of cinnamon. The Third Stairway is also dry and hot. There are 3 steps. Each step has a letter written in green that is blazing to look upon. The letter *B* is on the first step, *F* is on the second, and *K* is on the third. Recite the words written above the appropriate Third Stairway before ascending:

The time shall come, that the oak that is beaten with every storm shall be a Dining Table in the Princes' Hall.

Step 8. In the god-form of a Sephirothic Cross Angel of Fire, slowly repeat the magic word RI as you climb. Climb up to the top of the Third Stairway and say:

I am a Sephirothic Cross Angel of Fire. I am Sephirothic Cross Angel VADALI. I bear the Cross of Fire from Water to Air within Fire.

Step 9. As VADALI, slowly repeat the word RI and at the top of the Stairway, turn toward the center of the Fire-Tier, which is also the center of the mandala. If you are male, assume the naked god-form of the King of Fire, EDLPRNAA. If you are female, assume the naked god-form of the Goddess of Fire, BALOBAN.

Step 10. Same as Step 10 in Path 49.

Step 11. Same as Step 11 in Path 49.

Step 12. Turn from your consort and step outside of the red hexagram. Leave by the same path that you entered. After leaving the Mandala, conduct the banishing pentagram ritual. This completes the fifty-fourth initiatory path.

PATH FIFTY-FIVE

The Path of Healing Others leads through the 4 positions 69-75-81-84 as shown in Figure 81. It contains the specific atmospheres of healing, foreknowledge, and health. It is the Third Path of Right Action. Use this path for the power to heal others.

Step 1. Make a circle and conduct the invoking pentagram ritual.

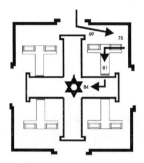

Figure 81: Path 55, The Path of Healing Others

Step 2. Face the South, and imagine the Mandala of the Watchtower of Fire clearly before you. You are facing the northern wall of the mandala. Imagine the walls and floors to be flame red. Recite the Centering Spell. Then say:

May I enter and safely pass through this red Watchtower of Fire.
May I obtain success in this, the fifty-fifth of my initiations.
In the threefold secret and holy name of OIPTEAAPDOKE
I make this request. OEKARIMI NOTAHOA IALAPEREGI
OD KA-KA-KOM DO-ZILODAREPE

Step 3. Visualize the closed Topaz Gate. say:

O TBRAP I invoke thee. Come unto me from the Watchtower of Water.

Visualize TBRAP materializing before you. Approach the Angel unafraid, open your arms and embrace him. Feel his body melt into your own body and become a part of you. Assume the god-form of the Angel TBRAP (Teh-bar-ah-peh) who guards the Topaz Gate (position 69) as follows:

The god-form of TBRAP: See page 243 for the god-form of TBRAP.

There are special words written above the Topaz Gate to be spoken before entering. say:

The soul was made spiritual and increasing, wherein the philosophers, the wise men of this world are deceived. This has been a secret shut up in the Book of Eldras, not fit for the world.[21]

Step 4. Visualize the gate opening at these words. Step within the Topaz Gate. Face the Earth-Tier. In the god-form of TBRAP, say:

I am the Angel of Fire. I am the Angel TBRAP. I am
the Guardian of the Topaz Gate. I enter into the Watchtower of Fire.

While slowly repeating the Threefold Holy Word, enter into the Watchtower of Fire and move across the Earth-Tier to the bottom of the Walnut Stairway leading up to the Water-Tier (position 75). The Threefold Word that you recite will protect you from the Demons who reside on the Earth-Tier.

Step 5. Face the Walnut Stairway. Visualize the Kerubic Angel AAAN materializing before you. Approach the Angel unafraid, open your arms and embrace him. Feel his body melt into your own body and become a part of you. Assume the god-form of AAAN who guards the Walnut Stairway as follows:

The god-form of AAAN: See page 235 for the god-form of AAAN.

Recite the words written over the Walnut Stairway:

Behold, the Doors stand open before thee, why entereth thou not?

Step 6. In the god-form of the Kerubic Angel of Fire, AAAN, while slowly reciting the magic word KUM, climb the 14 stetps of the Walnut Stairway to the Water-Tier. Then say:

I am a Kerubic Angel of Fire. I am Kerubic Angel AAAN. I am the
Guardian of the Walnut Stairway. I rise up through the Watchtower of Fire.
Throughout eternity I purify myself from Earth to Water within Fire.

Pathworking the Watchtower of Fire

Step 7. Slowly repeat the magic word KUM as you move across the Water-Tier. Approach the Stairway to the Air-Tier. Before entering the Second Stairway, say:

As the Sun deprives the Moon in respect of her end, which is to give light, but not of her self; so do the Angels and higher powers, drown and overshadow the soul in man when they are present.

Climb the Second Stairway, which has 10 steps, to the Air-Tier. Assume the Visualize the Sephirothic Cross Angel VADALI materializing before you. Approach the Angel unafraid, open your arms and embrace him. Feel his body melt into your own body and become a part of you. god-form of VADALI who guards the Air-Tier and Third Stairway (position 81) as follows:

The god-form of VADALI: See page 243 for the god-form of VADALI.

The Third Stairway is red and smells of cinnamon. The Third Stairway is also dry and hot. There are 3 steps. Each step has a letter written in green that is blazing to look upon. The letter *B* is on the first step, *F* is on the second, and *K* is on the third. Recite the words written above the appropriate Third Stairway before ascending:

The time shall come, that the oak that is beaten with every storm shall be a Dining Table in the Princes' Hall.

Step 8. In the god-form of a Sephirothic Cross Angel of Fire, slowly repeat the magic word RI as you climb. Climb up to the top of the Third Stairway and say:

I am a Sephirothic Cross Angel of Fire. I am Sephirothic Cross Angel VADALI. I bear the Cross of Fire from Water to Air within Fire.

Step 9. As VADALI, slowly repeat the word RI and at the top of the Stairway, turn toward the center of the Fire-Tier, which is also the center of the mandala. If you are male, assume the naked god-form of the King of Fire, EDLPRNAA. If you are female, assume the naked god-form of the Goddess of Fire, BALOBAN.

Step 10. Same as Step 10 in Path 49.

Step 11. Same as Step 11 in Path 49.

Step 12. Turn from your consort and step outside of the red hexagram. Leave by the same path that you entered. After leaving the Mandala, conduct the banishing pentagram ritual. This completes the fifty-fifth initiatory path.

Path Fifty-Six

The Path of Healing Power leads through the 4 positions 69-74-81-84 as shown in Figure 82. It contains the specific atmospheres of healing and love. It is the Fourth Path of Right Action. Use this path to enhance your healing power.

Step 1. Make a circle and conduct the invoking pentagram ritual.

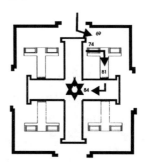

Figure 82: Path 56, The Path of Healing Power

The Angels' Message to Humanity

Step 2. Face the South, and imagine the Mandala of the Watchtower of Fire clearly before you. You are facing the northern wall of the mandala. Imagine the walls and floors to be flame red. Recite the Centering Spell. Then say:

> May I enter and safely pass through this red Watchtower of Fire.
> May I obtain success in this, the fifty-sixth of my initiations.
> In the threefold secret and holy name of OIPTEAAPDOKE
> I make this request. OEKARIMI NOTAHOA IALAPEREGI
> OD KA-KA-KOM DO-ZILODAREPE

Step 3. Visualize the closed Topaz Gate. say:

> O TBRAP I invoke thee. Come unto me from the Watchtower of Water.

Visualize TBRAP materializing before you. Approach the Angel unafraid, open your arms and embrace him. Feel his body melt into your own body and become a part of you. Assume the god-form of the Angel TBRAP (Teh-bar-ah-peh) who guards the Topaz Gate (position 69) as follows:

The god-form of TBRAP: See page 243 for the god-form of TBRAP.

There are special words written above the Topaz Gate to be spoken before entering. say:

> The soul was made spiritual and increasing, wherein the philosophers, the wise men of this world are deceived. This has been a secret shut up in the Book of Eldras, not fit for the world.

Step 4. Visualize the gate opening at these words. Step within the Topaz Gate. Face the Earth-Tier. In the god-form of TBRAP, say:

> I am the Angel of Fire. I am the Angel TBRAP. I am the Guardian
> of the Topaz Gate. I enter into the Watchtower of Fire.

While slowly repeating the Threefold Holy Word, enter into the Watchtower of Fire and move across the Earth-Tier to the bottom of the Olive Stairway leading up to the Water-Tier (position 74). The Threefold Word that you recite will protect you from the Demons who reside on the Earth-Tier.

Step 5. Face the Olive Stairway. Visualize the Kerubic Angel ANAA materializing before you. Approach the Angel unafraid, open your arms and embrace him. Feel his body melt into your own body and become a part of you. Assume the god-form of ANAA who guards the Olive Stairway as follows:

The god-form of ANAA: See page 237 for the god-form of ANAA.

Recite the words written over the Olive Stairway:

> Love therefore one another, and comfort one another, for he that comforts his brother, comforts himself.

Step 6. In the god-form of the Kerubic Angel of Fire, ANAA, while slowly reciting the magic word KUM, climb the 14 steps of the Olive Stairway to the Water-Tier. Then say:

> I am a Kerubic Angel of Fire. I am Kerubic Angel ANAA. I am the
> Guardian of the Olive Stairway. I rise up through the Watchtower of Fire.
> Throughout eternity I purify myself from Earth to Water within Fire.

Pathworking the Watchtower of Fire

Step 7. Slowly repeat the magic word KUM as you move across the Water-Tier. Approach the Stairway to the Air-Tier. Before entering the Second Stairway, say:

As the Sun deprives the Moon in respect of her end, which is to give light, but not of her self; so do the Angels and higher powers, drown and overshadow the soul in man when they are present.

Climb the Second Stairway, which has 10 steps, to the Air-Tier. Visualize the Sephirothic Cross Angel VADALI materializing before you. Approach the Angel unafraid, open your arms and embrace him. Feel his body melt into your own body and become a part of you. Assume the god-form of VADALI who guards the Air-Tier and Third Stairway (position 81) as follows:

The god-form of VADALI: See page 243 for the god-form of VADALI.

The Third Stairway is red and smells of cinnamon. The Third Stairway is also dry and hot. There are 3 steps. Each step has a letter written in green that is blazing to look upon. The letter *B* is on the first step, *F* is on the second, and *K* is on the third. Recite the words written above the appropriate Third Stairway before ascending:

The time shall come, that the oak that is beaten with every storm shall be a Dining Table in the Princes' Hall.

Step 8. In the god-form of a Sephirothic Cross Angel of Fire, slowly repeat the magic word RI as you climb. Climb up to the top of the Third Stairway and say:

I am a Sephirothic Cross Angel of Fire. I am Sephirothic Cross Angel VADALI. I bear the Cross of Fire from Water to Air within Fire.

Step 9. As VADALI, slowly repeat the word RI and at the top of the Stairway, turn toward the center of the Fire-Tier, which is also the center of the mandala. If you are male, assume the naked god-form of the King of Fire, EDLPRNAA. If you are female, assume the naked god-form of the Goddess of Fire, BALOBAN.

Step 10. Same as Step 10 in Path 49.

Step 11. Same as Step 11 in Path 49.

Step 12. Turn from your consort and step outside of the red hexagram. Leave by the same path that you entered. After leaving the Mandala, conduct the banishing pentagram ritual. This completes the fifty-sixth initiatory path.

THE AIR QUADRANT OF THE FIRE MANDALA

PATH FIFTY-SEVEN

The Path of Purification leads through the four positions 70-72-80-84 as shown in Figure 83. It contains the specific atmospheres of love, purification, power, and health. It is the First Path of Self-Manifestation. Use this path for the power of purification.

Step 1. Make a circle and conduct the invoking pentagram ritual.

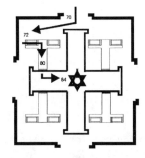

Figure 83: Path 57, The Path of Purification

The Angels' Message to Humanity

Step 2. Face the South, and imagine the Mandala of the Watchtower of Fire clearly before you. You are facing the northern wall of the mandala. Imagine the walls and floors to be flame red. Recite the Centering Spell. Then say:

> May I enter and safely pass through this red Watchtower of Fire.
> May I obtain success in this, the fifty-seventh of my initiations.
> In the threefold secret and holy name of OIPTEAAPDOKE
> I make this request. OEKARIMI NOTAHOA IALAPEREGI
> OD KA-KA-KOM DO-ZILODAREPE

Step 3. Visualize the closed Cedar Gate. say: O IOPMN I invoke thee. Come unto me from the Watchtower of Water. Visualize IOPMN materializing before you. Approach the Angel unafraid, open your arms and embrace him. Feel his body melt into your own body and become a part of you. Assume the god-form of the Angel IOPMN (Ee-oh-pem-neh) who guards the Cedar Gate (position 70) as follows:

> **The god-form of IOPMN:** See page 239 for the god-form of IOPMN.

There are special words written above the Cedar Gate to be spoken before entering. say:

> **Over the Cedar Gate is written: Now to the work intended, which is called the Holy Art GEBOFAL, which is not (as the philosophers have written) the first step supernatural, but it is the first supernatural step naturally limited unto the 48 Gates of Wisdom.**[22]

Step 4. Visualize the gate opening at these words. Step within the Cedar Gate. Face the Earth-Tier. In the god-form of IOPMN, say:

> **I am the Angel of Fire. I am the Angel IOPMN. I am the Guardian of the Cedar Gate. I enter into the Watchtower of Fire.**

While slowly repeating the Threefold Holy Word, enter into the Watchtower of Fire and move across the Earth-Tier to the bottom of the Ash Stairway leading up to the Water-Tier (position 72). The Threefold Word that you recite will protect you from the Demons who reside on the Earth-Tier.

Step 5. Face the Ash Stairway. Visualize the Kerubic Angel DOPA materializing before you. Approach the Angel unafraid, open your arms and embrace him. Feel his body melt into your own body and become a part of you. Assume the god-form of DOPA (Doh-pah) who guards the Water-Tier Stairway as follows:

> **The god-form of DOPA:** See page 238 for the god-form of DOPA.

Recite the words written over the Ash Stairway:

> **Art thou so become a little one, that thou are less than a King?**[23]

Step 6. In the god-form of the Kerubic Angel of Fire, DOPA, while slowly reciting the magic word KUM, climb the 13 steps of the Ash Stairway to the Water-Tier. Then say:

Pathworking the Watchtower of Fire

I am a Kerubic Angel of Fire. I am Kerubic Angel DOPA. I am the Guardian of the Ash Stairway. I rise up through the Watchtower of Fire. Throughout eternity I purify myself from Earth to Water within Fire.

Step 7. Slowly repeat the magic word KUM as you move across the Water-Tier. Approach the Stairway to the Air-Tier. Before entering the Second Stairway, say:

As the Sun deprives the Moon in respect of her end, which is to give light, but not of her self; so do the Angels and higher powers, drown and overshadow the soul in man when they are present.

Climb the Second Stairway, which has 14 steps, to the Air-Tier. Visualize the Sephirothic Cross Angel NOALMR materializing before you. Approach the Angel unafraid, open your arms and embrace him. Feel his body melt into your own body and become a part of you. Assume the god-form of NOALMR (Noh-al-mar) who guards the Air-Tier and Third Stairway (position 80) as follows:

The god-form of NOALMR: See page 241 for the god-form of NOALMR.

The Third Stairway is red and smells of cinnamon. The Third Stairway is also dry and hot. There are 3 steps. Each step has a letter written in green that is blazing to look upon. The letter *B* is on the first step, *F* is on the second, and *K* is on the third. Recite the words written above the appropriate Third Stairway before ascending:

I came from the Fountain of Light, where is no error or darkness. I am a piercing fire sent out as a flame. Such as rise up against my Spirit, I will destroy them in the midst of the same fire, and will deliver their ashes to the winds for a memory of their wickedness.[24]

Step 8. In the god-form of a Sephirothic Cross Angel of Fire, slowly repeat the magic word RI as you climb. Climb up to the top of the Third Stairway and say:

I am a Sephirothic Cross Angel of Fire. I am Sephirothic Cross Angel NOALMR. I bear the Cross of Fire from Water to Air within Fire.

Step 9. As NOALMR, slowly repeat the word RI and at the top of the Stairway, turn toward the center of the Fire-Tier, which is also the center of the mandala. If you are male, assume the naked god-form of the King of Fire, EDLPRNAA. If you are female, assume the naked god-form of the Goddess of Fire, BALOBAN.

Step 10. Same as Step 10 in Path 49.

Step 11. Same as Step 11 in Path 49.

Step 12. Turn from your consort and step outside of the red hexagram. Leave by the same path that you entered. After leaving the Mandala, conduct the banishing pentagram ritual. This completes the fifty-seventh initiatory path.

Path Fifty-Eight

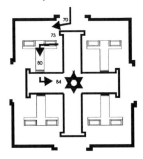

The Path of Happiness leads through the 4 positions 70-73-80-84 as shown in Figure 84. It contains the specific atmospheres of love, purification, happiness, and protection. It is the Second Path of Self-Manifestation. Use this path to generate happiness.

Figure 84: Path 58, The Path of Happiness

Step 1. Make a circle and conduct the invoking pentagram ritual.

Step 2. Face the South, and imagine the Mandala of the Watchtower of Fire clearly before you. You are facing the northern wall of the mandala. Imagine the walls and floors to be flame red. Recite the Centering Spell. Then say:

> **May I enter and safely pass through this red Watchtower of Fire.**
> **May I obtain success in this, the fifty-eighth of my initiations.**
> **In the threefold secret and holy name of OIPTEAAPDOKE**
> **I make this request. OEKARIMI NOTAHOA IALAPEREGI**
> **OD KA-KA-KOM DO-ZILODAREPE**

Step 3. Visualize the closed Cedar Gate. say: O IOPMN I invoke thee. Come unto me from the Watchtower of Water. Visualize IOPMN materializing before you. Approach the Angel unafraid, open your arms and embrace him. Feel his body melt into your own body and become a part of you. Assume the god-form of the Angel IOPMN who guards the Cedar Gate (position 70) as follows:

The god-form of IOPMN: See page 239 for the god-form of IOPMN.

There are special words written above the Cedar Gate to be spoken before entering. say: Over the Cedar Gate is written:

> **Now to the work intended, which is called the Holy Art GEBOFAL, which is not (as the philosophers have written) the first step supernatural, but it is the first supernatural step naturally limited unto the 48 Gates of Wisdom.**

Step 4. Visualize the gate opening at these words. Step within the Cedar Gate. Face the Earth-Tier. In the god-form of IOPMN, say:

> **I am the Angel of Fire. I am the Angel IOPMN. I am the Guardian of the Cedar Gate. I enter into the Watchtower of Fire.**

While slowly repeating the Threefold Holy Word, enter into the Watchtower of Fire and move across the Earth-Tier to the bottom of the Mahogany Stairway leading up to the Water-Tier (position 73). The Threefold Word that you recite will protect you from the Demons who reside on the Earth-Tier.

Step 5. Face the Mahogany Stairway. Visualize the Kerubic Angel PADO materializing before you. Approach the Angel unafraid, open your arms and embrace him.

Pathworking the Watchtower of Fire

Feel his body melt into your own body and become a part of you. Assume the god-form of PADO (Pah-doh) who guards the Mahogany Stairway as follows:

The god-form of PADO: See page 241 for the god-form of PADO.

Recite the words written over the Mahogany Stairway:

> **If thou follow the rules of calling them, thou shalt see that the Air is their habitation.**[25]

Step 6. In the god-form of the Kerubic Angel of Fire, PADO, while slowly reciting the magic word KUM, climb the 13 steps of the Mahogany Stairway to the Water-Tier. Then say:

> **I am a Kerubic Angel of Fire. I am Kerubic Angel PADO. I am the Guardian of the Mahogany Stairway. I rise up through the Watchtower of Fire. Throughout eternity I purify myself from Earth to Water within Fire.**

Step 7. Slowly repeat the magic word KUM as you move across the Water-Tier. Approach the Stairway to the Air-Tier. Before entering the Second Stairway, say:

> **As the Sun deprives the Moon in respect of her end, which is to give light, but not of her self; so do the Angels and higher powers, drown and overshadow the soul in man when they are present.**

Climb the Second Stairway, which has 14 steps, to the Air-Tier. Visualize the Sephirothic Cross Angel NOALMR materializing before you. Approach the Angel unafraid, open your arms and embrace him. Feel his body melt into your own body and become a part of you. Assume the god-form of NOALMR who guards the Air-Tier and Third Stairway (position 80) as follows:

The god-form of NOALMR: See page 241 for the god-form of NOALMR.

The Third Stairway is red and smells of cinnamon. The Third Stairway is also dry and hot. There are 3 steps. Each step has a letter written in green that is blazing to look upon. The letter *B* is on the first step, *F* is on the second, and *K* is on the third. Recite the words written above the appropriate Third Stairway before ascending:

> **I came from the Fountain of Light, where is no error or darkness. I am a piercing fire sent out as a flame. Such as rise up against my Spirit, I will destroy them in the midst of the same fire, and will deliver their ashes to the winds for a memory of their wickedness.**

Step 8. In the god-form of a Sephirothic Cross Angel of Fire, slowly repeat the magic word RI as you climb. Climb up to the top of the Third Stairway and say:

> **I am a Sephirothic Cross Angel of Fire. I am Sephirothic Cross Angel NOALMR. I bear the Cross of Fire from Water to Air within Fire.**

Step 9. As NOALMR, slowly repeat the word RI and at the top of the Stairway, turn toward the center of the Fire-Tier, which is also the center of the mandala. If you are male, assume the naked god-form of the King of Fire, EDLPRNAA. If you are female, assume the naked god-form of the Goddess of Fire, BALOBAN.

The Angels' Message to Humanity

Step 10. Same as Step 10 in Path 49.

Step 11. Same as Step 11 in Path 49.

Step 12. Turn from your consort and step outside of the red hexagram. Leave by the same path that you entered. After leaving the Mandala, conduct the banishing pentagram ritual. This completes the fifty-eighth initiatory path.

PATH FIFTY-NINE

The Path of Joy leads through the 4 positions 71-72-80- 84 as shown in Figure 85. It contains the specific atmospheres of love, health, and power. It is the Third Path of Self- Manifestation. Use this path to generate joy.

Step 1. Make a circle and conduct the invoking pentagram ritual.

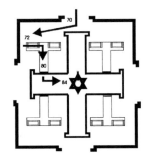

Figure 85: Path 59, The Path of Joy

Step 2. Face the East, and imagine the Mandala of the Watchtower of Fire clearly before you. You are facing the western wall of the mandala. Imagine the walls and floors to be flame red. Recite the Centering Spell. Then say:

> **May I enter and safely pass through this red Watchtower of Fire.**
> **May I obtain success in this, the fifty-nineth of my initiations.**
> **In the threefold secret and holy name of OIPTEAAPDOKE**
> **I make this request. OEKARIMI NOTAHOA**
> **IALAPEREGI OD KA-KA-KOM DO-ZILODAREPE**

Step 3. Visualize the closed Oak Gate. say: O IVASG I invoke thee. Come unto me from the Watchtower of Water. Visualize IVASG materializing before you. Approach the Angel unafraid, open your arms and embrace him. Feel his body melt into your own body and become a part of you. Assume the god-form of the Angel IVASG (Ee-vah-seh-geh) who guards the Oak Gate (position 71) as follows:

The god-form of IVASG: See page 239 for the god-form of IVASG.

There are special words written above the Oak Gate to be spoken before entering. say:

> **Three things to be considered: The place that every word occupies; the place that every letter occupies, and the number and place that every word and letter is referred unto. For here place and number are apart, and bear an Image of the work that they intreat of. But number and place must be joined together, and thereby shall you taste of that which follows—true wisdom.**[26]

Step 4. Visualize the gate opening at these words. Step within the Oak Gate. Face the Earth-Tier. In the god-form of IVASG, say:

> **I am the Angel of Fire. I am the Angel IVASG. I am the Guardian of the Oak Gate. I enter into the Watchtower of Fire.**

Pathworking the Watchtower of Fire

While slowly repeating the Threefold Holy Word, enter into the Watchtower of Fire and move across the Earth-Tier to the bottom of the Ash Stairway leading up to the Water-Tier (position 72). The Threefold Word that you recite will protect you from the Demons who reside on the Earth-Tier.

Step 5. Face the Ash Stairway. Visualize the Kerubic Angel DOPA materializing before you. Approach the Angel unafraid, open your arms and embrace him. Feel his body melt into your own body and become a part of you. Assume the god-form of DOPA who guards the Ash Stairway as follows:

>**The god-form of DOPA:** See page 238 for the god-form of DOPA.

Recite the words written over the Ash Stairway:

>**Art thou so become a little one, that thou are less than a King?**

Step 6. In the god-form of the Kerubic Angel of Fire, DOPA, while slowly reciting the magic word KUM, climb the 13 steps of the Ash Stairway to the Water-Tier. Then say:

>**I am a Kerubic Angel of Fire. I am Kerubic Angel DOPA. I am the Guardian of the Ash Stairway. I rise up through the Watchtower of Fire. Throughout eternity I purify myself from Earth to Water within Fire.**

Step 7. Slowly repeat the magic word KUM as you move across the Water-Tier. Approach the Stairway to the Air-Tier. Before entering the Second Stairway, say:

>**As the Sun deprives the Moon in respect of her end, which is to give light, but not of her self; so do the Angels and higher powers, drown and overshadow the soul in man when they are present.**

Climb the Second Stairway, which has 14 steps, to the Air-Tier. Visualize the Sephirothic Cross Angel NOALMR materializing before you. Approach the Angel unafraid, open your arms and embrace him. Feel his body melt into your own body and become a part of you. Assume the god-form of NOALMR who guards the Air-Tier and Third Stairway (position 80) as follows:

>**The god-form of NOALMR:** See page 241 for the god-form of NOALMR.

The Third Stairway is red and smells of cinnamon. The Third Stairway is also dry and hot. There are 3 steps. Each step has a letter written in green that is blazing to look upon. The letter *B* is on the first step, *F* is on the second, and *K* is on the third. Recite the words written above the appropriate Third Stairway before ascending:

>**The words written above this Stairway: I came from the Fountain of Light, where is no error or darkness. I am a piercing fire sent out as a flame. Such as rise up against my Spirit, I will destroy them in the midst of the same fire, and will deliver their ashes to the winds for a memory of their wickedness.**

Step 8. In the god-form of a Sephirothic Cross Angel of Fire, slowly repeat the magic word RI as you climb. Climb up to the top of the Third Stairway and say:

The Angels' Message to Humanity

I am a Sephirothic Cross Angel of Fire. I am Sephirothic Cross Angel NOALMR. I bear the Cross of Fire from Water to Air within Fire.

Step 9. As NOALMR, slowly repeat the word RI and at the top of the Stairway, turn toward the center of the Fire-Tier, which is also the center of the mandala. If you are male, assume the naked god-form of the King of Fire, EDLPRNAA. If you are female, assume the naked god-form of the Goddess of Fire, BALOBAN.

Step 10. Same as Step 10 in Path 49.

Step 11. Same as Step 11 in Path 49.

Step 12. Turn from your consort and step outside of the red hexagram. Leave by the same path that you entered. After leaving the Mandala, conduct the banishing pentagram ritual. This completes the fifty-nineth initiatory path.

Path Sixty

The Path of Bliss leads through the 4 positions 71-73- 80-84 as shown in Figure 86. It contains the specific atmospheres of love, health, happiness, and protection. It is the Fouorth Path of Self-Manifestation. Use this path to develope or enhance bliss (the amrita of the Tanras).

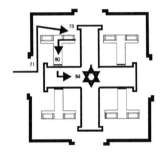

Figure 86: Path 60, The Path of Bliss

Step 1. Make a circle and conduct the invoking pentagram ritual.

Step 2. Face the East, and imagine the Mandala of the Watchtower of Fire clearly before you. You are facing the western wall of the mandala. Imagine the walls and floors to be flame red. Recite the Centering Spell. Then say:

> May I enter and safely pass through this red Watchtower of Fire.
> May I obtain success in this, the sixtieth of my initiations.
> In the threefold secret and holy name of OIPTEAAPDOKE
> I make this request. OEKARIMI NOTAHOA IALAPEREGI
> OD KA-KA-KOM DO-ZILODAREPE

Step 3. Visualize the closed Oak Gate. say: O IVASG I invoke thee. Come unto me from the Watchtower of Water. Visualize IVASG materializing before you. Approach the Angel unafraid, open your arms and embrace him. Feel his body melt into your own body and become a part of you. Assume the god-form of the Angel IVASG who guards the Oak Gate (position 71) as follows:

The god-form of IVASG: See page 239 for the god-form of IVASG.

There are special words written above the Oak Gate to be spoken before entering. say:

> **Three things to be considered: The place that every word occupies; the place that every letter occupies, and the number and place that every**

Pathworking the Watchtower of Fire

word and letter is referred unto. For here place and number are apart, and bear an Image of the work that they intreat of. But number and place must be joined together, and thereby shall you taste of that which follows — true wisdom.

Step 4. Visualize the gate opening at these words. Step within the Oak Gate. Face the Earth-Tier. In the god-form of IVASG, say:

I am the Angel of Fire. I am the Angel IVASG. I am the Guardian of the Oak Gate. I enter into the Watchtower of Fire.

While slowly repeating the Threefold Holy Word, enter into the Watchtower of Fire and move across the Earth-Tier to the bottom of the Mahogany Stairway leading up to the Water-Tier (position 73). The Threefold Word that you recite will protect you from the Demons who reside on the Earth-Tier.

Step 5. Face the Mahogany Stairway. Visualize the Kerubic Angel PADO materializing before you. Approach the Angel unafraid, open your arms and embrace him. Feel his body melt into your own body and become a part of you. Assume the god-form of PADO who guards the Mahogany Stairway as follows:

The god-form of PADO: See page 241 for the god-form of PADO.

Step 6. In the god-form of the Kerubic Angel of Fire, PADO, while slowly reciting the magic word KUM, climb the 13 steps of the Mahogany Stairway to the Water-Tier. Then say:

I am a Kerubic Angel of Fire. I am Kerubic Angel PADO. I am the Guardian of the Mahogany Stairway. I rise up through the Watchtower of Fire. Throughout eternity I purify myself from Earth to Water within Fire.

Step 7. Slowly repeat the magic word KUM as you move across the Water-Tier. Approach the Stairway to the Air-Tier. Before entering the Second Stairway, say:

As the Sun deprives the Moon in respect of her end, which is to give light, but not of her self; so do the Angels and higher powers, drown and overshadow the soul in man when they are present.

Climb the Second Stairway, which has 14 steps, to the Air-Tier. Visualize the Sephirothic Cross Angel NOALMR materializing before you. Approach the Angel unafraid, open your arms and embrace him. Feel his body melt into your own body and become a part of you. Assume the god-form of NOALMR who guards the Air-Tier and Third Stairway (position 80) as follows:

The god-form of NOALMR: See page 241 for the god-form of NOALMR.

The Third Stairway is red and smells of cinnamon. The Third Stairway is also dry and hot. There are 3 steps. Each step has a letter written in green that is blazing to look upon. The letter *B* is on the first step, *F* is on the second, and *K* is on the third. Recite the words written above the appropriate Third Stairway before ascending:

The Angels' Message to Humanity

> I came from the Fountain of Light, where is no error or darkness. I am a piercing fire sent out as a flame. Such as rise up against my Spirit, I will destroy them in the midst of the same fire, and will deliver their ashes to the winds for a memory of their wickedness.

Step 8. In the god-form of a Sephirothic Cross Angel of Fire, slowly repeat the magic word RI as you climb. Climb up to the top of the Third Stairway and say:

> I am a Sephirothic Cross Angel of Fire. I am Sephirothic Cross Angel NOALMR. I bear the Cross of Fire from Water to Air within Fire.

Step 9. As NOALMR, slowly repeat the word RI and at the top of the Stairway, turn toward the center of the Fire-Tier, which is also the center of the mandala. If you are male, assume the naked god-form of the King of Fire, EDLPRNAA. If you are female, assume the naked god-form of the Goddess of Fire, BALOBAN.

Step 10. Same as Step 10 in Path 49.

Step 11. Same as Step 11 in Path 49.

Step 12. Turn from your consort and step outside of the red hexagram. Leave by the same path that you entered. After leaving the Mandala, conduct the banishing pentagram ritual. This completes the sixtieth initiatory path.

THE FIRE QUADRANT OF THE FIRE MANDALA

PATH SIXTY-ONE

The Path of Benevolence leads through the 4 positions 66-79-83-84 as shown in Figure 87. It contains the specific atmospheres of happiness, protection, wealth, and love. It is the First Path of Energized Enthusiasm. Use this path to bestow prosperity and good will on others.

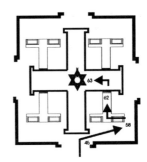

Figure 87: Path 61, The Path of Benevolence

Step 1. Make a circle and conduct the invoking pentagram ritual.

Step 2. Face the North, and imagine the Mandala of the Watchtower of Fire clearly before you. You are facing the southern wall of the mandala. Imagine the walls and floors to be flame red. Recite the Centering Spell. Then say:

> May I enter and safely pass through this red Watchtower of Fire.
> May I obtain success in this, the sixty-first of my initiations.
> In the threefold secret and holy name of OIPTEAAPDOKE
> I make this request. OEKARIMI NOTAHOA IALAPEREGI
> OD KA-KA-KOM DO-ZILODAREPE

Step 3. Visualize the closed Sulfur Gate. say: O MADRE I invoke thee. Come unto me from the Watchtower of Water. Visualize MADRE materializing before you.

Pathworking the Watchtower of Fire

Approach the Angel unafraid, open your arms and embrace him. Feel his body melt into your own body and become a part of you. Assume the god-form of the Angel MADRE (Mah-dar-eh) who guards the Sulfur Gate (position 66) as follows:

The god-form of MADRE: See page 240 for the god-form of MADRE.

There are special words written above the Sulfur Gate to be spoken before entering. say:

Lo, Light stands by me, and my words are medicine, and whatsoever I speak, Light bears witness of me. Therefore, my words are true.[27]

Step 4. Visualize the gate opening at these words. Step within the Sulfur Gate. Face the Earth-Tier. In the god-form of MADRE, say:

I am the Angel of Fire. I am the Angel MADRE. I am the Guardian of the Sulfur Gate. I enter into the Watchtower of Fire.

While slowly repeating the Threefold Holy Word, enter into the Watchtower of Fire and move across the Earth-Tier to the bottom of the Chestnut Stairway leading up to the Water-Tier (position 79). The Threefold Word that you recite will protect you from the Demons who reside on the Earth-Tier.

Step 5. Face the Chestnut Stairway. Visualize the Kerubic Angel ZAZI materializing before you. Approach the Angel unafraid, open your arms and embrace him. Feel his body melt into your own body and become a part of you. Assume the god-form of ZAZI (Zah-zee) who guards the Chestnut Stairway:

The god-form of ZAZI: See page 243 for the god-form of ZAZI.

Recite the words written over the Chestnut Stairway:

Cease for this time, for it is a time of Silence, for the wicked are confounded.[28]

Step 6. In the god-form of the Kerubic Angel of Fire, ZAZI, while slowly reciting the magic word KUM, climb the 12 steps of the Chestnut Stairway to the Water-Tier. Then say:

I am a Kerubic Angel of Fire. I am Kerubic Angel ZAZI. I am the Guardian of the Chestnut Stairway. I rise up through the Watchtower of Fire. Throughout eternity I purify myself from Earth to Water within Fire.

Step 7. Slowly repeat the magic word KUM as you move across the Water-Tier. Approach the Stairway to the Air-Tier. Before entering the Second Stairway, say:

As the Sun deprives the Moon in respect of her end, which is to give light, but not of her self; so do the Angels and higher powers, drown and overshadow the soul in man when they are present.

Climb the Second Stairway, which has 7 steps, to the Air-Tier. Visualize the Sephirothic Cross Angel RZIONR materializing before you. Approach the Angel unafraid, open your arms and embrace him. Feel his body melt into your own body and become a part of you. Assume the god-form of RZIONR (Rah-zee-oh-nar) who guards the Air-Tier and Third Stairway (position 83) as follows:

The god-form of RZIONR: See page 242 for the god-form of RZIONR.

The Third Stairway is red and smells of cinnamon. The Third Stairway is also dry and hot. There are 3 steps. Each step has a letter written in green that is blazing to look upon. The letter *B* is on the first step, *F* is on the second, and *K* is on the third. Recite the words written above the appropriate Third Stairway before ascending:

I am a flaming fire among you, and the Rod of Justice. Heave up your hands, and you shall be heard. May the peace of Him who is the Spirit of Wisdom inflame your mind with love and charity, and grant you continuance to His glory. Amen.[29]

Step 8. In the god-form of a Sephirothic Cross Angel of Fire, slowly repeat the magic word RI as you climb. Climb up to the top of the Third Stairway and say:

I am a Sephirothic Cross Angel of Fire. I am Sephirothic Cross Angel RZIONR. I bear the Cross of Fire from Water to Air within Fire.

Step 9. As RZIONR, slowly repeat the word RI and at the top of the Stairway, turn toward the center of the Fire-Tier, which is also the center of the mandala. If you are male, assume the naked god-form of the King of Fire, EDLPRNAA. If you are female, assume the naked god-form of the Goddess of Fire, BALOBAN.

Step 10. Same as Step 10 in Path 49.

Step 11. Same as Step 11 in Path 49.

Step 12. Turn from your consort and step outside of the red hexagram. Leave by the same path that you entered. After leaving the Mandala, conduct the banishing pentagram ritual. This completes the sixty-first initiatory path.

Path Sixty-Two

The Path of Power leads through the 4 positions 66-78- 83-84 as shown in Figure 88. It contains the specific atmospheres of happiness, protection, magical power, and psychic power. It is the Second Path of Energized Enthusiasm. Use this path to bestow magical power on others.

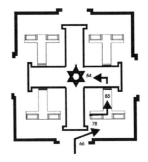

Figure 88: Path 62, The Path of Power

Step 1. Make a circle and conduct the invoking pentagram ritual.

Step 2. Face the North, and imagine the Mandala of the Watchtower of Fire clearly before you. You are facing the southern wall of the mandala. Imagine the walls and floors to be flame red. Recite the Centering Spell. Then say:

May I enter and safely pass through this red Watchtower of Fire. May I obtain success in this, the sixty-second of my initiations. In the

Pathworking the Watchtower of Fire

threefold secret and holy name of OIPTEAAPDOKE
I make this request. OEKARIMI NOTAHOA IALAPEREGI
OD KA-KA-KOM DO-ZILODAREPE

Step 3. Visualize the closed Sulfur Gate. say: O MADRE I invoke thee. Come unto me from the Watchtower of Water. Visualize MADRE materializing before you. Approach the Angel unafraid, open your arms and embrace him. Feel his body melt into your own body and become a part of you. Assume the god-form of the Angel MADRE who guards the Sulfur Gate (position 66) as follows:

The god-form of MADRE: See page 240 for the god-form of MADRE.

There are special words written above the Sulfur Gate to be spoken before entering. say:

Lo, Light stands by me, and my words are medicine, and whatsoever I speak, Light bears witness of me. Therefore, my words are true.

Step 4. Visualize the gate opening at these words. Step within the Sulfur Gate. Face the Earth-Tier. In the god-form of MADRE, say:

I am the Angel of Fire. I am the Angel MADRE. I am the Guardian of the Sulfur Gate. I enter into the Watchtower of Fire.

While slowly repeating the Threefold Holy Word, enter into the Watchtower of Fire and move across the Earth-Tier to the bottom of the Wormwood Stairway leading up to the Water-Tier (position 78). The Threefold Word that you recite will protect you from the Demons who reside on the Earth-Tier.

Step 5. Face the Wormwood Stairway. Visualize the Kerubic Angel ZIZA materializing before you. Approach the Angel unafraid, open your arms and embrace him. Feel his body melt into your own body and become a part of you. Assume the god-form of ZIZA (Zee-zah) who guards the Wormwood Stairway

The god-form of ZIZA: See page 244 for the god-form of ZIZA.

Recite the words written over the Wormwood Stairway:

VOOAN is spoken with them that fall, but VAOAN with them that are, and are glorified. The devils have lost the dignity of their sounds.[30]

Step 6. In the god-form of the Kerubic Angel of Fire, ZIZA, while slowly reciting the magic word KUM, climb the 12 steps of the Wormwood Stairway to the Water-Tier. Then say:

I am a Kerubic Angel of Fire. I am Kerubic Angel ZIZA. I am the Guardian of the Wormwood Stairway. I rise up through the Watchtower of Fire. Throughout eternity I purify myself from Earth to Water within Fire.

Step 7. Slowly repeat the magic word KUM as you move across the Water-Tier. Approach the Stairway to the Air-Tier. Before entering the Second Stairway, say:

As the Sun deprives the Moon in respect of her end, which is to give light, but not of her self; so do the Angels and higher powers, drown and overshadow the soul in man when they are present.

Climb the Second Stairway, which has 7 steps, to the Air-Tier. Visualize the Sephirothic Cross Angel RZIONR materializing before you. Approach the Angel unafraid, open your arms and embrace him. Feel his body melt into your own body and become a part of you. Assume the god-form of RZIONR who guards the Air-Tier and Third Stairway (position 83) as follows:

The god-form of RZIONR: See page 242 for the god-form of RZIONR.

The Third Stairway is red and smells of cinnamon. The Third Stairway is also dry and hot. There are 3 steps. Each step has a letter written in green that is blazing to look upon. The letter *B* is on the first step, *F* is on the second, and *K* is on the third. Recite the words written above the appropriate Third Stairway before ascending:

> **I am a flaming fire among you, and the Rod of Justice. Heave up your hands, and you shall be heard. May the peace of Him who is the Spirit of Wisdom inflame your mind with love and charity, and grant you continuance to His glory. Amen.**

Step 8. In the god-form of a Sephirothic Cross Angel of Fire, slowly repeat the magic word RI as you climb. Climb up to the top of the Third Stairway and say:

> **I am a Sephirothic Cross Angel of Fire. I am Sephirothic Cross Angel RZIONR. I bear the Cross of Fire from Water to Air within Fire.**

Step 9. As RZIONR, slowly repeat the word RI and at the top of the Stairway, turn toward the center of the Fire-Tier, which is also the center of the mandala. If you are male, assume the naked god-form of the King of Fire, EDLPRNAA. If you are female, assume the naked god-form of the Goddess of Fire, BALOBAN.

Step 10. Same as Step 10 in Path 49.

Step 11. Same as Step 11 in Path 49.

Step 12. Turn from your consort and step outside of the red hexagram. Leave by the same path that you entered. After leaving the Mandala, conduct the banishing pentagram ritual. This completes the sixty-second initiatory path.

PATH SIXTY-THREE

The Path of Riches leads through the 4 positions 67-79- 83-84 as shown in Figure 89. It contains the specific atmospheres of prophecy, love, and wealth. It is the Third Path of Energized Enthusiasm. Use this path to obtain riches or to bestow riches on others.

Step 1. Make a circle and conduct the invoking pentagram ritual.

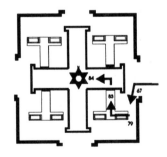

Figure 89: Path 63, The Path of Riches

Step 2. Face the West, and imagine the Mandala of the Watchtower of Fire clearly before you. You are facing the eastern wall of the mandala. Imagine the walls and floors to be flame red. Recite the Centering Spell. Then say:

Pathworking the Watchtower of Fire

May I enter and safely pass through this red Watchtower of Fire.
May I obtain success in this, the sixty-third of my initiations.
In the threefold secret and holy name of OIPTEAAPDOKE
I make this request. OEKARIMI NOTAHOA IALAPEREGI
OD KA-KA-KOM DO-ZILODAREPE

Step 3. Visualize the closed Amber Gate. say: O MAKAR I invoke thee. Come unto me from the Watchtower of Water. Visualize MAKAR materializing before you. Approach the Angel unafraid, open your arms and embrace him. Feel his body melt into your own body and become a part of you. Assume the god-form of the Angel MAKAR (Mah-kah-rah) who guards the Amber Gate (position 67) as follows:

The god-form of MAKAR: See page 240 for the god-form of MAKAR.

There are special words written above the Amber Gate to be spoken before entering. say:

Whatever I teach you has a Mystery. And I am a Mystery in my self. Even so, all things that you learn of me, you must be content to receive as mystical instructions comprehending Perfect Truth, and to be known to such as are true.[31]

Step 4. Visualize the gate opening at these words. Step within the Amber Gate. Face the Earth-Tier. In the god-form of MAKAR, say:

I am the Angel of Fire. I am the Angel MAKAR. I am the Guardian of the Amber Gate. I enter into the Watchtower of Fire.

While slowly repeating the Threefold Holy Word, enter into the Watchtower of Fire and move across the Earth-Tier to the bottom of the Chestnut Stairway leading up to the Water-Tier (position 79). The Threefold Word that you recite will protect you from the Demons who reside on the Earth-Tier.

Step 5. Face the Chestnut Stairway. Visualize the Kerubic Angel ZAZI materializing before you. Approach the Angel unafraid, open your arms and embrace him. Feel his body melt into your own body and become a part of you. Assume the god-form of ZAZI who guards the Chestnut Stairway:

The god-form of ZAZI: See page 243 for the god-form of ZAZI.

Step 6. In the god-form of the Kerubic Angel of Fire, ZAZI, while slowly reciting the magic word KUM, climb the 12 steps of the Chestnut Stairway to the Water-Tier. Then say:

I am a Kerubic Angel of Fire. I am Kerubic Angel ZAZI. I am the Guardian of the Chestnut Stairway. I rise up through the Watchtower of Fire. Throughout eternity I purify myself from Earth to Water within Fire.

Step 7. Slowly repeat the magic word KUM as you move across the Water-Tier. Approach the Stairway to the Air-Tier. Before entering the Second Stairway, say:

As the Sun deprives the Moon in respect of her end, which is to give light, but not of her self; so do the Angels and higher powers, drown and overshadow the soul in man when they are present.

The Angels' Message to Humanity

Climb the Second Stairway, which has 7 steps, to the Air-Tier. Visualize the Sephirothic Cross Angel RZIONR materializing before you. Approach the Angel unafraid, open your arms and embrace him. Feel his body melt into your own body and become a part of you. Assume the god-form of RZIONR who guards the Air-Tier and Third Stairway (position 83) as follows:

The god-form of RZIONR: See page 242 for the god-form of RZIONR.

The Third Stairway is red and smells of cinnamon. The Third Stairway is also dry and hot. There are 3 steps. Each step has a letter written in green that is blazing to look upon. The letter *B* is on the first step, *F* is on the second, and *K* is on the third. Recite the words written above the appropriate Third Stairway before ascending:

I am a flaming fire among you, and the Rod of Justice. Heave up your hands, and you shall be heard. May the peace of Him who is the Spirit of Wisdom inflame your mind with love and charity, and grant you continuance to His glory. Amen.

Step 8. In the god-form of a Sephirothic Cross Angel of Fire, slowly repeat the magic word RI as you climb. Climb up to the top of the Third Stairway and say:

I am a Sephirothic Cross Angel of Fire. I am Sephirothic Cross Angel RZIONR. I bear the Cross of Fire from Water to Air within Fire.

Step 9. As RZIONR, slowly repeat the word RI and at the top of the Stairway, turn toward the center of the Fire-Tier, which is also the center of the mandala. If you are male, assume the naked god-form of the King of Fire, EDLPRNAA. If you are female, assume the naked god-form of the Goddess of Fire, BALOBAN.

Step 10. Same as Step 10 in Path 49.

Step 11. Same as Step 11 in Path 49.

Step 12. Turn from your consort and step outside of the red hexagram. Leave by the same path that you entered. After leaving the Mandala, conduct the banishing pentagram ritual. This completes the sixty-third initiatory path.

Path Sixty-Four

The Path of Prophecy leads through the 4 positions 67- 78-83-84 as shown in Figure 90. It contains the specific atmospheres of prophecy, love, magical power, and psychic power. It is the Fourth Path of Energized Enthusiasm. Use this path to bestow the power of prophecy on others.

Step 1. Make a circle and conduct the invoking pentagram ritual.

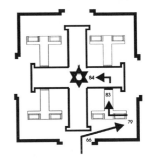

Figure 90: Path 64, The Path of Prophecy

Step 2. Face the West, and imagine the Mandala of the Watchtower of Fire clearly before you. You are facing the eastern wall of the mandala. Imagine the walls and floors to be flame red. Recite the Centering Spell. Then say:

Pathworking the Watchtower of Fire

> May I enter and safely pass through this red Watchtower of Fire.
> May I obtain success in this, the sixty-fourth of my initiations.
> In the threefold secret and holy name of OIPTEAAPDOKE
> I make this request. OEKARIMI NOTAHOA IALAPEREGI
> OD KA-KA-KOM DO-ZILODAREPE

Step 3. Visualize the closed Amber Gate. say: O MAKAR I invoke thee. Come unto me from the Watchtower of Water. Visualize MAKAR materializing before you. Approach the Angel unafraid, open your arms and embrace him. Feel his body melt into your own body and become a part of you. Assume the god-form of the Angel MAKAR who guards the Amber Gate (position 67) as follows:

The god-form of MAKAR: See page 240 for the god-form of MAKAR.

There are special words written above the Amber Gate to be spoken before entering. say:

> Whatever I teach you has a Mystery. And I am a Mystery in my self. Even so, all things that you learn of me, you must be content to receive as mystical instructions comprehending Perfect Truth, and to be known to such as are true.

Step 4. Visualize the gate opening at these words. Step within the Amber Gate. Face the Earth-Tier. In the god-form of MAKAR, say:

> I am the Angel of Fire. I am the Angel MAKAR. I am the Guardian of the Amber Gate. I enter into the Watchtower of Fire.

While slowly repeating the Threefold Holy Word, enter into the Watchtower of Fire and move across the Earth-Tier to the bottom of the Wormwood Stairway leading up to the Water-Tier (position 79). The Threefold Word that you recite will protect you from the Demons who reside on the Earth-Tier.

Step 5. Face the Wormwood Stairway. Visualize the Kerubic Angel ZIZA materializing before you. Approach the Angel unafraid, open your arms and embrace him. Feel his body melt into your own body and become a part of you. Assume the god-form of ZIZA who guards the Wormwood Stairway as follows:

The god-form of ZIZA: See page 244 for the god-form of ZIZA.

Recite the words written over the Wormwood Stairway:

> VOOAN is spoken with them that fall, but VAOAN with them that are, and are glorified. The devils have lost the dignity of their sounds.

Step 6. In the god-form of the Kerubic Angel of Fire, ZIZA, while slowly reciting the magic word KUM, climb the 12 steps of the Wormwood Stairway to the Water-Tier. Then say:

> I am a Kerubic Angel of Fire. I am Kerubic Angel ZIZA. I am the Guardian of the Wormwood Stairway. I rise up through the Watchtower of Fire. Throughout eternity I purify myself from Earth to Water within Fire.

Step 7. Slowly repeat the magic word KUM as you move across the Water-Tier. Approach the Stairway to the Air-Tier. Before entering the Second Stairway, say:

As the Sun deprives the Moon in respect of her end, which is to give light, but not of her self; so do the Angels and higher powers, drown and overshadow the soul in man when they are present.

Climb the Second Stairway, which has 7 steps, to the Air-Tier. Visualize the Sephirothic Cross Angel RZIONR materializing before you. Approach the Angel unafraid, open your arms and embrace him. Feel his body melt into your own body and become a part of you. Assume the god-form of RZIONR who guards the Air-Tier and Third Stairway (position 83) as follows:

The god-form of RZIONR: See page 242 for the god-form of RZOINR.

The Third Stairway is red and smells of cinnamon. The Third Stairway is also dry and hot. There are 3 steps. Each step has a letter written in green that is blazing to look upon. The letter B is on the first step, F is on the second, and K is on the third. Recite the words written above the appropriate Third Stairway before ascending:

I am a flaming fire among you, and the Rod of Justice. Heave up your hands, and you shall be heard. May the peace of Him who is the Spirit of Wisdom inflame your mind with love and charity, and grant you continuance to His glory. Amen.

Step 8. In the god-form of a Sephirothic Cross Angel of Fire, slowly repeat the magic word RI as you climb. Climb up to the top of the Third Stairway and say:

I am a Sephirothic Cross Angel of Fire. I am Sephirothic Cross Angel RZIONR. I bear the Cross of Fire from Water to Air within Fire.

Step 9. As RZIONR, slowly repeat the word RI and at the top of the Stairway, turn toward the center of the Fire-Tier, which is also the center of the mandala. If you are male, assume the naked god-form of the King of Fire, EDLPRNAA. If you are female, assume the naked god-form of the Goddess of Fire, BALOBAN.

Step 10. Same as Step 10 in Path 49.

Step 11. Same as Step 11 in Path 49.

Step 12. Turn from your consort and step outside of the red hexagram. Leave by the same path that you entered. After leaving the Mandala, conduct the banishing pentagram ritual. This completes the sixty-fourth initiatory path.

NOTES TO CHAPTER THIRTEEN

1. The last two lines contain a magical spell. This short spell is to be spoken aloud in the Enochian language. The words mean, "Praises sung in the midst of burning pain will flourish in conquest." Using gematria, the letters add up to 2,411 which reduces to 8 (2+4+1+1=8).

2. From Casaubon, page 360.

3. From Casaubon, page 407.

Pathworking the Watchtower of Fire

4. The Enochian word KUM is given in Table 21 of *Enochian Yoga* as an Enochian magic word associated with the Throat Center (Vishuddha Chakra).

5. This message was delivered to Dee by the Angel MADIMI (see Casaubon, page 226).

6. The letters on the steps correspond to the letters of the Throat Center as given in *Enochian Yoga*. For best results, these letters should be visualized in Enochian as follows:

    B = V̌ F = ⟩ K = ß

7. From Casaubon, page 56.

8. The Enochian word RI, like KUM, is given in Table 21 of *Enochian Yoga* as an Enochian magic word associated with the Throat Center (Vishuddha Chakra).

9. The names of the primary god and goddess of the Watchtower of Fire are from Table 21 of *Enochian Yoga*.

10. These god-forms are from *Enochian Yoga* (see page 170, the Throat Center).

11. This was said by the Angel GABRIEL to Dee (see Casaubon, page 93).

12. This was said by the Angel GABRIEL to Dee (see Casaubon, page 94).

13. From Causabon, page 360.

14. From Casaubon, page 77.

15. Steps 10 and 11 are identical for each of the exercises in the Watchtower of Fire. To conserve space, we refer you to those steps given fully in Path 49 rather than repeat them throughout.

16. From Casaubon, page 368.

17. From Casaubon, page 369.

18. From Casaubon, page 392.

19. From Casaubon, page 153.

20. From Casaubon, page 394.

21. From Casaubon, page 371.

22. From Casaubon, page 373. The word GEBOFAL equals 70 by Crowley's gematria. The words IAD (God) and OADO (to weave) also equal 70.

23. From Casaubon, page 391.

24. From Casaubon, page 56.

25. From Casaubon, page 398.

26. From Casaubon, page 364.

27. From Casaubon, page 251.

28. From Casaubon, page 81.

29. From Casaubon, page 40.

30. From Casaubon, page 80. This message was deliver by the Angel NALVAGE. Note that the word VAOAN means truth.

31. From Casaubon, page 361.

Chapter 14

PATHWORKING THE TABLET OF UNION

This is the fifth and final set of initiatory paths. This set of 24 paths (paths 65 to 88) uses the Complete Enochian Mandala as shown in Figure 91 and Color Plate V. Figure 91 shows the positions throughout these 24 paths (Watchtower position numbers are the same as from Figures 15, 34, 53, and 72) that we will use in our pathworking. Figure 91 also shows the two steps of the central Tablet of Union Mandala with the letters A and D in Enochian (𐤀 and 𐤃) as described in Step 6 of each exercise. Figures 92 through 115 show the 24 paths that you will take through the Complete Enochian Mandala.

THROUGH EARTH TO TABLET OF UNION

PATH SIXTY-FIVE

The Path of Retribution leads through the 3 positions 1-85-89 as shown in Figure 92. It contains the specific atmospheres of justice and manifestation. It is the High Path of Karmic Justice. Use it to ease your karmic burden.

Step 1. Make a circle and conduct the invoking pentagram ritual.

Step 2. Visualize the Complete Enochian Mandala with the Tablet of Union Mandala in the center clearly before you as shown in Figure 91. Face the Emerald Gate at position 1. Recite the Centering Spell.

Step 3. Assume the god-form of the Angel TOPNA standing before the Emerald Gate (position 1). At the entrance say:

> I pass safely through the Watchtower of Earth. I am the Angel TOPNA, the Guardian of the Emerald Gate and I vibrate the holy name MORDIALHKTGA DO-KIKIALE BAUNESA ZIMEZA PIRE, KHRISTEOS MIKAELZO NA-E-EL KHRISTEOS APILA.[1]

The Angels' Message to Humanity

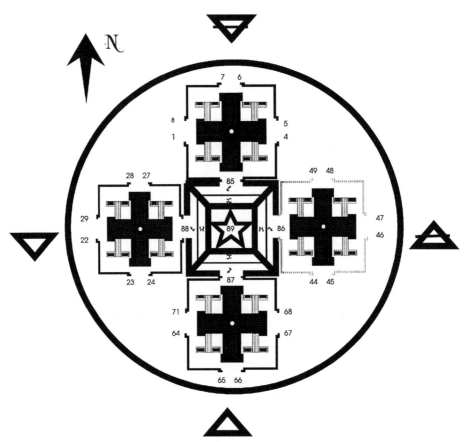

Figure 91: The Tablet of Union Showing Position Numbers

Step 4. Visualize the gate opening at these words. In the god-form of the Angel, alternate the Threefold Holy Name with the magic word DUM² (pronounced doom) as you move counter-clockwise across the Earth-Tier of the Watchtower of Earth toward the Inner Gate of Earth (posiiton 85) that opens to the truncated pyramid at the center of the mandala. These magic words will protect you from the Watchtower Demons. As you approach the Inner Gate of Earth (a combination of the Turquoise and Black Tourmaline Gates), say:

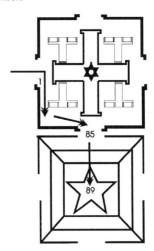

Figure 92: Path 65, The Path of Retribution

When the Earth lies opened unto your eyes, and when the Angels of Light shall offer the passages of the Earth unto the entrances of your senses (chiefly of seeing), then shall you see the Treasures of the Earth,

Pathworking the Tablet of Union

as you go. And the Caves of the Hills shall not be unknown unto you. Unto these, you may say, "Arise, be gone. You are of destruction and of the places of darkness." These are provided for the use of man. So shall you use the wicked, and no otherwise.[3]

When you reach the black Inner Gate of Earth, stop and say the following words:

Cease to plead when Judgement stands in place; For all things are determined already. The Seven Doors are opened. The Seven Governors have almost ended their Government. The Earth labors as sick, yea sick unto death. The Waters pour forth weepings, and have not moisture sufficient to quench their own furrows. The Air withers, for her heat is infected. The Fire consumes, and is scalded with its own heat. The Heavens die above, and are ready to say: "We are weary of our courses." Nature would fain creep again into the bosom of her good and gracious Master. Darkness is now heavy and sinks down all together: She has build up herself. Yea, I say, she has advanced herself into a mighty building. She says, "Have done, for I am ready to receive my burden." Hell itself is weary of Earth. For why? The Son of Darkness comes now to challenge his right, and seeing all things prepared and provided, desires to establish himself a kingdom, saying, "We are now strong enough. Let us now build us a kingdom upon Earth, and establish that which we could not confirm above." And therefore, behold, the End. When the time comes, there will be sweetness, but your sorrows shall be greater than the sweetness; the sorrows of that which you see—in respect of the sweetness of your knowledge. Then you will lament and weep for those you thought were just men. When you earnestly pray, it shall be said to you, "Labor." When you would take Mercy, Justice shall say, "Be it so." Therefore, thirst not overmuch: for fear lest your capacity be confounded. Neither move you Him, who has moved all things already to the End. But do you that which is commanded. Neither prescribe you any form to God, his building. All things shall be brought into an uniform Order.[4]

Step 5. Visualize the Inner Gate opening before you. Enter the Inner Gate and visualize its gaurdian, the sixth Senior of Earth, LIIANSA.

   The god-form of LIIANSA: See page 240 for the god-form of LIIANSA.

See LIIANSA approach you and embrace you in his arms. Feel him merge into you until you have assumed his god-form. As LIIANSA, face the truncated pyramid and say:

The Lord appeared unto them in a vision: But he cometh to you when you are awake: Unto them he came unlooked for, unto you he cometh requested. Arise up therefore, and be not forgetful what the Lord hath done for you; for the things of this World are not, until they be done, neither is there any thing assured, but by the end.[5]

Step 6. The truncated pyramid has two large white steps. Each step has a letter written in glossy black. The letter A is written on the first step, and the letter D is on the second.[6] In the god-form of LIIANSA, say the magic word HAM[7] (Hah-meh).

Climb to the first step and say SONDENNA.[8] Climb to the second step and say MADZILODARP.[9] When you reach the top of the truncated pyramid, stop and say these 6 words:[10] DLASOD ROXTAN RLODNR AUDKAL DARR LULO.

Step 7. If you are male, assume the god-form of the main deity of the Tablet of Union whose name is EHNB.[11] Visualize the goddess BABALON[12] standing naked before you at the center of the mandala which is a large white pentagram. Your consort is waiting for you. If you are female assume the god-form of BABALON and visualize the God, EHNB, standing naked at the center of the mandala and waiting for you.

The god-form of EHNB: See page 238 for the god-form of EHNB.

The god-form of BABALON: See page 238 for the god-form of BABALON.[13]

Step 8. Say the magic word OM[14] letting the final m trail off into silence. Enter the white pentagram and stand facing your consort who is naked and very beautiful before you. While you face each other, see yourself clearly at the center of the Enochian Mandala. Smile at each other as if in love. Then move together and hold each other. Merge God and Goddess of the Magical Universe together while holding a detailed awareness of the entire Tablet of Union Mandala around you. Remain this way for as long as you can and then say:

> **I am the Daughter of Fortitude, and ravished every hour from my youth. For behold, I am Understanding, and Science dwells in me, and the heavens oppress me, they covet and desire me with infinite appetite. Few or none that are earthly have embraced me, for I am shadowed with the Circle of the Stone, and covered with the morning Clouds. My feet are swifter than the winds, and my hands are sweeter than the morning dew. My garments are from the beginning, and my dwelling place is in my self. The Lion knows not where I walk, neither do the beasts of the field understand me. I am deflowered, and yet a virgin. I sanctify, and am not sanctified. Happy is he that embraces me, for in the night season I am sweet, and in the day full of pleasure. My company is a harmony of many Cymbals, and my lips sweeter than health itself. I am a harlot for such as ravish me, and a virgin with such as know me not. For lo, I am loved of many, and I am a lover to many, and as many as come unto me as that should do, have entertainment. And behold, I will bring forth children unto you, and they shall be the Sons of Comfort. I will open my garments, and stand naked before you, that your love may be more enflamed toward me. I will make a dwelling place among you, and I will be common with the father and the son, yea and with all them that truly favor you, for my youth is in her flowers, and my strength is not to be extinguished with men. Strong am I above and below, therefore provide for me.**[15]

Step 9. Step outside of the pentagram. Leave the mandala by the same path that you entered. Conduct the banishing pentagram ritual. This completes the sixty-fifth initiatory path.

Pathworking the Tablet of Union

PATH SIXTY-SIX

The Path of Judgement leads through the 3 positions 5-85-89 as shown in Figure 93. It contains the specific atmospheres of holiness and peace. It is the High Path of Magical Judgement. Use it to strengthen your ability to reason and to make right decisions.

Step 1. Make a circle and conduct the invoking pentagram ritual.

Step 2. Visualize the Complete Pathorking Enochian Mandala with the Tablet of Union Mandala in the center clearly before you as shown in Figure 91. Face the Magnolia Gate at position 5. Recite the Centering Spell.

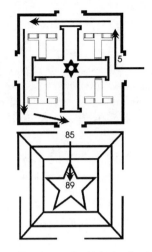

Figure 93: Path 66, The Path of Judgment

Step 3. Assume the god-form of the Angel NOMGG standing before the Magnolia Gate (position 5). At the entrance say:

> I pass safely through the Watchtower of Earth. I am the Angel NOMGG, the Guardian of the Magnolia Gate and I vibrate the holy name MORDIALHKTGA DO-KIKIALE BAUNESA ZIMEZA PIRE, KHRISTEOS MIKAELZO NA-E-EL KHRISTEOS APILA.

Step 4. Same as Step 4 in Path 65 except you pass through the Cypress, Green Jasper, Green Tourmaline, and Emerald Gates, which are all open to you.

Step 5. Visualize the Inner Gate opening before you. Enter the Inner Gate and visualize its gaurdian, the fifth Senior of Earth, AHMLLKV.

The god-form of AHMLLKV: See page 236 for the god-form of AHMLLKV.

See AHMLLKV approach you and embrace you in his arms. Feel him merge into you until you have assumed his god-form. As AHMLLKV, face the truncated pyramid and say:

> O Mother, Mother, if thou shouldst speak unto this poeple, out of and from the Clouds, they would melt before thee, yea, they would fall. But lo thou speakest unto them by thy daughter that they may stand and hear.[16]

Step 6. Same as Step 6 in Path 65 except you are in the god-form of AHMLLKV.

Step 7. Same as Step 7 in Path 65.

Step 8. Same as Step 8 in Path 65.

Step 9. Step outside of the pentagram. Leave the mandala by the same path that you entered. Conduct the banishing pentagram ritual. This completes the sixty-sixth initiatory path.

Path Sixty-Seven

The Path of Fruitfulness leads through the 3 positions 6-85-89 as shown in Figure 94. It contains the specific atmospheres of visions and wealth. It is the High Path of Spiritual Wealth. Use it gain general prosperity.

Step 1. Make a circle and conduct the invoking pentagram ritual.

Step 2. Visualize the Complete Patworking Enochian Mandala with the Tablet of Union Mandala in the center clearly before you as shown in Figure 91. Face the Cypress Gate at position 6. Recite the Centering Spell.

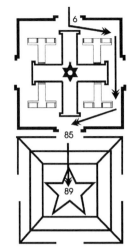

Figure 94: Path 67, The Path of Fruitfulness

Step 3. Assume the god-form of the Angel NIAHL standing before the Cypress Gate (position 6). At the entrance say:

> I pass safely through the Watchtower of Earth. I am the Angel NIAHL, the Guardian of the Cypress Gate and I vibrate the holy name **MORDIALHKTGA DO-KIKIALE BAUNESA ZIMEZA PIRE, KHRISTEOS MIKAELZO NA-E-EL KHRISTEOS APILA.**

Step 4. Same as Step 4 in Path 65 except you travel clockwise, passing through the Magnolia and Green Agate Gates, which are open to you.

Step 5. Visualize the Inner Gate opening before you. Enter the Inner Gate and visualize its gaurdian, the fourth Senior of Earth, ALHKTGA.

The god-form of ALHKTGA: See page 236 for the god-form of ALHKTGA.

See him approach you and embrace you in his arms. Feel him merge into you until you have assumed his god-form. As ALHKTGA, face the truncated pyramid and say:

> The Earth of itself bringeth forth nothing, for it is the lump and excrement of Darkness, whose bowels are a burning lake. But where the heavens yield, and the sun poureth down his force, she openeth herself, and becommeth spongy, receiving mixture to generation, and so is exalted above herself, and bringeth forth to the use of man.[17]

Step 6. Same as Step 6 in Path 65 except you are in the god-form of ALHKTGA.

Step 7. Same as Step 7 in Path 65.

Step 8. Same as Step 8 in Path 65.

Step 9. Step outside of the pentagram. Leave the mandala by the same path that you entered. Conduct the banishing pentagram ritual. This completes the sixty-seventh initiatory path.

PATH SIXTY-EIGHT

The Path of Past Lives leads through the 3 positions 7-85-89 as shown in Figure 95. It contains the specific atmospheres of purification, healing, and memory. It is the High Path of Self-Memory. Use it to recall your past lives.

Step 1. Make a circle and conduct the invoking pentagram ritual.

Step 2. Visualize the Complete Enochian Mandala with the Tablet of Union Mandala in the center clearly before you as shown in Figure 91. Face the Green Jasper Gate at position 7. Recite the Centering Spell.

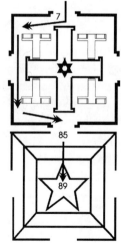

Figure 95: Path 68, The Path of Past Lives

Step 3. Assume the god-form of the Angel AAIRA standing before the Green Jasper Gate (position 7). At the entrance say:

> I pass safely through the Watchtower of Earth. I am the Angel AAIRA, the Guardian of the Green Jasper Gate and I vibrate the holy name MORDIALHKTGA DO-KIKIALE BAUNESA ZIMEZA PIRE, KHRISTEOS MIKAELZO NA-E-EL KHRISTEOS APILA.

Step 4. Same as Step 4 in Path 65 except you pass through the Green Tourmaline and Emerald Gates which are open to you.

Step 5. Visualize the Inner Gate opening before you. Enter the Inner Gate and visualize its gaurdian, the third Senior of Earth, LZINOPO.

> **The god-form of LZINOPO:** See page 240 for the god-form of LZINOPO.

See him approach you and embrace you in his arms. Feel him merge into you until you have assumed his god-form. As LZINOPO, face the truncated pyramid and say:

> **Consider, you are created by God. Consider, you are redeemed by God. Consider, also you are also left to the spiritual tuition and comfort of God.**[18]

Step 6. Same as Step 6 in Path 65 except you are in the god-form of LZINOPO.

Step 7. Same as Step 7 in Path 65.

Step 8. Same as Step 8 in Path 65.

Step 9. Step outside of the pentagram. Leave the mandala by the same path that you entered. Conduct the banishing pentagram ritual. This completes the sixty-eighth initiatory path.

Path Sixty-Nine

The Path of Altruism leads through the 3 positions 8- 85-89 as shown in Figure 96. It contains the specific atmospheres of foreknowledge, creativity, and generousity. It is the High Path of Self-Negation. Use it to strengthen your altruism and compassion.

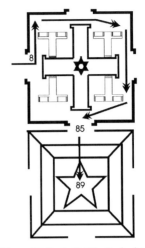

Figure 96: Path 69, The Path of Altruism

Step 1. Make a circle and conduct the invoking pentagram ritual.

Step 2. Visualize the Complete Enochian Mandala with the Tablet of Union Mandala in the center clearly before you as shown in Figure 91. Face the Green Tourmaline Gate at position 8. Recite the Centering Spell.

Step 3. Assume the god-form of the Angel RIZNR standing before the Green Tourmaline Gate (position 8). At the entrance say:

> I pass safely through the Watchtower of Earth. I am the Angel RIZNR, the Guardian of the Green Tourmaline Gate and I vibrate the holy name MORDIALHKTGA DO-KIKIALE BAUNESA ZIMEZA PIRE, KHRISTEOS MIKAELZO NA-E-EL KHRISTEOS APILA.

Step 4. Same as Step 4 in Path 65 except you go clockwise passing through the Green Jasper, Cypress, Magnolia, and Green Agate Gates, which are all open to you.

Step 5. Visualize the Inner Gate opening before you. Enter the Inner Gate and visualize its gaurdian, the second Senior of Earth, AKZINOR.

The god-form of AKZINOR: See page 236 for the god-form of AKZINOR.

See him approach you and embrace you in his arms. Feel him merge into you until you have assumed his god-form. As AKZINOR, face the truncated pyramid and say:

> **Love therefore one another, and comfort one another;
> for he that comforteth his brother, comforteth himself.**[19]

Step 6. Same as Step 6 in Path 65 except you are in the god-form of AKZINOR.

Step 7. Same as Step 7 in Path 65.

Step 8. Same as Step 8 in Path 65.

Step 9. Step outside of the pentagram. Leave the mandala by the same path that you entered. Conduct the banishing pentagram ritual. This completes the sixty-ninth initiatory path.

Pathworking the Tablet of Union

PATH SEVENTY

The Path of Will leads through the 3 positions 4-85-89 as shown in Figure 97. It contains the specific atmospheres of insight, health, and motivation. It is the High Path of the Magical Will. Use it to strengthen your True Will.

Step 1. Make a circle and conduct the invoking pentagram ritual.

Step 2. Visualize the Complete Enochian Mandala with the Tablet of Union Mandala in the center clearly before you as shown in Figure 91. Face the Green Agate Gate at position 4. Recite the Centering Spell.

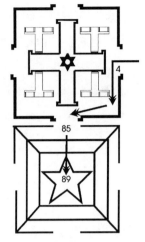

Figure 97: Path 70, The Path of Will

Step 3. Assume the god-form[20] of the Angel ASTIM standing before the Green Agate Gate (position 4). At the entrance say:

> **I pass safely through the Watchtower of Earth. I am the Angel ASTIM, the Guardian of the Green Agate Gate and I vibrate the holy name MORDIALHKTGA DO-KIKIALE BAUNESA ZIMEZA PIRE, KHRISTEOS MIKAELZO NA-E-EL KHRISTEOS APILA.**

Step 4. Same as Step 4 in Path 65 except you go clockwise to the Inner Gate.

Step 5. Visualize the Inner Gate opening before you. Enter the Inner Gate and visualize its guardian, the first Senior of Earth, LAIDROM.

> **The god-form of LAIDROM:** See page 239 for the god-form of LAIDROM.

See him approach you and embrace you in his arms. Feel him merge into you until you have assumed his god-form. As LAIDROM, face the truncated pyramid and say:

> **Invocation proceedeth of the good will of man,
> and of the heat and fervency of the spirit.**[21]

Step 6. Same as Step 6 in Path 65 except you are in the god-form of LAIDROM.

Step 7. Same as Step 7 in Path 65.

Step 8. Same as Step 8 in Path 65.

Step 9. Step outside of the pentagram. Leave the mandala by the same path that you entered. Conduct the banishing pentagram ritual. This completes the seventieth initiatory path.

Through Water to Tablet of Union

Path Seventy-One

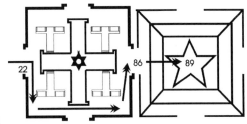

Figure 98: Path 71, The Path of Dream Control

The Path of Dream Control leads through the 3 positions 22-86-89 as shown in Figure 98. It contains the specific atmospheres of knowledge, dreams, and maturity. It is the High Path of Stable Dreams. Use it to gain the ability to consciously control your dreams.

Step 1. Make a circle and conduct the invoking pentagram ritual.

Step 2. Visualize the Complete Enochian Mandala with the Tablet of Union Mandala in the center clearly before you as shown in Figure 91. Face the Amethyst Gate at position 22. Recite the Centering Spell.

Step 3. Assume the god-form of the Angel MPAKO standing before the Amethyst Gate (position 22). At the entrance say:

> I pass safely through the Watchtower of Water. I am the Angel MPAKO, the Guardian of the Amethyst Gate and I vibrate the holy name MPHARSLGAIOL DO-KIKIALE BAUNESA ZIMEZA PIRE, KHRISTEOS MIKAELZO NA-E-EL KHRISTEOS APILA..

Step 4. Visualize the gate opening at these words. In the god-form of the Angel, alternate the Threefold Holy Name with the magic word DUM (pronounced doom) as you move counterclockwise across the Earth-Tier of the Watchtower of Water toward the Inner Gate of Water (position 86) that opens to the truncated pyramid at the center of the mandala. These magic words will protect you from the Watchtower Demons. Pass through the Jade and Rose Gates which are open to you. As you approach the Inner Gate of Water (a comination of the Coral and Crystal Gates), say:

> When the Earth lies opened unto your eyes, and when the Angels of Light shall offer the passages of the Earth unto the entrances of your senses (chiefly of seeing), then shall you see the Treasures of the Earth, as you go. And the Caves of the Hills shall not be unknown unto you. Unto these, you may say, "Arise, be gone. You are of destruction and of the places of darkness." These are provided for the use of man. So shall you use the wicked, and no otherwise.

When you reach the blue Inner Gate of Water, stop and say the following words:

> Wisdom is a piercing beam, which is the center of the spiritual being of the holy Spirit, touching from all parts from whence the Divinity sendeth it out; and is proper to the soul, or unto substances, that have beginning, but no ending; so that, whatsoever shall have end, can never attain unto that which is called Wisdom; Neither can things that are subject to the second death, receive any such influence, because they are already noted, and marked with the Seat of Destruction... for the soul of man is free from all passions and affections, until it enter into the body unto the which it is limited.[22]

Pathworking the Tablet of Union

Step 5. Visualize the Inner Gate opening before you. Enter the Inner Gate and visualize its gaurdian, the sixth Senior of Water, LIGDISA.

The god-form of LIGDISA: See page 239 for the god-form of LIGDISA.

Face the truncated pyramid and say:

> **Blessed are those that are comforted of me, for their strength is from above. For whosoever is rebuked of the Spirit of Truth, shall with time perish as a shadow.[23]**

Step 6. Same as Step 6 in Path 65 except you are in the god-form of LIGDISA.

Step 7. Same as Step 7 in Path 65.

Step 8. Same as Step 8 in Path 65.

Step 9. Step outside of the pentagram. Leave the mandala by the same path that you entered. Conduct the banishing pentagram ritual. This completes the seventy-first initiatory path.

PATH SEVENTY-TWO

The Path of the Self-Expression leads through the 3 positions 23-86-89 as shown in Figure 99. It contains the specific atmospheres of divination, love, and character. It is the High Path of Personality Styling. Use it to change your personality, to become the person that you want to be.

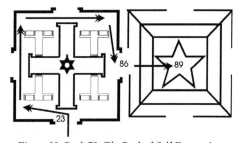

Figure 99: Path 72, The Path of Self Expression

Step 1. Make a circle and conduct the invoking pentagram ritual.

Step 2. Visualize the Complete Enochian Mandala with the Tablet of Union Mandala in the center clearly before you as shown in Figure 91. Face the Jade Gate at position 23. Recite the Centering Spell.

Step 3. Assume the god-form of the Angel MXRNH and stand at the Jade Gate (position 23). At the entrance say:

> **I pass safely through the Watchtower of Water. I am the Angel MXRNH, the Guardian of the Jade Gate and I vibrate the holy name MPHARSLGAIOL DO-KIKIALE BAUNESA ZIMEZA PIRE, KHRISTEOS MIKAELZO NA-E-EL KHRISTEOS APILA..**

Step 4. Same as Step 4 in Path 65 except you go clockwise through the Amethyst, Lapis Lazuli, Sapphire, and Lotus Gates, which are all open to you.

Step 5. Visualize the Inner Gate opening before you. Enter the Inner Gate and visualize its guardian, the fifth Senior of Water, SOAIZNT.

The god-form of SOAIZNT: See page 242 for the god-form of SOAIZNT.

The Angels' Message to Humanity

See him approach you and embrace you in his arms. Feel him merge into you until you have assumed his god-form. As SOAIZNT, face the truncated pyramid and say:

> **When God of very God, the true light, beauty and honor of his Father, contained or was full of the image of an heaven and earth, and by the omnipotent, conjoined, and equal power and strength of them both, joined in one, was brought forth, and had his real beginning, he determineth also, in the self-same Image and Idea, the due and proper order, just law and determination, of all things that were comprehended, which law and things together have their course co-essential both in heaven and earth, distinguishing all things into their real beginnings, limitation of time, and determination between their extremes.**[24]

Step 6. Same as Step 6 in Path 65 except you are in the god-form of SOAIZNT.

Step 7. Same as Step 7 in Path 65.

Step 8. Same as Step 8 in Path 65.

Step 9. Step outside of the pentagram. Leave the mandala by the same path that you entered. Conduct the banishing pentagram ritual. This completes the seventy-second initiatory path.

PATH SEVENTY-THREE

The Path of Sexual Currents leads through the 3 positions 27-86-89 as shown in Figure 100. It contains the specific atmospheres of strength, potency, and sexual desire. It is the High Path of Sexual Fulfillment. Use it to gain power of sexual currents that are located in the Watchtowers and to strengthen your sex drive and potency.

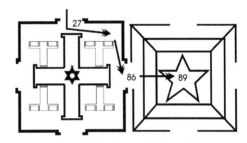

Figure 100: Path 73, The Path of Sexual Currents

Step 1. Make a circle and conduct the invoking pentagram ritual.

Step 2. Visualize the Complete Enochian Mandala with the Tablet of Union Mandala in the center clearly before you as shown in Figure 91. Face the Lotus Gate at position 27. Recite the Centering Spell.

Step 3. Assume the god-form of the Angel ORVLI standing before the Lotus Gate (position 27). At the entrance say:

> **I pass safely through the Watchtower of Water. I am the Angel ORVLI, the Guardian of the Lotus Gate and I vibrate the holy name MPHARSLGAIOL DO-KIKIALE BAUNESA ZIMEZA PIRE, KHRISTEOS MIKAELZO NA-E-EL KHRISTEOS APILA.**

Step 4. Same as Step 4 in Path 71 except you will go clockwise directly to the Inner Gate of Water.

Pathworking the Tablet of Union

Step 5. Visualize the Inner Gate opening before you. Enter the Inner Gate and visualize its gaurdian, the fourth Senior of Water, SLGAIOL.

The god-form of SLGAIOL: See page 242 for the god-form of SLGAIOL.

See him approach you and embrace you in his arms. Feel him merge into you until you have assumed his god-form. As SLGAIOL, face the truncated pyramid and say:

> **For pride is hateful before God: and to be in love with yourselves is the greatest ignorance.**[25]

Step 6. Same as Step 6 in Path 65 except you are in the god-form of SLGAIOL.

Step 7. Same as Step 7 in Path 65.

Step 8. Same as Step 8 in Path 65.

Step 9. Step outside of the pentagram. Leave the mandala by the same path that you entered. Conduct the banishing pentagram ritual. This completes the seventy-third initiatory path.

PATH SEVENTY-FOUR

The Path of Sensitivity leads through the 3 positions 28-86-89 as shown in Figure 101. It contains the specific atmospheres of love and receptivity. It is the High Path of Emotional Awareness. Use it to strengthen your sensitivity to the emotions of others.

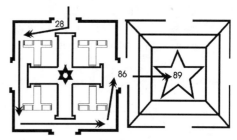

Figure 101: Path 74, The Path of Sensitivity

Step 1. Make a circle and conduct the invoking pentagram ritual.

Step 2. Visualize the Complete Enochian Mandala with the Tablet of Union Mandala in the center clearly before you as shown in Figure 91. Face the Sapphire Gate at position 28. Recite the Centering Spell.

Step 3. Assume the god-form of the Angel KTOKO standing before the Sapphire Gate (position 28). At the entrance say:

> **I pass safely through the Watchtower of Water. I am the Angel KTOKO, the Guardian of the Sapphire Gate and I vibrate the holy name MPHARSLGAIOL DO-KIKIALE BAUNESA ZIMEZA PIRE, KHRISTEOS MIKAELZO NA-E-EL KHRISTEOS APILA.**

Step 4. Same as Step 4 in Path 71 except you pass through the Lapis Lazuli, Amethyst, Jade, and Rose Gates which are all open to you.

Step 5. Visualize the Inner Gate opening before you. Enter the Inner Gate and visualize its gaurdian, the third Senior of Water, LAVAXRP.

The god-gorm of LAVAXRP: See page 239 for the god-form of LAVAXRP.

See him approach you and embrace you in his arms. Feel him merge into ou until you have assumed his god-form. As LAVAXRP, face the truncated pyramid and say:

The Angels' Message to Humanity

> You called for wisdom, God hath opened unto you, his Judgement: He hath delivered unto you the keys, that you may enter; But be humble. Enter not of presumption, but of permission.[26]

Step 6. Same as Step 6 in Path 65 except you are in the god-form of LAVAXRP.

Step 7. Same as Step 7 in Path 65.

Step 8. Same as Step 8 in Path 65.

Step 9. Step outside of the pentagram. Leave the mandala by the same path that you entered. Conduct the banishing pentagram ritual. This completes the seventy-fourth initiatory path.

PATH SEVENTY-FIVE

The Path of Compassion leads through the 3 positions 29-86-89 as shown in Figure 102. It contains the specific atmospheres of divination, love, and goodness. It is the High Path of Benovolence. Use it to strengthen your concern and compassion for others.

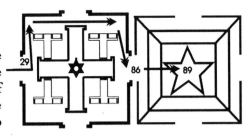

Figure 102: Path 75, The Path of Compassion

Step 1. Make a circle and conduct the invoking pentagram ritual.

Step 2. Visualize the Complete Enochian Mandala with the Tablet of Union Mandala in the center clearly before you as shown in Figure 91. Face the Lapis Lazuli Gate at position 29. Recite the Centering Spell.

Step 3. Assume the god-form of the Angel KSAIZ standing before the Lapis Lazuli Gate (position 29). At the entrance say:

> I pass safely through the Watchtower of Water. I am the Angel KSAIZ, the Guardian of the Lapis Lazuli Gate and I vibrate the holy name MPHARSLGAIOL DO-KIKIALE BAUNESA ZIMEZA PIRE, KHRISTEOS MIKAELZO NA-E-EL KHRISTEOS APILA.

Step 4. Same as Step 4 in Path 71 except you go clockwise passing through the Sapphire and Lotus Gates which are open to you.

Step 5. Visualize the Inner Gate opening before you. Enter the Inner Gate and visualize its gaurdian, the second Senior of Water, SAIINOV.

The god-form of SAIINOV: See page 242 for the god-form of SAIINOV.

See him approach you and embrace you in his arms. Feel him merge into you until you have assumed his god-form. As SAIINOV, face the truncated pyramid and say:

> Happy is he whose mind thirsteth after the knowledge of such things as are spiritual and celestial, of such things as are in the everlasting place and glory of him that is, and was, and shall be for ever: for unto him belongeth rest in the Harvest of the Highest, and comfort in the midst of many worldly sorrows.[27]

Pathworking the Tablet of Union

Step 6. Same as Step 6 in Path 65 except you are in the god-form of SAIINOV.

Step 7. Same as Step 7 in Path 65.

Step 8. Same as Step 8 in Path 65.

Step 9. Step outside of the pentagram. Leave the mandala by the same path that you entered. Conduct the banishing pentagram ritual. This completes the seventy-fifth initiatory path.

Path Seventy-Six

The Path of Magical Power leads through the 3 positions 24-86-89 as shown in Figure 103. It contains the specific atmospheres of enchantment, love, and occult power. It is the High Path of Magic. Use it to strengthen your magical powers.

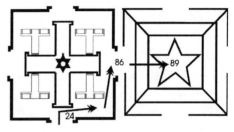

Figure 103: Path 76, The Path of Magical Power

Step 1. Make a circle and conduct the invoking pentagram ritual.

Step 2. Visualize the Complete Enochian Mandala with the Tablet of Union Mandala in the center clearly before you as shown in Figure 91. Face the Rose Gate at position 24. Recite the Centering Spell.

Step 3. Assume the god-form of the Angel AXPKN standing before the Rose Gate (position 24). At the entrance say:

> I pass safely through the Watchtower of Water. I am the Angel AXPKN, the Guardian of the Rose Gate and I vibrate the holy name MPHARSLGAIOL DO-KIKIALE BAUNESA ZIMEZA PIRE, KHRISTEOS MIKAELZO NA-E-EL KHRISTEOS APILA.

Step 4. Same as Step 4 in Path 71 except you go directly to the Inner Gate.

Step 5. Visualize the Inner Gate opening before you. Enter the Inner Gate and visualize its gaurdian, the first Senior of Water, LSRAHPM.

> **The god-form of LSRAHPM:** See page 240 for the god-form of LSRAHPM.

See him approach you and embrace you in his arms. Feel him merge into you until you have assumed his god-form. As LSRAPHM, face the truncated pyramid and say:

> I am the Daughter of Felicity. Remeber all ye, that are drunken with my pleasures, the character I have given you, and prepare yourselves to content with the Highest, set yourselves against him, as against the anointed, for you are become the Children of a Strong Champion: whose son shall garnish you with the Name of a Kingdom, and shall pour wonders amonst you from the stars, which shall put the Sun the Steward of his Waggon, and the Moon the handmaid of his servants.[28] Every Idea in eternity is become forever, and what is thought, is become a living creature. I teach you a mystery.[28]

Step 6. Same as Step 6 in Path 65 except you are in the god-form of LSRAHPM.

The Angels' Message to Humanity

Step 7. Same as Step 7 in Path 65.

Step 8. Same as Step 8 in Path 65.

Step 9. Step outside of the pentagram. Leave the mandala by the same path that you entered. Conduct the banishing pentagram ritual. This completes the seventy-sixth initiatory path.

THROUGH AIR TO TABLET OF UNION

PATH SEVENTY-SEVEN

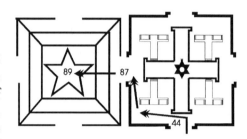

Figure 104: Path 77, The Path of Warding

The Path of Warding leads through the 3 positions 44- 87-89 as shown in Figure 104. It contains the specific atmospheres of magic power, protection, and preservation. It is the High Path of Self-Protection. Use it to protect yourself from all manner of harm.

Step 1. Make a circle and conduct the invoking pentagram ritual.

Step 2. Visualize the Complete Enochian Mandala with the Tablet of Union Mandala in the center clearly before you as shown in Figure 91. Face the Pumice Gate at position 44. Recite the Centering Spell.

Step 3. Assume the god-form of the Angel RSHAL standing before the Pumice Gate (position 44). At the entrance say:

> **I pass safely through the Watchtower of Air. I am the Angel RSHAL, the Guardian of the Pumice Gate and I vibrate the holy name OROIBAHAOZPI DO-KIKIALE BAUNESA ZIMEZA PIRE, KHRISTEOS MIKAELZO NA-E-EL KHRISTEOS APILA.**

Step 4. Visualize the gate opening at these words. In the god-form of the Angel, alternate the Threefold Holy Name with the magic word DUM (pronounced doom) as you move clockwise across the Earth-Tier of the Watchtower of Air toward the Inner Gate of Air (position 87) that opens to the truncated pyramid at the center of the mandala. These magic words will protect you from the Watchtower Demons. As you approach the yellow Inner Gate of Air (a combination of the Pine and Mica Gates), say:

> **When the Earth lies opened unto your eyes, and when the Angels of Light shall offer the passages of the Earth unto the entrances of your senses (chiefly of seeing), then shall you see the Treasures of the Earth, as you go. And the Caves of the Hills shall not be unknown unto you. Unto these, you may say, "Arise, be gone. You are of destruction and of the places of darkness." These are provided for the use of man. So shall you use the wicked, and no otherwise.**[29]

Pathworking the Tablet of Union

When you reach the yellow Inner Gate of Air, stop and say the following words:

> **I have been promised the secret knowledge and understanding of the Philosopher's Stone, of the Book of St. Dunstans, to have the knowledge of them. I am he who must deal with Devils, and with Sorcery, and with Witchcraft, even the devils Maserien and Hermeloe, the Four Wicked Ones, the which are accounted the four Rulers of the Air, whose names be Ories, Egym, Paynim, and Mayrary. They be the Devils that I must deal withall. Should I deal rightly, I shall have promises and wisdom, the Philospher's Stone of the Book of St. Dunstans, and the secret wisdom of that Jewel shall be delivered.**[30]

Step 5. Visualize the Inner Gate opening before you. Enter the Inner Gate and visualize its gaurdian, the sixth Senior of Air, HIPOTGA.

The god-form of HIPOTGA: See page 238 for the god-form of HIPOTGA.

See him approach you and embrace you in his arms. Feel him merge into you until you have assumed his god-form. As HIPOTGA, face the truncated pyramid and say:

> **Flesh can never be throughly mortified but with death.**[31]

Step 6. Same as Step 6 in Path 65 except you are in the god-form of HIPOTGA.

Step 7. Same as Step 7 in Path 65.

Step 8. Same as Step 8 in Path 65.

Step 9. Step outside of the pentagram. Leave the mandala by the same path that you entered. Conduct the banishing pentagram ritual. This completes the seventy-seventh initiatory path.

PATH SEVENTY-EIGHT

The Path of Understanding leads through the 3 positions 47-87-89 as shown in Figure 105. It contains the specific atmospheres of love, psychic power, and purposeful action. It is the High Path of Magical Intent. Use it to strengthen your understanding of magic.

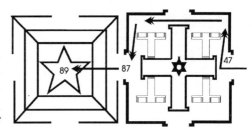

Figure 105: Path 78, The Path of Understanding

Step 1. Make a circle and conduct the invoking pentagram ritual.

Step 2. Visualize the Complete Enochian Mandala with the Tablet of Union Mandala in the center clearly before you as shown in Figure 91. Face the Acacia Gate at position 47. Recite the Centering Spell.

Step 3. Assume the god-form of the Angel AOYVB standing before the Acacia Gate (position 47). At the entrance say:

> **I pass safely through the Watchtower of Air. I am the Angel AOYVB, the Guardian of the Acacia Gate and I vibrate the holy name**

The Angels' Message to Humanity

OROIBAHAOZPI DO-KIKIALE BAUNESA ZIMEZA PIRE,
KHRISTEOS MIKAELZO NA-E-EL KHRISTEOS APILA.

Step 4. Same as Step 4 in Path 77 except you go counterclockwise through the Aspen and Papyrus Gates which are open to you.

Step 5. Visualize the Inner Gate opening before you. Enter the Inner Gate and visualize its gaurdian, the fifth Senior of Air, AVTOTAR.

> **The god-form of AVTOTAR:** This Senior is very masculine. His body is muscular with large wings for easy traveling. His features are fierce and terrible to look upon. He wears an orange robe. He carries the mighty Sword of AVTOTAR in his right hand and an oak staff in his left hand. He uses the Sword to create new forms and his staff to bestow creative power and energy.

See him approach you and embrace you in his arms. Feel him merge into you until you have assumed his god-form. As AVTOTAR, face the truncated pyramid and say:

> **Of this Knowledge I have laid a sure foundation, have taught what is, and the instrument wherewithal, and whereby it is. The manner of proceeding, and her Basis. So that there wanteth nothing but the simple and easy unknitting of those things that are wrapped, not with the bands of itself, but with the obscurity and caliginous Clouds of your own ignorance.**[32]

Step 6. Same as Step 6 in Path 65 except you are in the god-form of AVTOTAR.

Step 7. Same as Step 7 in Path 65.

Step 8. Same as Step 8 in Path 65.

Step 9. Step outside of the pentagram. Leave the mandala by the same path that you entered. Conduct the banishing pentagram ritual. This completes the seventy-eighth initiatory path.

PATH SEVENTY-NINE

The Path of Pattern leads through the 3 positions 48- 87-89 as shown in Figure 106. It contains the specific atmospheres of eloquence and a strong sense of purposeful arrangement. It is the High Path of Order. Use it to strengthen your sense of order and organization.

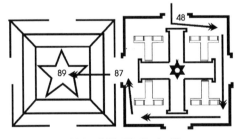

Figure 106: Path 79, The Path of Pattern

Step 1. Make a circle and conduct the invoking pentagram ritual.

Step 2. Visualize the Complete Enochian Mandala with the Tablet of Union Mandala in the center clearly before you as shown in Figure 91. Face the Aspen Gate at position 48. Recite the Centering Spell.

Step 3. Assume the god-form of the Angel ADIRL standing before the Aspen Gate (position 48). At the entrance say:

Pathworking the Tablet of Union

I pass safely through the Watchtower of Air. I am the Angel ADRIL, the Guardian of the Aspen Gate and I vibrate the holy name OROIBA-HAOZPI DO-KIKIALE BAUNESA ZIMEZA PIRE, KHRISTEOS MIKAELZO NA-E-EL KHRISTEOS APILA.

Step 4. Same as Step 4 in Path 77 except you pass through the Acacia, Maple, Aventurine, and Pumice Gates which are all open to you.

Step 5. Visualize the yellow Inner Gate of Air opening before you. Enter the Inner Gate and visualize its gaurdian, the fourth Senior of Air, AHAOZPI.

The god-form of AHAOZPI: This Senior is thin and delicate. He has large wings and he wears a violet robe that looks like the sky at sunset. He carries a Scepter made of cedar in his right hand and a poppy, the Opiate of AHAOZPI, in his left hand. He uses the narcotic to dispense lust and the Scepter to dispense compassion.

See him approach you and embrace you in his arms. Feel him merge into you until you have assumed his god-form. As AHAOZPI, face the truncated pyramid and say:

But understand that hoc opus unum receiveth Multiplication and dignification, by ascension through all the rest that are limited according to their proper qualities.[33]

Step 6. Same as Step 6 in Path 65 except you are in the god-form of AHAOZPI.

Step 7. Same as Step 7 in Path 65.

Step 8. Same as Step 8 in Path 65.

Step 9. Step outside of the pentagram. Leave the mandala by the same path that you entered. Conduct the banishing pentagram ritual. This completes the seventy-ninth initiatory path.

Path Eighty

The Path of Intuition leads through the 3 positions 49-87-89 as shown in Figure 107. It contains the specific atmospheres of powerful communication and spontaneity. It is the High Path of Magical Instinct. Use it to strengthen your intuitions.

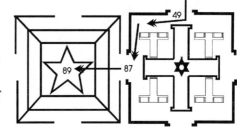

Figure 107: Path 80, The Path of Intuition

Step 1. Make a circle and conduct the invoking pentagram ritual.

Step 2. Visualize the Complete Enochian Mandala with the Tablet of Union Mandala in the center clearly before you as shown in Figure 91. Face the Papyrus Gate at position 49. Recite the Centering Spell.

Step 3. Assume the god-form of the Angel XKZNS standing before the Papyrus Gate (position 49). At the entrance say:

The Angels' Message to Humanity

> I pass safely through the Watchtower of Air. I am the Angel XKZNS, the Guardian of the Papyrus Gate and I vibrate the holy name OROIBA-HAOZPI DO-KIKIALE BAUNESA ZIMEZA PIRE, KHRISTEOS MIKAELZO NA-E-EL KHRISTEOS APILA.

Step 4. Same as Step 4 in Path 77 except you go counterclockwise directly to the Inner Gate of Air.

Step 5. Visualize the yellow Inner Gate of Air opening before you. Enter the Inner Gate and visualize its gaurdian, the third Senior of Air, HTNORDA.

The god-form of HTNORDA: See page 238 for the god-form of HTNORDA.

See him approach you and embrace you in his arms. Feel him merge into you until you have assumed his god-form. As HTNORDA, face the truncated pyramid and say:

> **But put all these things up amonst the secrets of your hearts, as though not seeing, yet feeling all things.**[34]

Step 6. Same as Step 6 in Path 65 except you are in the god-form of HTNORDA.

Step 7. Same as Step 7 in Path 65.

Step 8. Same as Step 8 in Path 65.

Step 9. Step outside of the pentagram. Leave the mandala by the same path that you entered. Conduct the banishing pentagram ritual. This completes the eightieth initiatory path.

PATH EIGHTY-ONE

The Path of Wisdom leads through the 3 positions 45-87- 89 as shown in Figure 108. It contains the specific atmospheres of knowledge, intelligence, and reason. It is the High Path of the Seer. Use it to gain wisdom in all things.

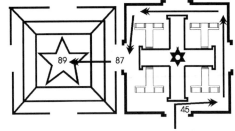

Figure 108: Path 81, The Path of Wisdom

Step 1. Make a circle and conduct the invoking pentagram ritual.

Step 2. Visualize the Complete Enochian Mandala with the Tablet of Union Mandala in the center clearly before you as shown in Figure 91. Face the Aventurine Gate at position 45. Recite the Centering Spell.

Step 3. Assume the god-form of the Angel PAKKA standing before the Aventurine Gate (position 45). At the entrance say:

> I pass safely through the Watchtower of Air. I am the Angel PAKKA, the Guardian of the Aventurine Gate and I vibrate the holy name OROIBAHAOZPI DO-KIKIALE BAUNESA ZIMEZA PIRE, KHRISTEOS MIKAELZO NA-E-EL KHRISTEOS APILA.

Step 4. Same as Step 4 in Path 77 except you go counterclockwise and you pass through the Maple, Acacia, Aspen, and Papyrus Gates which are all open to you.

Pathworking the Tablet of Union

Step 5. Visualize the Inner Gate opening before you. Enter the Inner Gate and visualize its gaurdian, the second Senior of Air, AAOZAIF.

The god-form of AAOZAIF: See page 235 for the god-form of AAOZAIF.

See him approach you and embrace you in his arms. Feel him merge into you until you have assumed his god-form. As AAOZAIF, face the truncated pyramid and say:

Thy mouth, O Lord, is a two-edged sword, thy judgements are perpetual and everlasting, thy words are the spirits of truth and understanding.[35]

Step 6. Same as Step 6 in Path 65 except you are in the god-form of AAOZAIF.

Step 7. Same as Step 7 in Path 65.

Step 8. Same as Step 8 in Path 65.

Step 9. Step outside of the pentagram. Leave the mandala by the same path that you entered. Conduct the banishing pentagram ritual. This completes the eighty-first initiatory path.

PATH EIGHTY-TWO

The Path of Courage leads through the 3 positions 46- 87-89 as shown in Figure 109. It contains the specific atmospheres of health and daring. It is the High Path of Daring. Use it to strengthen your courage and to banish fear.

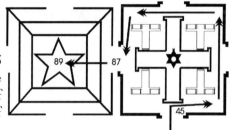

Figure 109: Path 82, The Path of Courage

Step 1. Make a circle and conduct the invoking pentagram ritual.

Step 2. Visualize the Complete Enochian Mandala with the Tablet of Union Mandala in the center clearly before you as shown in Figure 91. Face the Maple Gate at position 46. Recite the Centering Spell.

Step 3. Assume the god-form of the Angel PPMOX and stand at the Maple Gate (position 46). At the entrance say:

I pass safely through the Watchtower of Air. I am the Angel PPMOX, the Guardian of the Maple Gate and I vibrate the holy name OROIBAHAOZPI DO-KIKIALE BAUNESA ZIMEZA PIRE, KHRISTEOS MIKAELZO NA-E-EL KHRISTEOS APILA.

Step 4. Same as Step 4 in Path 77 except you pass through the Aventurine and Pumice Gates which are open to you.

Step 5. Visualize the Inner Gate opening before you. Enter the Inner Gate and visualize its gaurdian, the first Senior of Air, HABIORO.

The god-form of HABIORO: See page 238 for the god-form of HABIORO.

The Angels' Message to Humanity

See him approach you and embrace you in his arms. Feel him merge into you until you have assumed his god-form. As HABIORO, face the truncated pyramid and say:

> God hath spoken unto you, and hath gathered you together, and lo, you are become a strong Sword, with the which the Nations shall be cut down, and the God of Hosts shall stretch for his hands; And behold, you are come, and now is the time you Satan shall reap.[36]

Step 6. Same as Step 6 in Path 65 except you are in the god-form of HABIORO.

Step 7. Same as Step 7 in Path 65.

Step 8. Same as Step 8 in Path 65.

Step 9. Step outside of the pentagram. Leave the mandala by the same path that you entered. Conduct the banishing pentagram ritual. This completes the eighty-second initiatory path.

THROUGH FIRE TO TABLET OF UNION

PATH EIGHTY-THREE

The Path of Lust leads through the 3 positions 64-87-89 as shown in Figure 110. It contains the specific atmospheres of sexual energy and lust. It is the High Path of Ecstacy. Use it to attain spiritual ecstacy and to strengthen your bliss (amrita).

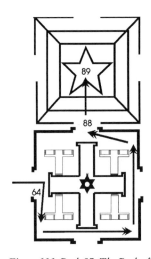

Figure 110: Path 83, The Path of Lust

Step 1. Make a circle and conduct the invoking pentagram ritual.

Step 2. Visualize the Complete Enochian Mandala with the Tablet of Union Mandala in the center clearly before you as shown in Figure 91. Face the Onyx Gate at position 64. Recite the Centering Spell.

Step 3. Assume the god-form of the Angel ODATT standing before the Onyx Gate (position 64). At the entrance say:

> I pass safely through the Watchtower of Fire. I am the Angel ODATT, the Guardian of the Onyx Gate and I vibrate the holy name IOPTEAAPDOKE DO-KIKIALE BAUNESA ZIMEZA PIRE, KHRISTEOS MIKAELZO NA-E-EL KHRISTEOS APILA.

Step 4. Visualize the gate opening at these words. In the god-form of the Angel, alternate the Threefold Holy Name with the magic word DUM (pronounced doom) as

Pathworking the Tablet of Union

you move counterclockwise across the Earth-Tier of the Watchtower of Fire toward the Inner Gate of Fire (position 88) that opens to the truncated pyramid at the center of the mandala. You will pass through the Diamond, Sulfur, Amber, Flint, Topaz, and Cedar Gates which are to be visualized as open to you. These magic words will protect you from the Watchtower Demons. As you approach the yellow Inner Gate of Air (a combination of the Cedar and Topaz Gates), say:

> **When the Earth lies opened unto your eyes, and when the Angels of Light shall offer the passages of the Earth unto the entrances of your senses (chiefly of seeing), then shall you see the Treasures of the Earth, as you go. And the Caves of the Hills shall not be unknown unto you. Unto these, you may say, "Arise, be gone. You are of destruction and of the places of darkness." These are provided for the use of man. So shall you use the wicked, and no otherwise.**

When you reach the red Inner Gate of Fire, stop and say the following words:

> **He that pawneth his soul for me, loseth it not, and he that dieth for me, dieth to eternal life. Behold you shall as Lambs be brought forth before men in your latter days, and shall be overthrown and slain, and your bodies tossed to and fro. But I will receive you again, and will be full of power. And you shall be comforted with the joys of your brethren, for I have many that secretly serve me, for I will lead you into the way of Knowledge and Understanding. And Judgment and Wisdom shall be upon you, and shall be restored unto you. And you shall grow every day, wise and mighty in me.**[37]

Step 5. Visualize the Inner Gate opening before you. Enter the Inner Gate and visualize its gaurdian, the sixth Senior of Fire, ARINNAP.

The god-form of ARINNAP: See page 237 for the god-form of ARINNAP.

See him approach you and embrace you in his arms. Feel him merge into you until you have assumed his god-form. As ARINNAP, face the truncated pyramid and say:

> **Wheresoever thou wilt, God doth prize thy willing desire.**[38]

Step 6. Same as Step 6 in Path 65 except you are in the god-form of ARINNAP.

Step 7. Same as Step 7 in Path 65.

Step 8. Same as Step 8 in Path 65.

Step 9. Step outside of the pentagram. Leave the mandala by the same path that you entered. Conduct the banishing pentagram ritual. This completes the eighty-third initiatory path.

PATH EIGHTY-FOUR

The Path of Versatility leads through the 3 positions 65-88-89 as shown in Figure 111. It contains the specific atmospheres of love, spirituality, and versatility. It is the High Path of Mobility and Change. Use it to strengthen your ability to adapt to new situations.

Step 1. Make a circle and conduct the invoking pentagram ritual.

Step 2. Visualize the Complete Enochian Mandala with the Tablet of Union Mandala in the center clearly before you as shown in Figure 91. Face the Diamond Gate at position 65. Recite the Centering Spell.

Step 3. Assume the god-form of the Angel ORGAN standing before the Diamond Gate (position 65). At the entrance say:

> **I pass safely through the Watchtower of Fire. I am the Angel ORGAN, the Guardian of the Diamond Gate and I vibrate the holy name IOPTEAAPDOKE DO-KIKIALE BAUNESA ZIMEZA PIRE, KHRISTEOS MIKAELZO NA-E-EL KHRISTEOS APILA.**

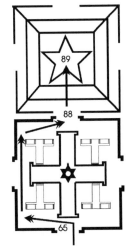

Figure 111: Path 84 The Path of Versatility

Step 4. Same as Step 4 in Path 83 except you pass through the Onyx and Oak Gates which are open to you.

Step 5. Visualize the red Inner Gate of Fire opening before you. Enter the Inner Gate and visualize its gaurdian, the fifth Senior of Fire, ANODOIN.

> **The god-form of ANODOIN:** See page 237 for the god-form of ANODOIN.

See him approach you and embrace you in his arms. Feel him merge into you until you have assumed his god-form. As ANODOIN, face the truncated pyramid and say:

> **If the Smith prove and temper his Gold by fire, his intent is to excell in the work that he hath in hand: that thereby it might be tried, refined, and made apt, to the end wherein it shall be used. Much more, think you, doth the God of Wisdom, forge, try, and beat out, such as he intendeth to use in the execution of his divine and eternal purposes.**[39]

Step 6. Same as Step 6 in Path 65 except you are in the god-form of ANODOIN.

Step 7. Same as Step 7 in Path 65.

Step 8. Same as Step 8 in Path 65.

Step 9. Step outside of the pentagram. Leave the mandala by the same path that you entered. Conduct the banishing pentagram ritual. This completes the eighty-fourth initiatory path.

PATH EIGHTY-FIVE

The Path of Appearances leads through the 3 positions 68-88-89 as shown in Figure 112. It contains the specific atmospheres of peace and enchantment. It is the High Path of Magical Illusions. Use it to strengthen your ability to see through illusions.

Pathworking the Tablet of Union

Step 1. Make a circle and conduct the invoking pentagram ritual.

Step 2. Visualize the Complete Enochian Mandala with the Tablet of Union Mandala in the center clearly before you as shown in Figure 91. Face the Flint Gate at position 68. Recite the Centering Spell.

Step 3. Assume the god-form of the Angel TGMNM standing before the Flint Gate (position 68). At the entrance say:

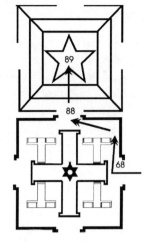

Figure 112: Path 85, The Path of Appearances

> I pass safely through the Watchtower of Fire. I am the Angel TGMNM, the Guardian of the Flint Gate and I vibrate the holy name **IOPTEAAPDOKE DO-KIKIALE BAUNESA ZIMEZA PIRE, KHRISTEOS MIKAELZO NA-E-EL KHRISTEOS APILA.**

Step 4. Same as Step 4 in Path 83 except you go counterclockwise directly to the Inner Gate of Fire.

Step 5. Visualize the red Inner Gate of Fire opening before you. Enter the Inner Gate and visualize its gaurdian, the fourth Senior of Fire, AAPDOKE.

> **The god-form of AAPDOKE:** See page 235 for the god-form of AAPDOKE.

See him approach you and embrace you in his arms. Feel him merge into you until you have assumed his god-form. As AAPDOKE, face the truncated pyramid and say:

> **Wo, wo, be unto them that are delivered, for their tribulation is great. There is horror and gnashing of teeth, there is misery and vengence for ever, there is horror and the Worm of Conscience. But two things are to be considered here, whether the temptation be greater than the resistance, or the resistance more dignified than the rigor of temptation.**[40]

Step 6. Same as Step 6 in Path 65 except you are in the god-form of AAPDOKE.

Step 7. Same as Step 7 in Path 65.

Step 8. Same as Step 8 in Path 65.

Step 9. Step outside of the pentagram. Leave the mandala by the same path that you entered. Conduct the banishing pentagram ritual. This completes the eighty-fifth initiatory path.

Path Eighty-Six

The Path of Imagination leads through the 3 positions 71-88-89 as shown in Figure 113. It contains the specific atmospheres of love and hallucinations. It is the High Path of Reality. Use it to enhance your magical imagination.

Step 1. Make a circle and conduct the invoking pentagram ritual.

Step 2. Visualize the Complete Enochian Mandala with the Tablet of Union Mandala in the center clearly before you as shown in Figure 91. Face the Oak Gate at position 71. Recite the Centering Spell.

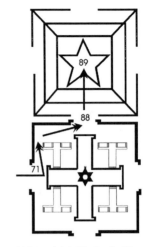

Figure 113: Path 86, The Path of Imagination

Step 3. Assume the god-form of the Angel IVASG standing before the Oak Gate (position 71). At the entrance say:

> **I pass safely through the Watchtower of Fire. I am the Angel IVASG, the Guardian of the Oak Gate and I vibrate the holy name IOPTEAAPDOKE DO-KIKIALE BAUNESA ZIMEZA PIRE, KHRISTEOS MIKAELZO NA-E-EL KHRISTEOS APILA.**

Step 4. Same as Step 4 in Path 83 except you directly to the Inner Gate of Fire.

Step 5. Visualize the Inner Gate opening before you. Enter the Inner Gate and visualize its gaurdian, the third Senior of Fire, ALNKVOD.

> **The god-form of ALNKVOD:** See page 236 for the god-form of ALNKVOD

See him approach you and embrace you in his arms. Feel him merge into you until you have assumed his god-form. As ALNKVOD, face the truncated pyramid and say:

> **Hath the Sun entered into your bowels, or have you tasted of the night-dew?**[41]

Step 6. Same as Step 6 in Path 65 except you are in the god-form of ALNKVOD.

Step 7. Same as Step 7 in Path 65.

Step 8. Same as Step 8 in Path 65.

Step 9. Step outside of the pentagram. Leave the mandala by the same path that you entered. Conduct the banishing pentagram ritual. This completes the eighty-sixth initiatory path.

Path Eighty-Seven

The Path of Enthusiasm leads through the 3 positions 66-88-89 as shown in Figure 114. It contains the specific atmospheres of happiness and eagerness. It is the High Path of Energized Enthusiasm. Use it to strengthen your magical enthusiasm and zest for life.

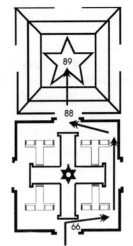

Step 1. Make a circle and conduct the invoking pentagram ritual.

Step 2. Visualize the Complete Enochian Mandala with the Tablet of Union Mandala in the center clearly before you as shown in Figure 91. Face the Sulfur Gate at position 66. Recite the Centering Spell.

Figure 114: Path 87, The Path of Enthusiasm

Step 3. Assume the god-form of the Angel MADRE standing before the Sulfur Gate (position 66). At the entrance say:

> I pass safely through the Watchtower of Fire. I am the Angel MADRE, the Guardian of the Sulfur Gate and I vibrate the holy name IOPTEAAPDOKE DO-KIKIALE BAUNESA ZIMEZA PIRE, KHRISTEOS MIKAELZO NA-E-EL KHRISTEOS APILA.

Step 4. Same as Step 4 in Path 83 except you go pass through the Amber and Flint Gates which are open to you.

Step 5. Visualize the Inner Gate opening before you. Enter the Inner Gate and visualize its gaurdian, the second Senior of Fire, ADAEOET.

The god-form of ADAEOET: See page 235 for the god-form of ADAEOET.

See him approach you and embrace you in his arms. Feel him merge into you until you have assumed his god-form. As ADAEOET, face the truncated pyramid and say:

Simple Faith excelleth all Science.[42]

Step 6. Same as Step 6 in Path 65 except you are in the god-form of ADAEOET.

Step 7. Same as Step 7 in Path 65.

Step 8. Same as Step 8 in Path 65.

Step 9. Step outside of the pentagram. Leave the mandala by the same path that you entered. Conduct the banishing pentagram ritual. This completes the eighty-seventh initiatory path.

Path Eighty-Eight

The Path of Desire leads through the 3 positions 67-88- 89 as shown in Figure 115. It contains the specific atmospheres of prophecy, love, and raw power. It is the High Path of Magical Wishes. Use it to control and direct your desires.

Step 1. Make a circle and conduct the invoking pentagram ritual.

Step 2. Visualize the Complete Enochian Mandala with the Tablet of Union Mandala in the center clearly before you as shown in Figure 91. Face the Amber Gate at position 67. Recite the Centering Spell.

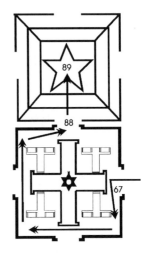

Figure 115: Path 88, The Path of Desire

Step 3. Assume the god-form of the Angel MAKAR standing before the Amber Gate (position 67). At the entrance say:

> I pass safely through the Watchtower of Fire. I am the Angel MAKAR, the Guardian of the Amber Gate and I vibrate the holy name IOPTEAAPDOKE DO-KIKIALE BAUNESA ZIMEZA PIRE, KHRISTEOS MIKAELZO NA-E-EL KHRISTEOS APILA.

Step 4. Same as Step 4 in Path 83 except you go clockwise and pass through the Sulfur, Diamond, Onyx, and Oak Gates which are all open to you.

Step 5. Visualize the Inner Gate opening before you. Enter the Inner Gate and visualize its gaurdian, the first Senior of Fire, AAETPIO.

The god-form of AAETPIO: See page 235 for the god-form of AAETPIO.

Face the truncated pyramid and say:

> Every letter in PARAOAN, is a living fire: but all of one quality and of one Creation: But unto N is delivered a Vial of Destruction, according to that part he is of PARAOAN the Governor.[43]

Step 6. Same as Step 6 in Path 65 except you are in the god-form of AAETPIO.

Step 7. Same as Step 7 in Path 65.

Step 8. Same as Step 8 in Path 65.

Step 9. Step outside of the pentagram. Leave the mandala by the same path that you entered. Conduct the banishing pentagram ritual. This completes the eighty-eighth initiatory path.

Pathworking the Tablet of Union

NOTES TO CHAPTER FOURTEEN

1. The last three lines contain a magical spell. This short spell is to be spoken aloud in the Enochian language. The words mean, "In the mystery of these vestures of the Holy Ones, may my power be mighty and may it endure for ever." Using gematria, the letters add up to 2,969 which reduces to 8 (2+9+6+9=26=2+6=8).

2. The Enochian word DUM is given in Table 21 of *Enochian Yoga* as an Enochian magic word associated with the Brow Center (Ajna Chakra).

3. These words were spoken by the Angel AVE. The message provides guidance on how/when to use the Demons (see Casaubon, page 188).

4. This passage was delivered by the Angel MURIFRI to Dee through Kelly in May 1583 (see page 4 of Casaubon).

5. From Casaubon, page 74.

6. The letters on the steps correspond to the letters of the Brow Center as given in *Enochian Yoga*. For best results, these letters should be visualized in Enochian as follows:

    A = ∂ D = ⊥

7. The Enochian word HAM, like DUM, is given in Table 21 of *Enochian Yoga* as an Enochian magic word associated with the Brow Center (Ajna Chakra).

8. This Angel's name is from Casaubon, page 185. SONDENNA—wicked but full of knowledge of future events—takes the form of a Giant. In both Golden Dawn gematria and in Greek gematria, the name has the value of 430, where in Greek, 430 = NOMOS (law) and ORNIS (prophecy).

9. This Angel's name is from Casaubon, page 216. MADZILODARP—"the God of Conquest"—in the 16th Call. With Crowley's gematria the name is equal to 326, the number for YARRY (providence, fate).

10. These words are from Casaubon, pages 363 and 386. DLASOD ROXTAN RLODNR AUDKAL DARR LULO = 1666 (using Crowley's gematria) which reduces to 1 (1+6+6+6=19=1+9=10=1+0=1). These words are "the mediating ways to the Center." Where, DLASOD = sulphur ROXTAN = wine AUDKAL = gold DAAR = Philosophers Stone LULO = Tartar

11. The name EHNB is found reading down the first (leftmost) column of letters in the Tablet of Union as shown in Table 5.

12. BABALON is the highest goddess in Enochian Magic. In a psychological sense, she can be considered as the feminine archetype of the collective unconscious.

13. During this supreme visualization, EHNB and BABALON are both to be seen as being perfect in form.

14. The Enochian word OM (which means understanding) is given in Table 21 of *Enochian Yoga* as an Enochian magic word associated with the Crown Center (Sahasrara Chakra).

15. This passage can be found in Casaubon, page 25 in ACTIO TERTIA. It was delivered to Dee on Saturday, May 23, 1587 and spoken by the "Daughter of Comfort."

16. From Casaubon, page 378.

17. From Casaubon, page 368.

18. From Casaubon, page 412.

19. From Casaubon, page 394.

The Angels' Message to Humanity

20. These god-forms are from our Enochian Tarot.
21. From Casaubon, page 188.
22. This passage is taken from Casaubon, page 26 in ACTIO TERTIA.
23. From Casaubon, page 419.
24. From Casaubon, page 383.
25. From Casaubon, page 373.
26. From Casaubon, page 145.
27. From Casaubon, page 24 in ACTIO TERTIA.
28. From Casaubon, page 410.
29. From Casaubon, page 24.
30. This passage is paraphrased from Casaubon, page 34 in ACTIO TERTIA.
31. From Casaubon, page 138.
32. From Casaubon, page 373.
33. From Casaubon, page 393.
34. From Casaubon, page 381.
35. From Casaubon, page 409.
36. From Casaubon, page 401.
37. This passage is taken from Casaubon, page 23 in ACTIO TERTIA.
38. From Casaubon, page 37 in ACTIO TERTIA.
39. From Casaubon, page 189.
40. From Casaubon, page 393.
41. From Casaubon, page 73.
42. From Casaubon, page 74.
43. From Casaubon, page 188.

Chapter 15

THE TABLET OF CHAOS

The proceeding chapters have described eighty-eight specific pathways through the Enochian Tablets. There are actually many additional paths that are possible from the Earth-Tiers leading to the Fire- Tiers and to the Tablet of Union. Furthermore, we have mentioned Demons that can be encountered through the Earth-Tier of each Watchtower Mandala. These Demons reside on the Tablet of Chaos, shown in Figure 116.[1] This tablet is created from the Tablet of Union (see Figure 5) by reversing its twenty letters. Just as the Tablet of Union was used to create the Tablet of Union Mandala as shown in Figures 11 and 12, so this tablet is used to create the Tablet of Chaos Mandala shown in Figures 13 and 14. So far, we have not made use of this mandala. We will now use this mandala as a polar or counter to the Tablet of Union Mandala in what we call the Enochian Cube. We will now describe the Enochian Cube.

The Enochian Cube is a six-sided cube with the four Watchtower Mandalas on each of the four sides, the Tablet of Union on the top, and the Tablet of Chaos on the bottom.[2] In this way, the spiritual forces found in the Tablet of Union are counterbalanced by the demonic forces found in the Tablet of Chaos.[3] They are separated from each other by the four Watchtowers. The cube thus represents a three-dimensional model of the entire magical universe as described in Enochian Magic.

The Tablet of Chaos is shown in Figure 116. Observe that it consists of twenty letters which are the same as those in Figure 5 except they are written backwards. In Enochian Magic, the demonic side

Fire	Earth	Water	Air	Spirit	
M	O	T	I	B	Fire
A	T	N	A	N	Earth
A	M	O	K	H	Water
P	R	A	X	E	Air

Figure 116: The Tablet of Chaos

The Angels' Message to Humanity

of any angelic being or force can sometimes be known simply by reversing the letters of its name. So in the Tablet of Chaos, the element Fire is called MOTIB, while in the Tablet of Union it is BITOM. The highest god of this Tablet is BNHE which is the reverse spelling of EHNB. The highest goddess is NOLABAB which is BABALON spelled backwards. To symbolize these demonic powers, we use a counterclockwise spiral with three and one half turns as shown in Figures 13 and 14. The sun moves in a clockwise direction and counterclockwise or widdershins is traditionally the direction of evil (it is also the direction of magic). In Tantra, the goddess Kundalini, in the form of a snake, is said to reside in our subtle body at a point corresponding to the base of the spine and she is said to be lying asleep in three and one half turns or coils. Thus three and one half is the number for our individual creative potential which is yet wild and untamed. It is exactly this chaotic creative potential, on a global scale, that resides in the Tablet of Chaos. [4]

Figure 117 shows the six Mandalas that comprise one version of the Enochian Cube. This version is called the Directional Enochian Cube. Each mandala forms one side of the cube. The figure shows the cube as if it had just been unfolded or opened

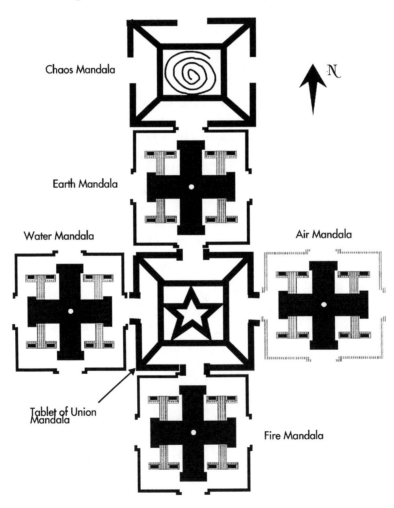

Figure 117: The Six Mandalas and the Directional Enochian Cube

The Tablet of Chaos

out flat with the Earth and Chaos Mandalas toward the North. If we look at the cube downward from the top, the four Watchtower Mandalas on the sides are arranged together in the four directions given by the Golden Dawn.[5] When we use the cube this way, we visualize ourselves as being at the center of the cube - i.e., every magician is at the center of the magical universe.

We have found that the directional cube is not the only version that is suitable for pathworking purposes. Figure 118 shows our second version of this cube, which we call the Serial Enochian Cube. Here the four Watchtower Mandalas are arranged in serial order so that we have Fire, Air, Water, and then Earth, connected together in a clockwise direction, the natural direction of all manifestation. They are also connected in a counterclockwise direction from Earth to Water, Air, and then Fire because this is the direction of magic. Most magical operations use the widdershins direction because most magic opposes the natural order of things. In both versions, the Tablet of Union and Tablet of Chaos are opposite each other and are connected only through one of the Watchtowers (the only difference between the two versions is that Air and

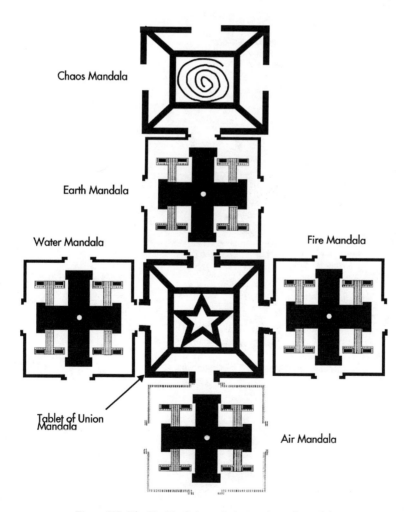

Figure 118: The Six Mandalas and the Serial Enochian Cube

The Angels' Message to Humanity

Fire have switched positions). We have found that the Directional Enochian Cube is especially suited to invoking or evoking operations, while the Serial Enochian Cube is especially suited to astral traveling or pathworking. However, both can be used for either, and the difference is largely personal. We do not recommend that anyone pathwork the Tablet of Chaos, nor do we see any need to move "through" the cube (which would be equivalent to traveling through our physical Earth). When using the directional cube, to pass from one Watchtower to another, we can either return to our body (the center of the cube) and then travel out again in another direction, or we can pass directly from one Watchtower to an adjacent Watchtower by making an appropriate "ninety-degree turn" which would be equivalent to passing through a cosmic Ring-Pass-Not.

In order to arrive at a larger number of possible pathways through the magical universe, we can allow each mandala or surface of the cube to rotate about a central pivot. Figure 119, for example, shows the Fire Mandala being rotated counterclockwise.

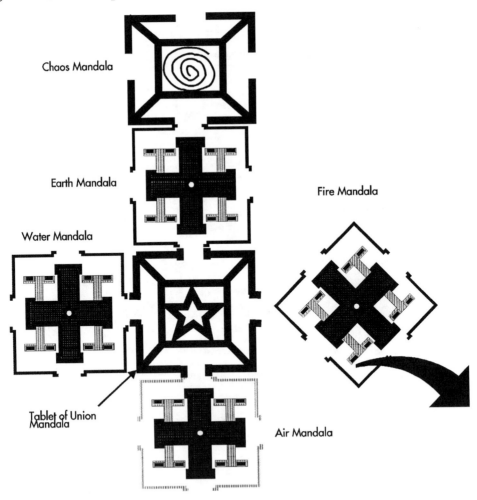

Figure 119: Rotating Fire on the Serial Enochian Cube

The Tablet of Chaos

Rotations of the Watchtowers allow the Gates to match up with different Gates of adjacent mandalas. Thus each Watchtower Mandala can connect to the Tablet of Union, for example, in eight ways or through eight separate paths because each of the eight Gates can be connected to the Tablet of Union. They can also connect to the Tablet of Chaos in eight ways. Each Watchtower Mandala can connect to an adjacent Watchtower Mandala in eight by eight, or sixty-four possible ways. In this way, the cube allows for a wide variety of pathways that can be taken through the magical universe. Also, rotation of each Watchtower mandala can give us four different Inner Gates for each Watchtower Mandala to make connection with the Tablet of Union.

Probably the easiest way to make an Enochian Cube for yourself is to use cardboard and construction paper. Cut six squares out of cardboard and glue them together to form a cube. Then cut six squares out of construction paper the same size as your cardboard squares. Draw the six mandalas on the squares of construction paper with as much detail as you can (you can simplify this step by using a copier machine to copy the mandalas shown in this book). Attach each mandala to an appropriate side of the cardboard cube using a small brad through the center. Your cube is now complete. By rotating the sides around the brad, you can discover a variety of possible pathways through the magical universe.

Another method is to use a standard plastic photo cube that you can purchase in many gift shops. Draw or copy scaled-down versions of the six mandalas given in this book to fit each of the sides of the photo cube. Insert the pictures in the appropriate faces of the cube and you will have a nice Enochian Cube. Figure 120 shows a cube that we made this way.

In a real sense, the Enochian Cube is a three-dimensional model of the Enochian magical universe. But it allows us access to pathways through the magical universe that are not traditional. For example, the Watchtower of Earth and the Watchtower of Fire are adjacent on the cube. This implies secret Gates that can take us directly from one to the other, rather like a wormhole in spacetime as defined in modern theoretical astronomy (in this case the "wormhole" would be located in the Great Outer Abyss).

The standard model of the magical universe used in Enochian Magic is similar to that shown in Figure 91 as well as in color plate V.[6] This model is two-dimensional and consists of John Dee's five Holy Tablets in the form of mandalas spread out, with each region facing the traditional four directions. Our new model comprises six mandalas by adding the Tablet of Chaos to the Earth Mandala as shown in Figures 117 and 118 as well as in color plates VI and VII. Then the six mandalas are folded into a three-dimensional cube. The Enochian Cube allows us to travel through each of the

Figure 120: Photo of an Enochian Cube

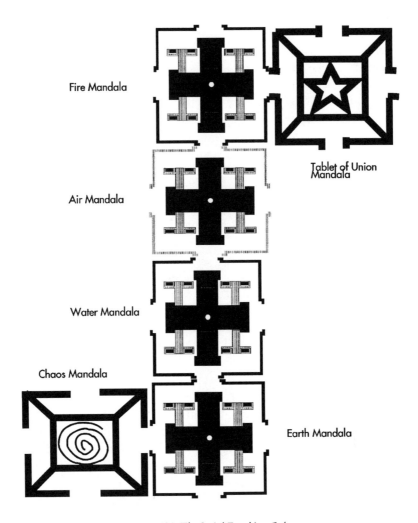

Figure 121: The Serial Enochian Cube

four Watchtowers and Tablet of Union in a wide variety of ways. Now, lets look at the cube in another way. Figure 121 shows what we call the Serial Enochian Cube which is unfolded in a serial order, from Earth to Water, then Air, then Fire, and then the Tablet of Union - in that order only. We must return backwards through the five areas, again in a serial order. This configuration conforms with pathworking experience and especially with a specific magical operation called Rising on the Planes.[7]

Using the cube as a model, secret pathways allow us to travel in previously unavailable paths. We can still go through the Watchtowers in the same way, but now we can also travel directly between Earth and Fire. We can also travel from any Watchtower to any other Watchtower by going through the Tablet of Union, which is now available from all four Watchtowers. The Tablet of Chaos (so called because it opposes the Tablet of Union which represents the foundation of order and pattern) is a new addition to the more traditional Enochian model. Understandably, little is

The Tablet of Chaos

known about this region, except that within it reside those demonic beings who thwart the creative order of the Kings, Seniors, and Angels of the Watchtowers. This Tablet can be said to correspond to the Qliphoth of the Qabala, the "shells" or shadowy side of the 10 Sephiroth. It thus contains the Tunnels of Set[8] which are said to contain the core of all Sethian or demonic forces in our universe.

NOTES TO CHAPTER FIFTEEN

1. We are suggesting that the Tablet of Chaos represents a separate region somewhere in the magical universe. It is unclear if this region is below our Earth (like the Avichi of modern theosophy) or above it (possibly the lowest subplane of the astral plane where some say Hell is located). It is even possible that the Tablet of Chaos represents our own Earth, or some other location on the physical plane. Further research is needed here.

2. The notion of top and bottom is, of course, completely arbitrary. We suggest that when you initially use the cube, the "top" should face upward toward your head, while the "bottom" should face downward toward your feet. During your operations, you will rotate the cube anyway, so its directional orientation will always be relative to how you are looking at it.

3. The idea of providing a balance of forces is not only esthetically pleasing, but it is also necessary for stability. In the same way, heaven balances hell, and spirit balances matter.

4. In *The Occult Power of Numbers*, W. Wynn Westcott says that 3+ is half of seven and thus represents "present suffering as compared with future joy." (Newcastle Publishing, p. 49) The tantric goddess, Kundalini, is equivalent to the Enochian TELOKH-VOVIN or "death-dragon," which James equates to the fallen one of the Great Outer Abyss called KHRONONZON (reference *The Enochian Evocation of Dr. John Dee*, ed. & trans. by Geoffrey James, p. 101. This excellent reference book has been recently released by Llewellyn under the title *The Enochian Magick of Dr. John Dee*).

5. We refer the reader to Donald Tyson's introduction for a good discussion of the problems associated with Watchtower directions. We have maintained the directions used by the Golden Dawn throughout this work, but we personally would prefer switching the Watchtowers of Air and Water so that Water is in the East (the direction of the rising sun and of birth) and Air is in the West (the direction of the setting sun and of death).

6. For the standard model, see our Cosmic Planes and Elements Model in Figure 12 on page 41 of our *Enochian Physics*.

7. Rising on the Planes was an exercise taught by the Golden Dawn and adopted by Crowley in his own magical school (see his *Liber O*).

8. The Tunnels of Set are described by Kenneth Grant in *Nightside of Eden*. Grants writes, "The qliphoth are not only the shells of the 'dead' but, more importantly they are the anti- forces behind the Tree and the negative substratum that underlies all positive life." (Frederick Muller Limited, p. 31). This is exactly the sense in which the Tablet of Chaos should be viewed.

Glossary

GOD-FORMS

The god-form of AAAN: A dark masculine Kerubic Angel with very large wings wearing an emerald green robe. AAAN wears a magical ring with an emerald set in copper that bestows foreknowledge.

The god-form of AAETPIO: This Senior has a fierce countenance and is awesome to behold. He has large wings and his entire body is enveloped in flames. He wears a deep violet robe. He carries the Rod of Love in his right hand and an olive branch in his left hand. The Rod bestows love, the strongest power known, to everyone it touches. If love already exists, then the Rod will magnify it sevenfold. The olive branch bestows acceptance.

The god-form of AAIRA: A masculine Angel with very large wings wearing a red-orange robe. He holds a censure with storax incense that purifies everyone who smells it.

The god-form of AAOZAIF: This Senior is thin and delicate. He has large wings and he wears a blood-red robe. He carries a pearl-studded Cup in his right hand and an opium poppy in his left hand. The Cup contains the Wine of Compassion. The opium poppy bestows an understanding of the World's Sorrow.

The god-form of AAPDOKE: This Senior is terrible to look upon. He is very strong and of fierce countenance. He has large wings and he wears a green robe studded with emeralds. He carries a Wand in his right hand and an aphrodisiac in his left hand. The Wand of AAPDOKE is used to cast bonds of attachment and spells of desire and lust. The aphrodisiac is used to bestow love.

The god-form of ABALPT: See yourself as "he who stoops down" because of your concern for those who are beneath you. You should wear an amber robe. ABALPT is masculine with large wings. In this god-form, you have the power to beautify anything you see before you.

The god-form of ADAEOET: This Senior has a fierce countenance and is terrible to look upon. He wears a deep yellow robe studded with agates. His entire body is covered with small darting flames. He carries an agate-studded Cup in his right hand and a large opal in his left hand. The Cup contains the Wine of Healing. The opal bestows strength and resolve.

The god-form of ADIRL: A beautiful, delicate, feminine Angel with small wings wearing a red-orange robe. She holds a topaz medallion that bestows protection from all harm.

The god-form of ADTA: A very handsome, masculine Kerubic Angel with large wings. He wears a blue robe and holds a pendant of brown zircon that transforms everything it touches into gold.

The god-form of AHAOZPI: This Senior is thin and delicate. He has large wings and he wears a violet robe that looks like the sky at sunset. He carries a Scepter made of cedar in his right hand and a poppy, the Opiate of AHAOZPI, in his left hand. He uses the narcotic to dispense lust and the Scepter to dispense compassion.

The god-form of AHMLLKV: This Senior combines masculine and feminine qualities. He is strong and dark in complexion, and very graceful in motion. He wears a scarlet robe. He carries a ram's horn, the Horn of AHMLLKV that purifies all who can hear it, in his right hand and a tiger lily in his left hand. His form should be accompanied by a sense of timelessness.

The god-form of AIAOAI: See yourself as "he who is within you," because you are more concerned with inner values than outer appearances. You should wear a scarlet robe. AIAOAI has masculine characteristics with large wings. In this form, you are completely purified of bad karma, and you can purify all who come before you.

The god-form of AKPS: A strong masculine Kerubic Angel with small wings wearing an amber robe. He holds a black rose that bestows protection from harm.

The god-form of AKZINOR: This Senior is very masculine; he is big and strong and his movements are powerful. He wears a rose pink robe and a wreath of laurel crowns his head. He carries a ceramic Cup in his right hand and a large yellow diamond in his left hand. The Cup contains the Wine of Harmony. The diamond bestows peace.

The god-form of ALHKTGA: This Senior combines masculine and feminine qualities. He is strong and his movements are graceful. He is very sexually attractive. He wears an emerald green robe. He carries a rose in his right hand and an aphrodisiac in his left hand. The aphrodisiac of ALHKTGA bestows great sexual desire and attraction.

The god-form of ALNKVOD: This Senior has dark hair and eyes. He is very strong and is beautiful to look upon. He wears an amber robe and crescent-shaped sandals. He carries a Wand in his right hand and a lotus in his left hand. ALNKVOD is passive. He has dedicated himself to serving others. The Wand of ALNKVOD is used to cast enchantments.

The god-form of ALOBABN: This beautiful Goddess of the Watchtower of Air wears a white tiara. She has golden-yellow hair. She holds a yellow Dagger in her right hand inscribed with the magical word MUM in blue. She holds a large topaz shewstone in her left hand.

Glossary

The god-form of AMSAL: A masculine Angel whose movements are graceful. He has large wings and wears an indigo robe. He holds a large quartz crystal through which you can see the secret workings of the universe.

The god-form of ANAA: A dark masculine Kerubic Angel with very large wings wearing an emerald green robe. ANAA holds a large emerald pendant that bestows love.

The god-form of ANAEEM: See yourself as "he who is nine times obedient" to emphasize your sense of obedience to law. ANAEEM combines masculine and feminine characteristics. In this god-form, you should see yourself with white wings and wearing a white robe. As ANAEEM, you have the power to enter samadhi and all manner of exalted states of consciousness.

The god-form of ANGPOI: See yourself as "he who divides thoughts." ANGPOI combines masculine and feminine characteristics. See yourself wearing a yellow robe. In this form you have the power to enter into the Knowledge and Conversation of your Holy Guardian Angel and you can attain your True Will.

The god-form of ANODOIN: This Senior has dark hair and eyes and he is very beautiful to look upon. He wears an orange robe that is made of fiery flames. He carries a Wand in his right hand and a Scourge in his left hand. ANODOIN reads the karma of all who come before him and he either punishes or rewards accordingly. The reward of ANODOIN is creative power.

The god-form of AOVRRZ: See yourself as "he who beautifies everything he sees." The god-form of AOVRRZ has hard, masculine characteristics. In this form, you should wear an indigo robe. As AOVRRZ, you have the power to quicken action, and can ease the karmic burden of anyone who comes before you.

The god-form of AOYVB: A dark, active, masculine Angel with small wings wearing an indigo robe. He holds a rose quartz pendant that stimulates love and sexuality.

The god-form of ARINNAP: This Senior has a dark silent aspect and is frightening to behold. He has large wings and his entire body is enveloped in flames. He wears a yellow robe. He carries the Wand of Wishes in his right hand and a flaming Sword in his left hand. The Wand bestows a wish to everyone it touches. The sword bestows protection and security.

The god-form of ARNIL: A dark, masculine Angel with small wings, wearing a violet purple robe. He holds an opal that bestows visions.

The god-form of ASTIM: A masculine Angel with small wings wearing a yellow robe. He holds a rock crystal through which you can see your inner divine nature.

The god-form of AVTOTAR: This Senior is very masculine. His body is muscular with large wings for easy traveling. His features are fierce and terrible to look upon. He wears an orange robe. He carries the mighty Sword of AVTOTAR in his right hand and an oak staff in his left hand. He uses the Sword to create new forms and his staff to bestow creative power and energy.

The god-form of AXPKN: A large, masculine Angel with small wings, wearing an amber robe. He holds a pendant of amber that casts enchantments.

The Angels' Message to Humanity

The god-form of BABALON: The god-form of BABALON is the most perfect and sexually attractive female that you can imagine.

The god-form of BALOBAN: This beautiful Goddess of the Watchtower of Fire wears a silver tiara. She has long red hair. She holds a red Wand in her right hand that is inscribed with the magical word RI in green. She holds a large fire opal in her left hand.

The god-form of BATAIVAH: The King of Air holding a Sword in his left hand and a Dagger in his right hand. He wears a yellow crown. He stands with his right foot out in a stance of action. BATAIVAH is merciful and loving, and speaks with a beautiful voice that is both pleasant and seductive. No one can lie to this King, who sees through all deception immediately.

The god-form of BATN: A dark, active, masculine Kerubic Angel with small wings wearing an amber robe. BATN wears a ring with a large emerald set in silver that bestows love.

The god-form of BOZA. A very masculine and active Kerubic Angel with small wings. He wears an orange robe and holds a red ruby that bestows magic power.

The god-form of DOPA: An attractive Kerubic Angel with both masculine and feminine characteristics. DOPA has small wings and wears a blue robe. DOPA holds a rutilated quartz crystal that bestows energy and power.

The god-form of EDLPRNAA: The King of Fire holding a Wand in his right hand and a flaming torch in his left hand. He wears a red crown. EDLPRNAA is dangerous and quick to anger. He has a violent temper. His nature is to change things. He can destroy things with his touch.

The god-form of EHNB: The god-form of EHNB is the most perfect and sexually attractive male that you can imagine.

The god-form of GLMA: A graceful, beautiful, feminine Kerubic Angel with small wings, wearing a deep violet robe. She holds an amethyst that bestows sexual love.

The god-form of HABIORO: This Senior is active and very energetic. He has small wings and he wears an amber robe. He carries the Rod of Life in his right hand and a rose in his left hand. The Rod bestows life to whatever it touches. The rose bestows beauty and harmony.

The god-form of HIPOTGA: This Senior has feminine characteristics. He has small wings and he wears an elegant pink robe. He carries the Wand of Well-Being in his right hand and a large yellow diamond in his left hand. The Wand bestows health and harmony to whatever it touches. The yellow diamond bestows joy.

The god-form of HTNORDA: This Senior has a soft and loving face with dark hair and eyes. His body is heavy but well proportioned. He wears a light blue robe that looks like thin clouds or a light mist. He carries a Dagger in his right hand and a sprig of hashish, the Herb of HTNORDA, in his left hand. He uses the hashish to dispense dreams and visions.

The god-form of IAAASD: See yourself as "he who is in truth." The god-form of IAAASD has clearly masculine characteristics. This god-form has large wings and wears an orange robe. In this form you have the power to foretell the future, and like an oracle, can answer one question from anyone who comes before you.

The god-form of IAOM: This Kerubic Angel combines masculine and feminine characteristics, wears a scarlet robe, and holds a ram's horn. When this Angel blows the horn, the clear sound bestows purification.

The god-form of IDOIGO: See yourself as "she who sits on the holy throne." IDOIGO has soft, feminine characteristics. In this god-form, you should wear a yellow robe. In the form of IDOIGO, you have an inner power of communication with all living beings, and can bestow this power on all who come before you.

The god-form of IKZHIKAL: The King of Earth holds a black Pantacle in his left hand. He wears a black crown. IKZHIKAL lives in the past and hates change. His nature is to make things remain as they are. He seeks to describe and define all things by giving them a name. His presence enhances the sense of identity and clarifies memory. His nature is to give all who come before him a sense of identity and purpose.[14]

TThe god-form of IMTD: A very beautiful, delicate, feminine Kerubic Angel without wings, wearing a yellow robe. She holds a lily whose fragrance bestows mystic experiences.

The god-form of IOPMN: A fierce feminine Angel without wings wearing an emerald green robe. She holds a large turquoise that bestows love.

The god-form of IVASG: A dark handsome masculine Angel with small wings wearing an amber robe. He holds a large emerald pendant that bestows love.

The god-form of KSAIZ: A very masculine Angel with small wings, wearing a blue robe. He holds a string of pearls that bestows the power of divination.

The god-form of KTOKO: A strong, active, and very masculine Angel. He has no wings and wears a violet robe. He holds a stone of lapis lazuli that bestows fame.

The god-form of LAIDROM: This Senior has strong feminine characteristics; he is delicate and his movements are graceful.[20] He wears a light green robe. He carries a Pantacle made from a sunflower in his right hand and a large Cats Eye in his left hand. The Pantacle bestows raw animalistic power while the Cats Eye bestows control of that power.

The god-form of LARZ: A graceful, masculine Kerubic Angel with small wings wearing a pink robe. LARZ holds a sprig of acacia that bestows psychic powers.

The god-gorm of LAVAXRP: This Senior is masculine and moves about with graceful strength. He has dark hair and large wings and he wears a deep blue robe that looks like flowing water. He carries a Cup in his right hand and a lotus in his left hand. By means of his Cup, he bestows prophecy and foreknowledge.

The god-form of LIGDISA: This Senior has feminine characteristics. He is very beautiful and his countenance is peaceful and loving. He wears an indigo robe and sandals. He carries the Wand of Working in his right hand and a mandrake in his left hand. The Wand bestows the power of proper functioning on whatever it touches. The mandrake bestows harmonious energy.

The Angels' Message to Humanity

The god-form of LIIANSA: This Senior has strong feminine characteristics; he is delicate and his large wings are graceful. He wears a violet purple robe. He carries the Wand of Wonder in his right hand and a large Fire Opal in his left hand. The Wand bestows the sense of awe and delight while the Fire Opal bestows transcendence.

The god-form of LLAKZA: See yourself as "he who is first to precipitate," to emphasize your creative nature. LLAKZA has hard, masculine characteristics. This god-form should wear a blue robe. In this form, you have the power of clairvoyance, and can bestow clairvoyance to all who come before you.

The god-form of LOBABAN: The beautiful Goddess of the Watchtower of Water wears a violet tiara. She has blue hair, and holds a blue Cup in her right hand that is inscribed in yellow with the magical word TRAM. She holds a mirror in her left hand.[12]

The god-form of LSRAHPM: This Senior has feminine characteristics. He has small wings and his body is graceful and beautiful. He wears an orange robe. He carries the Rod of Power in his right hand and a lightening bolt in his left hand. The Rod bestows occult powers. The lightening bolt slays all who oppose him.

The god-form of LZINOPO: This Senior combines masculine and feminine qualities. He is thin and his movements are graceful. He wears a yellow-orange robe. He carries a Pantacle in his right hand and a large topaz in his left hand. The Pantacle of LZINOPO bestows great strength.

The god-form of MADRE: A fiery feminine Angel with small wings wearing a crimson robe. He holds a large amethyst that bestows beauty and happiness.

The god-form of MAGL: A graceful, beautiful, feminine Kerubic Angel with small wings, wearing a deep violet robe. She holds an amethyst that bestows true and lasting love.

The god-form of MAKAR: A heavy, strong, masculine Angel with large wings wearing an amber robe. He holds a yellow rose whose fragrance bestows prophecy.

The god-form of MALADI: See yourself as "she who shoots arrows" to emphasize your nature as a hunter. In this form you should wear a crimson robe. The god-form of MALADI has soft, feminine characteristics and large wings. In this form you will understand sorrow and suffering and all manner of feeling, and can dispense feelings to those who come before you.

The god-form of MPAKO: A strong, masculine Angel with short wings, wearing a yellow robe. He holds an opal that bestows knowledge.

The god-form of MXRNH: A dark, masculine Angel without wings, wearing a pale yellow robe. He holds a topaz that bestows the power of divination.

The god-form of NELAPR: See yourself as "he who has his way." The god-form of NELAPR combines masculine and feminine characteristics. You should wear a deep violet robe. In this form, you are filled with love, and can cause love to enter the hearts of all who come before you.

The god-form of NIAHL: A feminine, graceful, delicate Angel with small wings. She wears a violet purple robe and holds a fire opal that bestows visions.

Glossary

The god-form of NKRO: A strong. dark, masculine Kerubic Angel wearing a yellow robe. He holds an agate that bestows knowledge.

The god-form of NLRX: A dark, graceful, masculine Kerubic Angel without wings, wearing an amber robe. He holds a lotus that he uses to cast enchantments.

The god-form of NOALMR: See yourself as "he who is first to bring torment" to emphasize your fierce aspect. The god-form of NOALMR has predominately hard masculine characteristics. In this form you should wear a violet purple robe. As NOALMR, you have the power to manifest your thoughts and desires, and you can bestow the power of manifestation to all who come before you.

The god-form of NOMGG: A feminine Angel of great beauty without wings and wearing a scarlet robe. She holds a red ruby that consecrates everything it touches.

The god-form of OBGOTA: See yourself as "he who is like a garland," because your presence is like beautiful flowers. The god-form of OBGOTA has strong, masculine characteristics. You should wear a red-orange robe. In this form you have awesome strength, and can bestow strength upon all who come before you.

241

The god-form of ODATT: A fierce active masculine Angel with small wings wearing a blue robe. He holds a large pearl that bestows love and sexual attraction.

The god-form of OIAGM: A beautiful, feminine Angel with small wings, wearing an emerald green robe. She holds an emerald vase containing a powerful love potion.

The god-form of OMIA: This Kerubic Angel combines masculine and feminine characteristics, wears a scarlet robe, and holds a ram's horn. When this Angel blows the horn, the clear sound bestows harmony.

The god-form of OPMNIR: See yourself as "he who increases knowledge." The god-form of OPMNIR combines masculine and feminine characteristics. You should wear a pink robe. In this form you have the power to bring harmony to yourself and to all who come before you.

he god-form of ORABALN: The beautiful Goddess of the Watchtower of Earth wears a golden tiara. She has black hair. She holds a black Pantacle in her right hand with the letters AH inscribed in white. She holds a lotus bud ready to bloom in her left hand.

The god-form of ORGAN: A dark masculine Angel with small wings wearing a blue robe. He holds a large moonstone that bestows love and sexual attraction.

The god-form of ORVLI: A dark, masculine Angel without wings, wearing a red-orange robe. He holds a topaz that bestows physical strength.

The god-form of PADO: An attractive Kerubic Angel with both masculine and feminine characteristics. PADO has small wings and wears a blue robe. PADO holds a smoky quartz crystal that bestows happiness.

The god-form of PAKKA: A big, strong, masculine Angel with large wings, wearing an indigo robe. He holds a quartz crystal that bestows the secrets of the universe.

The god-form of PAYT: An active Kerubic Angel who has both masculine and feminine characteristics. PAYT has small wings, wears a yellow robe, and holds a fire opal that bestows riches.

The god-form of PHRA: A heavy, hermaphroditic Kerubic Angel wearing a violet purple robe. He holds an opal that bestows visions.

The god-form of PPMOX: This is a fierce-looking feminine Angel, terrible to behold. She has no wings and wears a red-orange robe. She holds a large topaz that bestows health and healing.

The god-form of PSAK: A strong masculine Kerubic Angel with small wings wearing an amber robe. He holds a red rose that bestows beauty.

The god-form of RAAGIOSL:. The King of Water is shown holding a golden Cup in his left hand. He wears a blue crown. RAAGIOSL is highly creative; his nature is to make things. He seeks, through life-giving creativity, to express infinite spiritual ideas through finite forms. He has the power to place living beings into bodies, and is a master of the forces of life. He can bestow the gifts of healing and longevity.

The god-form of RABMO: An active, masculine Angel with small wings wearing a pink robe. He holds a yellow diamond that bestows harmony.

The god-form of RAPH: A heavy, hermaphroditic Kerubic Angel wearing a violet purple robe. He holds an opal that bestows truthfulness.

The god-form of RIZNR: A heavy, masculine Angel without wings wearing a blue robe. He holds a moonstone that bestows clairvoyance.

The god-form of RONK: A strong, dark, masculine Kerubic Angel wearing a yellow robe. He holds an agate that bestows healing.

The god-form of RSHAL: A graceful yet masculine Angel with small wings wearing an orange robe. He holds a deep red ruby that bestows magical powers.

The god-form of RXNL: A dark, masculine Angel with small wings, wearing a violet purple robe. He holds a mandrake that bestows occult visions.

The god-form of RZIONR: See yourself as "he who is in the waters of the sun" to emphasize your solar nature. The god-form of RZIONR has definite masculine characteristics. In this form, you should wear a red robe. As RZIONR, you have a mighty inner strength, and you can give strength to all who come before you.

The god-form of RZLA: A graceful, masculine Kerubic Angel with small wings wearing a pink robe. He holds a sprig of laurel which bestows protection for evil.

The god-form of SAIINOV: This Senior has dark complexion. He has small wings with dark hair and eyes and he wears a blue robe and he carries a crystal Cup in his right hand and a large moonstone in his left hand. The Cup contains the Wine of Clairvoyance. The moonstone bestows insight.

The god-form of SLGAIOL: This Senior moves about with grace and beauty. He has large wings with light hair and eyes and he wears a yellow robe and he carries a large crystal shewstone in his right hand and a willow staff in his left hand. With his shewstone he bestows visions, and with his staff he creates desires.

The god-form of SOAIZNT: This Senior is very masculine and moves about with pride and confidence. He has small wings. He wears an indigo robe and sandals. He carries a quartz shewstone in his right hand and an orchid in his left hand. By means of the shewstone, he bestows wisdom and knowledge.

Glossary

The god-form of TAAD: A very handsome, masculine Kerubic Angel with large wings. He wears a blue robe and holds a pendant of yellow zircon that bestows the power to transform emotions into love.

The god-form of TAXIR: A masculine Angel with small wings wearing a red-orange robe. He holds a topaz that bestows great physical strength.

The god-form of TBRAP: A fierce masculine Angel with small wings wearing a yellow robe. He holds a large blood agate that bestows the power of healing.

The god-form of TGMNM: A beautiful feminine Angel without wings wearing a blue robe. She holds a large blue quartz crystal that bestows peace and tranquility.

The god-form of TNBA: A dark, active, masculine Kerubic Angel with small wings wearing an amber robe. He holds a large emerald that bestows beauty and sexual attraction.

The god-form of TDIM: A very beautiful, delicate, feminine Kerubic Angel without wings, wearing a yellow robe. She holds a lily whose fragrance bestows awareness of divinity.

The god-form of TOPNA: A strong, dark, masculine Angel with small wings wearing an orange robe. He holds a nettle in his left hand and a scourge in his right.

The god-form of VADALI: See yourself as "he who has the Secret Truth." The god-form of VADALI combines masculine and feminine characteristics and should have large wings. In this form you should wear a yellow robe. As VADALI, every action you make is with meaning and purpose. You can bestow the power of proper action to all who come before you.

The god-form of VOLXDO: See yourself as "he whose name is annihilation" because you seek to annihilate forms. In this form you should wear a green robe. As VOLXDO, you have predominately masculine characteristics. You can make yourself invisible, and can bestow the power of invisibility on all who come before you.

The god-form of XFMND: A dark, handsome, masculine Angel without wings, wearing a red-orange robe. He wears a topaz ring on his right hand that bestows protection from all harm.

The god-form of XGZD: A beautiful Kerubic Angel who combines both masculine and feminine characteristics. XGZD has no wings, wears an amber robe, and holds a red rose that bestows love.

The god-form of XKZNS: A strong, dark, masculine Angel without wings wearing a greenish-yellow robe. He holds a cat's eye medallion that bestows power over all lower life forms, including animals and demons.

The god-form of YTPA: An active Kerubic Angel who has both masculine and feminine characteristics. YPTA has small wings, wears a yellow robe, and holds a black opal that bestows magical powers.

The god-form of ZABO: A very masculine and active Kerubic Angel with small wings. He wears an orange robe and holds a red ruby that bestows creative energy.

The god-form of ZAZI: A thin delicate masculine Kerubic Angel with small wings wearing a yellow robe. He holds a fire opal that bestows beauty and great wealth.

The Angels' Message to Humanity

The god-form of ZDXG: A beautiful Kerubic Angel who combines both masculine and feminine characteristics. ZDXG has no wings, wears an amber robe, and holds a black rose that bestows psychic powers.

The god-form of ZIZA: A thin, delicate, masculine Kerubic Angel with small wings wearing a yellow robe. He holds a large black opal that bestows magical powers.

INDEX

AAAN, 170
AAETPIO, 36
AAOZAIF, 35
AAPDOKE, 36
ABALPT, 39
ADAEOET, 36
ADIRL, 137
AH, 27
AHAOZPI, 35
AHMLLKV, 34
AIAOAI, 123
Air-Tier, 21
AKPS, 164
AKZINOR, 34
ALHKTGA, 34
ALNKVOD, 36
ALOBABN, 35
AMSAL, 39
ANAA, 172
ANAEEM, 39
ANGPOI, 39
ANODOIN, 36
AOVRRZ, 151
AOYVB, 132
ARINNAP, 36
ARNIL, 114
ASTIM, 39
astral, 1
ATH, 15
aura, 17
AVE, 5
AVTOTAR, 35
AXPKN, 110
BABALON, 26
BALOBAN, 36
banishing, 13
BATAIVAH, 15
BATN, 126

BITOM, 13
Body of Bliss, 29
Body of Light, 17
BOZA, 39
causal, 1
centering spell, 36
Circle, 9
cosmic elements, 2
cosmic planes, 1
demons, 16
Dispositors, 10
DOPA, 178
duality, 9
Earth-Tier, 21
ecstasy, 29
EDLPRNAA, 15
Egypt, 15
EHNB, 13
Einstein, 30
Enochian, 2
etheric, 1
EXARP, 13
feminine current, 30
Fire-Tier, 21
GABRIEL, 5
Gate, 11
Acacia, 132
Amber, 159
Aspen, 137
Aventurine, 150
Black Tourmaline, 39
Cedar, 159
Coral, 89
Crystal, 19
Cypress, 39
Diamond, 79
Emerald, 39
Flint, 159

Green Agate, 39
Green Jasper, 39
Green Tourmaline, 39
Jade, 84
Lapis Lazuli, 104
Lotus, 94
Magnolia, 39
Maple, 154
Mica, 122
Oak, 159
Papyrus, 141
Pine, 145
Pumice, 128
Rose, 110
Sapphire, 99
Sulfur, 159
Topaz, 159
GLMA, 82
god-form, 17
Golden Dawn, 3
Great Cross, 3
HABIORO, 35
HAM, 225
hexagram, 21
HIPOTGA, 35
HKOMA, 13
HTNORDA, 35
HUM, 35
IAAASD, 111
IAOM, 39
IDOIGO, 142
IKZHIKAL, 15
imagination, 15
IMTD, 90
initiation, 2
invoking, 13
Earth, 1
Fire, 1
Water, 1
mandalas, 2
mantra, 18
mantras, 27
masculine current, 30
mental, 1
Mercury, 4

microcosm, 9
Moon, 4
MORDIALHKTGA, 27
MOR-DIAL-HKTGA, 27
MPAKO, 78
MPHARSLGAIOL, 78
MPH-ARSL-GAIOL, 34
MUM, 35
MXRNH, 84
NANTA, 13
NELAPR, 91
NIAHL, 39
NKRO, 39
NLRX, 112
NOALMR, 179
NOMGG, 39
OBGOTA, 101
occult, 1
occultism, 1
ODATT, 160
OIAGM, 90
OIPTEAAPDOKE, 160
OIP-TEAA-PDOKE, 36
OM, 225
OMIA, 39
OPMNIR, 39
ORABALN, 34
ORGAN, 165
OROIBAHAOZPI, 122
ORO-IBAH-AOZPI, 35
ORVLI, 94
PADO, 180
PAKKA, 150
PAYT, 133
pentagram, 13
PHRA, 39
PPMOX, 154
Prince, 11
PSAK, 161
psychic, 1
QUM, 34
RAAGIOSL, 15
RABMO, 122
RAPH, 39
RI, 36

Index

RIZNR, 62
RONK, 39
RSHAL, 128
RXNL, 110
RZIONR, 187
RZLA, 142
SAIINOV, 34
Senior, 25
Sephirothic Cross, 3
sexual currents, 26
sexual union, 29
SLGAIOL, 35
SOAIZNT, 35
Stairway, 21
Almond Stairway, 141
Anise Stairway, 144
Aquamarine Stairway, 100
Ash, 159
Azurite, 102
Banyan, 135
Bloodstone, 159
Carnelian, 163
Chalcedony, 92
Chestnut, 159
Coal, 39
Elm, 110
Grain, 29
Green Calcite, 39
Hazel, 132
Kunzite, 39
Moonstone, 90
Mulberry, 123
Oleander, 39
Olive, 159
Palm, 150

Pecan, 152
Pimpernel, 126
Salt, 39
Sandalwood, 112
Walnut, 159
Willow, 82
Wormwood, 159
Stalagmite, 39
Sun, 2
TAAD, 100
talisman, 10
TAXIR, 39
TBRAP, 174
TDIM, 92
TGMNM, 170
TNBA, 123
TOPNA, 39
TRAM, 34
Trumpeter, 10
VADALI, 171
Venus, 4
visualization, 26
VOLXDO, 161
Watchtowers, 3
Water-Tier, 21
XFMND, 145
XGZD, 152
XKZNS, 141
XUM, 34
yoga, 16
YTPA, 135
ZABO, 39
ZAZI, 187
ZDXG, 150
ZIZA, 189

247

STAY IN TOUCH...
Llewellyn publishes hundreds of books on your favorite subjects

On the following pages you will find listed some books now available on related subjects. Your local bookstore stocks most of these and will stock new Llewellyn titles as they become available. We urge your patronage.

ORDER BY PHONE

Call toll-free within the U.S. and Canada, 1–800–THE MOON. In Minnesota call (612) 291–1970. We accept Visa, MasterCard, and American Express.

ORDER BY MAIL

Send the full price of your order (MN residents add 7% sales tax) in U.S. funds to:

Llewellyn Worldwide,
P.O. Box 64383, Dept. K 605–X
St. Paul, MN 55164–0383, U.S.A.

POSTAGE AND HANDLING

- ★ $4.00 for orders $15.00 and under
- ★ $5.00 for orders over $15.00
- ★ No charge for orders over $100.00

We ship UPS in the continental United States. We cannot ship to P.O. boxes. Orders shipped to Alaska, Hawaii, Canada, Mexico, and Puerto Rico will be sent first-class mail.

International orders: Airmail—add freight equal to price of each book to the total price of order, plus $5.00 for each non-book item (audiotapes, etc.).

Surface mail: Add $1.00 per item

Allow 4–6 weeks delivery on all orders. Postage and handling rates subject to change.

DISCOUNTS

We offer a 20% quantity discount to group leaders or agents. You must order a minimum of 5 copies of the same book to get our special quantity price.

FREE CATALOG

Get a Free copy of our color catalog, *New Worlds of Mind and Spirit*. Subscribe for just $10.00 in the United States and Canada ($20.00 overseas, first class mail). Many bookstores carry *New Worlds*—ask for it!

ENOCHIAN MAGIC
A PRACTICAL MANUAL

GERALD J. SCHUELER, PH.D.

The powerful system of magic introduced in the 16th century by Dr. John Dee, Astrologer Royal to Queen Elizabeth I, and as practiced by Aleister Crowley and the Hermetic Order of the Golden Dawn, is here presented for the first time in a complete, step-by-step form. There has never before been a book that has made *Enochian Magic* this easy!

In this book you are led carefully along the path from "A brief history of the Enochian Magical System," through "How to Speak Enochian," "How to Invoke," "The Calls," "Egyptian Deities," and "Chief Hazards," to "How to visit the Aethyrs in Spirit Vision (Astral Projection)." Not a step is missed; not a necessary instruction forgotten.

0–87542–710–3, 288 pp., 5¼ x 8, illus., softcover $12.95

To Order call 1-800-THE-MOON
Prices subject to change without notice

The Enochian Workbook
The Enochian Magickal System Presented in 43 Easy Lessons

Gerald J. Schueler, Ph.D.,
and Betty Schueler, Ph.D.

Enochian Magic is an extremely powerful and complex path to spiritual enlightenment. Here, at last, is the first book on the subject written specifically for the beginning student. Ideally suited for those who have tried other books on Enochia and found them to be too difficult, *The Enochian Workbook* presents the basic teachings of Enochian Magic in a clear, easy-to-use workbook.

The authors have employed the latest techniques in educational psychology to help students master the information in this book. The book is comprised of 11 sections, containing a total of 43 lessons, with test questions following each section so students can gauge their progress. You will learn how to conduct selected rituals, skry using a crystal, and use the Enochian Tarot as a focus for productive meditation. Also explore Enochian Chess, Enochian Physics (the laws and models behind how the magic works), and examine the dangers associated with Enochian Magic. Readers who complete the book will be ready to tackle the more complex concepts contained in the other books in the series.

One of the reasons why Enochian Magic is so hard to understand is that it has a special, complex vocabulary. To help beginning students, Enochian terms are explained in simple, everyday words, wherever possible.

0-87542-719-7, 360 pp., 7 x 10, illus.,
16 color plates, softcover $19.95

To Order call 1-800-THE-MOON
Prices subject to change without notice

The Enochian Tarot: A New System of Divination for a New Age

Gerald J. Schueler, Ph.D., and Betty Schueler, Ph.D.

The popular deck of cards known as the Tarot has been used for many centuries for divination, fortunetelling and self-initiation through meditation. *The Enochian Tarot*, an 86-card deck, is the first to utilize the mystery and magical power inherent in Enochian Magic.

The Enochian Tarot explains in detail the meaningful correspondences behind the structure of this deck. It discusses, for example, the difference between the 22 Paths on the Qabalistic Tree of Life, on which traditional Tarot decks are based, and the 30 Aethyrs of Enochian Magick (the Enochian deck has 8 extra cards because there are 8 more Aethyrs than Paths). The book also includes tables and figures for easy comprehension of an otherwise difficult subject, as well as tips for reading the cards for fun or profit.

The unique system of Enochian Magick was revealed to John Dee, court astrologer to Queen Elizabeth I of England, and his partner Edward Kelly by the Enochian Angels who inhabit the Watchtowers and Aethyrs of the subtle regions of the universe. The authors are foremost authorities on this subject and have published a number of books that have made a fascinating magical system accessible to a wide audience.

0–87542–709–X, 352 pgs., 5¼ x 8, illus., softcover $12.95

To Order call 1-800-THE-MOON
Prices subject to change without notice

THE ENOCHIAN TAROT DECK

**GERALD J. SCHUELER, PH.D.,
AND BETTY SCHUELER, PH.D.
PAINTED BY SALLIE ANN GLASSMAN**

The Enochian Tarot is a deck of cards which is primarily used to foretell the future. Forecasting the future, however, is only a superficial use of the massive powers of *The Enochian Tarot*. Here is a powerful tool which allows you to look deep inside your subconscious and "see" the direction your life is taking. *The Enochian Tarot* is an easy-to-use system of self-discovery which allows you to see your relationship to God and the universe.

The Tarot is your map of life. With it you can choose the road you want to wander. Instead of being an uninformed victim of your subconscious will, you can gather your inner strength and consciously change the path your life is to take. The Tarot is your key to self-determination, and with that key you can open any door.

The Enochian Tarot Deck consists of 86 cards which are divided into 2 main sections: a Major Arcana and a Minor Arcana. The Major Arcana is a set of 30 picture cards which are also called The Greater Arcana, Trumps, Atouts, or Triumphs. These cards are symbolic representations of various cosmic forces such as Doubt, Intuition, Glory, etc. The Minor Arcana contains 56 cards that represent the Four Enochian Watchtowers. The Minor Arcana is divided into 4 "suits" called Earth, Water, Air, and Fire.

0-87542-708-1, boxed set: 86 cards with booklet　　　　　　　　　　　　$12.95

To Order call 1-800-THE-MOON
Prices subject to change without notice

ECSTASY THROUGH TANTRA

DR. JOHN MUMFORD

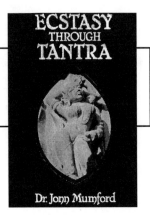

Dr. Jonn Mumford makes the occult dimension of the sexual dynamic accessible to everyone. One need not go up to the mountaintop to commune with Divinity: its temple is the body, its sacrament the communion between lovers. *Ecstasy Through Tantra* traces the ancient practices of sex magick through the Egyptian, Greek and Hebrew forms, where the sexual act is viewed as symbolic of the highest union, to the highest expression of Western sex magick.

Dr. Mumford guides the reader through mental and physical exercises aimed at developing psychosexual power; he details the various sexual practices and positions that facilitate "psychic short-circuiting" and the arousal of Kundalini, the Goddess of Life within the body. He shows the fundamental unity of Tantra with Western Wicca, and he plumbs the depths of Western sex magick, showing how its techniques culminate in spiritual illumination. Includes 14 full-color photographs.

0-87542-494-5, 190 pp., 6 x 9, 14 color plates, softcover   **$16.00**

To Order call 1-800-THE-MOON
Prices subject to change without notice

THE ENOCHIAN MAGICK OF DR. JOHN DEE
THE MOST POWERFUL SYSTEM OF MAGICK
IN ITS ORIGINAL, UNEXPURGATED FORM

GEOFFREY JAMES

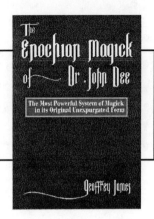

(formerly *The Enochian Evocation of Dr. John Dee*)

Dr. John Dee's system of Enochian Magick is among the most powerful in the Western tradition, and it has been enormously influential in the practices of the Order of the Golden Dawn. Though long out-of-print, this book has become an occult classic because it holds all the secrets of Dee's private magical workbooks, just as Dee recorded them in the late 16th century.

This indispensable treasure of Enochian lore offers the only definitive version of the famous Angelical Calls or Keys, conjurations said to summon the angels of the heavenly sphere—as well as all the practical information necessary for the experienced magician to reproduce Dee's occult experiments, with details on how to generate the names of the angels, create Enochian talismans, and set up an Enochian temple. Here readers will find the only available version of Dee's system of planetary and elemental magic, plus other material sure to fascinate a new generation of students of Enochian Magick. Explore the source texts that inspired MacGregor Mathers, Aleister Crowley, Israel Regardie, and a host of others and learn to practice angelic magick!

1–56718–367–0, 6 x 9, 248 pp., illus. $14.95

To Order call 1-800-THE-MOON
Prices subject to change without notice

TETRAGRAMMATON: THE SECRET OF EVOKING ANGELIC POWERS AND THE KEY TO THE APOCALYPSE

DONALD TYSON

In Western magick, *Tetragrammaton* is the holiest name of God. It is composed of the four Hebrew letters IHVH and is the occult key that unlocks the meaning behind astrological symbolism, the tarot, the mysteries of the Old Testament and the Book of Revelation, the kabbalah, the Enochian magick of John Dee, and modern ritual magick. It is nothing less than the archetypal blueprint of creation, the basis for such fundamental forms as the DNA double helix and the binary language of modern computers. Its true structure is the great arcanum of occultism, which has never before been explicitly revealed but only hinted at in obscure religious and alchemical emblems. Now, for the first time, its true structure is laid bare in a clear and unambiguous manner, allowing this potent key to open astounding vistas of understanding.

Tetragrammaton is a book for kabbalists, ritual occultists and anyone fascinated by the magic of the Bible. Those seeking proof for the coming of the Apocalypse will be captivated by the justification for Revelation in the Keys.

1-56718-744-7, 320 pp., 7 x 10, softcover $19.95

To Order call 1-800-THE-MOON
Prices subject to change without notice